Mental Illness Defined

Understanding the true nature of mental illness is essential for interpreting disparate research results, establishing accurate diagnostic profiles, setting robust research agendas, and optimizing therapeutic interventions. Psychopathology currently lacks a unifying framework. *Mental Illness Defined: Continuums, Regulation, and Defense* provides such a framework by filling the knowledge gap. Continuums, as opposed to numerous discrete entities, characterize mental illness. Impaired regulation fosters extreme expressions of mental illness continuums, an occurrence that can be compensated for by "cognitive regulatory control therapies." Defenses tend to moderate behavior, although excessive levels foster dysfunction, as with personality disorders. The model presented aligns with neuroscience and other relevant data, thereby placing psychopathology on a more scientific foundation to advance the aims of both researchers and treatment providers.

Brad Bowins, MD, directs the Centre for Theoretical Research in Psychiatry & Clinical Psychology, which he founded to advance theoretical research, provide guidelines, and support research on mental illness.

Mental Illness Defined

Continuums, Regulation, and Defense

Brad Bowins

Routledge
Taylor & Francis Group
NEW YORK AND LONDON

First published 2016
by Routledge
605 Third Avenue, New York, NY 10017

and by Routledge
2 Park Square, Milton Park, Abingdon, Oxon, OX14 4RN

Routledge is an imprint of the Taylor & Francis Group, an informa business

Library of Congress Cataloging in Publication Data
Names: Bowins, Brad, author.
Title: Mental illness defined : continuums, regulation, and defense / Brad Bowins.
Description: New York, NY : Routledge, 2016. | Includes bibliographical references and index.
Identifiers: LCCN 2016019738| ISBN 9781138200593 (hardback : alk. paper) | ISBN 9781138200609 (pbk. : alk. paper) | ISBN 9781315514130 (ebook)
Subjects: | MESH: Mental Disorders | Models, Psychological | Defense Mechanisms
Classification: LCC RC454.4 | NLM WM 140 | DDC 616.89--dc23
LC record available at https://lccn.loc.gov/2016019738

ISBN: 978-1-138-20059-3 (hbk)
ISBN: 978-1-138-20060-9 (pbk)
ISBN: 978-1-315-51413-0 (ebk)

Typeset in Minion
by Saxon Graphics Ltd, Derby

Dedicated to those who advance theoretical research in science, for the betterment of science.

Contents

Author Biography

Dr. Bowins is a psychiatrist, researcher, and founder of The Centre For Theoretical Research In Psychiatry & Clinical Psychology. His research and writings foster paradigm shifts crucial to the advancement of science and knowledge. Several theoretical perspectives, presented in peer-reviewed papers, have advanced the way that key aspects of mental illness are understood including, psychosis and schizophrenia, hypomania-mania, depression, personality disorders, repetitive maladaptive behavior, defensive mechanisms, and dissociation. Dr. Bowins provides effective interventions for mental illness that follow from the theoretical advances.

Acknowledgment

I thank Dr. Irwin Kleinman for his feedback on my theoretical perspectives, and acting as devil's advocate.

CHAPTER 1

Introduction

Defining the true nature of mental illness is essential for interpreting disparate research results, establishing accurate diagnostic profiles, setting robust research agendas, and advancing treatments. Presently, mental health research is characterized by numerous results lacking a unifying framework. One of the key issues underlying this occurrence is the atheoretical (or antitheoretical) orientation of psychiatry and clinical psychology, embodied in major diagnostic systems. We are still very much in the post-psychoanalytic era, with the overthrow of psychoanalysis several decades ago also entailing a rejection of theory. However, it is really a matter of throwing the baby out with what is perceived by some to be the bathwater, due to the crucial role that theory plays in science. Robust science moves ahead with a healthy balance of theoretical and empirical approaches, such as in the so-called ultimate science of physics. Theory is an integral part of physics, providing a meaningful framework for interpreting disparate empirical findings, setting key research directions and testable hypotheses, and linking past and present knowledge.

As valuable as empirical results are, they simply cannot provide a comprehensive perspective, and in the absence of theory often just accumulate, filling academic journals. It might be opined that empirical results move knowledge ahead simply by the weight of the findings, but a sobering reality is that about 80% of medical research results are false (see the chapter "Diagnostic Considerations"), and this is for top tier results in areas where there are hard endpoints! It only takes a little imagination to realize how weak the empirical results likely are in mental health research with mostly soft endpoints, such as points on a rating scale. Theory can compensate for this sad reality by providing workable models divorced from financial and political influences. The current book defines mental illness by linking empirical findings to advanced theoretical models. In this regard, three major concepts, which combined yield a robust picture of psychopathology, stand out: Continuums, regulation, and defense.

Continuums

Due to our perceptual processes, discreteness is preferred, and current diagnostic systems (DSM-5 and ICD-10) for the most part reflect this occurrence. However, natural systems almost uniformly gravitate toward a continuous organization, in line with how natural selection operates on the basis of trait variation. Given how natural events tend to be organized, the evidence for discreteness must be very solid, consistent with the Continuum Principle, which holds that natural phenomena tend to occur on a continuum, and any hypothesized instance of discreteness requires unassailable proof (see the chapter "Depression"). For each of the proposed categories of mental illness, research evidence is reviewed to determine whether discreteness or continuums apply. Consistent with the vast majority of natural phenomena, mental illness appears to be characterized by a limited number of continuums, there being insufficient evidence to support most discrete diagnoses, and none that comes even close to that required by the Continuum Principle.

A model of mental illness is proposed that defines naturally occurring continuums, based on solid empirical data from neuroscience and other sources such as emotional information processing. These continuums consist of:

- Depression
- Anxiety
- Hypomania-Mania
- Psychosis
- Negative Symptoms
- Dissociation
- Eating Disorders
- Reinforcement Based Disorders
- Personality Disorders

These continuums align quite extensively with the general content of current diagnostic systems, demonstrating that while the emphasis on numerous discrete conditions is misguided, being influenced by our perceptual tendencies, mental health practitioners and researchers have for the most part identified naturally occurring forms of mental illness. The alternative proposed in this book helps to synthesize the discrete and continuous perspectives. Each of the continuums is based on naturally occurring processes: Depression and anxiety involve emotional information processing; hypomania-mania is a defensive response to depression and even anxiety; psychosis arises from cognitive and perceptual distortions; negative symptoms are linked to human-specific cognition, including executive functions, social cognition, and motivational states; dissociation is a stress response; eating disorders stem from evolutionarily derived motivational platforms supporting food consumption and related reproductive strategies; reinforcement based addictive, impulsive, and compulsive behaviors derive from reward systems; and personality disorders are extreme and enduring expressions of defensive responses. Within these major mental health continuums are various sub-dimensions described in the relevant chapter, and also summarized in the chapter "Diagnostic Considerations." Along with, first, the processes of circumstances activating continuums, and second qualitative variation arising from quantitative variation as an emergent property (see the chapters "Depression" and "Anxiety" for more complete explanations of both processes), these sub-dimensions further assist in synthesizing the continuous and discrete approaches to psychopathology.

Some of the proposed continuums align very closely with current perspectives, while others entail a shift in how mental illness is viewed. As an example of the latter, negative symptoms are currently largely neglected, whereas they actually play a robust role in schizophrenia, bipolar disorder, severe depression, and several other conditions. The proposed model elevates negative symptoms to the prominent position warranted. Current diagnostic systems and perspectives are oriented to viewing addictive, impulsive, and compulsive patterns pluralistically, involving various substances and behaviors including sexual. However, practically and conceptually these terms are difficult to distinguish, and the underlying issue applicable to all is reinforcement. In addition, current methods of identifying, classifying, and researching addictive/impulsive/compulsive behavior are hopelessly inadequate in the rapidly changing computer era. The proposed reinforcement based model is capable of describing novel instances of dysfunctional behavior of this form immediately. Conditions with clear organic impairments, such as dementia, delirium, and sleep disorders are excluded, on the basis of insufficient psychological import. However, it is common for there to be psychological reactions to these problems, such as depression and anxiety, and these expressions are covered. Consistent with most natural occurrences, each of the organic conditions also appears to be organized in a continuous fashion, such as varying degrees of dementia. Negative symptoms are largely organic, but are included because they have a profound impact on many conditions.

In an imperfect world, no method of conceptualizing mental illness will be perfect. Critiques of continuous models typically pertain to the distinction between the discrete and continuous. Everything in nature is interconnected; we live in an entangled world. Due to this reality everything probably merges at a quantum level. However, at a macro level form emerges from the quantum interconnectedness. For example, planets are distinct instead of being compressed into one large mass. Likewise, mental illness entities emerge that are distinguishable from one another, organized continuously due to the nature of natural selection with trait variation, one of the most powerful forces applicable to biological entities. Related to the interconnectedness of everything, there will inevitably be fuzziness at the borders of these mental illness entities. While such fuzziness may be disturbing from a purely academic perspective, it is necessary to accept it. The interconnectedness might best be viewed as dimensions or continuums interfacing (see the chapter "Diagnostic Considerations"). For example, anxiety and depression are distinct continuums derived from the underlying emotional information processing, with fear being the root emotion of anxiety and sadness the root emotion of depression. Due to overlap in the emotional information processing circumstances—conditions that entail threat commonly also convey loss and vice versa—anxiety disorders and depression commonly overlap; the continuums interface with one another. Hence, we have naturally occurring continuums that in our interconnected universe must interact with one another.

An additional critique of continuous models related to the constitution of continuous and discrete entities is that continuums actually represent discrete entities due to limited horizontal capacity, although with vastly better vertical range. This occurrence might even be referred to as meta-discreteness. This is to some extent a valid critique. However, since form does arise from quantum interconnectedness, as with the example of planets discussed earlier, then the task is to distinguish naturally occurring forms, while accepting that at a very fundamental level, often beyond our sensory capabilities, everything is linked. Forms of mental illness must be distinguished on the basis of natural processes, such as emotional information processing and neuroscientific data, and not political or financial agendas, as with discrete entities favoring the marketing of medications. If the latter is the basis of the definition of mental illness, then the field represents a captured discipline removed from science. The model of mental illness proposed provides what appear to be naturally occurring dimensions, with the understanding that their inevitable interfacing with one another does not compromise their unique form.

Regulation

All biological systems rely on regulatory control over essential processes. Within our own bodies physiological parameters such as electrolyte composition, blood sugar levels, temperature, and blood pressure are tightly controlled. When this regulation falters disease occurs, as with diabetes involving deficient control of blood sugar levels and hypertension sustained high blood pressure. Even the growth of cells is controlled by various signals to keep the system in balance. Cancer arises when cells remove themselves from this regulation and divide without restraint. Regulation in biological systems also transpires at the ecosystem level, such as with temperate riparian systems. For example, salmon mature in rivers and then enter the sea where they live for a few years before returning to the same river system they grew up in. After spawning they die, their bodies providing a crucial source of nitrogen and carbon for their developing offspring, and other animals such as bears that eat the salmon. Partially eaten salmon and the feces of animals that eat them return minerals to the soil, enabling the growth of trees and plants, which in turn shade the river, cooling the water so that salmon can survive.

The role of regulation in mental health is also profound but vastly underappreciated. To adequately define mental illness, the contribution of psychological regulation is explored and described for each of the mental illness continuums. Evidence supports the position that impaired regulation is instrumental in the shift from mild and adaptive expressions of continuous behavior to extreme and maladaptive levels, with adaptive/maladaptive defined in terms of the functioning of the individual, and in some instances evolutionary fitness implications, such as mania being incompatible with relationships that could lead to reproduction. Perhaps most evident is how the prefrontal cortex (PFC) and higher cortical structures regulate limbic system structures to limit emotional reactions. Anxiety and depression entail deficient PFC-limbic connectivity, and treatments such as cognitive behavioral therapy actually appear to reverse this impairment to restore mental health. On a somewhat more speculative note, the distinction between schizophrenia and bipolar disorder might actually hinge on regulation over a natural defensive response to depression in the case of bipolar disorder, and over psychotic level cognitions. When this regulation fails hypomania progresses to mania, and psychotic cognitions and sensory perceptual experiences intrude into the conscious and awake state. Healthy defensive responses to stress can extend to extreme and enduring expressions, producing personality and dissociative disorders when regulation falters. Eating disorders and reinforcement based conditions arise when regulation of food consumption and reward continuums is compromised. A key contribution of the proposed model is to elevate regulation to a role of prominence commensurate with that it occupies in mental health and illness.

Psychological Defense

Classical psychoanalytic defense mechanisms automatically come to mind when the term psychological defense is raised. Indeed, defense mechanisms qualify as one of the most robust and enduring of all psychoanalytic concepts, an occurrence anticipated by Freud when he mentioned in a personal communication to his friend Wilhelm Fliess that in identifying them he had touched upon one of the greatest secrets in nature. A key reason why these psychoanalytic defense mechanisms are so robust is that they are actually part of a much larger process, namely compensation and resilience to stressors. To a large extent compensation for stressors characterizes life, and when compensation fails illness and death ensue. For instance, when blood sugar levels rise so does insulin to compensate by storing the excess sugar. When there is a lack of insulin or insulin resistance, blood sugar levels rise to toxic levels. Defenses applicable to mental health compensate for stressors in a similar fashion, and when they fail mental illness occurs.

If we are to understand the true role of defense, it is necessary to break free from the notion of psychological defense consisting only of classical psychoanalytic defense mechanisms. In line with this conceptual shift, classical defense mechanisms are likely only components of two much broader psychological defense templates, positive cognitive distortions and dissociation, concepts developed in the chapters "Psychosis" and "Dissociation." These defense mechanism templates operate largely at the level of emotions, defending against excessive negative emotions, such as fear and sadness. The evolution of human intelligence appears to have amplified emotional states, making us the most emotional of all creatures, with amplified fear and sadness contributing respectively to anxiety disorders and depression. To attenuate and compensate for excessive negative emotions, psychological defense mechanisms evolved. At the level of mental illness defensive processes have also evolved, and in particular hypomania for depression and even anxiety, at least that derived from social sources.

Extreme expressions of psychological defenses play a major role in bipolar disorder, psychosis, dysfunctional dissociation (including Post-Traumatic Stress Disorder), eating disorders, and personality disorders, as covered in the given chapter. Readers definitely should not take from this that the various forms of mental illness represent defenses, as most have no defensive value, such as anxiety disorders and depression. Some, such as psychosis, mania, and extreme dissociation, can provide a defensive capacity under limited circumstances, and several have pronounced defensive value in a mild form, as with hypomania, dissociation, and the processes underlying personality disorders. Nor should readers assume a set role for defensive processes applicable to all of the naturally occurring mental illness continuums. Researchers prefer ideal symmetry, but nature can be much more "messy," and models accurately describing it often reflect this, as with the Standard Model of particle physics, which while quite "messy" is very accurate.

Conceptualizing and applying psychological defense in terms of compensation for stressors reveals the natural and robust role that defense processes play in mental health and illness. Restricting psychological defense to classical psychoanalytic defense mechanisms obscures their significance, particularly since these defenses apply to many emotional states, and are hence not specific to given disorders, other than perhaps as trends in highly limited scenarios. A potential critique of expanding defense to compensation for stressors is that it can become so general and diffuse as to lose meaning and relevance. In this regard a high threshold of relevance as a compensatory process has to be applied. This high threshold entails not citing psychological defense when other more parsimonious explanations are available. For example, you come home from work and express anger towards your spouse for an unnecessary purchase when money is tight. Is this a defense against stress? The answer is no because the occurrence can much more parsimoniously be explained by emotional information processing, whereby you perceive a violation. In contrast, hypomania, at least understood in terms of its modal time frame and ensuing expression, compensates very well in the moment for depressive inhibition, and lacks other more parsimonious explanations. When the compensatory role is clearly identified, and alternative more parsimonious explanations are lacking or weak, the adaptive value is clear and meaningful, as it is restricted to a particular circumstance. The applicable role of psychological defense is explored in each chapter, focusing on compensation for stress when other more parsimonious explanations are lacking.

Continuums, Regulation, and Defense

By defining mental illness on the basis of continuums, regulation, and defense, a vastly different picture of psychopathology emerges, and one that aligns very well with neuroscience and other relevant data. This occurrence will allow mental illness categorization to move ahead, and not be structured on the basis of preferences and political agendas. Diagnostic profiles will need to shift in the direction of far fewer conditions emphasizing the naturally occurring continuums identified here. However, the notion of categories can to some extent be maintained based on primary continuums, sub-dimensions within these, qualitative variation arising from quantitative variation, and also eliciting mechanisms.

To enhance practical applications, in line with the saying by the social psychologist Kurt Lewin that there is nothing so practical as a good theory, novel psychotherapeutic techniques are presented. Several of these techniques, falling under the umbrella of cognitive regulatory control therapies, are designed to restore compromised regulation occurring with anxiety, depression, mania, and psychosis. In addition, the chapters on dissociation, eating disorders, reinforcement based disorders, and personality disorders provide novel approaches to managing these conditions. By embracing theory, in combination with empirical results, a unique conceptual framework with practical treatment applications is thus generated. An unfortunate consequence of the current-day rejection of theory in mental health research is that there is little impetus or capacity for paradigm shifts, so crucial for the advancement of science. The current book facilitates this crucial paradigm shift, and will hopefully open up much needed dialogue while providing an informed direction for the necessary changes.

CHAPTER 2

Depression

Throughout recorded history there is evidence of depression, and it comprises one of the most common conditions mental health professionals treat, supporting the position that it is a naturally occurring entity, at least for humans. However, how it is structured is debatable. Throughout the history of psychiatry there has been a tendency to view depression as consisting of discrete types. Two types have traditionally been identified: Endogenous, vital, or melancholic, and reactive, neurotic, or dysthymic (Healy, 2013; Kiloh et al, 1972; Parker et al, 1988; Paykel, 2008). Melancholia was identified at the time of Hippocrates and persisted as a diagnosis through Galenic and medieval times (Paykel, 2008). In 1621, Richard Burton wrote *The Anatomy of Melancholia* (in Paykel, 2008). Carl Lange, in 1880, identified a disorder with neurovegetative features that became known as endogenous or vital depression (in Healy, 2013). Psychoanalysts led by Freud were instrumental in advancing the notion of reactive depression, in which the actual or symbolic loss of a love object gives rise to depression (in Shorter, 1997). According to Alfred Meyer all psychiatric illness consists of a psychobiological reaction to stress (in Paykel, 2008).

Discrete endogenous and reactive forms of depression are consistent with the medical disease model, whereby distinct conditions demonstrating etiological, symptom, course, and treatment differences occur (Paykel, 2008). The alternative—the unitary perspective maintaining that depression is a single entity with various manifestations—aligns with the overlapping features of depression (Parker et al, 1991; Parker, 2013). Diagnostic systems such as the Diagnostic and Statistical Manual (DSM) and the International Classification of Diseases (ICD) have proposed discrete forms of depression—understandably, given that the disease model is the basis for these classification systems. DSM-IV-TR identified major depression, minor depression, and dysthymia, with DSM-5 keeping the first and adding persistent depressive disorder to replace dysthymia (First et al, 2002; American Psychiatric Association, 2013). ICD-10 includes depressive episodes, dysthymia (under persistent mood disorder), and recurrent depression (World Health Organization, 1992).

In attempting to resolve the issue of whether depression consists of discrete types or constitutes a unitary entity, factor analytic methodology has been applied. Although the technique of factor analysis does not allow for one "correct" solution for any data set, an infinite number of solutions being viable, Eysenck (1970) indicated that the unitary/binary debate can be "translated into factor analytic logic quite simply and clearly." The unitary view predicts a single large general factor with positive loadings, and no interpretable bipolar factor (not to be confused with bipolar disorder), and the binary position entails a bipolar factor (Eysenck, 1970: 243). The position taken by Eysenck was that a two-factor solution is supported (Eysenck, 1970). Reviewing factor analytic studies, Parker et al (1991) conclude that there is evidence for both positions, with the most support for an endogenous/melancholic type (Parker et al, 1991). Based on their own research and reviews of other studies, Parker and colleagues believe that there is a single depressive factor (melancholic/endogenous), and a non-endogenous factor that includes anxiety, personality, and other non-specific contributors (Parker et al, 1988; Parker et al, 1991; Parker, 2013). A psychoanalytically oriented empirical study by Cochrane also supports this conclusion, finding evidence for only one type of depression (endogenous), with all other versions indistinguishable from non-depressed psychiatric states (Cochrane, 1977).

Considering that the discrete model is largely derived from the disease model it is reasonable to expect that the various forms of depression would exhibit different etiologies, symptom profiles, courses, and responses to treatment. Research, however, does not support this interpretation, with for example endogenous/melancholic and reactive/neurotic depression not being clearly distinguishable on the basis of these parameters (Bech, 1988; Benazzi, 2006; Brodaty et al, 2001; Bronisch & Klerman, 1988; Healy, 2013; Kessing, 2004; Kessing, 2007; O'Leary, 1996; Parker, 2013; Paykel, 2008; Ramana et al, 1995; Su et al, 2011; Surtees & Barkley, 1994; Welch & Ellis, 1991). Nor has research supported the idea of dysthymia (and its continuation as persistent depressive disorder in DSM-5) and minor depression as distinct forms of depression (Rhebergen & Graham, 2014; Rhebergen et al, 2012; Newman & Bland, 2009). Regarding etiology, research has not revealed any clear differences that hold out over repeated studies. Supporting the unitary perspective, a neuroscience study by Su et al (2011) examining levels of brain-derived neurotrophic factor (BDNF), tumor necrosis factor (TNF), adinopectin, interleukin-6 (IL-6), all hypothesized to play a role in depression, found no differences between reactive depression, major depression (believed to be equivalent to endogenous), and bipolar depression.

Symptom profiles likewise do not seem to clearly differentiate types of depression. Parker and colleagues, despite years of attempting to do so, have been unable to distinguish melancholic from non-melancholic types on the basis of symptoms (Parker, 2013). As pertains to the course of depression, various indicators (such as risk of relapse, likelihood of recurrence, probability of readmission, and suicide) fail overall to distinguish types of depression, such as melancholic and non-melancholic, with studies yielding varying results (Brodaty et al, 2001; Kessing, 2004; O'Leary, 1996; Ramana et al, 1995; Surtees

& Barkley, 1994). Suicide is an indicator of how severe depression can become, and hence of the progression, but Kessing did not find any differences in completed suicide between melancholic and non-melancholic forms (Kessing, 2004). Research indicates that the course and symptom profile of depression often changes over time, fulfilling criteria for various subtypes including major, minor, and dysthymic (Angst et al, 2000; Angst & Merkangas, 1997; Judd et al, 1998; Kessing, 2007). Types of depression should also vary in their respond to treatment. Early research by Parker and colleagues suggested that endogenous/ melancholic depression responded better to ECT and tricyclic antidepressants (TCA), but they later learned that their "pristine" results were actually an effect of aging, with older patients responding better to these two treatment modalities regardless of the type of depression (Parker, 2013).

While proposed types of depression are not clearly distinguishable on the basis of etiology, symptom profile, course, and response to treatment, research does provide some support for the position that melancholic depression is a subtype. Select studies indicate that with melancholic depression there is more extensive psychomotor impairment, consisting of cognitive and physical slowing, anergia, anhedonia, suicide risk, agitation, fewer anxiety symptoms, higher cortisol levels and failure to suppress with dexamethasone treatment, and a greater response to ECT and TCAs along with a lesser response to SSRIs (Harris et al, 2011; Harris et al, 2013; Healy, 2013; Parker, 2013; Parker et al, 2010; Parker et al, 2013). Some taxometric studies have also found that melancholic depression is distinguishable (Ambrosini et al, 2002; Haslam & Beck, 1994), although others have found evidence for a dimensional latent structure (Ruscio et al, 2004; Slade, 2007). Taxometrics are a set of mathematical techniques that help determine if there is a continuous distribution, by looking for abrupt changes in the structure of a data set (Beauchaine, 2007). Abrupt changes indicate the presence of latent subtypes, with latency referring to the pathological processes underlying manifest symptoms (Beauchaine, 2007). Regarding other proposed subtypes of depression, such as self-criticality, hopelessness, and social defeat, taxometric research indicates that a continuous latent structure applies (Haslam & Beck, 1994; Ruscio et al, 2004). We thus have a situation where there is insufficient evidence for truly discrete types of depression, but yet a suggestion that there are distinctions of some type. It is an intriguing scenario that at first glance seemingly is without a method to resolve it.

Fortunately, by clarifying conceptual issues pertaining to discrete and continuous characterizations of disease entities, we can resolve this intriguing puzzle. The first conceptual issue is whether natural phenomena including psychological variables tend to be discrete or continuous. If nature gravitates to discreteness, then we might expect depression to be organized into discrete types. On the other hand, if it tends to be continuous then depression is more likely to be organized on the basis of a spectrum rather than discretely. Natural phenomena do tend to be continuous and not discrete, although we prefer to see discreteness (Darwin, 1858/1958; Kinsey et al, 1948; Kinsey et al, 1953). Discovering that human sexual orientation is organized continuously, Kinsey and colleagues commented on how despite our tendency to see discreteness, continuums characterize nature (Kinsey et al, 1948; Kinsey et al, 1953). In *Sexual Behavior in the Human Male* (Kinsey et al, 1948: 130) they state, "Males do not represent two discrete populations, heterosexual and homosexual. The world is not divided into sheep and goats. It is a fundamental of taxonomy that nature rarely deals with discrete categories…The living world is a continuum in each and every one of its aspects." In *Sexual Behavior in the Human Female* (Kinsey et al, 1953: 469), it is added, "It is a characteristic of the human mind that it tries to dichotomize in its classification of phenomena…Sexual behavior is either normal or abnormal, socially acceptable or unacceptable, heterosexual or homosexual; and many persons do not want to believe that there are gradations in these matters from one to the other extreme." These statements capture how nature, human psychology included, is organized in a continuous fashion, while our perception of discrete categories is an illusion arising from a natural psychological inclination to dichotomize when classifying. Discrete entities are easier to process mentally, accuracy being traded off for simplicity (Bowins, 2015).

Even a straightforward single gene trait involving dominant and recessive alleles—eye color—that should be fully discrete with brown and blue categories, gravitates to a continuum evidenced by the phenotypes of hazel and green eye color when brown and blue genes mix. Variation in traits is the phenomenon acted upon by natural selection, allowing for their evolution (Darwin, 1858/1958). Continuums provide for trait variation, whereas truly discrete entities do not. This means that if nature were organized discretely and not continuously, there would be no variation, and hence no evolution (Darwin, 1858/1958). Traits lacking any variation (truly discrete) either persist, if selection pressures favor the given characteristics, or perish if it does not, an either/or scenario. Ample trait variation provided by a continuous organization of forms allows for the most adaptive variant/s to become more represented in succeeding generations, the hallmark of natural selection and evolution (Darwin, 1858/1958). Due to our automatic tendency to apply discreteness to what are almost universally continuous variables, a "Continuum Principle" is warranted: Natural phenomena tend to occur on a continuum, and any instance of hypothesized discreteness requires unassailable proof (Bowins, 2015). Hence, any researcher or theorist positing discrete forms of depression must provide unambiguous evidence. Evidence for discrete types of depression clearly does not even come close to achieving this standard.

The second conceptual issue requiring clarification is that continuous and discrete methods of categorization are ironically not all that distinct. This occurrence arises from an important emergent property of quantitative dimensions: Quantitative dimensions produce different qualitative states (Bowins, 2015). For example, blood pressure demonstrates quantitative variation ranging from very low to very high. Both extremely low and high levels produce disease states as emergent properties: low levels unconsciousness and circulatory collapse, and extremely high levels strokes. Dimensional quantitative variation yields qualitatively different disease states as emergent properties. Likewise, with varying quantitative levels of depression, different qualitative "types" can manifest as emergent properties. Supporting this perspective, Schotte et al (1997) found that non-melancholic and melancholic depression are organized continuously, with melancholic symptoms emerging as depression severity increases.

Clarifying the concepts of how well dimensions or discreteness apply to natural phenomena, and how quantitative differences yield qualitative variation as an emergent property, thus helps resolve the question of whether or not depression (or for that matter probably any psychiatric condition) is organized discretely or continuously. It represents a synthesis replacing the polar extremes, and one supporting a dimensional organization while allowing for some qualitative distinctions as emergent properties. It implies that adjectives such as major, minor, dysthymia, endogenous, melancholic, and reactive cannot be applied to depression. As a continuous entity depression must be simply identified as "depression" in any diagnostic system, although it can be understood that the more severe manifestations have a greater probability of producing classic melancholic signs and symptoms. Let us now look at the dimensional nature of depression.

Depression as a Dimensional Entity

There are a number of possible ways that depression might be organized dimensionally. One possibility is as a single dimension, but according to what characteristic? Perhaps severity? But if so, what about duration? Every experienced clinician intuitively considers the dimensions of severity and duration when evaluating and describing depression. Even diagnostic systems incorporate this distinction to an extent, with DSM characterizing major depressive episode as typically more severe and of relatively limited duration (First et al, 2002; American Psychiatric Association, 2013). Dysthymia (DSM-IV-TR) and its continuation as persistent depressive disorder (DSM-5), on the other hand, are usually understood to be of lesser severity and longer duration (First et al, 2002; American Psychiatric Association, 2013). Hence, two dimensions of severity and duration need be incorporated to describe a depressive episode (Bowins, 2015).

Severity Dimension

How might we set up a severity dimension? Mild, moderate, and severe comprises a solid starting point, already being built into the ICD-10 system (World Health Organization, 1992). Research by Kessing (2004) supports the ICD-10 mild, moderate, and severe distinctions: The risk of suicide and relapse increases significantly moving from the mild to moderate range, and then from the moderate to severe range. Greater diagnostic stability was found for the moderate and severe distinctions, indicating the difficulty often encountered in distinguishing normal dysphoric mood from milder depression (Kessing, 2004).

The difficulty experienced by Kessing (2004) in distinguishing milder depression underscores the importance of having a solid means of characterizing depression severity. I have previously suggested that depression severity as a dimension be characterized by "depressive inhibition," a term originating with Kraepelin (in Himmelhoch, 1998) that with modifications consistent with current research appears to suit our purpose very well (Bowins, 2015). Kraepelin (in Himmelhoch, 1998: 209) believed that the entire phenomenology of manic-depressive illness derives from depressive inhibition, and that impediment of volition is the predominant clinical feature of depression: "All action of the will is extremely difficult…the transformation of impulses of the will into action meets with obstacles that cannot be overcome without difficulty, and often not at all by the patient's own strength." Updating the concept of depressive inhibition, modern research indicates that impeded cognitive, emotional, social, and physical behavior are involved: Cognitive consisting of thought slowing, and impairments to attention, memory, and learning processes (executive functions); emotional entailing diminished positive emotions, excessive negative emotions, restricted affective range, and limitations to emotional information processing; social consisting of reduced social activity and impaired social cognition; and physical including fatigue, lethargy, sleep problems, appetitive changes, and psychomotor slowing (Benazzi, 2004, 2007; Bilder et al, 2000; Elvevag & Goldberg, 2000; Fiszdon et al, 2007; Himmelhoch, 1998).

The concept of depressive inhibition helps separate milder depression from normal dysphoric mood states, such as uncomplicated bereavement, because with the former there will be some degree of cognitive, social, emotional, and/or physical impairment, whereas with the latter there will not be, or negligibly so. Furthermore, as the severity of depressive inhibition progresses so do the impairments. Severe depressive inhibition involves profound changes such as greatly reduced memory and information processing capacity, blunted emotions and highly restricted range of affect, minimal or no social interactions, and pronounced psychomotor slowing or agitation (Benazzi, 2004, 2007; Bilder et al, 2000; Elvevag & Goldberg, 2000; Fiszdon et al, 2007; Himmelhoch, 1998). Psychometric research has been applied to the issue of whether or not clinical depression is continuous with or distinct from sub-clinical depression related symptoms. The bulk of the evidence clearly supports a continuous latent structure (Andrews et al, 2007; Gibb et al, 2004; Okumura et al, 2009; Prisciandaro & Roberts, 2005; Ruscio & Ruscio, 2002; Slade, 2007; Slade & Andrews, 2005). Okumura et al (2009) applied taxometric procedures to the responses of 20,987 Japanese citizens to a questionnaire regarding depression, and found that the latent structure of depression is dimensional. Prisciandaro and Roberts (2005) assessed 4,577 National Comorbidity Survey participant responses indicating depression or anhedonia, finding a dimensional structure. Slade and Andrews (2005) evaluated the responses of 1,933 citizens to the Australian National Survey of Mental Health and Well-Being, and ascertained by taxometric procedures that there was a latent dimensional structure. Regarding core symptoms, Gibb et al (2004) found that negative cognitive styles have a continuous latent structure extending from mild in the non-clinical population to more severe in the clinical population.

Some taxometric studies have found a more discrete structure, with depression related symptoms in the normal population being distinct from clinical depression symptoms. An example is that of Solomon et al (2006), who analyzed 1,400 responses to the Oregon Adolescent Depression Project, and found evidence for a taxonic latent structure. It has been commented that taxonic results are more likely to emerge with small and very specific sample populations, such as Oregon adolescents, and when potential confounding variables are not well controlled (Haslam et al, 2012; Okumura et al, 2009). Hence, the evidence tends to support a continuum of depression related symptoms from the normal to the clinical population. At a certain level of symptom quantity and severity, clinical depression occurs (Solomon et al, 2001).

Fundamental motivational parameters, known as the Behavioral Activation System (BAS) and Behavioral Inhibition System (BIS), support the validity of the use of depressive inhibition to characterize the severity dimension of depression. BAS and BIS are very ancient general motivational systems, with the former approach oriented and based on positive appetitive incentive; and the latter regulating sensitivity to threat and non-reward cues, and guiding inhibition or avoidance responses (Fowles, 1988; Gray, 1987; Johnson et al, 2000; Kasch et al, 2002). BAS and positive affectivity are related concepts, sometimes used interchangeably, as are BIS and negative affectivity (Gray, 1987; Kasch et al, 2002). Positive and negative affectivity can be viewed as expressions of BAS and BIS, respectively (Kasch et al, 2002). BIS is increased in a range of psychiatric conditions including depression, anxiety, schizophrenia, and disordered attachment states (Campbell-Sills et al, 2004; Kasch et al, 2002; Mineka et al, 1998; Scholten et al, 2006). BAS on the other hand appears more specific to depression with lower levels found in this condition (Fowles, 1988; Kasch et al, 2002). BIS and BAS typically operate in a fashion that is complementary, even synergistic. For example, increased aversive motivation lowers appetitive motivation (Fowles, 1988).

BIS and BAS align well with the concept of depressive inhibition, and add support to the notion that it can be used to characterize depression severity. Scales assessing BIS and BAS assist in linking these motivational parameters to depressive inhibition (Bowins, 2012a; Carver & White, 1994). In addition, the BIS/BAS Scales can be applied to improve behavioral activation treatments for depression, by more clearly identifying specific components of BAS and BIS that are impaired (Bowins, 2012a). Behavioral activation therapy is oriented to increasing activity and access to reinforcement. The two main versions, Behavioral Activation (BA) and Behavioral Activation Treatment for Depression (BATD) (Hopko et al, 2003; Jacobson et al, 1996; Lejuez et al, 2001), are highly effective for depression (Chartier & Provencher, 2013; Kanter et al, 2012; Ly et al, 2013; McEvoy et al, 2013), and work just as well for cognitions as does Cognitive Behavioral Therapy (Jacobson et al, 1996). Future research can help devise measurement strategies for assessing the different components of depressive inhibition beyond BIS and BAS—cognitive, emotional, social, and physical. It is suggested that low, moderate, and high severity ratings be applied, with the severity ratings averaged to provide a composite score for depressive inhibition. Three levels of ratings are suggested because most experienced clinicians can distinguish low, moderate, and severe, whereas finer gradients become unreliable, and certainly without extensive training that is very unlikely to occur outside of a research setting. Treatment strategies addressing the separate components of depressive inhibition can also be devised and tested.

Despite the similarity of the terms depressive inhibition and behavioral inhibition, the two should not be considered synonymous (Bowins, 2015). Behavioral inhibition is linked to negative affectivity in general, emerges at an early age in relation to attachment states, and is present in a range of psychiatric conditions (Campbell-Sills et al, 2004; Kasch et al, 2002; Mineka et al, 1998; Scholten et al, 2006). Depressive inhibition pertains to depression only and describes impairments to cognitive, emotional, social, and physical behaviors. Even the combination of high behavioral inhibition and low behavioral activation (high BIS/low BAS) is not equivalent to depressive inhibition, although if sustained can lead to a state of depressive inhibition.

Psychological, genetic, epigenetic, and neural influences appear to play a role in the development and persistence of depressive inhibition (Azorin et al, 2010; Du et al, 2013; Pandya et al, 2012; Treadway & Pizzagalli, 2014). Via the Amplification Effect (described in the chapter "Anxiety"), loss-oriented cognitions contribute to depression by amplifying sadness, the root emotion of depression (Bowins, 2004, 2006a). Likewise, cognitions such as, "I know I can't succeed" intensify BIS and diminish BAS, further strengthening depressive inhibition (Bowins, 2008). Depression, in turn, increases both loss-oriented and high BIS/low BAS cognitions, with this mutually reinforcing process helping to lock in depressive inhibition (Bowins, 2008).

A crucial neural influence contributing to depressive inhibition appears to be impaired regulation: Deficient prefrontal cortex (PFC), and frontal cortices more generally, regulation of excessive limbic based feelings of sadness and related emotions (Arnsten, 2009; Arnsten, 2011; Beauregard et al, 2006; Brambilla et al, 2005; Hartley & Phelps, 2010; Philippot & Brutoux, 2008; Salzman & Fusi, 2010; Schardt et al, 2010). Excessive activation of limbic and other emotion-related structures, and attenuated activity of frontal regions implicated in emotion regulation, is revealed by neuroimaging studies, suggesting deficient top-down regulation of emotion-related structures (Arnsten, 2009; Arnsten, 2011; Beauregard et al, 2006; Cusi et al, 2012; Hamilton et al, 2012). Beauregard et al (2006) found that compared to non-depressed controls, depressed subjects demonstrated impaired down-regulation of sad feelings, ensuring that they had difficulty containing depression related emotions. Interestingly, deficits pertaining to cognitive control might even increase with each depressive episode and persist after remission, suggesting a 'scar' on cognitive regulatory processes (Vanderhasselt & DeRaedt, 2009). Negative symptoms (see the chapter "Negative Symptoms") occur with depression, and can be primary or secondary, the latter comprising a reaction to depression, such as reduced motivation. Primary negative symptoms, on the other hand, might be instrumental in depression, by impairing top-down regulation of excessive limbic system responses (see the chapter "Negative Symptoms" for more extensive coverage of the role of these symptoms in impaired regulation). Supporting this notion, the presence of primary negative symptoms indicates a more severe illness, as expressed by psychosis (Coryell, 1997). Conceivably, the same process might apply to anxiety.

Impaired regulation, from whatever source, offers a unique therapeutic opportunity for both depression and anxiety disorders—so-called cognitive regulatory control therapies (Bowins, 2013). Cognitive behavioral and related techniques are well suited to bolstering deficient regulation, and likely succeed largely via this mechanism (Beauregard, 2007; Bowins, 2013; Goldin, 2009; Hermann et al, 2007; Schardt et al, 2010). For example, cognitive reappraisal, a key cognitive behavioral technique, reduces or eliminates the perception of loss or threat, linked to depression and anxiety respectively, by altering negative automatic thoughts and underlying schemata (Beck, 1991; Beck & Clark, 1997). Loss and threat oriented cognitive activating appraisals, playing such a pivotal role in the mutually reinforcing cognitive-emotional cycles initiating and maintaining depression and anxiety, are if anything replaced by cognitive activating appraisals for positive emotions (Beck, 1991; Beck & Clark, 1997; Bowins, 2013).

By opposing or terminating the mutually reinforcing cognitive-emotional cycles via cognitive regulatory control techniques, the frontal cortex appears to be able to reestablish regulation of limbic system activity (Beauregard, 2007; Bowins, 2013), a process involving enhanced frontal cortical-limbic connectivity (Schardt et al, 2010). In line with this cognitive regulatory control mechanism, cognitive reappraisal improves emotional self-regulation (Beauregard, 2007). Greater PFC and reduced amygdala activation has been observed in social anxiety disorder patients who completed Cognitive Behavioral Therapy (Goldin, 2009). PFC-amygdala connectivity also regulates phobic reactions derived from excessive amygdala activity (Hermann et al, 2007). In effect, by enhancing cognitive regulatory control, cognitive behavioral and related techniques restore the naturally positive spin characterizing good mental health, which with depression and anxiety shifts to a negative spin (see the chapter "Psychosis") (Beck, 1991; Beck & Clark, 1997; Bowins, 2004; Bowins, 2013).

Dissociation based techniques, such as willful detachment, suppression therapy, attention shifts of metacognitive therapy, compartmentalization, and absorption in a positive focus, also constitute forms of cognitive regulatory control therapy, because they help to improve regulation of negative emotional states by psychologically distancing or removing a person from them (Bowins, 2012c, 2013). The first four dissociation based techniques involve consciously attenuating the negative focus by mentally detaching from it (willful detachment), suppressing it in the moment (suppression therapy), shifting attention to another input (attention shifts of metacognitive therapy), or walling it off psychologically (compartmentalization), whereas the latter involves immersing oneself in a positive or at least not negative focus (Bowins, 2012c, 2013). Absorption in a positive focus often follows from the first four techniques, the combination helping with cognitive regulation over negative emotional states.

Duration Dimension

As pertains to the duration dimension of depression, time units distinguish short, moderate, and long (Bowins, 2015). Perhaps short might be set at less than 3 months, moderate at 3-6 months, and long greater than 6 months, although research might have to establish the optimal time frame parameters for these three levels, and with the understanding that there is a continuous structure. For a fully comprehensive picture of a depressive episode both severity and duration should be described in relationship to each other. As with anxiety (see the "Anxiety" chapter) severity and duration are to be rated low, moderate, high (or low, moderate, and severe), with the numbers 1, 2, 3 assigned respectively. The product of the assigned values gives a fairly accurate picture of the quantitative and qualitative differences. For example, a short-lived and low severity episode can be listed as $1 \times 1 = 1$, and a long-lived and high severity episode $3 \times 3 = 9$. Between these two extremes are various scenarios such as shorter range/high severity episodes ($1 \times 3 = 3$), moderate length/moderate severity ($2 \times 2 = 4$), short duration/moderate severity ($1 \times 2 = 2$), moderate duration/high severity ($2 \times 3 = 6$), and longer range/mild severity ($3 \times 1 = 3$). Given that the same numeric value can describe different states, the rating assigned for duration and severity should both be recorded. The ratings are for each episode, and as such do not indicate recurrent episodes, necessitating that they be recorded separately.

A crucial feature of this characterization is that varying qualitative experiences emerge from different quantitative levels (Bowins, 2015). For example, playing your favorite music at low volume for an hour ($1 \times 1 = 1$) is vastly different, both numerically and qualitatively, than the same music at high volume for a day straight ($3 \times 3 = 9$): Whereas the former is highly pleasing and soothing, the latter is very annoying and draining. Likewise, depressions of varying quantitative levels differ qualitatively. For example, a short duration/mild severity depression is qualitatively very different to a long duration/high severity episode. In the case of the former there is typically much less overall suffering and disruption to the person's life compared to the latter. The dimensional nature of depression is then captured by the duration × severity model, with severity based on depressive inhibition in terms of cognitive, emotional, social, and physical behavior. Rating duration and severity on three levels provides a measure of each dimension. The product of these values yields invaluable information pertaining to the quantitative and related qualitative aspects of a depressive episode. For instance, melancholic depression, being high in severity and often also duration, is qualitatively distinct as an emergent property of the quantitative variation.

Should the Depression Dimension Include Other Conditions?

Evidence for depression as a unitary entity ironically comes from the research by Parker and colleagues (Parker, 2013; Parker et al, 1988; Parker et al, 1991), purportedly supporting melancholic/endogenous depression as a discrete type. The non-endogenous factor they identified consisting of anxiety, personality, and other condition variables is used to support the position that a discrete form of depression—melancholic/endogenous—alone exists, with reactive/neurotic "depression" a composite of anxiety and personality symptoms (Parker, 2013; Parker et al, 1988; Parker et al, 1991). The results of Cochrane (1977) also align with this perspective, the non-endogenous form of depression being indistinguishable from non-depressed psychiatric states. But then how are we to characterize scenarios where depression involves anxiety, hypomania-mania, psychosis, and personality disorders? Depression is commonly mixed with anxiety, hypomanic-manic symptoms, psychosis in some instances, and personality disorder symptoms (Benazzi, 2004; Benazzi, 2007; Bilder et al, 2000; Elvevag & Goldberg, 2000; Fava et al, 2000; Fiszdon et al, 2007; Freeman & McElroy, 1999; Himmelhoch, 1998; Judd et al, 1998). One solid option for explaining the overlap between depressive and other symptoms is separate continuums interfacing with one another (Bowins, 2015). Hence, the depression continuum can interface with other continuums, such as that for anxiety, hypomania-mania, psychosis, and personality disorders.

Interfacing of the anxiety and depression continuums provides an example of how this process can work. Depression and anxiety commonly overlap, as with depression and social anxiety (Fava et al, 2000). This is not surprising given the emotional information processing overlap between anxiety and depression: Circumstances that entail threat or danger also frequently involve loss (Bowins, 2004). We might arrange depression and anxiety on a single dimension, placing them at either extreme, a seemingly viable option. However, this arrangement produces serious obstacles. First, it would imply that depressive and anxiety symptoms must trade off against each other, such that greater depression means lesser anxiety, a clearly false scenario since both symptom types can occur together with varying severity levels. Second, moderate levels on the single dimension, representing a true mix of symptoms, must mean less severe depression than at the depression pole, and less severe anxiety than at the anxiety pole. This occurrence is not compatible with the comorbidity of depression and anxiety, because mixed scenarios commonly involve both intense depression and anxiety; indeed, comorbidity is often a sign of greater severity generally. The perspective might be taken that placement on the same dimension only pertains to the presence or absence of depressive and anxiety symptoms, such that depressive symptoms are maximal at that pole and decline to the anxiety pole. However, the dimension we are now considering is severity and not just presence of symptoms.

Watson (2005) presents another way that anxiety and depression overlap based on the interpretation of factor analytic studies: Certain types of anxiety,

GAD and posttraumatic stress disorder (PTSD), and depression, major and dysthymic, are linked on the basis of distress (distress disorders), while panic disorder, agoraphobia, social phobia, and specific phobia are distinct as "fear" disorders. This comorbidity perspective can only account for depression and anxiety, and hence is limited in its applicability to the overlap between depression and other disorders. As pertains to depression and anxiety together, a major problem is that it fails to consider the different emotional information processing underlying depression and anxiety: Depression as amplified sadness with the root emotion triggered by loss-oriented cognitive activating appraisals, and anxiety as amplified fear with the root emotion derived from threat or danger oriented cognitive activating appraisals (Beck, 1991; Bowins, 2004, 2006a; Clore & Ortony, 2000; Eley & Stevenson, 2000; Finlay-Jones & Brown, 1981; Lazarus, 1984; Lazarus, 1991; Shrout et al, 1989). A more specific problem with Watson's (2005) model pertaining to the realities of comorbidity is that depression frequently co-exists with "fear" conditions such as social phobia (Fava et al, 2000). Social anxiety actually appears to represent the primary trigger for depression in many instances (Schneier et al, 2002). In addition, panic disorder, agoraphobia, social phobia, and specific phobia can involve equal or greater levels of distress than with generalized anxiety disorder, PTSD, or depression. For instance, those with panic disorder often experience great distress. Hence, the notion of interfacing depression and anxiety continuums is more parsimonious and compatible with the realities of depression and anxiety comorbidity.

Depression and Specific Circumstances

We have examined how different mental health conditions might overlap with depression, and concluded that the interfacing of dimensions provides the best of fit. Depression also interacts with various specific circumstances, and an explanation of this process is required. Specific circumstances appear to have the capacity to activate the depressive continuum, at least in those predisposed. For example, social stressors, physiological disease processes, and environmental cues relevant to behavioral inhibition and behavioral activation (BIS and BAS) each appear capable of activating the depressive continuum. Social stressors, such as trauma, and physical disease processes including hypothyroidism, cancer, pain, and inflammation (likely via pain), amongst others, often trigger depression.

BIS and BAS relevant environmental cues underlie seasonal affective disorder, known as SAD (Bowins, 2008). In the case of SAD, there appears to be a pronounced sensitivity to environmental cues relevant to BIS and BAS, with low light levels and related winter stimuli, such as cold days with few signs of life, substantially increasing behavioral inhibition and reducing behavioral activation, thereby initiating depression (Bowins, 2008). Lesser mood and behavioral changes in response to environmental cues for high BIS and low BAS do not constitute depression. SAD might conceivably represent a different subtype of depression. However, support for discrete types of depression is lacking, as we have seen, and a depressive continuum is more viable.

Furthermore, as with other proposed subtypes there is too much symptom overlap. For example, with SAD so-called "atypical" depressive symptoms involving excessive sleep and carbohydrate cravings occur, but many people with non-SAD depression oversleep and consume high calorie sweetened foods over healthier alternatives, this occurrence contributing to the problem of excess weight found in those with depression (Davidson & Kaplan, 2012). Research also does not fully support SAD as being a separate disease entity. Examining a population in Northern Norway living without sun for two months, Hansen et al (2008) did not find evidence that depression is higher than in any other population in winter, and suggested that "depression with seasonal pattern" be used to describe depression that recurs in winter. Hence, it appears that the depressive component of SAD does not represent a distinct clinical entity, but more properly depression elicited by environmental cues for high BIS and low BAS in those who are highly sensitive to these stimuli.

Specific circumstances associated with depression are then best conceptualized as eliciting mechanisms or triggers activating the depression continuum (Bowins, 2015). Reversal of those inputs can improve or resolve depression. For example, with SAD reversal of cues for behavioral inhibition/behavioral activation can help resolve the depressive state: When low light levels, cold, and dreary environmental stimuli are replaced with sun, warmth, and vibrant stimuli, such as when a person vacations to the Caribbean, cues for high BIS and low BAS rapidly shift to low BIS and high BAS. Consequently, activation of the depressive continuum shifts to deactivation. In a similar fashion, reversal of social stressors or a triggering disease process helps resolve depression. For example, correcting thyroid hormone deficiency can improve or remedy depression that was initiated by the illness. However, if depressive inhibition becomes too severe and/or too long-term (locked in), reversal of the input mechanism is often insufficient to reverse it, and other means such as antidepressant medication are required. This latter point is a very important one because, with depressive inhibition, the cognitive, emotional, social, and physical impairments can persist, even with reversal of any specific circumstances that activated depression. This occurrence clearly separates depressive inhibition from behavioral inhibition.

The Dimensional Nature of Depression

Although there are certainly various ways to understand depression, the most reasonable appears to be as a continuum with severity and duration dimensions, the former characterized by depressive inhibition based on cognitive, emotional, social, and physical symptoms. There are no specific types of depression, but quantitative variation can produce qualitative variance as an emergent property, making it appear that different types actually exist. For instance, so-called endogenous depression seems qualitatively different based on the greater quantitative severity, although it resides on a single continuum of depression. Therefore, in any diagnostic system there should only be "depression" with low, moderate, and high (or mild, moderate, and severe) ratings for severity and duration. The composite of severity and duration ratings ranging from 1-9 (1 × 1 to 3 × 3) provides an accurate perspective regarding the quantitative and related qualitative aspects, and the degree of impairment associated with a given episode of depression.

A dimensional characterization of depression aligns with the Continuum Principle discussed, expressing how natural phenomena tend to be organized on the basis of continuums, and any suggestion of discreteness requires overwhelming proof. Such evidence is definitely lacking in the case of depression, with 100 years of research failing to clearly distinguish discrete types of depression. The notion of depression, and other mental health conditions such as anxiety, being organized dimensionally provides a parsimonious and robust understanding of comorbidity, based on the interfacing of continuums. It can also explain why specific circumstances are often associated with depression, in that they activate the depressive continuum, and their reversal can often deactivate depression.

References

Ambrosini, P.J., Bennett, D.S., Cleland, C.M., & Haslam, N. (2002). Taxonicity of adolescent melancholia: A categorical or dimensional construct? *Journal of Psychiatric Research, 36*(4), 247-256.

American Psychiatric Association (2013). *Diagnostic & Statistical Manual 5*. Washington, DC: American Psychiatric Publishing Inc.

Andrews, G., Brugha, T., Thase, M.E., Duffy, F.F., Rucci, P., & Slade, T. (2007). Dimensionality and the category of major depressive episode. *International Journal of Methods in Psychiatric Research, 16*(Suppl 1), S41-S51.

Angst, J. & Merikangas, K.R. (1997). The depressive spectrum: diagnostic classification and course. *Journal of Affective Disorders, 45*, 31-39.

Angst, J., Sellaro, R., & Merikangas, K.R. (2000). Depressive spectrum diagnoses. *Comprehensive Psychiatry, 41*(Supplement), 39-47.

Arnsten, A. (2009). Stress signaling pathways that impair prefrontal cortex structure and function. *Nature Reviews Neuroscience, 10*, 410-422.

Arnsten, A. (2011). Prefrontal cortical network connections: Key sites of vulnerability in stress and schizophrenia. *International Journal of Developmental Neuroscience, 29*(3), 215-223.

Azorin, J.M., Kaladjian, A., Fakra, E., DaFonseca, D., Adida, M., Maurel, M., Richieri, R., Bottai, T., & Pringuey, D. (2010). Gene-environment interactions in affective disorders. *Encephale, 36*(Suppl 6), 162-172.

Beauchaine, T.P. (2007). A brief taxometrics primer. *Journal of Clinical Child & Adolescence Psychology, 36*(4), 654-676.

Beauregard, M. (2007). Mind does really matter: Evidence from neuroimaging studies of emotional self-regulation, psychotherapy, and placebo effect. *Progress in Neurobiology, 81*(4), 218-236.

Beauregard, M., Paquette, V., & Levesque, J. (2006). Dysfunction in the neural circuitry of emotional self-regulation in major depressive disorder. *Neuroreport, 17*(8), 843-846.

Bech, P. (1988). Rating scales for mood disorders: Applicability, consistency, and construct validity. *Acta Psychiatrica Scandinavica, Supplementum, 345*, 45-55.

Beck, A. (1976). *Cognitive Therapy and the Emotional Disorders.* New York: Meridian Books.

Beck, A. (1991). Cognitive therapy: A 30-year retrospective. *American Psychologist, 46*(4), 368-375.

Beck, A. & Clark, D. (1997). An information processing model of anxiety: Automatic and strategic processes. *Behavior Research and Therapy, 35*(1), 49-58.

Benazzi, F. (2004). Factor structure of recalled DSM-IV hypomanic symptoms of bipolar disorder. *Comprehensive Psychiatry, 45,* 441-446.

Benazzi, F. (2006). Various forms of depression. *Dialogues of Clinical Neuroscience, 8,* 151-161.

Benazzi, F. (2007). Is overactivity the core feature of hypomania in bipolar II disorder? *Psychopathology, 40,* 54-60.

Bilder, R.M., Goldman, R.S., Robinson, D., Reiter, G., Bell, L., Bates, J.A. et al (2000). Neuropsychology of first-episode schizophrenia: Initial characterization and clinical correlates. *American Journal of Psychiatry, 157,* 549-559.

Bowins, B.E. (2004). Psychological defense mechanisms: A new perspective. *American Journal of Psychoanalysis, 64,* 1-26.

Bowins, B.E. (2006a). How psychiatric treatments can enhance psychological defense mechanisms. *American Journal of Psychoanalysis, 66,* 173-194.

Bowins, B. (2008). Hypomania: A depressive inhibition override defense mechanism. *Journal of Affective Disorders, 109,* 221-232.

Bowins, B.E. (2012a). Augmenting behavioural activation treatment with the behavioural activation and inhibition scales. *Behavioural and Cognitive Psychotherapy, 40,* 233-237.

Bowins, B.E. (2012c). Therapeutic dissociation: Compartmentalization and absorption. *Counselling Psychology Quarterly, 25*(1), 307-317.

Bowins, B.E. (2013). Cognitive regulatory control therapies. *American Journal of Psychotherapy, 67*(3), 215-236.

Bowins, B.E. (2015). Depression: Discrete or continuous? *Psychopathology, 48*(2), 69-78.

Brambilla, P., Glahn, D., Balestrieri, M., & Soares, J. (2005). Magnetic resonance findings in bipolar disorder. *Psychiatric Clinics of North America, 28*(2), 443-467.

Brodaty, H., Luscombe, G., Peisah, C., Anstey, K., & Andrews, G. (2001). A 25-year longitudinal, comparison study of the outcome of depression. *Psychological Medicine, 31,* 1347-1359.

Bronisch, T. & Klerman, G.L. (1988). The current status of neurotic depression as a diagnostic category. *Psychiatric Developments, 6*(4), 245-275.

Campbell-Sills, L., Liverant, G.I., & Brown, T.A. (2004). Psychometric evaluation of the behavioral inhibition/behavioral activation scales in a large sample of outpatients with anxiety and mood disorders. *Psychological Assessment, 16,* 244-254.

Carver, C.L. & White, T.L. (1994). Behavioral inhibition, behavioral activation, and affective responses to impending reward and punishment: The BIS/BAS scales. *Journal of Personality and Social Psychology, 67,* 319-333.

Chartier, S. & Provencher, M.D. (2013). Behavioural activation for depression: Efficacy, effectiveness and dissemination. *Journal of Affective Disorders, 145*(3), 292-299.

Clore, G. & Ortony, A. (2000). Cognition in emotion: Always, sometimes, or never? In *Cognitive Neuroscience of Emotion.* New York: Oxford University Press.

Cochrane, N. (1977). A contribution from the field of psychodynamics to the controversy over reactive and endogenous depression. *British Journal of Medical Psychology, 50*(1), 87-94.

Coryell, W. (1997). Do psychotic, minor, and intermittent depressive disorders exist on a continuum? *Journal of Affective Disorders, 45*(1-2), 75-83.

Cusi, A., Nazarov, A., Holshausen, K., MacQueen, G., & McKinnon, M. (2012). Systematic review of the neural basis of social cognition in patients with mood disorders. *Journal of Psychiatry & Neuroscience, 37*(3), 154-169.

Davidson, K. & Kaplan, B. (2012). Nutrient intakes are correlated with overall psychiatric functioning in adults with mood disorders. *Canadian Journal of Psychiatry, 57*(2), 85-92.

Darwin, C. (1858/1958). *The Origin of Species*. New York: Signet Classic.

Du, X., Pang, T.Y., & Hannan, A.J. (2013). A tale of two maladies? Pathogenesis of depression with and without the Huntington's disease gene mutation. *Frontiers in Neurology, 4*(81). http://doi.org/10.3389/fneur.2013.00081.

Ekman, P. (1972). *Emotions in the Human Face*. New York: Cambridge University Press.

Ekman, P. (1994). Antecedent events and emotion metaphors. In *Nature of Emotions*. Oxford: Oxford University Press.

Ekman, P. & Friesen, W. (1971). Constants across cultures in the face and emotion. *Journal of Personality and Social Psychology, 17*, 124-129.

Eley, T. & Stevenson, J. (2000). Specific life events and chronic experiences differentially associated with depression and anxiety in young twins. *Journal of Abnormal Child Psychology, 28*(4), 383-394.

Elvevag, B. & Goldberg, T.E. (2000). Cognitive impairment in schizophrenia is the core of the disorder. *Critical Reviews of Neurobiology, 14*, 1-21.

Eysenck, H.J. (1970). The classification of depressive illness. *British Journal of Psychiatry, 117*, 241-250.

Fava, M., Rankin, M.A., & Wright, E.C. (2000). Anxiety disorders in major depression. *Comprehensive Psychiatry, 41*, 97-102.

Finlay-Jones, R. & Brown, G. (1981). Types of stressful life event and the onset of anxiety and depressive disorders. *Psychological Medicine, 11*, 803-815.

First, M.B., Frances, A., & Pincus, H.A. (2002). *DSM-IV-TR Handbook of Differential Diagnosis*. Washington, DC: American Psychiatric Publishing.

Fiszdon, J.M., Richardson, R., Greig, T., & Bell, M.D. (2007). A comparison of basic and social cognition between schizophrenia and schizoaffective disorder. *Schizophrenia Research, 91*, 117-121.

Fowles, D.C. (1988). Psychophysiology and psychopathology: A motivational approach. *Psychophysiology, 25*, 373-391.

Freeman, M.P. & McElroy, S.L. (1999). Clinical picture and etiologic models of mixed states. *Psychiatric Clinics of North America, 22*, 535-546

Gibb, B.E., Alloy, L.B., Abramson, L.Y., Beevers, C.G., & Miller, I.W. (2004). Cognitive vulnerability to depression: A taxometric analysis. *Journal of Abnormal Psychology, 113*(1), 81-89.

Goldin, P. (2009). Effects of cognitive-behavioral therapy on neural bases of emotion regulation in social anxiety disorder. *Biological Psychiatry, 65*(Suppl. 1), 1215-1221.

Gray, J.A. (1987). Perspectives on anxiety and impulsivity: A commentary. *Journal of Research in Personality, 21*, 493-509.

Hamilton, J., Etkin, A., Furman, D., Lemus, M., Johnson, R., & Gotlib, I. (2012). Functional neuroimaging of major depressive disorder: A meta-analysis and new integration of baseline activation and neural response data. *American Journal of Psychiatry, 169*(7), 693-703.

Hansen, V., Skre, I., & Lund, E. (2008). What is this thing called "SAD"? A critique of the concept of seasonal affective disorder. *Epidemiology Psychiatry Society, 17*(2), 120-127.

Harmer, C., Hill, S., Taylor, M., Cowen, P., & Goodwin, G. (2003). Toward a neuropsychological theory of antidepressant drug action: Increase in positive emotional bias after potentiation of norepinephrine activity. *The American Journal of Psychiatry, 160*(5), 990-992.

Harris, M., Farquhar, F., Healy, D., LeNoury, J., Baker, D., Whitaker, C. et al (2011). The incidence and prevalence of admissions for melancholia in two cohorts (1875-1924 and 1995-2005). *Journal of Affective Disorders, 134*(1-3), 45-51.

Harris M., Farquhar F., Healy D., LeNoury J., Linden S., Hughes J.A., & Roberts A.P. (2013). The morbidity and mortality linked to melancholia: Two cohorts compared, 1875-1924 and 1995-2005. *History & Psychiatry, 24*(1), 3-14.

Hartley, C. & Phelps, E. (2010). Changing fear; the neurocircuitry of emotion regulation. *Neuropsychopharmacology, 35*, 136-146.

Haslam, N. & Beck, A.T. (1994). Subtyping major depression: A taxometric analysis. *Journal of Abnormal Psychology, 103*(4), 686-692.

Haslam, N., Holland, E., & Kuppens, P. (2012). Categories versus dimensions in personality and psychopathology: A quantitative review of taxometric research. *Psychological Medicine, 42*(5), 902-920.

Healy, D. (2013). Melancholia: Past and present. *The Canadian Journal of Psychiatry, 58*(4), 190-194.

Hermann, A., Schafer, A., Walter, B., Stark, R., Vaitl, D., & Schienle, A. (2007). Diminished medial prefrontal cortex activity in blood-injection-injury phobia. *Biological Psychiatry, 75*(2), 124-130.

Himmelhoch, J.M. (1998). Social anxiety, hypomania and the bipolar spectrum: Data, theory and clinical issues. *Journal of Affective Disorders, 50*, 203-213.

Hopko, D.R., Lejuez, C.W., Ruggiero, K.J., & Eifert, G.H. (2003). Contemporary behavioral activation treatments for depression: Procedures, principles, and progress. *Clinical Psychology Review, 23*, 699-717.

Izard, C. (1977). *Human Emotions*. New York: Plenum

Jacobson, N.S., Dobson, K.S., Truax, P.A., Addis, M.E., Koerner, K., Gollan, J.K. et al (1996). A component analysis of cognitive-behavioral treatment for depression. *Journal of Consulting & Clinical Psychology, 64*, 295-304.

Johnson, S.L., Sandrow, D., Meyer, B., Winters, R., Miller, I., Solomon, D., & Keitner, G. (2000). Increases in manic symptoms after life events involving goal attainment. *Journal of Abnormal Psychology, 109*, 721-727.

Judd, L.L., Akiskal, H.S., & Maser, J.D. (1998). A prospective 12-year study of subsyndromal and syndromal depressive symptoms in unipolar major depressive disorders. *Archives of General Psychiatry, 55*, 694-700.

Kanter, J.W., Puspitasari, A.J., Santos, M.M., & Nagy, G.A. (2012). Behavioural activation: History, evidence, and promise. *British Journal of Psychiatry, 200*, 361-363.

Kasch, K.L., Rottenberg, J., Arnow, B.A., & Gotlib, I.H. (2002). Behavioral activation and inhibition systems and the severity and course of depression. *Journal of Abnormal Psychology, 111*, 589-597.

Kendler, K.S., Thornton, L.M., & Gardner, C.O. (2000). Stressful life events and previous episodes in the etiology of major depression in women: An evaluation of the "kindling" hypothesis. *American Journal of Psychiatry, 157*, 1243-1251.

Kessing, L.V. (2004). Endogenous, reactive and neurotic depression—diagnostic stability and long-term outcome. *Psychopathology, 37*, 124-130.

Kessing, L.V. (2007). Epidemiology of subtypes of depression. *Acta Psychiatrica Scandinavica, 115*(Suppl. 433), 85-89.

Kiloh, L.G., Andrews, G., Neilson, M., & Bianchi, G.N. (1972). The relationship of the syndromes called endogenous and neurotic depression. *British Journal of Psychiatry, 121*, 183-196.

Kinsey, A.C., Pomeroy, W.B., & Martin, C.E. (1948). *Sexual Behavior in the Human Male*. Philadelphia: W.B. Saunders.

Kinsey, A.C., Pomeroy, W.B., Martin, C.E., & Gebhard, P.H. (1953). *Sexual Behavior in the Human Female*. Philadelphia: W.B. Saunders.

Lazarus, R. (1984). On the primacy of cognition. *American Psychologist, 39*(2), 124-129.

Lazarus, R. (1991). Cognition and emotion in motivation. *American Psychologist, 46*(4), 352-367.

Lejuez, C.W., Hopko, D.R., & Hopko, S.D. (2001). A brief behavioral activation treatment for depression. *Behavior Modification, 25*, 255-286.

Ly, K.H., Truschel, A., Jarl, L., Magnusson, S., Windahl, T., Johansson, R., Carlbring, P., & Andersson, G. (2013). Behavioural activation versus mindfulness-based guided self-help treatment administered through a smartphone application: A randomised controlled trial. *BMJ, 4*(1), e003440.

McEvoy, P., Law, A., Bates, R., Hylton, K., & Mansell, W. (2013). Using behavioural activation in the treatment of depression: A control theory perspective. *Journal of Psychiatric Mental Health Nursing, 20*(10), 890-895.

Mineka, S., Watson, D., & Clark, L.A. (1998). Comorbidity of anxiety and unipolar mood disorders. *Annual Review of Psychology, 49*, 377-412.

Newman, S.C. & Bland, R.C. (2009). A population-based family study of minor depression. *Depression & Anxiety, 26*(4), 389-392.

Okumura, Y., Sakamoto, S., & Ono, Y. (2009). Latent structure of depression in a Japanese population sample: Taxometric procedures. *Australian & New Zealand Journal of Psychiatry, 43*(7), 666-673.

O'Leary, D. (1996). The endogenous subtype and naturalistic course in depression. *Journal of Affective Disorders, 41*, 117-123.

Pandya, M., Altinay, M., Malone, D.A., & Anand, A. (2012). Where in the brain is depression? *Current Psychiatry Reports, 14*(6), 634-642.

Parker, G. (2013). A case for reprising and redefining melancholia. *The Canadian Journal of Psychiatry, 58*(4), 183-189.

Parker, G., Blignault, I., & Manicavasagar, V. (1988). Neurotic depression: Delineation of symptom profiles and their relation to outcome. *British Journal of Psychiatry, 152*, 15-23.

Parker, G., Fletcher, K., Barrett, M., Synnott, H., Breakspear, M., Rees, A.M., & Hadzi-Pavlovic, D. (2013). Inching toward Bethlehem: Mapping melancholia. *Journal of Affective Disorders, 123*(1-3), 291-298.

Parker, G., Hall, W., Boyce, P., Hadzi-Pavlovic, D., Mitchell, P., Wilhelm, K. et al (1991). Depression sub-typing: Unitary, binary, or arbitrary? *Australian & New Zealand Journal of Psychiatry, 25*, 63-76.

Parker, G., McCraw, S., Blanch, B., Hadzi-Pavlovic, D., Synnott, H., & Rees, A.M. (2013). Discriminating melancholic and non-melancholic depression by prototypic clinical features. *Journal of Affective Disorders, 144*(3), 199-207.

Paykel, E.S. (2008). Basic concepts of depression. *Dialogues of Clinical Neuroscience, 10*(3), 279-289.

Philippot, P. & Brutoux, F. (2008). Induced rumination dampens executive processes in dysphoric young adults. *Journal of Behavior, Therapy, and Experimental Psychiatry, 39*(3), 219-227.

Post, R.M. (1992). Transduction of psychosocial stress into the neurobiology of recurrent affective disorder. *American Journal of Psychiatry, 149*, 999-1010.

Prisciandaro, J.J. & Roberts, J.E. (2005). A taxometric investigation of unipolar depression in the national comorbidity survey. *Journal of Abnormal Psychology, 114*(4), 718-728.

Ramana, R., Paykel, E.S., Cooper, Z., Hayhurst, H., Saxty, M., & Surtees, P.G. (1995). Remission and relapse in major depression: A two-year prospective follow-up study. *Psychological Medicine, 25*, 1161-1170.

Rhebergen, D. & Graham, R. (2014). The re-labelling of dysthymic disorder to persistent depressive disorder in DSM-5: Old wine in new bottles? *Current Opinions in Psychiatry, 27*(1), 27-31.

Rhebergen, D., Graham, R., Hadzi-Pavlovic, D., Stek, M., Friend, P., Barrett, M., & Parker, G. (2012). The categorisation of dysthymic disorder: Can its constituents be meaningfully apportioned? *Journal of Affective Disorders, 143*(1-3), 179-186.

Ruscio, A.M. & Ruscio, J. (2002). The latent structure of analogue depression: Should the Beck Depression Inventory be used to classify people? *Psychological Assessment, 14*(2), 135-145.

Ruscio, J., Ruscio, A.M., & Keane, T.M. (2004). Using taxometric analysis to distinguish a small latent taxon from a latent dimension with positively skewed indicators: The case of involuntary defeat syndrome. *Journal of Abnormal Psychology, 113*(1), 145-154.

Salzman, D. & Fusi, S. (2010). Emotion, cognition, and mental state representation in amygdala and prefrontal cortex. *Annual Review of Neuroscience, 33*, 173-202.

Schardt, D., Erk, S., Nusser, C., Nothen, M., Cichon, S., Rietschel, M. et al (2010). Volition diminishes genetically mediated amygdala hyperreactivity. *Neuroimage, 53*(3), 943-951.

Schneier, F.R., Blanco, C., Antia, S.X., & Liebowitz, M.R. (2002). The social anxiety spectrum. *Psychiatric Clinics of North America, 25*, 757-774.

Scholten, M.R., van Honk, J., Aleman, A., & Kahn, R.S. (2006). Behavioral Inhibition System (BIS), the Behavioral Activation System (BAS) and schizophrenia: Relationship with psychopathology and physiology. *Journal of Psychiatric Research, 40*, 638-645.

Schotte, C.K., Maes, M., Cluydts, R., & Cosyns, P. (1997). Cluster analytic validation of the DSM melancholic depression. The threshold model: Integration of quantitative and qualitative distinctions between unipolar depressive subtypes. *Psychiatry Research, 71*(3), 181-195.

Shorter, E. (1997). *A History of Psychiatry*. Toronto: John Wiley & Sons, Inc.

Shrout, P., Link B., Dohrenwend, B., Skodol, A., Stueve A., & Mirotznik J. (1989). Characterizing life events as risk factors for depression: The role of fateful loss events. *Journal of Abnormal Psychology, 98*(4), 460-467.

Slade, T. (2007). Taxometric investigation of depression: Evidence of consistent latent structure across clinical and community samples. *Australian & New Zealand Journal of Psychiatry, 41*(5), 403-410.

Slade, T. & Andrews, G. (2005). Latent structure of depression in a community sample: A taxometric analysis. *Psychological Medicine, 35*(4), 489-497.

Solomon, A., Haaga, D.A., & Arnow, B.A. (2001). Is clinical depression distinct from subthreshold depressive symptoms? A review of the continuity issue in depression research. *Journal of Nervous & Mental Disease, 189*(8), 498-506.

Solomon, A., Ruscio, J., Seeley, J.R., & Lewinsohn, P.M. (2006). A taxometric investigation of unipolar depression in a large community sample. *Psychological Medicine, 36*(7), 973-985.

Su, S., Sun, M., Wen., M., Lin, C., Chen, Y., & Hung, Y. (2011). Brain-derived neurotrophic factor, adiponectin, and proinflammatory markers in various subtypes of depression in young men. *International Journal of Psychiatry in Medicine, 42*(3), 211-226.

Surtees, P.G. & Barkley, C. (1994). Future imperfect: The long-term outcome of depression. *British Journal of Psychiatry, 164*, 327-341.

Tomkins, S. (1962). *Affect, Imagery, Consciousness: The Positive Effects* (Volume 1). New York: Springer.

Tomkins, S. (1963). *Affect, Imagery, Consciousness: The Negative Effects* (Volume 2). New York: Springer.

Treadway, M.T. & Pizzagalli, D.A. (2014). Imagining the pathophysiology of major depressive disorder—from localist to circuit-based analysis. *Biological Mood & Anxiety Disorders, 4*(1). http://doi.org/10.1186/2045-5380-4-5.

Vanderhasselt, M. & DeRaedt, R. (2009). Impairments in cognitive control persist during remission from depression and are related to the number of past episodes: An event related potentials study. *Biological Psychiatry, 81*(3), 169-176.

Watson, D. (2005). Rethinking the mood and anxiety disorders: A quantitative hierarchical model for DSM-V. *Journal of Abnormal Psychology, 114*(4), 522-536.

Welch, G.W. & Ellis, P.M. (1991). FACTOREP: a new tool to explore the dimensions of depression. *Journal of Affective Disorders, 21*(2), 101-108.

World Health Organization (1992). *The ICD-10 Classification of Mental and Behavioral Disorders: Clinical Descriptions and Diagnostic Guidelines*. Geneva: World Health Organization.

CHAPTER 3
Anxiety

Evidence from neuroscience and emotional information processing, reviewed later in this chapter, demonstrates that anxiety is a naturally occurring entity. Current diagnostic systems embrace the concept of discrete types of anxiety. DSM-IV-TR includes social anxiety disorder, generalized anxiety disorder (GAD), specific phobia, panic disorder with or without agoraphobia, obsessive-compulsive disorder (OCD), and posttraumatic stress disorder (PTSD) as primary disorders (First et al, 2002). DSM-5 cleaves off OCD and PTSD as separate entities (American Psychiatric Association, 2013). ICD-10 describes phobic anxiety disorders including social phobias and agoraphobia, specific phobias, panic disorder, generalized anxiety disorder, OCD, and reaction to stress disorders such as PTSD (World Health Organization, 1992). Disorders with anxiety at the core appear to include GAD, social anxiety disorder, specific phobia, and panic disorder, whereas OCD and PTSD involve components beyond anxiety, such as compulsive behavior with OCD, and re-experiencing a traumatic event with PTSD (American Psychiatric Association, 2013; First et al, 2002; World Health Organization, 1992).

Characterization of anxiety disorders as discrete or continuous pertains to, first, within specific types such as distinct versions of social anxiety, and second, anxiety in general. Regarding the latter, a question rarely asked is whether or not specific disorders are invalid, with anxiety just consisting of one continuum. A consideration of whether continuums or discreteness applies within specific anxiety disorders makes it easier to address the very intriguing, but more complex topic of how anxiety in general can be characterized. Hence, we will first examine specific disorders.

Specific Anxiety Disorders

Social Anxiety Disorder (SAD)

SAD can be viewed as consisting of discrete forms, such as fear of public speaking, or a single continuum with various expressions (Aderka et al, 2012; Furmark et al, 2000; Ha et al, 2011; Piqueras et al, 2008; Rettew, 2000; Vriends et al, 2007). A popular perspective regarding social anxiety is that there are generalized and non-generalized subtypes (Aderka et al, 2012; Ha et al, 2011; Aderka et al, 2012; Piqueras et al, 2008; Rettew, 2000; Vriends et al, 2007). In everyday clinical practice this distinction tends to be applied, with fear of public speaking being perceived and addressed differently than a general fear of social situations. But what position is best supported by research?

Despite how common it is to view social anxiety as being separable into generalized and non-generalized forms (or various specific types), the research evidence does not support this perspective. For instance Aderka et al (2012) applied admixture analyses to generalized and non-generalized SAD subjects' responses to the Liebowitz Social Anxiety Scale. The results support the perspective that the two subtypes belong to the same underlying population of origin (Aderka et al, 2012). The authors noted that apparent differences between generalized and non-generalized subtypes of SAD, including depression and other comorbidities, were no longer significant when social anxiety severity was controlled for.

Support for the importance of illness severity comes from additional studies, such as that by Ha et al (2011) focused on Korean SAD patients. These researchers administered the Liebowitz Social Anxiety Scale, Anxiety Sensitivity Index, and Trait Form of the State-Trait Anxiety Inventory to 273 SAD patients. Scores differed between generalized and non-generalized SAD patients, but the differences vanished after adjusting for illness severity (Ha et al, 2011). The authors suggest that the two subtypes are actually on the same continuum, and differentiated only by symptom severity. A study by Vriends et al (2006) examining a very different patient population—1,877 young German females—found that the number of feared situations was distributed continuously. The researchers could not identify any clear-cut delineations considering functional impairment, comorbidity, subjective need for psychotherapy, help seeking (psychotherapy), level of social support, and overall mental health (Vriends et al, 2006). They examined subtype models, based on number of feared social situations (1, 2-4, and >4), and type such as fear of public speaking. These models did not add anything significant beyond a continuum model of social phobia. Vriends et al (2006) conclude that variation within social phobia is best understood as a continuum of severity, with greater functional, social, and psychological disability associated with an increasing number of feared situations. Supporting this perspective, El-Gabalawy et al (2010) using the National Comorbidity Survey Replication (9,282 subjects), discovered that as the number of feared social situations increased so did severity, based upon comorbidity and suicidal ideation. Turner et al (1992) also found that more generalized social fears are linked to greater symptom severity. Applying multiple taxometric procedures to the National Comorbidity Survey Replication data, also used by El-Gabalawy et al (2010), Ruscio (2010) found that social anxiety disorder is continuous with milder social anxiety.

A study by Furmark et al (2000) applied the technique of cluster analysis to Social Phobia Scale and Social Interaction Anxiety Scale scores, completed by

188 individuals with social phobia. They found three clusters of scores: High (generalized subtype), intermediate (non-generalized subtype), and low (discrete subtype). They concluded that although categorical distinctions might apply, their data supports the position that social phobia subtypes are distributed dimensionally in the general population, along a mild-moderate-severe continuum, and that the number of cases declines with increasing severity (Furmark et al, 2000). Research that does not assess severity, such as the factor analytic study of adolescence by Piqueras et al (2008), can erroneously conclude that discrete generalized and specific distinctions are valid.

Research studies examining whether social anxiety is organized discretely or continuously thus support the position that a continuum applies. Generalized and non-generalized types cannot be clearly separated (Aderka et al, 2012; Ha et al, 2011). Nor can social anxiety be organized discretely on the basis of number and types of fears (Vriends et al, 2006). Of critical importance, social anxiety appears to be characterized by severity—greater severity is associated with an increasing number of specific social fears (Aderka et al, 2012; El-Gabalawy et al, 2010; Furmark et al, 2000; Ha et al, 2011; Vriends et al, 2006). Generalized social anxiety is more severe due to the greater number of social fears involved (Aderka et al, 2012; Furmark et al, 2000; Ha et al, 2011).

Panic Disorder

In comparison to social anxiety disorder, panic disorder has received far less attention pertaining to whether or not discrete subtypes apply, an occurrence also true for the remaining anxiety disorders. However, some attention has been paid to this matter. Buller et al (1986) looked at whether panic attacks with agoraphobia are distinct from panic attacks without agoraphobia. Investigating a sample of 97 patients with panic attacks, they found support for a continuum, in that panic attacks with agoraphobia constituted a more severe illness, based on symptoms experienced both at the assessment and at a one-year follow-up. Results of research by Scheibe and Albus (1992) examining 178 outpatients support this perspective, finding that panic attacks with agoraphobia represents a more severe illness. Gelernter et al (1992) report results suggesting that agoraphobia might derive at least to some extent from social phobia, providing further support for the perspective that panic attacks with and without agoraphobia are not distinct entities.

Specific Phobia

Regarding phobias, fear inducing situations have been the main consideration when it comes to subdividing into types. Himle et al (1989) investigated the subtypes of animal-insect, blood-injury, situational, and choking-vomiting. These researchers found significant gender differences, in that all animal-insect and the majority of choking-vomiting phobias occurred in females, whereas blood-injury and situational occurred with equal frequency between females and males. Methodological limitations of this study prevent definitive conclusions: There were more females than males, and there were too few patients in blood-injury and choking-vomiting (9 and 8, respectively) (Himle et al, 1989). Furthermore, the differences were not related to actual clinical symptoms of anxiety, but only the phobia focus. The number of fears, irrespective of type, appears to be an indicator of greater severity, being related to impairment, comorbidity, illness course, and family psychopathology (Curtis et al, 1998). This occurrence supports specific phobia as being on a continuum.

Generalized Anxiety Disorder (GAD)

The term "generalized" in itself suggests that GAD cannot be subdivided, and research supports this notion. Worry is a core feature of GAD. Research by Olatunji et al (2010) demonstrates that it is continuous in distribution, having an equal association with anxiety, stress, and depression. Investigating the feasibility of subdividing GAD on the basis of duration, Angst et al (2006) utilized data from the Zurich Cohort Study. Their results did not support the subdivision approach, and they concluded that duration of GAD forms a continuum, and hence the DSM-III and DSM-IV-TR criteria of 6 months are not valid (Angst et al, 2006). Applying three taxometric procedures, Kertz et al (2014) found that generalized anxiety is a dimensional construct, and indicate that ongoing conceptualization, assessment, and treatment might be hampered by a categorical approach. Using data from the Midlife in the United States study and multiple taxometric procedures, Marcus et al (2014) did not find any evidence for GAD being organized categorically, the results favoring a continuous arrangement. Adding further to the notion of GAD constituting a continuum, as opposed to discrete subtypes, is how subthreshold anxiety extends to GAD (Rickels & Schweizer, 1998).

Other Forms of Anxiety

Obsessive-compulsive disorder and posttraumatic stress disorder are now considered to be different than core anxiety disorders, a categorization supported by the presence of non-anxiety components (American Psychiatric Association, 2013). Hence, a discussion of these two conditions will be presented when we examine the concept of anxiety as a single entity.

Anxiety in General

Considering that the evidence overwhelmingly suggests dimensionality within anxiety disorders "types," it is valid to examine whether or not anxiety in general is dimensional. Despite the validity of this issue, there is virtually a complete absence of research and discussion in the scientific literature, the implicit assumption being that anxiety disorders must be discrete, although the precise categorization can vary between diagnostic systems, and even over time in the same one (American Psychiatric Association, 2013; First et al, 2002; World Health Organization, 1992). Furthermore, the discrete model is based on studies comparing one supposed type to another, as opposed to whether or not there is any evidence for one continuous distribution. Noyes et al (1992) compared 41 GAD patients to 71 panic disorder patients. GAD patients experienced a more gradual and earlier onset than occurred with panic disorder patients. Associated symptoms tended to be milder with GAD, such as simple phobias, whereas with panic disorder agoraphobia and depersonalization were more common (Noyes et al, 1992). However, Noyes et al (1992) did not find any absolute separation between GAD and panic disorder, but rather degrees in terms of age of onset and associated symptoms. Scheibe and Albus (1992) also found that panic disorder had a later age of onset, in this instance compared to both simple and social phobia. There is the possibility that the greater severity of panic disorder takes time to manifest. In addition, panic disorder does arise at an early age (younger than 20 years) in some instances (Goodwin & Hamilton, 2002; Segui et al, 1999). Early-onset does tend to involve greater comorbidities, likely due to greater severity (Goodwin & Hamilton, 2002; Segui et al, 1999).

Comorbidity patterns have been used to support discrete types of anxiety disorders, for example, GAD associated with affective disorders, social phobias linked to agoraphobia (Angst, 1993), and OCD not involving GAD (Austin et al, 1990). However, attempts to separate anxiety disorders based on comorbidity break down under closer analysis. For instance, agoraphobia is also associated with specific phobia (Wittchen et al, 1998). Affective disorders, personality disorders, substance abuse, OCD, PTSD, and various anxiety disorders frequently comingle (Austin et al, 1990; Chapman et al, 1993; Maes et al, 1998; Merikangas & Angst, 1995; Segui et al, 1999; Skodol et al, 1995; Strarcevic et al, 1994; Tilfors & Ekselius, 2009).

To a great extent the distinguishing criteria of anxiety disorders involve circumstances consistent with the name of the condition that might not be core to the underlying illness. For example, Social Anxiety Disorder entails fear of social situation/s. Consistent with the name we would expect fear of social situations, and anxiety reactions involving a social emotional component such as shame, embarrassment, and humiliation. While this says something clear about the focus or contributing circumstances, it does not prove that the underlying core fear/anxiety process is different. Likewise, with specific phobia there is fear of a specific circumstance, with the fear/anxiety reaction linked to this circumstance. When the specific circumstance involves a social component it becomes a social phobia, but why is this different than a specific phobia? Obviously, both are specific phobias. When there is more than one specific fear focus we say there is Social Anxiety Disorder if these are social, and multiple specific phobias or GAD if non-social. The entire process appears to be a creation based predominantly on the fear circumstances and not the underlying fear/anxiety process, and one that produces absurdities such as how we deal with a specific phobia that is social in nature, and why there should be such a clear-cut separation of one fear focus from multiple ones instead of a severity gradient.

In response to this perspective some will suggest that there are clear-cut qualitative symptom differences, with the strongest contenders being worry in the case of GAD, and pronounced autonomic and physiological reactions with panic disorder. Worry does appear to be associated with GAD, and this symptom is included in diagnostic systems (American Psychiatric Association, 2013; First et al, 2002; World Health Organization, 1992). Research suggests that worry is actually continuous, being present in everyone to a greater or lesser extent (Olatunji et al, 2010). Utilizing two large samples each consisting of over 1,000 subjects, Olatunji et al (2010) examined the latent structure of worry by applying three taxometric procedures. They found that there is a continuous distribution of worry, rather than it being either present or absent, a result also found by other researchers using taxometrics (Kertz et al, 2014; Ruscio et al, 2001). An additional finding by Olatunji et al (2010) was that worry has an equal association with anxiety, depression, and stress.

Relevant to strictly anxiety disorders, an analysis by Zinbarg and Barlow (1996) found that in addition to fear and anxiety, these disorders share worry as a symptom. Hence, it does not appear that worry can distinguish GAD from other disorders. It might be more a matter of degree, in that the greater number of specific fears the more extensive the worry. For example, a person with multiple social fears is likely to be more worried than someone with fear of a specific social situation. Multiple social situations usually cannot be avoided except by a full retreat into an agoraphobic lifestyle, whereas an isolated social situation frequently can, such as a person with a fear of public speaking declining jobs that require presentations. The less feasible it is that a fearful scenario be avoided, the more extensive the worry that is likely to transpire, at least in the short term. With GAD fear inducing situations typically include those that are difficult to avoid, such as fear of death or illness.

Panic attacks consist of autonomic and physiological symptoms including palpitations, sweating, shaking, shortness of breath, lightheadedness, and intense fear such as of dying (First et al, 2002; American Psychiatric Association, 2013). Panic disorder involves more than the occasional panic attack. When mammals, non-human primates, and humans are highly stressed by threatening circumstances a fight/flight/freeze response is automatically activated (Ledoux, 2014; Sapolsky, 1990). Many panic attack symptoms can be understood in the context of this survival mechanism. For example, increased heart rate and sweating prepare the body for a rapid response. A panic attack can then be viewed as a quantitatively different, more severe fear/anxiety reaction activating the fight/flight/freeze system. Another way of viewing the process is that a qualitative variation (the fight/flight/freeze response) arises as an emergent property from quantitative variation in terms of anxiety severity. At a certain point of severity the fight/flight/freeze response is activated, and this is what distinguishes panic attacks. Even within panic attacks there is a range of severity, such as with and without agoraphobia, and also the intensity of symptoms. DSM-5 does recognize that panic attacks serve as a marker of severity (American Psychiatric Association, 2013).

It might be suggested that panic attacks only occur in the absence of other anxiety disorders, validating panic disorder as a distinct entity. However, research reveals that panic attacks are quite common in other anxiety conditions. Specific phobia frequently involves panic attacks (Chapman et al, 1993). Social Anxiety Disorder and specific social phobias are associated with panic attacks (Angst, 1993; Merikangas & Angst, 1995; Provencher et al, 2006; Segui et al, 1999). GAD often occurs with other anxiety disorders including panic attacks (Goisman et al, 1995; Provencher et al, 2006). Panic attacks also occur with OCD (Austin et al, 1990). Hence, panic attacks are associated with various anxiety disorders, and not just on their own in panic disorder.

With research evidence only providing weak support for distinct types of anxiety disorders, despite the popularity of this approach for diagnosis, the case for a single continuum of anxiety is strengthened. However, it is necessary to identify common ingredients underlying all "anxiety disorders" to support the case for a dimensional interpretation of anxiety. We have already seen how worry is distributed continuously in the population (Olatunji et al, 2010), and that it is present in the different anxiety disorders, not just GAD (Zinbarg & Barlow, 1996). Perhaps not surprisingly, Zinbarg and Barlow (1996) also found that fear and anxiety occur in each anxiety disorder. Their finding, while seemingly self-evident for "anxiety" disorders, highlights the all-important but little discussed role of emotional information processing. Ultimately, support for anxiety being dimensional in nature resides in four categories of evidence: Emotional information processing, classical and operant conditioning, cognitive-behavioral therapy, and neuroscience data.

Emotional Information Processing

Research strongly suggests that some form of conscious or unconscious cognitive activating appraisal is involved in the vast majority, or even all, emotional responses (Clore & Ortony, 2000; Lazarus, 1984, 1991). Primary emotions are those every person with intact cognitive functioning expresses, typically from a very early age: Fear, sadness, anger, disgust, surprise, happiness, interest, and probably shame (Ekman, 1972, 1994; Ekman & Friesen, 1971; Izard, 1977; Tomkins, 1962, 1963). Research in preliterate cultures having limited contact with the larger world, thereby minimizing the possibility of acquisition through learning, demonstrates the universality of several emotions. Focusing on an isolated New Guinea society, Ekman and Friesen (1971) gave male and female adults and children three photographs at once, each containing facial expressions of either happiness, sadness, anger, disgust, surprise, and fear, and told them a story that involved one emotion. Subjects were able to match stories to facial expressions for the six emotions with an accuracy greater than that predicted by chance. The researchers went one step further and had nine New Guineans demonstrate how their face would appear if they were the person in the story. The unedited videotapes were shown to college students in the United States. Except for the poses of fear and surprise, which the New

Guineans found difficult to consciously produce facial expressions of, the students accurately recognized the displayed emotion (Ekman, 1972). Supporting the work of Ekman and colleagues, Boucher and Carlson (1980) studied Malaysian aboriginals, and found that the same six emotions were recognized in facial expressions with an above average frequency.

A crucial aspect of emotional information processing is a so-called deep structure, reflected in the content of the cognitive activating appraisals (Clore & Ortony, 2000). These deep structures do not seem to be influenced by culture, as evidenced by research demonstrating that members of one culture can accurately identify primary emotions from antecedent conditions provided by members of a completely different culture (Boucher & Brandt, 1981). When conscious or unconscious cognitive appraisal processes detect the deep structure characterizing a given emotion, the feeling state pertaining to the emotion arises (Clore & Ortony, 2000). This feeling state provides motivation consistent with the emotion and the psychological situation that contributed to the emotional response. For fear, the deep structure is threat or danger (Eley & Stevenson, 2000; Finlay-Jones & Brown, 1981; Mathews & Klug, 1993; Rapee, 1997; Shaver et al, 1987). The deep structure to sadness is loss (Beck, 1991; Eley & Stevenson, 2000; Finlay-Jones & Brown, 1981; Konner, 1982; Shrout et al, 1989). For anger, the deep structure appears to be violation or damage (Rozin et al, 1999; Shaver et al, 1987; Vrana, 1993). Disgust is indicative of some form of contamination whether physical or moral (Rozin et al, 1994; Rozin et al, 2000; Rozin & Fallon, 1987; Vrana, 1993). The deep structure for shame is likely commission of a significant social or moral transgression (Keltner & Buswell, 1997). Surprise indicates the sudden presence of an unexpected occurrence either positive or negative (Izard, 1991; Tomkins, 1962). For happiness, the corresponding deep structure is gain or success (Beck, 1991; Shaver et al, 1987). The deep structure for interest is probably the detection of something offering the potential for reward (Izard, 1991).

Evolutionary selection pressures likely established which emotions are primary, based on the adaptive value of detecting and responding to the circumstances characterizing the corresponding deep structures (Ely & Stevenson, 2000; Izard, 1991; Keltner & Buswell, 1997; Konner, 1982; Rapee, 1997: Rozin et al, 1994; Rozin & Fallon, 1987; Shaver et al, 1987; Tomkins, 1972; Vrana, 1993). For fear the adaptive value is responding to threats or danger with withdrawal, avoidance, or fight/flight/freeze responses (Eley & Stevenson, 2000; Finlay-Jones & Brown, 1981; Mathews & Klug, 1993; Rapee, 1997; Shaver et al, 1987). The evolution of human intelligence beyond that of other species, including Great Apes, based on advanced conceptual reasoning ability, has amplified emotions by making the cognitive activating appraisals more intensive, extensive, and adding a temporal dimension—The Amplification Effect (Bowins, 2004). For example, a critical job review is interpreted as a threat. The person thinks about all the mistakes made, thereby intensifying the threat. The threat is also extended in scope by thoughts pertaining to how additional personnel at the place of employment might become critical. These fear generating thoughts can play out over days, months, and even years, adding a temporal dimension to the fear. The overall impact is to amplify fear, transforming it into anxiety (Bowins, 2004). Cycles of fear based thoughts and emotional reactions also play a role in amplifying fear to produce clinical anxiety: Threat or danger oriented cognitions produce a feeling of fear, which in turn creates an emotional climate conducive to the perception of threats and danger, leading to further feelings of fear, and so on and so forth (Beck & Clark, 1997; Rachman, 1998). The process of deducing a threat from the feeling of fear or anxiety has been referred to as ex-consequentia reasoning (Rachman, 1998). Anxiety reduces the ability to inhibit emotional information processing of threat-related stimuli, further contributing to the persistence of anxiety (Fox et al, 2005).

Emotional information pertaining to threat and danger, producing fear, is clearly highly relevant for anxiety disorders. There is a continuum from mild to excessive perceptions of threat and danger. Those with anxiety disorders perceive greater threat in situations such as meeting unfamiliar people. Those low on the dimension of threat and danger perception are more likely to interpret this occurrence in a positive way, as a chance to socialize, have fun, and maybe make new friends, producing feelings of happiness and interest. The perception of such an experience as a threat to the self, perhaps an opportunity for ridicule or humiliation, triggers fear and an anxious response. Likewise, elevators are to most people an easier and faster means than stairs to ascend or descend the stories in a building. They might even be perceived as safe if the stairwells could conceal unsavory people, or the individual concerned has a heart or breathing illness. A person with a specific phobia of elevators instead sees threat or danger in his mode of vertical transportation, and avoids them if feasible.

When the perception of threat or danger is extreme, the fight/flight/freeze response of panic attacks is triggered (Eley & Stevenson, 2000; Finlay-Jones & Brown, 1981; Mathews & Klug, 1993; Rapee, 1997; Shaver et al, 1987). Starcevic et al (2012) found that a "cognitive style" characterized by exaggerated perceptions of threat, and appraisal of the future as unpredictable (and hence threatening), occurs in GAD, Social Anxiety Disorder, and panic disorder, although it is not as pronounced in the last, likely due to how the autonomic and physiological symptoms of the fight/flight/freeze response dominate. Panic Disorder patients frequently cite threat-oriented interpretations of physical symptoms, such as benign palpitations or indigestion perceived as a heart attack, as triggers for the panic response.

Amplified cognitive activating appraisals, or at least those that are conscious, are experienced as worry, linking this shared feature of anxiety to emotional information processing. Worrying produces further fear and anxiety responses, generating an emotional climate enhancing the perception of threats and danger. The mutually reinforcing cycles of fearful cognitions and emotional reactions then involve worrying as the conscious cognitive component. Anxiety sensitivity is another aspect of emotional information processing that plays a key role in exaggerated fear and anxiety responses, such as are embodied in worry (Asmundson et al, 2011; Reiss, 2013; Reiss & McNally, 1985; Reiss et al,

1986). Reiss and McNally (1985) have found that fear of fear is often involved in anxiety, such as that expressed in panic attacks, phobias, PTSD, and other anxiety conditions. It represents a metacognition pertaining to how a person interprets fear. So, for example, palpitations quite commonly produce a mild fear response in people on the basis of the potential threat, at least those who are unfamiliar with them. If this is interpreted as a benign occurrence the fear fades, but if the fear is perceived as a sign of true danger (a heart attack), then the emotional response can rapidly escalate to panic (Reiss, 2013; Reiss & McNally, 1985; Reiss et al, 1986).

Anxiety sensitivity amplifies fear responses, thereby contributing to anxiety disorders. Various researchers have applied taxometrics to determine if anxiety sensitivity is continuously distributed from normal to abnormal. Research by Asmundson et al (2011), utilizing both undergraduate student and community samples, found that anxiety sensitivity has a latent dimensional structure that is continuously distributed in the population. Additional taxometric research results support the position that anxiety sensitivity is continuously distributed (Broman-Fulks et al, 2008; Broman-Fulks et al, 2010), but some studies have suggested subtypes such as high and low categories (Bernstein et al, 2005; Bernstein et al, 2006). It has been noted that with more recent, methodologically sound studies controlling for possible confounding influences, the number of categorical results has steadily dropped while dimensional outcomes have increased (Haslam et al, 2012). Those experiencing anxiety disorders more commonly place on the upper end of the anxiety sensitivity continuum (Asmundson et al, 2011; Broman-Fulks et al, 2008; Broman-Fulks et al, 2010; Reiss, 2013; Reiss & McNally, 1985; Reiss et al, 1986). Hence, considering anxiety sensitivity, worry, and cognitive activating appraisals for fear, it is clear that there are common continuously distributed cognitive-emotional processes that underlie anxiety and anxiety disorders.

In total then the evidence indicates that excessive fear based emotional information processing is a core feature of all anxiety disorders. Psychological defense mechanisms likely evolved to moderate the intensity of negative emotions, such as fear and sadness (Bowins, 2004, 2006). In their absence or impairment, the root emotions of fear and sadness are more likely to be amplified such that anxiety disorders and depression, respectively, develop (Bowins, 2004, 2006). For the most part psychological defenses, including classical psychoanalytic ones, that operate at the level of emotions fit into the defense mechanism templates of positive cognitive distortions and dissociation (Bowins, 2004, 2006), as described in the chapters "Psychosis" and "Dissociation" respectively.

Classical and Operant Conditioning

Conditioning paradigms of both a classical and operant nature are capable of eliciting anxiety responses. Pavlov induced dogs to salivate to the sound of a bell by pairing the sound with food (Pavlov, 1927). Food is an unconditioned stimulus triggering the unconditioned reflex of salivation. The sound of the bell normally does not elicit salivation because it is not associated with food. However, the repeated sound of the bell just prior to food endows the bell sound with the capacity to trigger salivation, making it a conditioned stimulus (Pavlov, 1927). This form of associative learning is known as Pavlovian or classical conditioning. When a conditioned stimulus such as a tone is paired with a noxious stimulus, like a mild electric shock, the tone comes to elicit a fear response. Behaviorists, such as Watson (1925), believe that the behavioral responses involved in fear are conditioned responses. For example, a neutral stimulus, such as presenting to a group of people, is linked to adverse responses inducing humiliation, causing the previously neutral stimulus to elicit fear reactions. According to strict behaviorists, fear as an emotion does not exist, or in latter versions of conditioning, is treated as an intervening variable (Tolman, 1935). The topic of how emotions fit into conditioning paradigms is a very complex one and is covered in some reviews such as that by Ledoux (2014).

Operant conditioning, initially described by Skinner (1938), occurs when an organism acts, and the response influences whether the behavior repeats or decreases in frequency. If the response is reinforced by either the receipt of something positive or the reduction of negative circumstances (positive and negative reinforcement, respectively), then it increases in frequency. Adverse responses, on the other hand, reduce the behavior or eliminate it. For instance, if a person gives a talk to a group of people and the audience is enthusiastic, showing interest and the like, the response to the behavior of presenting is reinforcing, and the presenter is more likely to want to do more talks. However, if the audience is disinterested, talking amongst themselves, or heckling, there is an aversive response making it less likely that the presenter will give another talk.

Many animal and human studies over decades have demonstrated that both classical and operant conditioning paradigms are capable of eliciting fear/anxiety responses (Ledoux, 2014). Ledoux (2014), who has done extensive work on the neural basis of fear, views fear responses as defensive survival or motivational circuits based on conditioning paradigms. A defensive organismic state is triggered by activity in survival circuits detecting threats and generating defensive responses (Ledoux, 2014). Conditioned responses can generalize to similar situations and stimuli, accounting for fear/anxiety responses to circumstances not directly involved in a conditioning process (Lissek, 2012). For example, fear of being trapped in a closed space might generalize from the closet a person was locked in as a child to elevators or similar situations. As with most behaviorists, Ledoux (2014) rejects the idea of the existence of fear as a motivational entity in and of itself, instead viewing emotions as an emergent property of the neural processing underlying fear responses. Countering the negligible role in motivation attributed to emotions by most behaviorists, emotional information processing is a very real occurrence based on the research data presented earlier, adding to the motivational strength of adaptive responses (Clore & Ortony, 2000; Ely & Stevenson, 2000; Izard, 1991; Keltner & Buswell, 1997; Konner, 1982; Lazarus, 1984, 1991; Rapee, 1997: Rozin et al,

1994; Rozin & Fallon, 1987; Shaver et al, 1987; Tomkins, 1972; Vrana, 1993). The debate regarding the relative contribution to motivation of emotional information processing and strictly reinforcement parameters is beyond the scope of the present treatment, but a reasonable perspective is that emotional information processing (as opposed to some abstract conceptualization of emotions) and reinforcement paradigms both contribute to motivation.

For our purposes the key point of examining the role of conditioning in fear/anxiety responses is to appreciate that, as with emotional information processing, a cognitive system that underlies all such responses has evolved for fear and anxiety. This cognitive system was in place a long time prior to our relatively arbitrary divisions of anxiety into subtypes, such as Social Anxiety Disorder and specific phobia. The associative learning processes underlying fear conditioning apply to fear/anxiety responses across species (Ledoux, 2014). There is even evidence that associative learning occurs in single cell organisms (Hennessey et al, 1979). Associative learning derived classical and operant conditioning paradigms for fear have thus evolved over many years and in countless species, providing a neural-cognitive basis for fear/anxiety responses in general, not specifically tailored to the subtypes we assign.

Cognitive-Behavioral Therapy (CBT)

CBT approaches to anxiety disorders have traditionally been focused on specific conditions, both in terms of the understanding and treatment protocol (Rector et al, 2014). For example, Social Anxiety Disorder is said to arise from threat amplifying automatic thoughts and underlying schemata pertaining to social scenarios, activated in the presence of the situation/s (Rapee & Heimberg, 1997). Intervention strategies focus on reappraising these underlying social cognitions, enhancing approach behavior and reducing social anxiety responses (Rapee & Heimberg, 1997). This tailored CBT approach is based on the assumption that anxiety disorders represent valid distinct entities, with the application of these treatment strategies in turn reinforcing the perspective that they are true entities. However, treatments tailored to one "type" do have significant benefits for other anxiety disorders, an occurrence that would be improbable if the "types" were clearly distinct (Barlow et al, 2004).

In contrast to this disorder-specific CBT approach, transdiagnostic approaches to anxiety disorders have been developed, based on the notion that they share certain underlying features (Barlow et al, 2011; Rector et al, 2014). For example, negative affectivity (often referred to as the Behavioral Inhibition System (BIS)) is intensified in anxiety disorders, whereas a combination of diminished positive affectivity (Behavioral Activation System (BAS)) and increased negative affectivity (BIS) distinguishes depression (Fowles, 1988; Kasch et al, 2002; Mineka et al, 1998; Watson, 2005). Hence, a CBT approach focused on negative affect, such as the Unified Protocol (Barlow et al, 2011) treats various anxiety disorders, and can also help with depression (Rector et al, 2014). Both disorder-specific and transdiagnostic CBT approaches appear effective, and it is highly unlikely that the latter would be beneficial if there were no solid common elements underlying all anxiety disorders, such as elevated negative affectivity, combined with relatively intact positive affectivity (Rector et al, 2014). Hence, even though a transdiagnostic CBT approach does not rule out specific anxiety disorders, it lends some support to the notion of a single continuum of anxiety characterized, at least in part, by elevated negative affectivity (BIS).

Neuroscience Data

The extent and complexity of neuroscience data pertaining to anxiety disorders is enormous, and extensive coverage of it is not feasible within the context of the current chapter; for detailed information the following articles are helpful (Atmaca, 2013; Fisher & Hariri, 2013; Holzschneider & Mulert, 2011; Ledoux, 2014; Linares et al, 2012; Martin et al, 2009; Shizukuishi et al, 2013). In reviewing the extensive data the initial impression is that unique neural structures apply to the various anxiety disorders, but what emerges is that despite some differences there are core structures that reliably repeat across conditions, these structures comprising a so-called fear circuit (DeCarvalho et al, 2010; Dresler et al, 2013; Holzschneider et al, 2012; Mathew & Ho, 2006).

The fear circuit includes limbic, paralimbic, and cortical structures (DeCarvalho et al, 2010; Dresler et al, 2013; Holzschneider et al, 2012; Mathew & Ho, 2006). The main components include the amygdala, insula, anterior cingulated cortex, hippocampus, and prefrontal cortex (PFC). All of these structures seem to play a role in emotional information processing and motivation pertaining to emotions (DeCarvalho et al, 2010; Dresler et al, 2013; Holzschneider et al, 2012; Mathew & Ho, 2006). Depending on the investigator other structures might or might not be included, such as the thalamus involved in gating of sensory information pertinent to emotional states (Ledoux, 1994, 2014). The role of the structures consistently identified as part of the fear circuit include:

> Amygdala: A group of nuclei in the medial temporal lobe involved in emotional information processing, and in particular that pertaining to fear (Delgado et al, 2006; Holzschneider & Mulert, 2011; Linares et al, 2012). The amygdala seems to assess the value or relevance of information, such as whether it indicates threat (Morrison & Salzman, 2010; Sabatinelli et al, 2011).
>
> Insula: Involved in emotional information processing, feeling states, and interoceptive awareness (Craig, 2002; Ferrari et al, 2008; Phan et al, 2002).
>
> Anterior cingulated cortex (ACC): Plays a major role in approach and avoidance, and fear learning (Buchanan & Powell, 1982; Freeman et al, 1996).
>
> Hippocampus: Highly involved in emotional memories and providing context to memories and emotional information (Atmaca, 2013; Ferrari et al, 2008; Shizukuishi et al, 2013).

Prefrontal cortex (PFC): Crucial to information processing and regulation of emotional states, certainly those involving fear (Arnsten, 2011, 2009; Delgado et al, 2006; Goldin, 2009; Goldin et al, 2009; Holzschneider & Mulert, 2011; Larson et al, 2006; Linares, 2012).

Fear and anxiety responses rely on each of these structures. Of crucial significance, research has identified a consistent pattern in how these structures interact with each other: Fear/anxiety involves amplified activity in limbic and paralimbic structures, and decreased activity in the PFC (Delgado et al, 2006; Freitas-Ferrari et al, 2010; Goldin, 2009; Goldin et al, 2009; Hartley & Phelps, 2010; Larson et al, 2006; Martin et al, 2009). This pattern is typically interpreted as the PFC failing to exert sufficient top-down regulation of limbic system fear/anxiety responses (Arnsten, 2009; Arnsten, 2011; Goldin, 2009; Goldin et al, 2009; Hartley & Phelps, 2010; Kim & Hamann, 2007; Larson et al, 2006; Martin et al, 2009). Excessive limbic and paralimbic system based anxiety reactions likely occur, at least in part, due to the amplification effect of human intelligence on emotional information processing (see the section on emotional information processing) (Bowins, 2004, 2013), and these reactions cannot be contained when top-down regulation is impaired. The PFC represents the brain's master controller, accounting for a third of the human cortex, and uncontrollable acute and chronic stress impede normal PFC functioning, impairing regulation (Arnsten, 2009; Arnsten, 2011). A negative feedback loop might even apply: With sufficient stress the regulatory function of the PFC is impeded, preventing excessive fear/anxiety responses from being dampened, with the heightened fear/anxiety adding additional stress, further impairing PFC regulation (Arnsten, 2009; Arnsten, 2011).

The presence of a fear circuit common to all fear/anxiety responses, and the pattern of impaired top-down PFC regulation of limbic system activity, both suggest that a single continuum of fear/anxiety is the case, and not specific types. However, proponents of the idea of specific types of anxiety disorders might argue that certain neural structures are linked to types of anxiety. For example, specific phobia might involve increased activity in the cerebellum (Ipser et al, 2013). Likewise, with OCD the striatum appears to be involved along with a cortico-striatal pathway (Holzschneider & Mulert, 2011). Various researchers have identified problems with neuroimaging investigations, including small sample sizes, the influence of patient characteristics, non-pure samples of a specified type of anxiety disorders, and variation of technique applied such as with magnetic resonance scanning (Linares et al, 2012; Martin et al, 2009; Shizukuishi et al, 2013). The practical significance of these limitations is that for a result to be considered robust it must repeat over many studies, using various neuroimaging techniques and subject samples. In contrast to many findings for discrete types of anxiety disorders, both the fear circuit and PFC-limbic system regulatory based connectivity have been established over countless studies using a wide range of subjects and approaches. Hence, they appear to be robust, and demonstrate that there is a set of structures having a particular type of interaction that applies to all anxiety disorders.

A rarely addressed limitation of neuroimaging investigations, of profound relevance to the issue of whether anxiety exists as a continuum or discrete disorders, is how features beyond the "type" of anxiety are involved. When studies of, for example, Social Anxiety Disorder patients are conducted, the assumption is that differences between subjects and controls (or subjects and those with other types of anxiety disorders) reflect the anxiety problem. Rarely is there a consideration that many features related to the anxiety problem, but not the anxiety itself, are confounding the results (Martin et al, 2009; Schwartz & Rauch, 2004). With social anxiety there can be attachment, social status, self-confidence, personality, and other variables that play a key role and will influence the neuroimaging findings. For example, if a person is high on neuroticism and introversion then social anxiety is more likely (Schwartz & Rauch, 2004). Do the results indicate neural changes associated with social anxiety or neuroticism and/or introversion? Likewise, impaired attachment during childhood can impact on social relationships as an adult, and increase the likelihood of social anxiety (as can childhood anxiety problems related to attachment and separation, such as separation anxiety and selective mutism), but are the neural changes noted due to the attachment issue, social anxiety itself, or both? The question is largely left unanswered because it is rarely addressed (Martin et al, 2009).

Neuroimaging investigations pertaining to attachment reveal how the influence of this variable, and others, need be separated from those cited for types of anxiety disorders: It appears that many of the key structures involved in the fear circuit are also integral to attachment, potentially confounding the results for any socially derived form of anxiety. Swain et al (2007) implicate hypothalamus-midbrain-limbic-paralimbic-cortical circuits in parents' attachment to infants. Linking grief to attachment, O'Connor (2012) shows how the anterior cingulated cortex, posterior cingulated cortex, and insula play a role in grief. Eisenberger and Lieberman (2004) suggest that the anterior cingulated cortex is involved in the overlap of physical and social pain, linking physical-social pain to a common circuit. Hypofunctioning of the amygdala during infancy seems to prevent infants from learning aversion to caregivers (aversion conditioning), demonstrating a clear role for the amygdala in attachment (Moriceau & Sullivan, 2005). These results for attachment related behaviors and processes, demonstrate that interpretations of neuroimaging results for postulated specific types of anxiety disorders need to disentangle the confounding impact of related influences before we can conclude that activity in any neurological structure is uniquely linked to a "type" of anxiety. The neuroimaging findings for attachment suggest that limbic, paralimbic, and cortical structures provide overlapping functions, supporting the notion of a common fear circuit.

The Dimensional Nature of Anxiety Disorders

Given the dimensional structure within specific "types" of anxiety disorders, the highly limited evidence in support of discrete forms of anxiety, and the robust evidence for common ingredients (emotional information processing, classical and operant conditioning, common ingredients to CBT, and neuroscience data), it appears that anxiety exists on a single continuum. A continuous approach to assessing anxiety disorders has been found to increase reliability and validity (Markon et al, 2011). Such an approach runs counter to the current classification schemes emphasizing discrete types of anxiety disorders (American Psychiatric Association, 2013; First et al, 2002; World Health Organization, 1992), but we have seen how the differences are often an illusion, such as trying to separate specific phobias from social phobias. Therefore, assuming that there is only one anxiety continuum, how would this look, and how to incorporate anxiety linked to specific circumstances, PTSD, and OCD?

Considering the intuitive tendency of every experienced clinician to automatically assess length of illness and severity, it is proposed that there are two sub-dimensions of duration and severity. In addition, as with depression (see the "Depression" chapter), it is best to set three levels of duration (short, medium, and long), and three levels of severity (mild, moderate, and severe) with the numbers 1, 2, and 3 applied respectively to the levels. This will produce an interactive description, such as a short-term and mild illness being $1 \times 1 = 1$, a moderate duration and moderate severity illness $2 \times 2 = 4$, and a long duration and severe illness $3 \times 3 = 9$. The three levels are suggested because most experienced clinicians can distinguish between mild, moderate and severe, but finer distinctions are unreliable without intensive training highly unlikely to occur outside of a research setting. Duration might be set at short = 1-3 months, medium = 3-6 months, and long = greater than 6 months, although research might be necessary to establish the ideal parameters. Considering that the multiplied value can result from different combinations (for instance moderate duration × high severity having the same value as long duration × moderate intensity), the ratings for duration and severity both need to be recorded. Furthermore, since the rating scheme applies to a given episode, separate ones need to be performed for each episode of the illness. Isolated anxiety occurrences such as a single panic attack do not constitute a mental illness, and hence do not warrant the application of this system. However, panic attacks extending over months do, with a high severity rating given the intensity.

While duration is clearly understood in terms of time units, severity is more complex. How might we evaluate the severity dimension of anxiety? Research will be required to answer this question more definitively, but the number of feared situations and symptom intensity need to be part of this evaluation.

Number of Fears

Intuitively, it does make sense that the more situations a person fears, the more severe will be the overall anxiety. Regarding SAD, research reveals that greater severity is linked to the number of feared social situations, with more feared situations increasing illness severity (El-Gabalawy et al, 2010; Turner et al, 1992; Vriends et al, 2006). Regarding specific phobia, Curtis et al (1998) have found that the number of fears, irrespective of type, appears to be an indicator of greater severity, being related to impairment, comorbidity, illness course, and family psychopathology. In the case of panic disorder it follows that the more situations and stimuli there are that trigger panic attacks, the more severe the illness will be. GAD involves less readily identifiable circumstances, but worry does have a focus. While the focus might not be as circumscribed and clear as public speaking or elevators, there nonetheless are identifiable themes, such as worry about death, or career issues. If a person worries about a single issue, or even a few, this occurrence is not typically viewed as a disorder. It is when the number of themes increases such that functioning is impaired that the diagnosis of GAD is given. This occurrence indicates that severity within GAD is associated with the number of feared situations. Hence, based on research findings and common sense, severity of anxiety can be assessed on the basis of the number of feared situations, at least in conjunction with symptom intensity.

Symptom Intensity

With any illness the intensity of symptoms is crucial for diagnosis, progression, and risks. For example, a blood pressure of 140/90, borderline high with no symptoms, is radically different than 180/130 with dizziness. In the case of SAD more intense symptoms are linked to greater illness severity (Ha et al, 2011; Piqueras et al, 2008; Vriends et al, 2006). Panic disorder with agoraphobia is a more severe condition than panic disorder without agoraphobia (Buller et al, 1986; Scheibe & Albus, 1992). A crucial symptom highly relevant to anxiety as a single continuum is the degree of negative affectivity (Kasch et al, 2002; Mineka et al, 1998; Watson, 2005). The greater the negative affectivity, the higher a person places on the severity dimension of the anxiety continuum. Other indicators of symptom intensity that might be assessed include avoidance behavior, autonomic and physiological manifestations of anxiety, and the strength of the feeling component (subjective distress). Ratings on each can be averaged to provide an overall intensity rating. A very important aspect of symptom intensity is panic attacks. As discussed earlier, highly threatening circumstances (or those perceived to be so) often trigger defensive fight/flight/freeze responses that we refer to as panic attacks. Quantitative variation in anxiety produces an apparently qualitatively different entity (panic attacks) as an emergent property. A range of intensity is demonstrated for panic attacks, from distressing but tolerable (at least for someone familiar with them) to a level where a person is completely dysfunctional, often with pronounced agoraphobia. Panic attacks occur with other Anxiety Disorder "types" (Angst, 1993; Chapman et al, 1993; Merikangas & Angst, 1995; Austin et al, 1990; Goisman et al, 1995; Provencher et al, 2006; Segui et al, 1999), revealing how panic disorder is not a discrete form of anxiety.

The number of fears and symptom intensity can then serve as a basis for evaluating the severity dimension of the anxiety continuum. Severity × duration gives a solid overall perspective on the quantitative and related qualitative aspects of an episode of anxiety. However, a couple of potentially problematic issues remain: Anxiety associated with specific circumstances and how to incorporate conditions related to anxiety, namely PTSD and OCD.

Anxiety Associated With Specific Circumstances

On the surface it appears that anxiety is tightly linked to certain circumstances, and this forms the entire basis of modern classification systems such as DSM-IV-TR, DSM-5, and ICD-10 (American Psychiatric Association, 2013; First et al, 2002; World Health Organization, 1992). However, as we have seen, anxiety appears to be distributed continuously. So how might we conceptualize the linkage between anxiety and specific circumstances? Perhaps the most accurate way is that specific circumstances activate the anxiety continuum, and also influence how the anxiety is expressed. For instance, social circumstances might activate anxiety in those with early-life attachment issues and/or certain personality profiles, such as high introversion and neuroticism. In children this can manifest as separation anxiety and/or selective mutism. In adults it might be expressed in the form of social avoidance or nervousness around people. Non-social circumstances activate the anxiety dimension due to experiences, like being trapped in a confined space, perhaps in combination with personality characteristics such as being closed to experience and high in harm avoidance. Fear responses can generalize to related stimuli, helping explain why actual experience with a source of fear is not required (Lissek, 2012). When more generalized stressors activate anxiety it is often expressed as brooding, tension, and self-absorption. If anxiety from any of these sources intensifies, panic attacks can be triggered, representing a qualitatively different anxiety response as an emergent property of the quantitative level. Hence, the specific circumstances now used as a basis to distinguish "types" of anxiety disorders are best viewed as circumstances that activate the anxiety continuum.

Posttraumatic Stress Disorder (PTSD)

PTSD (along with OCD) was listed as an Anxiety Disorder in DSM-IV-TR but shifted (as with OCD) into a separate category with DSM-5 (First et al, 2002; American Psychiatric Association, 2013). The separation of PTSD from anxiety disorders appears logical because anxiety is only one component of PTSD, other key ones including re-experiencing the trauma in various ways, avoidance of trauma-related stimuli, and heightened arousal (First et al, 2002; American Psychiatric Association, 2013). The traumatic experience likely activates the anxiety continuum (and also the depressive continuum) in many instances. PTSD actually appears to align more closely with dissociation, an occurrence that will surprise some readers. The reasons for this designation are presented in the "Dissociation" chapter.

Obsessive-Compulsive Disorder (OCD)

As with PTSD, OCD involves anxiety plus other key elements. Obsessions increase anxiety (Rachman & Hodgson, 1980), but compulsions can contain anxiety via negative reinforcement: Performing a cognitive or physical behavior linked to the obsession temporarily reduces or eliminates the anxiety (Abed & de Pauw, 1998/1999; Bowins, 2010b; Rachman & Hodgson, 1980; Stein et al, 1992; Storch et al, 2008). For example, when a person fears contamination by germs, hand washing reduces the anxiety, providing negative reinforcement (reduction or elimination of an adverse state). As will be discussed in more detail in the chapter "Personality Disorder," generalized anxiety can be funneled into a much more focused obsession, and the anxiety contained by compulsive behavior (Bowins, 2010b). For instance, fear of death or having some severe illness might be narrowed to an obsession about contamination by germs, and then compulsive hand washing helps contain the anxiety. Consistent with this process compulsive ritualistic behavior has been found to maintain tension at a manageable level (Rachman & Hodgson, 1980).

The Dimensional Nature of Anxiety Disorders

Although on the surface anxiety disorders appear to be just that—disorders plural—the evidence in support of this assertion is limited. The codification of discrete types in DSM and ICD (American Psychiatric Association, 2013; First et al, 2002; World Health Organization, 1992) helps perpetuate the notion that nature has set forth distinct types of anxiety. However, when evidence such as age of onset, course, symptoms, and comorbidity is examined, the distinctions between discrete types do not reliably hold up (Angst et al, 2006; Austin et al, 1990; Goodwin & Hamilton, 2002; Maes et al, 1998; Merikangas & Angst, 1995; Provencher et al, 1992; Rickels & Schweizer, 1998; Scheibe & Albus, 1992; Segui et al, 1999; Skodol et al, 1995; Strarcevic et al, 1994; Tilfors & Ekselius, 2009; Wittchen et al, 1998). Even worry, commonly considered to be largely diagnostic of GAD, is continuous in distribution, and equally associated with anxiety, stress, and depression (Olatunji et al, 2010). Panic attacks can occur in various conditions (Angst, 1993; Chapman et al, 1993; Goisman et al, 1995; Merikangas & Angst, 1995; Provencher et al, 2006; Segui et al, 1999), and represent an instance of a qualitative difference arising from a greater quantitative level (severity) as an emergent property, rather than an entirely distinct entity.

While the evidence is not strong for discrete types of anxiety disorders, several lines of evidence provide robust support for the notion of common processes underlying anxiety. These include emotional information processing, classical and operant conditioning, cognitive-behavioral therapy, and neuroscience data. Anxiety as a continuum can be comprehensively captured by duration × severity, with the latter assessed on the basis of the number of fears and symptom intensity. Differences in anxiety can arise from quantitative variation producing qualitative differences as an emergent property (panic attacks), or circumstances associated with anxiety, such as social fear situations social anxiety, non-social fear scenarios phobias, and less discrete sources of fear generalized anxiety. These circumstances can be seen as activating the anxiety continuum. Consistent with the notion of anxiety representing a continuum, the evidence supports a continuous organization within existing discrete anxiety disorders. Deficient PFC regulation of limbic and paralimbic system activity pertaining to fear responses appears to be instrumental in clinically relevant levels of anxiety. Understanding anxiety as a single continuum simplifies our understanding and approach, and avoids the complexities of trying to distinguish disorders that are not valid.

References

Abed, R.T. & de Pauw, K.W. (1998/1999). An evolutionary hypothesis for obsessive compulsive disorder: A psychological immune system. *Behavioral Neurology, 11*, 245-250.

Aderka, I.M, Nickerson, A., & Hofmann, S.G. (2012). Admixture analysis of the diagnostic subtypes of the social anxiety disorder for the DSM-V. *Journal of Behavioral Therapy & Experimental Psychiatry, 43*(2), 752-757.

American Psychiatric Association (2013). *Diagnostic & Statistical Manual 5*. Washington, DC: American Psychiatric Publishing.

Angst, J. (1993). Comorbidity of anxiety, phobia, compulsion, and depression. *International Journal of Clinical Psychopharmacology, 8*(Suppl. 1), 21-25.

Angst, J., Gamma, A., Bienvenu, J., Eaton, W.W., Ajdacic, V., Eich, D., & Rossler, W. (2006). Varying temporal criteria for generalized anxiety disorder: Prevalence and clinical characteristics in a young age cohort. *Psychological Medicine, 36*(9), 1283-1292.

Arnsten, A. (2009). Stress signaling pathways that impair prefrontal cortex structure and function. *Nature Reviews Neuroscience, 10*, 410-422.

Arnsten, A. (2011). Prefrontal cortical network connections: Key sites of vulnerability in stress and schizophrenia. *International Journal of Developmental Neuroscience, 29*(3), 215-223.

Asmundson, G.J., Weeks, J.W., Carleton, R.N., Thibodeau, M.A., & Fetzner, M.G. (2011). Revisiting the latent structure of the anxiety sensitivity construct: More evidence of dimensionality. *Journal of Anxiety Disorders, 25*(1), 138-147.

Atmaca, M. (2013). What about the neuroimaging findings in social anxiety disorder? *Review of Recent Clinical Trials, 8*(2), 124-127.

Austin, L.S., Lydiard, R.B., Fossey, M.D., Zealberg, J.J., Laraia, M.T., & Ballenger, J.C. (1990). Panic and phobic disorders in patients with obsessive-compulsive disorder. *Journal of Clinical Psychiatry, 51*(11), 456-458.

Barlow, D.H., Allen, L.B., & Choate, M.L. (2004). Toward a unified treatment for anxiety disorders. *Behavior Therapy, 35*, 205-230.

Barlow, D.H., Farchione, T.J., & Farchione, C.P. (2011). *The Unified Protocol for Transdiagnostic Treatment of Emotional Disorders: Therapist Guide*. New York: Oxford University Press.

Beck, A. (1991). Cognitive therapy: A 30-year retrospective. *American Psychologist, 46*(4), 368-375.

Beck, A. & Clark, D. (1997). An information processing model of anxiety: Automatic and strategic processes. *Behavior Research and Therapy, 35*(1), 49-58.

Bernstein, A., Zvolensky, M.J., Kotov, R., Arrindell, W.A., Taylor, S., Sandin, B. et al (2006). Taxonicity of anxiety sensitivity: A multinational analysis. *Journal of Anxiety Disorders, 20*(1), 1-22.

Bernstein, A., Zvolensky, M.J., Weems, C., Stickle, T., & Leen-Feldner, E.W. (2005). Taxonicity of anxiety sensitivity: An empirical test among youth. *Behavioral Research & Therapy, 43*(9), 1131-1155.

Boucher, J. & Brandt, M. (1981). Judgment of emotion: American and Malay antecedents. *Journal of Cross-Cultural Psychology, 12*(3), 272-283.

Boucher, J. & Carlson, G. (1980). Recognition of facial expression in three cultures. *Journal of Cross-Cultural Psychology, 11*, 263-280.

Bowins, B. (2004). Psychological defense mechanisms: A new perspective. *American Journal of Psychoanalysis, 64*, 1-26.

Bowins, B.E. (2010b). Personality disorders: A dimensional defense mechanism approach. *American Journal of Psychotherapy, 64*(2), 153-169.

Bowins, B.E. (2013). Cognitive regulatory control therapies. *American Journal of Psychotherapy, 67*(3), 215-236.

Bowlby, J. (1988). Developmental psychiatry comes of age. *American Journal of Psychiatry, 145*, 1-10.

Broman-Fulks, J.J., Deacon, B.J., Olatunji, B.O., Bondy, C.L., Abramowitz, J.S., & Tolin, D.F. (2010). Categorical or dimensional: A reanalysis of the anxiety sensitivity construct. *Behavior Therapy, 41*(2), 154-171.

Broman-Fulks, J.J., Green, B.A., Olatunji, B.O., Berman, M.E., Arnau, R.C., Deacon, B.J., & Sawchuk, C.N. (2008). The latent structure of anxiety sensitivity—revisited. *Assessment, 15*(2), 188-203.

Buchanan, S.L. & Powell, D.A. (1982). Cingulate cortex: Its role in Pavlovian conditioning. *Journal of Comprehensive Physiology & Psychology, 96*, 755-774.

Buller, R., Maier, W., & Benkert, O. (1986). Clinical subtypes in panic disorder: Their descriptive and prospective validity. *Journal of Affective Disorders, 11*(2), 105-114.

Chapman, T.F., Fyer, A.J., Mannuzza, S., & Klein, D.F. (1993). A comparison of treated and untreated simple phobia. *American Journal of Psychiatry, 150*(5), 816-818.

Clore, G. & Ortony, A. (2000). Cognition in emotion: Always, sometimes, or never? In *Cognitive Neuroscience of Emotion*. New York: Oxford University Press.

Craig, A.D. (2002). How do you feel? Interoception: The sense of the physical condition of the body. *Nature Reviews Neuroscience, 3*, 655-666.

Curtis, G.C., Magee, W.J., Eaton, W.W., Wittchen, H.U., & Kessler, R.C. (1998). Specific fears and phobias: Epidemiology and classification. *British Journal of Psychiatry, 173*, 212-217.

DeCarvalho, M.R., Dias, G.P., Cosci, F., De-Melo-Neto, V.L., Bevilaqua, M.C., Gardino, P.F., & Nardi, A.E. (2010). Current findings of fMRI in panic disorder: Contributions for the fear neurocircuitry and CBT effects. *Expert Reviews Neurotherapeutics, 10*(2), 291-303.

Delgado, M.R., Olsson, A., & Phelps, E.A. (2006). Extending animal models of fear conditioning to humans. *Biological Psychology, 73*(1), 39-48.

Dresler, T., Guhn, A., Tupak, S.V., Ehlis, A.C., Hermann, M.J., Fallgatter, A.J. et al (2013). Revise the revised? New dimensions of the neuroanatomical hypothesis of panic disorder. *Journal of Neural Transmission, 120*(1), 3-29.

Eisenberger, N.I. & Lieberman, M.D. (2004). Why rejection hurts: A common neural alarm system for physical and social pain. *Trends in Cognitive Science, 8*(7), 294-300.

Ekman, P. (1972). *Emotions in the Human Face*. New York: Cambridge University Press.

Ekman, P. (1994). Antecedent events and emotion metaphors. In *Nature of Emotions*. Oxford: Oxford University Press.

Ekman, P. & Friesen, W. (1971). Constants across cultures in the face and emotion. *Journal of Personality and Social Psychology, 17*, 124-129.

Eley, T. & Stevenson, J. (2000). Specific life events and chronic experiences differentially associated with depression and anxiety in young twins. *Journal of Abnormal Child Psychology, 28*(4), 383-394.

El-Gabalaway, R., Cox, B., Clara, I., & MacKenzie, C. (2010). Assessing the validity of social anxiety disorder subtypes using a nationally representative sample. *Journal of Affective Disorders, 24*(2), 244-249.

Ferrari, M.C., Busatto, G.F., McGuire, P.K., & Crippa, J.A. (2008). Structural magnetic resonance imaging in anxiety disorders: An update of research findings. *Review Brasil Psiquiatry, 30*(3), 251-264.

Finlay-Jones, R. & Brown, G. (1981). Types of stressful life event and the onset of anxiety and depressive disorders. *Psychological Medicine, 11*, 803-815.

First, M.B., Frances, A., & Pincus, H.A. (2002). *DSM-IV-TR Handbook of Differential Diagnosis*. Washington, DC: American Psychiatric Publishing.

Fisher, P.M. & Hariri, A.R. (2013). Identifying serotonergic mechanisms underlying the corticolimbic response to threat in humans. *Philosophical Transactions of the Royal Society London B Biological Science, 368*(1615), 1615-1621.

Fowles, D.C. (1988). Psychophysiology and psychopathology: A motivational approach. *Psychophysiology, 25*, 373-391.

Fox, E., Russo, R., & Georgiou, G. (2005). Anxiety modulates the degree of attentive resources required to process emotional faces. *Cognitive Affective and Behavioral Neuroscience, 5*(4), 396-404.

Freeman, J.H., Cuppernell, C., Flannery, K., & Gabriel, M. (1996). Limbic thalamic, cingulated cortical and hippocampal neuronal correlates of discriminate approach learning in rabbits. *Behavioral Brain Research, 80*, 123-136.

Freitas-Ferrari, M.C., Hallak, J.E., Trzesniak, C., Filho, A.S., Machado-De-Sousa, J.P., Chagas, M.H., Nardi, A.E., & Crippa, J.A. (2010). Neuroimaging in social anxiety disorder: A systematic review of the literature. *Progress in Neuropsychopharmacology & Biological Psychiatry, 34*(4), 565-580.

Furmark, T., Tillfors, M., Stattin, H., Ekselius, L., & Fredrikson, M. (2000). Social phobia subtypes in the general population revealed by cluster analysis. *Psychological Medicine, 30*(6), 1335-1344.

Gelernter, C.S., Stein, M.B., Tancer, M.E., & Uhde, T.W. (1992). An examination of syndromal validity and diagnostic subtypes in social phobia. *Journal of Clinical Psychiatry, 53*(1), 23-27.

Goisman, R.M., Goldenberg, I., Vasile, R.G., & Keller, M.B. (1995). Comorbidity of anxiety disorders in a multicenter anxiety study. *Comprehensive Psychiatry, 36*(4), 303-311.

Goldin, P. (2009). Effects of cognitive-behavioral therapy on neural bases of emotion regulation in social anxiety disorder. *Biological Psychiatry, 65*(Suppl. 1), 1215-1221.

Goldin, P.R., Manber, T., Halimi, S., Canli, T., & Gross, J. (2009). Neural bases of social anxiety disorder: Emotional reactivity and cognitive regulation during social and physical threat. *Archives of General Psychiatry, 66*(2), 170-180.

Goodwin, R.D. & Hamilton, S.P. (2002). The early-onset fearful panic attack as a predictor of severe psychopathology. *Psychiatry Research, 109*(1), 71-79.

Ha, J., Lim, S.W., Shin, Y.C., & Oh, K.S. (2011). Comparison of anxiety-related traits between generalized and nongeneralized subtypes of social anxiety disorder. *Journal of Nervous Mental Disorders, 199*(6), 390-393.

Hartley, C. & Phelps, E. (2010). Changing fear: The neurocircuitry of emotion regulation. *Neuropsychopharmacology, 35*, 136-146.

Haslam, N., Holland, E., & Kuppens, P. (2012). Categories versus dimensions in personality and psychopathology: A quantitative review of taxometric research. *Psychological Medicine, 42*(5), 902-920.

Hennessey, T.M., Rucker, W.B., & McDiarmid, C.G. (1979). Classical conditioning in paramecia. *Animal Learning Behavior, 7*(4), 417-423.

Himle, J.A., McPhee, K., Cameron, O.G., & Curtis, G.C. (1989). Simple phobia: Evidence for heterogeneity. *Psychiatric Research, 28*(1), 25-30.

Holzschneider, K. & Mulert, C. (2011). Neuroimaging in anxiety disorders. *Dialogues Of Clinical Neuroscience, 13*(4), 453-461.

Ipser, J.C., Singh, L., & Stein, D.J. (2013). Meta-analysis of functional brain imaging in specific phobia. *Psychiatry & Clinical Neuroscience, 67*(5), 311-322.

Izard, C. (1977). *Human Emotions*. New York: Plenum.

Izard, C. (1991). *The Psychology of Emotions*. New York: Plenum Press.

Kasch, K.L., Rottenberg, J., Arnow, B.A., & Gotlib, I.H. (2002). Behavioral activation and inhibition systems and the severity and course of depression. *Journal of Abnormal Psychology, 111*, 589-597.

Keltner, D. & Buswell, B. (1997). Embarrassment: Its distinct form and appeasement functions. *Psychological Bulletin, 122*(3), 250-270.

Kertz, S.J., McHugh, R.K., Lee, J., & Bjorgvinsson, T. (2014). Examining the latent structure of worry and generalized anxiety in a clinical sample. *Journal of Anxiety Disorders, 28*(1), 8-15.

Kim, S. & Hamann, S. (2007). Neural correlates of positive and negative emotion regulation. *Journal of Cognitive Neuroscience, 19*(5), 776-798.

Konner, M. (1982). *The Tangled Wing: Biological Constraints on the Human Spirit*. New York: Harper & Row.

Larson, C., Schaefer, H., Siegle, G., Jackson, C., Anderle, M., & Davidson, R. (2006). Fear is fast in phobic individuals: Amygdala activation in response to fear-relevant stimuli. *Biological Psychiatry, 60*(4), 410-417.

Lazarus, R. (1984). On the primacy of cognition. *American Psychologist, 39*(2), 124-129.

Lazarus, R. (1991). Cognition and emotion in motivation. *American Psychologist, 46*(4), 352-367.

Ledoux, J. (1994). Cognitive-emotional interactions in the brain. In *Nature of Emotions*. Oxford: Oxford University Press.

Ledoux, J.E. (2014). Coming to terms with fear. *Proceedings of the National Academy of Science USA, 111*(8), 2871-2878.

Linares, I.M., Trzesniak, C., Chagas, M.H., Hallak, J.E., Nardi, A.E., & Crippa, J.A. (2012). Neuroimaging in specific phobia disorder: A systematic review of the literature. *Review Brasil Psiquiatry, 34*(1), 101-111.

Lissek, S. (2012). Toward an account of clinical anxiety predicated on basic, neurally mapped mechanisms of Pavlovian fear-learning: The case for conditioned overgeneralization. *Depression & Anxiety, 29*(4), 257-263.

Maes, M., Delmeire, L., Schotte, C., Janca, A., Creten, T., Mylle, J. et al (1998). The two-factorial symptom structure of post-traumatic stress disorder: Depression-avoidance and arousal-anxiety. *Psychiatry Research, 81*(2), 195-210.

Marcus, D.K., Sawaqdeh, A., & Kwon, P. (2014). The latent structure of generalized anxiety disorder in midlife adults. *Psychiatric Research, 28*(2), 366-371.

Markon, K.E., Chmielewski, M., & Miller, C.J. (2011). The reliability and validity of discrete and continuous measures of psychopathology. *Psychological Bulletin, 137*(5), 856-879.

Martin, E.I., Ressler, K.J., Binder, E., & Nemeroff, C.B. (2009). The neurobiology of anxiety disorders: Brain imaging, genetics, and psychoneuroendocrinology. *Psychiatry Clinics of North America, 32*(3), 549-575.

Mathew, S.J. & Ho, S. (2006). Etiology and neurobiology of social anxiety disorder. *Journal of Clinical Psychiatry, 67*(Suppl 12), 9-13.

Mathews, A. & Klug, F. (1993). Emotionality and interference with color-naming in anxiety. *Behavior Research and Therapy, 31*(1), 57-62.

Merikangas, K.R. & Angst, J. (1995). Comorbidity and social phobia: Evidence from clinical, epidemiologic, and genetic studies. *European Archives of Psychiatry and Clinical Neuroscience, 244*(6), 297-303.

Mineka, S., Watson, D., & Clark, L.A. (1998). Comorbidity of anxiety and unipolar mood disorders. *Annual Review of Psychology, 49*(1), 377-412.

Moriceau, S. & Sullivan, R.M. (2005). Neurobiology of infant attachment. *Developmental Psychobiology, 47*(3), 230-242.

Morrison, S.E. & Salzman, C.D. (2010). Re-evaluating the amygdala. *Current Opinion in Neurobiology, 20*, 221-230.

Noyes, R., Woodman, C., Garvey, M.J., Cook, B.L., Suelzer, M., Clancy, J., & Anderson, D.J. (1992). Generalized anxiety disorder vs. panic disorder: Distinguishing characteristics and patterns of comorbidity. *Journal of Nervous & Mental Disorders, 180*(6), 369-79.

O'Connor, M.F. (2012). Immunological and neuroimaging biomarkers of complicated grief. *Dialogues of Clinical Neuroscience, 14*(2), 141-148.

Olatunji, B.O., Broman-Fulks, J.J., Bergman, S.M., Green, B.A., & Zlomke, K.R. (2010). A taxometric investigation of the latent structure of worry: Dimensionality and associations with depression, anxiety, and stress. *Behavioral Therapy, 41*(2), 212-228.

Pavlov, I.P. (1927). *Conditioned Reflexes.* New York: Dover.

Phan, K.L., Wager, T., Taylor, S.F., & Liberzon, I. (2002). Functional neuroanatomy of emotion: A meta-analysis of emotion activation studies in PET and fMRI. *Neuroimage, 16*, 331-348.

Piqueras, J.A., Olivares, J., & Lopez-Pina, J.A. (2008). A new proposal for the subtypes of social phobia in a sample of Spanish adolescents. *Journal of Anxiety Disorders, 22*(1), 66-77.

Provencher, M.D., Ladouceur, R., & Dugas, M.J. (2006). Comorbidity in generalized anxiety disorder: Prevalence and course after cognitive-behavioral therapy. *Canadian Journal of Psychiatry, 51*(2), 91-99.

Rachman, S. (1998). A cognitive theory of obsessions: Elaborations. *Behavior Research and Therapy, 36*, 385-401.

Rachman, S. & Hodgson, R. (1980). *Obsessions and Compulsions.* Englewood Cliffs: Prentice-Hall.

Rapee, R. (1997). Perceived threat and perceived control as predictors of the degree of fear in physical and social situations. *Journal of Anxiety Disorders, 11*(5), 455-461.

Rapee, R.M. & Heimberg, R.G. (1997). A cognitive-behavioral model of anxiety in social phobia. *Behavioral Research & Therapy, 35*, 741-756.

Rector, N.A., Man, V., & Lerman, B. (2014). The expanding cognitive-behavioural therapy treatment umbrella for the anxiety disorders: Disorder-specific and transdiagnostic approaches. *Canadian Journal of Psychiatry, 59*(6), 301-309.

Reiss, S. (2013). *The Reiss Motivational Profile: What Motivates You?* Columbus, OH: IDS Publishing.

Reiss, S. & McNally, R.J. (1985). Expectancy model of fear. In *Theoretical Issues in Behavior Therapy*. New York: Academic Press.

Reiss, S., Peterson, R.A., Gursky, D.M., & McNally, R.J. (1986). Anxiety sensitivity, anxiety frequency, and the prediction of fear. *Behavior Research and Therapy, 24*, 1-8.

Rettew, D.C. (2000). Avoidant personality disorder, generalized social phobia, and shyness: Putting the personality back into personality disorders. *Harvard Review of Psychiatry, 8*(6), 283-297.

Rickels, K. & Schweizer, E. (1998). The spectrum of generalized anxiety in clinical practice: The role of short-term, intermittent treatment. *British Journal of Psychiatry, 34*(Suppl), 49-54.

Rozin, P. & Fallon, A. (1987). A perspective on disgust. *Psychological Review, 94*(1), 23-41.

Rozin, P., Haidt, J., & McCauley, C. (2000). Disgust. In *Handbook of Emotions* (2nd ed.). New York: The Guilford Press.

Rozin, P., Lowery, L., & Ebert, R. (1994). Varieties of disgust faces and the structure of disgust. *Journal of Personality and Social Psychology, 66*(5), 870-881.

Rozin, P., Lowery, L., Imada, S., & Haidt, J. (1999). The CAD triad hypothesis: A mapping between three moral emotions (contempt, anger, disgust) and three moral codes (community, autonomy, divinity). *Journal of Personality and Social Psychology, 76*(4), 574-586.

Ruscio, A.M. (2010). The latent structure of social anxiety disorder: Consequences of shifting to a dimensional diagnosis. *Journal of Abnormal Psychology, 119*(4), 662-671.

Ruscio, A.M., Borkovec, T.D., & Ruscio, J. (2001). A taxometric investigation of the latent structure of worry. *Journal of Abnormal Psychology, 110*(3), 413-422.

Sabatinelli, D., Fortune, E.E., & Li, Q. (2011). Emotional perception: Meta-analyses of face and natural scene processing. *Neuroimage, 54*, 2524-2533.

Sapolsky, R. (1990). Stress in the wild. *Scientific American*, January, 116-123.

Scheibe, G., & Albus, M. (1992). Age at onset, precipitating events, sex distribution, and co-occurrence of anxiety disorders. *Psychopathology, 25*(1), 11-18.

Schwartz, C.E. & Rauch, S.L. (2004). Temperament and its implications for neuroimaging of anxiety disorders. *CNS Spectrum, 9*(4), 284-291.

Segui, J., Marquez, M., Garcia, L., Canet, J., Salvador-Carulla, L., & Ortiz, M. (1999). *Journal of Affective Disorders, 54*(1-2), 109-117.

Shaver, P., Schwartz, J., Kirson, D., & O'Connor, C. (1987). Emotion knowledge: Further exploration of a prototype approach. *Journal of Personality and Social Psychology, 52*(6), 1086-1091.

Shizukuishi, T., Abe, O., & Aoki, S. (2013). Diffusion tensor imaging analysis for psychiatric disorders. *Magnetic Resonance Medical Science, 12*(3), 153-159.

Shrout, P., Link B., Dohrenwend, B., Skodol, A., Stueve A., & Mirotznik J. (1989). Characterizing life events as risk factors for depression: The role of fateful loss events. *Journal of Abnormal Psychology, 98*(4), 460-467.

Skinner, B.F. (1938). *The Behavior of Organisms: An Experimental Analysis.* New York: Appleton-Century-Crofts.

Skodol, A.E., Oldham, J.M., Hyler, S.E., Stein, D.J., Hollander, E., Gallaher, P.E., & Lopez, A.E. (1995). Patterns of anxiety and personality disorder comorbidity. *Journal of Psychiatric Research, 29*(5), 361-374.

Starcevic, V., Sammut, P., Berle, D., Hannan, A., Milicevic, D., Moses, K. et al (2012). Can levels of a general anxiety-prone cognitive style distinguish between various anxiety disorders? *Comprehensive Psychiatry, 53*(5), 427-433.

Stein, D.J., Shoulberg, N., Helton, K., & Hollander, E. (1992). The neuroethological approach to obsessive-compulsive disorder. *Comprehensive Psychiatry, 33*(4), 274-281.

Storch, E.A., Abramowitz, J., & Goodman, W.K. (2008). Where does obsessive-compulsive disorder belong in DSM-V? *Depression & Anxiety, 25*, 336-347.

Swain, J.E., Lorberbaum, J.P., Kose, S., & Strathearn, L. (2007). Brain basis of early parent-infant interactions: Psychology, physiology, and in vivo functional neuroimaging studies. *Journal of Child Psychology & Psychiatry, 48*(3-4), 262-287.

Tilfors, M. & Ekselius, L. (2009). Social phobia and avoidant personality disorder: Are they separate diagnostic entities or do they reflect a spectrum of anxiety? *Israel Journal of Psychiatry & Relational Science, 46*(1), 25033.

Tolman, E.C. (1935). Psychology vs immediate experience. *Philosophical Science, 2*, 356-380.

Tomkins, S. (1962). *Affect, Imagery, Consciousness: The Positive Effects* (Volume 1). New York: Springer.

Tomkins, S. (1963). *Affect, Imagery, Consciousness: The Negative Effects* (Volume 2). New York: Springer.

Turner, S.M., Beidel, D.C., & Townsley, R.M. (1992). Social phobia: A comparison of specific and generalized subtypes and avoidant personality disorder. *Journal of Abnormal Psychology, 101*(2), 326-331.

Vrana, S. (1993). The psychophysiology of disgust: Differentiating negative emotional contexts with facial EMG. *Psychophysiology, 30*, 279-286.

Vriends, N., Becker, E.S., Meyer, A., Michael, T., & Margraf, J. (2007). Subtypes of social phobia: Are they of any use? *Journal of Anxiety Disorders, 21*(1), 59-75.

Watson, D. (2005). Rethinking the mood and anxiety disorders: A quantitative hierarchical model for DSM-V. *Journal of Abnormal Psychology, 114*(4), 522-536.

Watson, J.B. (1925). *Behaviorism*. New York: W.W. Norton.

Wittchen, H.U., Reed, V., & Kessler, R.C. (1998). The relationship of agoraphobia and panic in a community sample of adolescents and young adults. *Archives of General Psychiatry, 55*(11), 1017-1024.

World Health Organization. (1992). *The ICD-10 Classification of Mental and Behavioral Disorders: Clinical Descriptions and Diagnostic Guidelines*. Geneva: World Health Organization.

Zinbarg, R.E. & Barlow, D.H. (1996). Structure of anxiety and the anxiety disorders: A hierarchical model. *Journal of Abnormal Psychology, 105*(2), 181-193.

CHAPTER 4

Hypomania-Mania

Occurring in the context of depression, and also anxiety in some instances, is what appears to be another naturally occurring entity, hypomania-mania. In contrast to depression and anxiety, the issue of whether hypomania-mania symptoms are continuous seems to provoke less controversy. This occurrence is reflected in the diagnostic criteria of DSM-IV, DSM-5, and ICD-10 (American Psychiatric Association, 2013; First et al, 2002; World Health Organization, 1992). In DSM-IV and DSM-5 the criteria are for manic/hypomanic episodes, and not just one or the other (American Psychiatric Association, 2013; First et al, 2002). Symptoms consist of inflated self-esteem or grandiosity, decreased need for sleep, more talkative than usual or pressure to keep talking, flight of ideas or subjective experience that thoughts are racing, distractibility, and increase in goal directed behavior or psychomotor agitation. With mania there must be marked impairment in functioning or psychosis, although the criteria for hypomania also include marked impairment in functioning. For both, there needs to be abnormally elevated, expansive, or irritable mood lasting a week, with DSM-5 including increased energy or activity (American Psychiatric Association, 2013; First et al, 2002). A hypomanic episode must last at least 4 days (American Psychiatric Association, 2013; First et al, 2002).

ICD-10 also links hypomania and mania, and focuses on elevated mood, increased energy and activity, enhanced sense of wellbeing, and both physical and mental efficiency (World Health Organization, 1992). There is often increased sociability, familiarity, talkativeness, sexual energy, and decreased need for sleep. With hypomania the symptoms are less severe and do not involve psychosis, and episodes must last for several days. Mania can occur with or without psychosis, and involves essentially the same symptoms as hypomania, but simply more intense and interfering with functional capacity (World Health Organization, 1992).

Both DSM and ICD diagnostic systems largely focus on the same symptom types, including elevated mood, more expansive sense of self, increased energy and activity, reduced need for sleep, increased sociability such as with talkativeness and familiarity, and increased goal directed activity (American Psychiatric Association, 2013; First et al, 2002; World Health Organization,

1992). These symptoms shed light on an additional aspect of a continuous organization: Whether there is a direct linkage with the normal population. All of the symptom types listed clearly apply to the normal population, and there is considerable variation within the normal range. For example, people naturally vary in their mood state, energy and activity level, and sense of wellbeing, with some people being to the higher side. Level of sociability varies, such as with extroverted people being more outgoing, talkative, and generating a greater sense of familiarity. Need for sleep and sexual energy also vary widely. In addition, the cognitive features such as enhanced self-perspectives occur in a range within the normal population. We typically consider those on the higher end of the scale in these regards to be functioning more optimally, such as being more socially gifted or possessing a robust libido. This occurrence can actually help us understand why hypomanic-manic symptoms transpire, at least when hypomania is focused on.

Hypomania is distinct from many conditions listed as disorders in that it does not actually appear to be dysfunctional (Akiskal, 2005; Akiskal & Pinto, 1999; Bowins, 2008; Eckblad and Chapman, 1986; Jamison et al, 1980; Johnson et al, 2000; Koukopoulos et al, 2003). Diagnostic systems seem somewhat confused about this point, suggesting that the distinction between hypomania and mania is compromised social or occupation functioning, although somehow hypomania also involves compromised functioning (American Psychiatric Association, 2013; First et al, 2002; World Health Organization, 1992). Psychosis cannot reliably distinguish mania from hypomania because mania does not always involve psychosis. The DSM (IV and 5) criterion of a minimum of 4 days for hypomania and ICD-10 requirement of "several days" (American Psychiatric Association, 2013; First et al, 2002; World Health Organization, 1992) actually do not appear to be valid, and skew the focus towards dysfunctional expressions of hypomania, likely capturing the transition to mania (Bowins, 2008). Research reveals that the modal time frame for hypomania is 1-3 days (Akiskal and Pinto, 1999; Benazzi & Akiskal, 2001; Perugi & Akiskal, 2002; Wicki & Angst, 1991).

Diagnostic criteria designations are largely political in nature, based on consensus, and it seems that to date those involved remain closed to the perspective that hypomania might be adaptive. Perhaps this is not surprising given that the focus in psychiatry and clinical psychology is on dysfunctional states. Another major reason is pressure from the pharmaceutical industry to expand the range of dysfunction, and hence conditions requiring pharmaceutical intervention. The latter influence should not be discounted, because research has found that DSM panel members frequently have extensive ties with the pharmaceutical industry (Cosgrove et al, 2009). Cosgrove et al (2009) revealed that 100% of the DSM-IV "mood disorders" and "schizophrenia and other psychotic disorders" panel members had one or more financial associations with companies in the pharmaceutical industry. This influence is important to note when it comes to determining the actual validity of diagnostic criteria, because even a small financial influence sets up a powerful motivation to reciprocate (Bowins, 2014, pp. 213-279). Shifting to a position that hypomania is largely adaptive takes panel members into unfamiliar territory, and reduces the domain of what might be treatable by pharmaceuticals.

It is one thing to state that hypomania is mostly adaptive, but another to show proof. What does research reveal about the adaptive potential of hypomania, particularly when we remove the criterion of a minimum of 4 or several days, emphasizing more severe variants that actually appear to represent a crossover into mania? In this regards it is important to appreciate, consistent with the notion of continuums, that there is a progression from fully normal variants of hypomanic-manic symptoms, as discussed above, to subthreshold hypomania, to hypomania, to subthreshold mania, to mania of varying degrees, with extensive overlap between adjacent expressions (Bowins, 2008). There is a continuum, and we designate hypomania and mania as falling at certain arbitrary points along it (Angst et al, 2003; Angst et al, 2010; Bowins, 2008).

A substantial body of research supports the position that hypomania is typically adaptive, even when a several day criterion is applied (Akiskal, 2005; Akiskal & Pinto, 1999; Bowins, 2008; Eckblad and Chapman, 1986; Jamison et al, 1980; Johnson et al, 2000; Koukopoulos et al, 2003; Kraepelin 1921, cited in Jamison et al, 1980). Behaviors characterizing hypomania, such as cheerfulness and jocularity, gregariousness and people seeking, increased sexual drive and behavior, talkativeness and eloquence, confidence and optimism, adaptive disinhibition and carefree attitudes, reduced need for sleep, eutonia and vitality, and over-involvement in new projects, are adaptive under a wide range of circumstances (Akiskal & Pinto, 1999). Johnson et al (2000) have found that whereas goal attainment in non-bipolars leads to "coasting," the same success in bipolars produces intensified goal seeking. Koukopoulos et al (2003) describe how in rapid cyclers a "nuance" of hypomania, including slightly less need for sleep and higher activity and talkativeness, always remains, not impairing functioning or quality of life and having many positive aspects.

Jamison et al (1980) looked at whether hypomania is adaptive from a self perspective. Interviewing 35 bipolar and 26 unipolar depressed patients, they asked set questions about perceived short and long-term benefits in regards to psychological sensitivity, sexual enjoyment, productivity, creativity, and social outgoingness and ease. Depressed patients only indicated an increase in sensitivity, but the vast majority of bipolar men and women believed each of the attributes had increased either somewhat or very much during hypomania. For men the most significant change was increased social outgoingness and ease during hypomania, followed by creativity. Women were equally divided on increased sexual intensity, productivity, and social outgoingness and ease. Jamison et al (1980) suggest that a baseline effect applies, insofar as the lower the level of functioning prior to the hypomanic episode the greater the change with it. Prior to a hypomanic episode social anxiety and inhibition in men might be worse than their libido, resulting in a greater improvement in social outgoingness and ease than libido during a hypomanic state. By maximally increasing performance in areas of weakness, hypomanic episodes can be highly beneficial and adaptive. Noting the adaptive aspects of hypomania, Kraepelin (1921, cited in Jamison et al, 1980: 198) indicated that "the volitional excitement which accompanies the disease may under certain circumstances set powers free which otherwise are constrained by all kinds of inhibitions," although the use of the term "disease" suggests that Kraepelin did not fully appreciate the mostly adaptive nature of hypomania.

A comparison to depression further reveals the adaptive aspects of hypomania. Depression is widely understood as a maladaptive condition requiring treatment. In more than 20 years as a psychiatrist I have never encountered anyone requesting to become depressed, nor have I ever heard of such an occurrence. Instead, depression is one of the most common indications for seeking assistance from mental health professionals. Although there is the notion of secondary reinforcement for depression, it appears highly overstated, because beyond the very short range people withdraw from those who are depressed, enhancing the person's sense of isolation and worsening depression. When a person experiences and demonstrates sadness, the root emotion of depression, people frequently offer assistance, but sadness is a short lived state lasting seconds to perhaps days as an extended mood state. Depression involves weeks, months, and even years of suffering, a time frame that few other than quite rare codependent partners are likely to reinforce with assistance.

The maladaptive aspects of depression are inherent in impairments to sleep, appetite, concentration, motivation, energy, activity, functioning (including sexual, social, and occupational), and also suicidal behavior (Bowins, 2008). Depressive inhibition (see the "Depression" chapter), a concept proposed by Kraepelin (1904, cited in Himmelhoch, 1998: 209), captures the maladaptive nature of depression: "All action of the will is extremely difficult...the transformation of impulses of the will into action meets with obstacles that cannot be overcome without difficulty, and often not at all by the patient's own strength." During our evolution a depressed state would likely have reduced a person's capacity to cope with the demands of the physical environment, and the social hunting-gathering group context (Bowins, 2008).

In contrast to depression (and even normal behavior in many instances) hypomania is typically adaptive. Akiskal and Pinto (1999: 520) indicate that when there is depression with hypomania (BP II) there can be "supernormal periods of functioning," and that a "considerable number of these patients are able to rebound from their difficult periods, to attain new conjugal or occupational status." When preceded by depression, hypomanic episodes were observed by Akiskal et al (1979) to be ego-syntonic, usually pleasurable, socially adaptive, and described by some clinicians as a "flight into health."

The adaptive aspect of hypomania compared to depression is also evident by examining the Behavioral Activation System (BAS) and Behavioral Inhibition System (BIS), also covered in the "Depression" and "Anxiety" chapters (Fowles, 1988; Gray, 1987). The combination of low BAS and high BIS is said to characterize depression (Fowles, 1988; Kasch et al, 2002), whereas BIS is increased irrespective of BAS in conditions such as anxiety and schizophrenia (Campbell-Sills et al,

2004; Kasch et al, 2002; Mineka et al, 1998; Scholten et al, 2006). Hypomania involves the opposite BIS/BAS profile to depression: Enhanced BAS and reduced BIS (Bowins, 2008; Meyer et al, 2001). High BAS is associated with hypomania, and was in one study found to account for 27% of the variance for hypomania (Meyer et al, 2001). The tendency of those with hypomania to intensify goal seeking with goal attainment (Johnson et al, 2000) was described by the authors as due to increased BAS associated with hypomania-mania.

In addition to depression, hypomania is adaptive for managing social anxiety, or, based on the continuum perspective of anxiety presented in the "Anxiety" chapter, anxiety activated by social circumstances. Himmelhoch (1998) believes that social phobia and the volitional inhibitions of depression are similar states, and that in some cases social anxiety is an intrinsic presentation of the depressed phase of BP II disorder. With depressive inhibition there is difficulty initiating action, and with social anxiety inhibition related to fear of humiliation. Himmelhoch (1998) noted that treatment with MAOI's triggered hypomania in 14 subjects with social anxiety. In the hypomanic state these individuals became much more self-assertive, to the point where several relatives and friends were offended, and in 6 of the 14 the change was described as "optimal adaptation." Social anxiety and major depression are frequently comorbid, with more than a quarter of patients with major depressive disorder reporting social anxiety (Fava et al, 2000). Regarding the temporal sequence, social anxiety often starts at an earlier age than depression, and many comorbid patients attribute their depression to the suffering imposed by social anxiety (Schneier et al, 2002). Perugi et al (1999) found that in their sample generalized social phobia preceded the onset of bipolar disorder, and showed a complete remission during hypomania.

Additional research evidence supports the adaptive aspects of hypomania for social anxiety. Himmelhoch (1998) found that those with social phobia who became hypomanic demonstrated extroversion and good social skills, such as warmth and humor. Eckblad and Chapman (1986) evaluated undergraduate psychology students and compared those scoring high on the Hypomanic Personality Scale to a lower scoring control group. Those with hypomanic personality reported twice the number of close friends in high school, more social interactions, greater propensity to be a leader, and rated themselves more highly on sociability and outgoingness than did controls. During the interview the hypomanic group was described as poised and articulate, relaxed, and acting older than their age. These individuals tended to experience "speeded up" periods once or twice a month lasting 2-3 days. In the Jamison et al (1980) study both men and women felt more social outgoingness and ease during hypomania, and for men this was the most significant change. According to Benazzi and Akiskal (2003), social activation accounts for a large part of the variance of the phenomenology of hypomania.

Hypomania exists not only as a state but also as a personality variant or trait (Akiskal, 1996; Akiskal & Akiskal, 2005), as focused on in the Eckblad and Chapman (1986) study. Hypomanic personality, more commonly known as hyperthymic temperament (hyperthymia), is to a great extent the personality equivalent to hypomania, representing a permanently elevated baseline of hypomanic adjustment (Akiskal, 1996). Hyperthymic temperament is positively associated with leadership qualities and novelty seeking, and negatively associated with harm avoidance (Akiskal & Akiskal, 2005). Akiskal (2005) describes extroversion, proficiency in three or more languages, eminence, creativity, novelty seeking and enhanced activity as prominent facets of hyperthymia. Akiskal and Pinto (1999) indicate that a hyperthymic temperament protects against clinical depression, and hyperthymic individuals who succumb to depression usually do so later in life.

Given that hypomania (at least when lasting less than 4 days, consistent with its normal presentation) and hyperthymic temperament appear to be adaptive, the question arises as to why this capacity evolved. Dysfunctional conditions usually arise from impairments to normal functioning, whereas adaptive traits evolve in response to evolutionary fitness challenges (Darwin, 1858). The typically maladaptive consequences of depression, adaptive aspects of hypomania, and linkage of hypomania-mania to depression suggest that hypomania evolved as a defensive response to depression compensating for impairments to evolutionary fitness. Many researchers seem not to grasp the potential of hypomania to defensively compensate for depression, despite defensive compensation being a well-established fact of nature. As a simple example, the immune system evolved to manage challenges from invading organisms. Let us examine how hypomania might defensively compensate for the maladaptive aspects of depression, and how mania might fit into this scenario.

The Defensive Role of Hypomania

During our evolution in hunting-gathering groups survival was not a sure thing. There were predators not opposed to including humans in their range of edible species, and often competing hunting-gathering groups. Given the nature of depressive inhibition, including impairments to cognitive, emotional, social, and physical behaviors, depression almost certainly impacted negatively on evolutionary fitness, reducing a person's capacity to be vigilant for predators and other threats and to respond in an effective way to challenges (Bowins, 2008). In addition, within the social context of a hunting-gathering group a depressed person would usually have fared quite poorly (Bowins, 2008). People often idealize life in these groups seeing an affinity with nature, but much of a person's reality was comprised of contending with the social milieu involving politics, alliance formation, competition for key resources, and—of crucial significance—reciprocity (Glantz & Pearce, 1989).

Hunting-gathering groups emphasized reciprocity because resources could not be relied on. If your hunt goes well and you share with others who come up empty handed, then they will share with you when circumstances are reversed (Glantz & Pearce, 1989). The lack of refrigeration and impossibility of travelling with many resources ensured that reciprocity was a key social force. Reciprocity might even be the basis of empathy, because it requires an appreciation of another person's state of being. Mental processing is required for both empathy and reciprocity. Within hunting-gathering groups, a significant portion of mental activity goes into keeping track of debts and entitlements (Glantz & Pearce, 1989). Among the modern day Kung Bushmen of the Kalahari exchange relationships can last a lifetime—and even beyond, being passed on to a person's children (Glantz & Pearce, 1989). The cognitive limitations of depression would make it very difficult to keep track of debts and entitlements, particularly considering that tracking was completely memory based. In addition, the motivation, energy, and physical activity impairments of depression related to low BAS and high BIS would limit a person's capacity to seek resources required for repayment, and even pursue the repayment of debts.

When it came to deciding on partners for reciprocal exchanges and mates, a depressed person would likely have been passed over in favor of more upbeat and energetic individuals. Verbal and non-verbal expressions of the depressive inhibition state would have signaled to others that obligations might not be repaid, and that the person lacked desirable genes, given that a positive upbeat appearance and manner is suggestive of desirable characteristics, attracting potential mates and allies (Hess & Kirouac, 2000). Even in our modern era few will select a depressed person for a friend or mate. Healthy social functioning is largely characterized by reciprocity, and the capacity to reciprocate is impaired with depression. In contrast to depression hypomania entails solid energy, activity, motivation, and typically a much more positive presentation, consistent with elevated BAS and reduced BIS (Bowins, 2008). In a hypomanic state a person would be more likely to share resources and effectively call in debts, and be much more likely to be selected as a partner for reciprocal exchanges and mating (Bowins, 2008).

One crucial issue in appreciating the potential of hypomania to compensate for the evolutionary fitness impairments of a depressive inhibition state is the time frame. The typical time frame of a manic episode is 1-3 days (Akiskal and Pinto, 1999; Benazzi & Akiskal, 2001; Perugi & Akiskal, 2002; Wicki & Angst, 1991). Since hypomania cannot fully eliminate depression in this time frame, how might it compensate? Although scientists and philosophers endlessly debate the nature of time, at least from our perspective there is a past, present, and future. The future might be conceptualized as consisting of potential occurrences, and the past those potential occurrences that have been actualized. For example, many things might potentially occur tomorrow, but only those that actually do will form a person's past. Of crucial significance, the now or present is a very brief period during which potential occurrences are actualized. For instance, with a predator about there are several potential occurrences, one being that a person neglects the threat and is attacked, and another that the threat is responded to with an alarm call, motivating nearby group members to help scare the predator off. What happens in the moment guides what potential occurrence is actualized.

In a depressed state a person is more likely to miss the predator, or not respond appropriately, resulting in an evolutionary fitness-impairing potential occurrence being actualized. In a hypomanic state a person is more likely to detect a threat and respond appropriately, increasing the probability of evolutionary fitness-enhancing potential occurrences being actualized in the now. The same scenario applies to the social environment, such as an opportunity for a reciprocal partner, alliance formation, or status challenge. In a state of depression a person is more likely to actualize less adaptive potential social occurrences, while in a hypomanic state a person engages in the more adaptive options. From an evolutionary fitness perspective, it all happens in the moment, and hypomania active within a brief time frame can offset the increased likelihood of evolutionary fitness-impairing actions resulting from depression (Bowins, 2008).

Hypomania might then be conceptualized as a depressive inhibition override defense mechanism (Bowins, 2008). Templates for an override or interrupt defense mechanism exist in nature, with predator detection systems being able to override sleep, and, perhaps more relevant to depression and hypomania, physiological or emotional states being able to override behavioral inhibition (Cosmides & Tooby, 2000). For example, intense hunger, thirst, and anger can override inhibition against approaching a source of water or food (Cosmides & Tooby, 2000). In a similar fashion, hypomania can override depressive inhibition in the moment to restore adaptive functioning (Bowins, 2008). The increased likelihood of maladaptive potential occurrences being actualized due to a depressive state shifts to a much greater probability of adaptive outcomes being actualized in the now. No long-range solution to depression is required, as by operating in the brief now hypomania can offset many of the maladaptive consequences of depression. As a personality variant of hypomania, hyperthymia increases the probability of adaptive outcomes on an ongoing basis, and genes for it are quite likely undergoing rapid allelic spread (Bowins, 2008).

The depressive inhibition override perspective on hypomania explains the simultaneous presence of depressive and hypomanic-manic symptoms: Given that the defense works by briefly overriding depressive inhibition, it cannot fully eliminate depressive symptoms, and both types routinely occur together (Benazzi & Akiskal, 2001). Interestingly, the co-occurrence of these symptom types likely accounts for irritability being one of the key mood states in bipolar disorder, as the simultaneous presence of opposing states likely induces cognitive dissonance expressed as irritability (Bowins, 2008). A potential critique of the proposed override defense mechanism model is the maladaptive nature of mania.

The Problem with Mania

Whereas limited intensity and brief hypomania, typically lasting 1-3 days, tends to be adaptive, and relative to depression is certainly so, it is much harder to argue that full-blown mania with unrestrained energy and behavior, often complete lack of sleep, psychosis, and bizarre social behavior can be adaptive. It represents a defense over the edge (Bowins, 2008). In certain select instances throughout evolution it is possible that while in a manic but still coherent state a person could achieve adaptive outcomes not feasible when depressed. For example, with the increased energy and confidence forthcoming from mania, a low ranking male might successfully attack and overthrow a high ranking leader, acquiring key resources such as increased mating opportunities, also feasible given the enhanced sexual behavior that commonly occurs with hypomania-mania. However, in most instances mania appears to be maladaptive, compromising social and occupational functioning.

With a continuum of hypomania-mania it is not a matter of one discrete form being replaced with another, but instead an extension along the continuum. Increasing duration and intensity of symptoms shifts hypomania to subthreshold mania and then mania. The DSM-IV and DSM-5 requirement of 4 days' duration and focus on functional impairment (First et al, 2002; American Psychiatric Association, 2013) appear more properly to describe the transition from hypomania to subthreshold mania, emphasizing maladaptive expressions (Bowins, 2008). There are several possible reasons why hypomania might shift to subthreshold mania and even mania. One is that if the hypomanic defense does not succeed in overriding depressive inhibition in the moment, the defense might intensify, in much the way that, if a limited immune system response does not eliminate an invading pathogen, there is intensification. Another reason is exposure to substances not present during our evolution that can potentially trigger an intensification of hypomanic-manic symptoms, such as antidepressants, alcohol, and illicit substances. Antidepressants are well-recognized agents in triggering mania (Altshuler et al, 2006).

A key reason why antidepressants, alcohol, and illicit substances might trigger mania is impaired regulation over the proposed hypomanic depressive inhibition override defense. We learned in the "Depression" and "Anxiety" chapters how impaired top-down regulation of excessive limbic system activity is highly implicated in these disorders. As pertains to the hypomanic defense, adequate regulatory control ensures that the response is contained to a level that overrides depressive inhibition in the moment to restore adaptive functioning (Bowins, 2008). Adequate regulation likely represents BPII, whereas deficient regulatory control produces BPI—although, with its predominantly adaptive features, and certainly relative to depression, hypomania should not be listed as a disorder at all (Bowins, 2008). A specific way that this regulatory control process might operate is by monitoring the costs/benefits of hypomanic defense activation. When the benefits exceed the costs, such as by overriding maladaptive depressive behavior in the moment, the defense is activated and maintained. However, if costs are exceeding benefits, such as radically reduced sleep, unsustainable energy, and impairments to reality testing as with manic states, the defense is down-regulated or deactivated (Bowins, 2008). Genetically induced vulnerabilities and also environmental influences, such as antidepressants, alcohol, and illicit substances, quite likely impair regulatory control, allowing mostly adaptive hypomania to progress to largely maladaptive mania. Impairments to basic cognition (executive functions), social cognition, and motivational states—negative symptoms—also play a key role in impairing regulation over the hypomanic defense (see the chapter "Negative Symptoms"). Psychosis commonly occurs with mania, and hence the regulatory control issues proposed for psychosis (see the "Psychosis" chapter) also seem to be relevant.

Assuming that impaired regulatory control is a factor in hypomania progressing to mania, cognitive regulatory control therapy techniques may help to compensate, or even restore some of this functioning (Bowins, 2013). Some patients with BPI prefer not to be medicated on an ongoing basis, and wish to be more in control of their illness. With select patients that are self-aware and able to self-monitor on an ongoing basis, the techniques described can work quite well, compensating for impaired regulatory control over hypomania-mania. Psycho-education pertaining to hypomania, mania, and depression is crucial, with hypomania-mania understood as a continuum. The person must appreciate what symptoms they experience in each of these states, and monitor their mood on an ongoing basis. Collaboration and frequent contact with the treatment provider is also necessary. Prior to the onset of a manic episode, strategies are agreed on to help deactivate or minimize an evolving manic episode once the prelude is detected. This intervention can involve a range of options suited to the individual, such as relaxation strategies, minimizing stimulation, and reduction or elimination of mind-altering substances. Frequently it entails the use of medication on an as needed (prn) basis, with both antipsychotics and benzodiazepines, alone or in combination, being effective options. When an evolving manic episode is terminated the prn medications can be withdrawn. With motivated and self-aware patients these techniques can eliminate the need for ongoing medication that is often capable of producing severe problems, such as thyroid and kidney failure with lithium, and metabolic syndrome or tardive dyskinesia with antipsychotics.

A brief patient example will help illustrate the application of this technique. Amy (not her real name) is a mid-thirties intelligent woman with three clear manic episodes, multiple hypomanic episodes lasting 1-3 days typically, and a couple of severe depressive episodes. She has tried several different medications including lithium, valproic acid, and antipsychotics, but does not like the side effects. She prefers natural ways of dealing with her problems, but accepts being on escitalopram (a Selective Serotin Reuptake Inhibitor—SSRI) because it sustains her mood at a solid level. She is motivated to play a role in her own treatment, and through our discussions is very aware of her symptoms pertaining to depression, hypomania, and mania, understanding that there is a gradient of hypomanic-manic symptoms (and also depressive symptoms). When depressed she has little motivation, loses energy, and sleeps excessively, not wanting to get out of bed even to exercise or engage in other activities she typically enjoys. When hypomanic she is motivated, energetic, gets out of bed easily, and is more functional. She does online cognitive exercises and has recorded significantly better performance when hypomanic than depressed.

Amy's manic episodes have been triggered primarily by relationship/romance stress, and in the past, alcohol/drug abuse. Early in treatment we focused on the role that chemical substances play, and consistent with her motivation she joined

Alcoholics Anonymous, now having been clean and sober for approximately 2 years. This change alone greatly reduces the likelihood of her experiencing a manic episode. In addition, since romance stress and excessive alcohol/drug use often occurred together, managing the substance abuse issues also reduces risk of mania arising from relationship issues. When Amy detects intensifying hypomanic-manic symptoms (impaired sleep, confusion, and lesser cognitive capacity) she starts prn aripiprazole, a second generation antipsychotic, plus lorazepam (a benzodiazepine) if required, as agreed upon. Quetiapine (another second generation antipsychotic) worked remarkably well on its own, but was too heavily sedating. She also adjusts her workouts, as the timing and extent can either relax or overly activate her. Consistent with her clean and sober state, she now avoids stimulating party scenarios and engages in relaxation strategies. These techniques have enabled her to defuse a few instances of hypomania escalating to mania.

Given that hypomania is generally adaptive and brief, another novel therapeutic option consists of inducing hypomania when a person is depressed (Bowins, 2008). Essentially, this technique consists of increasing physical, social, and mental activity (Bowins, 2008). This process is consistent with what most experienced clinicians suggest, such as by getting patients to walk, exercise, socialize, and start to read again. It also aligns with behavioral activation therapy, covered in the "Depression" chapter, oriented to increasing activity. BAS is enhanced and BIS diminished by increasing physical, social, and mental activity. If hypomania routinely transitioned to mania this technique would be problematic, but hypomania rarely progresses to mania, at least when taken in its proper duration of 1-3 days (Akiskal, 2005; Akiskal, 1996; Bowins, 2008; Cassano et al, 1992; Coryell et al, 1989; Klein et al, 1996). Akiskal (2005) estimated that hypomania occurs in 50% of all depressions in clinical practice, while mania only occurs in 1% of the population (Weissman & Myers, 1978). Hypomania usually does not progress to mania, even in those with prior manic episodes—50%-60% of those who have experienced manic episodes also experience milder hypomanic episodes not leading to mania (Cassano et al, 1992; Coryell et al, 1989). Klein et al (1996) found that most adolescent bipolar individuals remain stable with hypomania that does not transition to mania. Amongst cyclothymics only 6% will develop mania (Akiskal, 1996). Hence, the risks associated with attempting to induce hypomania via increased physical, social, and mental activity are very low, and the gains in terms of improving functioning within the context of depression, and even anxiety from social sources, high.

The Hypomania-Mania Continuum

Hypomania and mania do appear to be continuous as is embodied in major diagnostic systems (American Psychiatric Association, 2013; First et al, 2002; World Health Organization, 1992). In addition, the symptoms of subthreshold hypomania run continuous with normal states. In contrast to the evidently maladaptive nature of mental illness, hypomania is generally adaptive, at least within the time frame of 1-3 days consistent with research evidence (Akiskal &

Pinto, 1999; Benazzi & Akiskal, 2001; Perugi & Akiskal, 2002; Wicki & Angst, 1991). This interesting occurrence does require a shift in perspective from the traditional view that it is only an illness. One viable option presented is that hypomania comprises a defensive compensation for depression and anxiety (at least of social origins). Given that hypomania typically lasts 1-3 days, and hence cannot completely eliminate depression, the most likely option is that it acts by overriding depression (and anxiety) to restore adaptive behavior in the moment. Natural precedents for an override defense mechanism support the plausibility of such a mechanism (Cosmides & Tooby, 2000). Mania probably arises due to defective or impaired regulation over the hypomanic defensive process, resulting for the most part in maladaptive behavior.

References

Akiskal, H.S. (1996). The prevalent clinical spectrum of bipolar disorders: Beyond DSM-IV. *Journal of Clinical Psychopharmacology, 16*, 4S-15S.

Akiskal, H.S. (2005). Searching for behavioral indicators of bipolar II in patients presenting with major depressive episodes: The "red sign," the "rule of three" and other biographic signs of temperamental extravagance, activation and hypomania. *Journal of Affective Disorders, 84*, 279-290.

Akiskal, K.K. & Akiskal, H.S. (2005). The theoretical underpinnings of affective temperaments: Implications for evolutionary foundations of bipolar disorder and human nature. *Journal of Affective Disorders, 85*, 231-239.

Akiskal, H. & Pinto, O. (1999). The evolving bipolar spectrum: Prototypes I, II, III, and IV. *Psychiatric Clinics of North America, 22*, 517-534.

Altshuler, L.L., Suppes, T., & Black, D.O. (2006). Lower switch rate in depressed patients with bipolar II than bipolar I disorder treated adjunctively with second-generation anti-depressants. *American Journal of Psychiatry, 163*, 313-315.

American Psychiatric Association (2013). *Diagnostic & Statistical Manual 5*. Washington, DC: American Psychiatric Publishing.

Angst, J., Cui, L., & Swendsen, J. (2010). Major depressive disorder with subthreshold bipolarity in the national comorbidity survey replication. *American Journal of Psychiatry, 167*, 1194-1201.

Angst, J., Gamma, A., Benazzi, F., Ajdacic, V., Eich, D., & Rossler, W. (2003). Toward a re-definition of subthreshold bipolarity: Epidemiological and proposed criteria for bipolar-II, minor bipolar disorders and hypomania. *Journal of Affective Disorders, 73*(1-2), 133-146.

Benazzi, F. & Akiskal, H. (2001). Delineating bipolar II mixed states in the Ravenna-San Diego collaborative study: The relative prevalence and diagnostic significance of hypomanic features during major depressive episodes. *Journal of Affective Disorders, 67*, 115-122.

Benazzi, F. & Akiskal, H.S. (2003). The dual factor structure of self-rated MDQ hypomania: Energized-activity versus irritable-thought racing. *Journal of Affective Disorders, 73*, 59-64.

Bowins, B. (2008). Hypomania: A depressive inhibition override defense mechanism. *Journal of Affective Disorders, 109*, 221-232.

Bowins, B. (2013). Cognitive regulatory control therapies. *American Journal of Psychotherapy, 67*(3), 215-236.

Bowins, B. (2014). *At the Tipping Point: How to Save Us from Self-Destruction*. West Conshohocken, PA: Infinity.

Campbell-Sills, L., Liverant, G.I., & Brown, T.A. (2004). Psychometric evaluation of the behavioral inhibition/behavioral activation scales in a large sample of outpatients with anxiety and mood disorders. *Psychological Assessment, 16*, 244-254.

Cassano, G.B., Akiskal, H.S., Savino, M., Musetti, L., & Perugi, G. (1992). Proposed subtypes of bipolar II and related disorders: With hypomanic episodes (or cyclothymia) and with hyperthymic temperament. *Journal of Affective Disorders, 26*, 127-140.

Coryell, W., Endicott, J., Keller, M., Andreasen, N., Grove, W., Hirshfeld, R.M., & Scheftner, W. (1989). Bipolar affective disorder and high achievement: A familial association. *American Journal of Psychiatry, 146*, 983-988.

Cosgrove, L., Bursztajn, H., Krimsky, S., Anaya, M., & Walker, J. (2009). Conflicts of interest and disclosure in the American psychiatric association's clinical practice guidelines. *Psychotherapy and Psychosomatics, 78*, 228-232.

Cosmides, L. & Tooby, J. (2000). Evolutionary psychology and the emotions. In *Handbook of Emotions* (2nd ed.). New York, NY: The Guilford Press.

Darwin, C. (1858/1958). *The Origin of Species*. New York: Signet Classic.

Eckblad, M. & Chapman, L.J., (1986). Development and validation of a scale for hypomanic personality. *Journal of Abnormal Psychology, 95*, 214-222.

Fava, M., Rankin, M.A., & Wright, E.C. (2000). Anxiety disorders in major depression. *Comprehensive Psychiatry, 41*, 97-102.

First, M.B., Frances, A., & Pincus, H.A. (2002). *DSM-IV-TR Handbook of Differential Diagnosis*. Washington, DC: American Psychiatric Publishing.

Fowles, D.C. (1988). Psychophysiology and Psychopathology: A motivational approach. *Psychophysiology, 25*, 373-391.

Glantz, K. & Pearce, J. (1989). *Exiles from Eden: Psychotherapy from an Evolutionary Perspective*. New York: W.W. Norton & Company.

Gray, J.A. (1987). Perspectives on anxiety and impulsivity: A commentary. *Journal of Research in Personality, 21*, 493-509.

Hess, U. & Kirouac, G. (2000). Emotion expression in groups. In *Handbook of Emotions* (2nd ed.). New York, NY: The Guilford Press.

Himmelhoch, J. (1998). Social anxiety, hypomania and the bipolar spectrum: Data, theory and clinical issues. *Journal of Affective Disorders, 50*, 203-213.

Jamison, K., Gerner, R., Hammen, C., & Padesky, C. (1980). Clouds and silver linings: Positive experiences associated with primary affective disorders. *American Journal of Psychiatry, 137*, 198-202.

Johnson, S.L., Sandrow, D., Meyer, B., Winters, R., Miller, I., Solomon, D., & Keitner, G. (2000). Increases in manic symptoms after life events involving goal attainment. *Journal of Abnormal Psychology, 109*, 721-727.

Kasch, K.L., Rottenberg, J., Arnow, B.A., & Gotlib, I.H. (2002). Behavioral activation and inhibition systems and the severity and course of depression. *Journal of Abnormal Psychology, 111*, 589-597.

Klein, D.N., Lewinsohn, P.M., & Seeley, J.R. (1996). Hypomanic personality traits in a community sample of adolescents. *Journal of Affective Disorders, 38*, 135-143.

Koukopoulos, A., Sani, G., Koukopoulos, A.E., Minnai, G.P., Girardi, P., Pani, L. et al (2003). Duration and stability of the rapid-cycling course: A long-term personal follow-up of 109 patients. *Journal of Affective Disorders, 73*, 75-85.

Meyer, B., Johnson, S.L., & Winters, R. (2001). Responsiveness to threat and incentive in bipolar disorder: Relations of the BIS/BAS scales with symptoms. *Journal of Psychopathology & Assessment, 23*, 133-143.

Mineka, S., Watson, D., & Clark, L.A. (1998). Comorbidity of anxiety and unipolar mood disorders. *Annual Review of Psychology, 49*, 377-412.

Perugi, G. & Akiskal, H.S. (2002). The soft bipolar spectrum redefined: Focus on the cyclothymic, anxious-sensitive, impulse-dyscontrol, and binge-eating connection in bipolar II and related conditions. *Psychiatric Clinics of North America, 25*(4), 713-737.

Perugi, G., Toni, C., & Akiskal, H.S., (1999). Anxious-bipolar comorbidity diagnostic and treatment challenges. *Psychiatric Clinics of North America, 22*, 565-583.

Schneier, F.R., Blanco, C., Antia, S.X., & Liebowitz, M.R. (2002). The social anxiety spectrum. *Psychiatric Clinics of North America, 25*, 757-774.

Scholten, M.R., Van Honk, J., Aleman, A., & Kahn, R.S. (2006). Behavioral Inhibition System (BIS), the Behavioral Activation System (BAS) and schizophrenia: Relationship with psychopathology and physiology. *Journal of Psychiatric Research, 40*, 638-645.

Weissman, M.M., & Myers, J.K. (1978). Affective disorders in a US urban community. *Archives of General Psychiatry, 35*, 1304-1311.

Wicki, E. & Angst, J. (1991). The Zurich study: Hypomania in a 28- to 30-year-old cohort. *European Archives of Psychiatry and Clinical Neuroscience, 240*, 339-348.

World Health Organization (1992). *The ICD-10 Classification of Mental and Behavioral Disorders: Clinical Descriptions and Diagnostic Guidelines.* Geneva: World Health Organization.

CHAPTER 5

Psychosis

Psychosis is one of the most dramatic and evident expressions of mental illness, frequently obscuring less colorful manifestations, such as negative symptoms (see the "Negative Symptoms" chapter). When it comes to whether psychosis is structured continuously or discretely, there are two main overlapping foci: The extension of psychosis to the general population, and the process/structure of psychotic symptoms. Substantial research efforts have been directed at determining if psychosis is continuous between the non-clinical and clinical populations, and much of this research focuses on auditory hallucinations. Depending on the methods employed and group studied, the prevalence of auditory hallucinations can range from nearly zero to very high (Beavan et al, 2011; Linscott & Van Os, 2010; Kelleher et al, 2012). For instance, Beavan et al (2011) reported on 17 surveys from nine countries, conducted over an extensive period (from the late 19th to early 21st century), that showed a range of verbal auditory hallucination from 0.6% to 84%, the differences due to various definitions, methodologies, and cultural factors. A more extensive cross-cultural review involving data from 52 countries produced a figure of 5.8%, with a substantial range from near zero to 31.4% in Nepal (Linscott & Van Os, 2010). The prevalence of auditory verbal hallucinations appears to be somewhat higher in children and adolescents, with one study finding 14.8% (Kelleher et al, 2012).

Trauma seems to account for a substantial percentage of auditory hallucinations, with Romme and Escher (1989) reporting that 70% of voice hearers first had the experience following a traumatic event. Escher et al (2004), studying auditory verbal hallucinations in children and adolescents, discovered that for 75%, the onset of the hallucination occurred after a trauma, or difficult circumstances beyond their control. Furthermore, the content of auditory verbal hallucinations has been found to relate directly to traumatic experiences in 13% of instances, and indirectly in 58% (Hardy et al, 2005).

Assuming that the figures reported are fairly accurate, and trauma accounts for a substantial percentage of auditory verbal hallucinations in the "normal" population, it certainly appears that there is discreteness between the clinical and non-clinical populations, since not everyone experiences auditory hallucinations and many people have not been traumatized. There has been much less research effort devoted to other types of hallucinations, with one New Zealand nationwide survey finding 5.5% prevalence for visual hallucinations, compared to 2.8% for auditory hallucinations (Gale et al, 2011). This latent class analysis study found evidence for normal, hallucinatory, and psychotic classes, but the authors indicated that the presence of sub-threshold events and variation in the frequency of events suggests a psychosis continuum (Gale et al, 2011). Overall it appears that the prevalence of hallucinations within the wider population is in the range of 10%-25% (Johns & Van Os, 2001).

A key feature distinguishing between clinical and non-clinical hallucinations appears to be excessive negative emotional valence in the clinical instances (Bernstein & Putman, 1986; Dalman et al, 2011). Dalman et al (2011) found that negative emotional valence predicted the presence of psychotic disorder in 88% of cases. Bernstein and Putman (1986) ascertained that all schizophrenics in their sample, but only 53% of non-patients, reported negative voices. However, positive voices are also present in clinical psychosis, so emotional valence is not a perfect predictor of clinical and non-clinical status (Bernstein & Putman, 1986). However, hallucinations in the population at large tend to be positive and self-limited (Stip & Letourneau, 2009). Hallucinations in the non-clinical population are self-perceived as being more controllable, perhaps because of their more positive nature (Dalman et al, 2011).

Delusional thoughts also appear to occur in the general population. Nuevo et al (2012) assessed 256,445 people from 52 countries, as part of the World Health Organization's World Health Survey. Of the delusions assessed there was a range from 4.8% for delusions of control, to 8.37% for delusions of reference and persecution (Neuvo et al, 2012). Since the health status of many reporting these experiences was diminished, it is difficult to conclude how prevalent delusions are in the healthy population. A study of Iranian medical students demonstrated an average of 9.4 psychotic-like ideas per student, and a range of 0%-28% (Sharifi et al, 2008). In one very unique study, Peters et al (1999) compared delusional ideation between those in new religious movements (Hare Krishnas and Druids), non-religious individuals, Christians, and psychotic inpatients. Their results showed that the new religious movement group had a higher rate of delusions than the non-religious and Christian groups, comparable to the psychotic inpatients but less distressed and preoccupied by their delusions (Peters et al, 1999). Relevant to the linkage of delusions and religion, another study found that delusion like beliefs in the general population are linked to paranormal and religious beliefs (Pechey & Halligan, 2011).

Thought patterns related to delusions, including grandiosity and persecution, occur in the normal population (Knowles et al, 2011). Delusions of grandeur, commonly believed to distinguish mania, occur in several psychiatric disorders (bipolar 75%, schizophrenia 50%, and lesser but still substantial numbers of those with addictions), with grandiose thoughts present in about 10% of the normal population (Knowles et al, 2011). Regarding persecutory delusions, distrustful and suspicious ideation forming the basis of paranoia is quite common in the population, with a sixth of people distrusting friends and colleagues, and 10% believing that people might be watching them, or trying to harm them in some way (Bebbington et al, 2013). Bebbington et al (2013) believe that more extreme paranoid ideas build on lesser ones.

Delusions and hallucinations in combination appear to occur in a small percentage of the population. Van Os et al (2000) conducted a random sample of 7,076 adults aged 18-64, and discovered 17.5% had evidence of some type of psychosis, with delusions and hallucinations being tightly linked. As would be expected, delusions and hallucinations are less common in the normal population than in the clinical psychotic population, with the pattern of distribution being quantitative and not qualitative (Van Os et al, 1999). Amongst adolescents, psychotic like experiences such as perceptual abnormalities, persecutory ideas, magical thinking, and bizarre experiences occur, but actual psychotic experiences are uncommon (Yung et al, 2009). Of the psychotic experiences that do occur during development 75%-90% are transitory, fading over time (Van Os et al, 2009).

Subclinical psychotic experiences appear to have a median prevalence of about 5% (Johns et al, 2004; Van Os et al, 2009). Interviewing 8,580 respondents aged 16-74, applying the Psychosis Screening Questionnaire, Johns et al (2004) found that 5.5% of the respondents endorsed one or more items on the questionnaire. In some studies population rates of psychosis are higher. For example, surveying 1,464 Brazilian adults, Loch et al (2011) found that 38% had at least one lifetime psychotic symptom, with 5.4% clinically relevant, 38% not clinically relevant, and 1.9% meeting the ICD-10 criteria for non-affective psychosis.

Evidence generally supports a continuous distribution of psychotic like and psychotic symptoms in the general population, through to clinical psychosis (Shevlin et al, 2007; Stip & Letourneau, 2009). Shevlin et al (2007) applying latent class analysis found a four-class solution (psychosis, hallucinatory, intermediate, and normative) said to reflect an underlying continuum. Social adversity and trauma appear to influence the shift from subclinical to clinical (Garety et al, 2007; Johns et al, 2004; Kuipers & Bebbington, 2006; Shevlin et al, 2007; Van Os et al, 2009). An urban setting also seems to be a factor in the development of clinical psychosis, at least for adolescents and young adults (Spauwen et al, 2004). These variables might advance psychosis by triggering adverse emotional and behavioral reactions, and also reasoning biases (Kuipers & Bebbington, 2006). Consistent with this perspective, negative emotional reactions and delusion level interpretations of adverse events increase the risk of developing clinical psychosis (Krabbendam et al, 2005). Interestingly, a long-standing proneness to psychosis (schizotypy) reduces subjective distress, probably by giving the person more time to adapt (Kline et al, 2012). Negative self-esteem is also linked to psychosis, perhaps by increasing stressful interpretations of events (Taylor et al, 2013). Aligning with this finding, the content of delusions reflects self-esteem, with lower self-esteem being linked to more negative self-diminishing and discomforting delusional content (Bowins & Shugar, 1998). At a biological level psychosis proneness is associated with increasing soft neurological signs that are continuously distributed in the population (Barkus et al, 2006).

Clearly a large amount of research focuses on whether psychosis runs continuous between the non-clinical and clinical populations, and most seems to conclude that there is an underlying continuum. Interestingly, though, discreteness actually is evident because no study has found that 100% of the population has psychosis, subclinical psychosis, or even definitively psychotic-like symptoms. Hence, there must be a discrete aspect to psychosis in that some people have it and others do not. This perspective aligns with evidence for both a continuous and discrete organization to psychosis between the normal and clinical populations (Gale et al, 2011; Linscott & Van Os, 2010). As none of the relevant research adopts a psychoanalytic perspective, there is no mention of the role that dreams, said to be psychotic equivalents (Balestriere, 2007; Freud, 1900; Robbins, 2008) might play, a topic that we will get to shortly.

The second main focus of research pertaining to the continuous or discrete nature of psychosis—process/structure—has also received much attention. This area of research takes into account psychotic expressions both within an individual and between different people, as well as types and severity. In general terms, the structure of psychosis consists of thought content, thought form, and sensory perceptual expressions. Each of these symptom types resides on somewhat separate continuums. Psychotic thought content involves delusions that might be thought of as cognitive distortions inconsistent with reality (Bowins, 2004, 2011). Perspectives regarding delusion formation can be divided into belief positive and belief negative (Bell et al, 2006). Belief positive originate from a neuroscience perspective examining delusions in neurological conditions, and are based on the notion that distorted perceptual processes underlie delusional thinking (Bell et al, 2006; Maher, 2005). Langdon and Coltheart (2000) believe that perceptual distortions are a necessary first factor, and that cognitive biases in the interpretation of the perception are the second factor. According to Langdon and Coltheart (2000), there is a deficit resulting in an incorrect evaluation of the perception. A flaw in at least the first part of the model is that many delusional patients do not report unusual perceptions (Bell et al, 2006).

Belief negative models are based on more functional psychosis not related to evident brain pathology (Bell et al, 2006). Specific types of cognitive distortions characterize functional psychosis (Balzan et al, 2012; Balzan et al, 2013; Garety & Freeman, 1999; Kuipers et al, 2006). One form is evidence-hypothesis mismatches or illusory correlations. Balzan et al (2013) compared schizophrenics with a history of delusions to non-clinical subjects with delusional proneness, and subjects without a history of delusions, on tasks designed to elicit illusory correlations and illusions of control. The schizophrenic group was more susceptible to evidence-hypothesis mismatches, derived from illusory correlations and perceptions of control when none or little existed (Balzan et al, 2013). In another experiment Balzan et al (2012) found that schizophrenics are vulnerable to evidence-hypothesis mismatches, due to reliance on apparent representativeness (outcome based on similarity) and availability (outcome based on what comes to mind). Distorted appraisals of events, such as evidence-hypothesis mismatches, are instrumental in the formation of delusions (Garety & Freeman, 1999; Kuipers et al, 2006). Appraisals pertain to both the reason for an occurrence, and also how serious and threat relevant the event is (Garety & Freeman, 1999; Kuipers et al, 2006). Probabilistic reasoning biases have been found to result in "jumping to conclusions" common in persecutory delusions (Garety & Freeman, 1999). A jumping to conclusions bias occurs in about 20% of the non-clinical population, demonstrating a linkage of the process/structure underlying psychosis to the general population (Freeman et al, 2008).

Psychotic cognitive distortions pertaining to attributions are also a feature of delusions (Allen et al, 2006; Houran & Lange, 2004; Kuipers et al, 2006; Sno, 1994). Misattributions for events are generated that are inconsistent with reality (Allen et al, 2006; Houran & Lange, 2004; Sno, 1994)—for example, "The street lights came on early tonight so that those watching me would be sure to see me." Houran and Lange (2004) argue that attributional processes are adaptive by reducing fear of ambiguous stimuli, with delusional thinking occurring on a continuum with normal forms. Likewise, Bentall et al (1994) present the position that misattributions are a form of protective self-bias, positing that persecutory delusions help minimize actual-self/ideal-self inconsistencies via excessive external-person attributions. They distinguish between implicit and explicit self-esteem, and suggest that external-person attributions can defend implicit self-esteem (Bentall et al, 1994). However, there is little support for self-esteem being divided into implicit and explicit (Bell et al, 2006).

More generally, misattributions to external or other generated sources occur, including for both delusions and hallucinations (Allen et al, 2006). Patients with delusions and hallucinations, when played distorted recordings of their own speech, tend to attribute the origin to an external source (Allen et al, 2006). Attribution to external sources is a theme with persecutory delusions (Kuipers et al, 2006). Related to misattribution is misidentification, where a person makes an erroneous identification (Sno, 1994). Demonstrating an overlap between the belief positive and negative models, Freeman and Garety (2003) propose that delusions are maintained by relief of cognitive dissonance derived through the acquisition of an explanation for unusual experiences. Other cognitive distortions present in delusions include altered representations of the mental state of others (Frith, 1992), and seeking specific types of information such as threat related (Kaney & Bentall, 1992).

Some of the theories proposed for delusions also apply to hallucinations, because the two occurrences can be quite closely linked (Allen et al, 2006; Shinn et al, 2012). Appraisals often determine how distressful a sensory perceptual experience is (Mawson et al, 2010). For example, voices appraised to be high in malevolence, supremacy, disapproval, and involving a personal acquaintance lead to more distress (Mawson et al, 2010). Hallucinations might actually result from failure to identify self-generated occurrences, such as inner speech being falsely attributed to an external source (Bentall, 1990; Ford & Mathalon, 2004). Regarding visual hallucinations it has been suggested that there is an evolutionary value to false positives for threatening stimuli, and hence the brain is structured to detect visual stimuli that might not correspond exactly to real objects (Coy & Hutton, 2012).

The various cognitive and perceptual processes underlying delusions and hallucinations do appear to be widely distributed in the population (Langer et al, 2011). For example, vivid daydreams, perceptual distortions, and intrusive thoughts are common (Langer et al, 2011). In children imaginary companions frequently occur, and other unusual perceptual experiences are not uncommon (Jardi et al, 2014). Approximately 25% of childhood visual hallucinations persist into adolescence (Jardi et al, 2014). In addition, various mystical and religious experiences, such as feeling in communion with the divine, are found in a wide segment of the population (Buckley, 1981). Hence, there is solid evidence that much of what undergirds the process and structure of psychosis is distributed continuously in the population, but given that actual psychosis is dysfunctional, we need a template to understand this occurrence, and as with anxiety and depression, that appears to reside in the evolution of human intelligence.

The Evolution of Human Intelligence and Psychosis

In the "Depression" and "Anxiety" chapters we examined how human intelligence has amplified emotional information processing, and via this process contributed to depression and anxiety disorders. In a similar fashion the evolution of human intelligence has instilled the capacity for psychosis in each of us (Bowers, 1973; Bowins, 2011, 2012b). As expressed by Bowers (1973: 97), "The central nervous system appears to possess a latent capacity, neurobiologically speaking, for a pattern of functioning, which experientially is human psychotic consciousness." Underlying this innate capacity is a naturally occurring and extensive spectrum of thought content (cognitive distortions), thought form, and sensory perceptual experiences, derived from the evolution of human intelligence (Bowins, 2004, 2006a, 2011, 2012b).

Regarding cognitive distortions, we have so far considered the various processes and structural aspects, but not examined why cognitive distortions actually occur. The story links to the evolution of human intelligence and defense mechanisms. With intensified negative emotional states related to the amplification of emotional information processing, in turn derived from the evolution of human intelligence, psychological defense mechanisms appear to have evolved as a compensatory strategy (Bowins, 2004, 2006a). I have previously proposed (Bowins, 2004, 2006a) that two main templates of psychological defense mechanisms evolved: Positive cognitive distortions and dissociation (see the "Dissociation" chapter). A starting point in understanding cognitive distortions is an appreciation that completely objective reality is virtually impossible to capture, and certainly when it comes to human intentions, motivations, and social interactions. Instead of capturing objective reality, we perceive and process it according to our cognitive abilities, which are highly influenced by emotional needs (Bowins, 2004, 2006a). Positive cognitive distortions (a positivity bias) characterize good mental health, while depression involves a negativity bias (Beck, 1991). Cognitive distortions like most psychological events occur on a continuum from mild to extreme. Mild positive variants consist of placing a sugar coating on events, seeing the world through rose colored glasses, placing a self-enhancing spin on experience, and favorable attribution biases (Bowins, 2004, 2006a). People also tend to be excessively optimistic about the probability of positive outcomes in the future (Tiger, 1979), and selectively recall the past in a positive fashion (Nelson & Craighead, 1977).

More moderate level cognitive distortions consist of extensive fantasy involvement, superstition, many religious beliefs, magical thinking, and over-valued ideas (Bowins, 2004, 2006a). For example, numerous people are superstitious, as with believing that wearing a certain shirt to a game will increase the chances of their team winning, and countless people believe in an afterlife despite absolutely no evidence for such an occurrence. On the extreme end of the continuum, cognitive distortions actually lose contact with reality, transforming into delusions (Bowins, 2004, 2006a). Delusions then represent the extreme end of a naturally occurring range of cognitive distortions (thought content) made possible by the evolution of human intelligence, and advanced by psychological defense needs.

Classical psychological defenses constitute a form of positive cognitive distortion, in that they reduce the impact of negative states and protect conscious system functioning (Bowins, 2004, 2006a). An inverse relationship exists between the sophistication, or maturity level, of a defense and the degree of cognitive distortion: More sophisticated defenses such as humor and sublimation only attenuate unpleasant states (mild cognitive distortion), while very immature ones such as schizoid fantasy and projection greatly alter the perception of reality (Bowins, 2004). Cognitive distortions provide a psychological defense against excessive negative emotions and the onset of depression and anxiety, but can be turned against the self with the illness capturing the defense, as occurs in the case of the negative distortions associated with depression (Bowins, 2004, 2006a). In a similar fashion the immune system evolved to provide defensive capacity against pathogens, but can be turned against the body in the case of autoimmune conditions. In clinical psychosis, the cognitive distortions are extreme and typically negative.

Much less attention has been paid to the role of thought form in psychosis, but alterations are a crucial aspect (Bowins, 2011). As with cognitive distortions, there is a naturally occurring range of thought form, from tight, very logical thinking to looser associations, circumstantial thought, tangentiality, blocking, derailment, and complete fragmentation (Bowins, 2004, 2006a). Psychosis involves more extreme deviations of thought form, such as very loose associations, blocking, derailment, and fragmentation. To a certain extent looser thought form is required for some of the more extreme cognitive distortions, such as with jumping to conclusions and bizarre attributions, given that tight logical connections might counter the thought stream (Bowins, 2012b). This occurrence implies that the continuums for thought content and thought form are linked. There is also an extensive range of sensory perceptual experiences, from those such as illusions, vivid daydreams, imaginary companions, perceiving concrete forms in abstract entities such as clouds, hallucination like perceptions entering into sleep and while waking up, to full blown hallucinations (Choong et al, 2007; Jardi et al, 2014; Johns & Van Os, 2001; Langer et al, 2011; Olson et al, 1985; Stip & Letourneau, 2009). Hence, we all have the capacity for cognitive distortions, thought form variants, and sensory perceptual experiences extending from mild to extreme, ultimately derived from the evolution of human intelligence (Bowers, 1973; Bowins, 2004, 2006a).

The Role of Cognitive Regulation

Given that there is a naturally occurring extensive range of thought content or cognitive distortions, thought form, and sensory perceptual experiences, the question arises as to why the more extreme psychotic variations are quite uncommon outside of psychotic illnesses. If we have such an extensive range of these cognitive events, why do we not routinely experience delusion level cognitive distortions, extremely loose and fragmented thought form, and hallucinations as a regular occurrence? In one sense we do in the form of dream content that psychoanalysts have long identified as being a form of psychosis, or psychotic equivalents (Balastreire, 2007; Freud, 1900; Frosch, 1976; Robbins, 2008). According to Freud (1907, cited in Frosch, 1976) dreams are the physiological delusions of normal people. Dreams routinely involve bizarre content equivalent to delusions. The form of thought is very loose and often fragmented. During dreams we see and hear things that are not present, but just creations of the mind.

A key distinction between dreaming and being awake is that we do not have to be reality congruent during dreams (Bowins, 2011, 2012b). In the conscious and awake state we must be reality congruent to function in an adaptive manner, reality incongruent behavior leading to maladaptive actions detracting from evolutionary fitness (Bowins, 2011, 2012b). During dreaming we are asleep, and although conscious, there is no impact on adaptive functioning and evolutionary fitness. Likewise, if psychotic level cognitions remain in unconsciousness, being blocked from consciousness when awake, reality congruent functioning is not adversely impacted (Bowins, 2012b). The presence of psychotic equivalents in dreams, and how they vanish upon awakening, implies that there is a regulatory function ensuring that psychotic level cognitions are blocked from the conscious and awake state (Bowins, 2011, 2012b).

Regulation over cognitive processes is an integral aspect of adaptive and healthy psychological functioning, as we learned in the preceding chapters. If it is the case that we have a natural capacity for psychotic level cognitive distortions, thought form variants, and sensory perceptual experiences, and these extreme expressions are maladaptive due to being reality incongruent, it follows that there must be some regulation over psychotic level cognitions, at least when expressed in the conscious and awake state (Bowins, 2011, 2012b).

When asleep the regulatory control processes can be relaxed, and typically are, resulting in the expression of psychotic equivalents in dreams (Bowins, 2011, 2012b). To provide an example of the importance of regulation over psychotic level states, image a person believing that his boss and coworkers are conspiring against him, and hearing voices discussing plans to kill him. While this will only be a nightmare during sleep, if present during the conscious and awake state the person will not be able to function, perhaps shouting at the voices, hiding, or attacking. Suspicious and distrustful ideas are quite common in the population, but rarely progress to full blown persecutory delusions, at least in the conscious and awake state (Bebbington et al, 2013).

During schizophrenia and other psychotic illnesses, extreme cognitive distortions, very loose and even fragmented thought form, and bizarre sensory perceptual experiences routinely extend into the conscious and awake state, impairing adaptive functioning. It is quite feasible that regulatory control processes blocking psychotic level cognitions from the conscious and awake state are impaired or damaged in illnesses such as schizophrenia and psychotic mania (Bowins, 2011, 2012b). This approach to understanding psychotic illnesses such as schizophrenia represents a novel approach. It also aligns with the poor regulation over sexual and aggressive urges and behavior frequently observed in those with schizophrenia who are actively psychotic.

The frontal cortices, and in particular the prefrontal cortex (PFC), appear to be a key site for the cognitive regulatory control processes over psychosis, as the PFC plays an important role in cognitive control generally (Brass et al, 2005; Dumontheil et al, 2010; Morsella et al, 2010; Savine & Braver, 2010), and inhibitory control over inappropriate or maladaptive emotional and cognitive behaviors (Dietrich, 2003; Lhermitte et al, 1986). There is research evidence supporting the notion of impaired cognitive regulatory control over psychotic level cognitions, and for the PFC being a key site for these regulatory processes (Carhart-Harris et al, 2012; Chrysikou & Thompson-Schill, 2011; Solms & Turnbill, 2002). During dreaming when psychotic equivalents are expressed there is less PFC activity (Solms & Turnbill, 2002), and the bizarreness of a dream is directly related to the degree of hypofunction of the prefrontal cortex (Hobson et al, 2000). Creativity has often been linked to psychotic thought capacity, and this linkage appears related to cognitive regulation, or reductions thereof, over cognitive distortions: Research has revealed that during creative idea generation the PFC is less active, but more active when the products of creative thought are implemented (Chrysikou & Thompson-Schill, 2011). For many years psychedelic drugs were believed to induce psychosis by increasing brain activity, but it appears that reduced cognitive control is pivotal (Carhart-Harris et al, 2012). Carhart-Harris et al (2012) discovered that psilocybin, the hallucinogenic in magic mushrooms, reduces activity in control centers of the brain such as the PFC, thalamus, and anterior and posterior cingulated cortices, and that the greater the reduction in activity within these control regions, the more intense the self-reported psychedelic experiences. Conceivably the link between marijuana use and psychosis might work in the same way.

In the course of schizophrenia, the PFC undergoes extensive changes that could damage or impair the functioning of cognitive regulatory control processes residing there (Arnsten, 2009, 2011; Fuster, 2001; Molina et al, 2005; Morice & Delahunty, 1996; Ragland et al, 2009; Weinberger et al, 1986; Woo & Crowell, 2005). This impaired regulation appears to involve dopamine. Sustained elevations of dopamine in the PFC and other brain structures are a reliable finding in schizophrenia, and antipsychotics work primarily by dopamine blockage, thereby reducing levels in the impacted structures (Arnsten, 2009, 2011; Diamond, 2011). Research by Arnsten (2009, 2011) reveals that sustained elevations of dopamine in the PFC disrupt the normal regulatory and coordination functions. The dopamine system of the PFC is actually quite vulnerable to dysfunction or alteration (Diamond, 2011), helping to explain impairments to regulation over psychotic level cognitions. Work by Flegr (2007) has found that the main impact of *Toxoplasma gondii* (*T. gondii*), long implicated in the development of schizophrenia, is elevated levels of dopamine. In all animals except cats that are required for the life cycle of *T. gondii*, the organism seems to disrupt normal behavioral control, with the infected individual acting in accordance with the needs of the organism, such as mice approaching cat urine (Flegr, 2007).

The cognitive distortions, thought form variants, and sensory perceptual experiences underlying psychosis involve elevated dopamine. This neurotransmitter is linked to greater cognitive flexibility, including abstraction and neural plasticity (Previc, 1999; Volkow et al, 1998). Previc (1999) asserts that there are four lines of evidence supporting the role of dopamine in cognitive flexibility. The first is that dopaminergic mechanisms in the prefrontal cortex exert the inhibitory action on subcortical centers required for the cessation of current behavior. The second is that lesions to dopaminergic systems in rats prevent switching from one behavior to another. Thirdly, dopaminergic levels in clinical and aging populations are highly correlated with cognitive-shifting ability, and the administration of dopaminergic agonists results in improved cognitive flexibility, while removal of them or administration of dopaminergic antagonists reduces cognitive-shifting ability. The final line of evidence consists of disturbances in cognitive shifting being one of the principal intellectual deficits in dopaminergic disorders, such as Parkinsonism (Previc, 1999). Dopamine is involved in other cognitive processes that seem related to cognitive flexibility, including working memory, abstract representation, temporal analysis/sequencing, and generativity (Previc, 1999). Elevated levels of dopamine likely reduce regulatory control over cognitive distortions, thought form variants, and sensory perceptual experiences, facilitating extensive cognitive flexibility, with very high dopamine levels allowing psychotic level versions to routinely intrude into the conscious and awake state, producing psychosis. Although speculative, it is also possible that impaired PFC GABAergic activity might also be involved in compromised regulation, given that it is the brain's primary inhibitory neurotransmitter and counters excessive dopamine levels (Wobrock et al, 2008).

Regulation over psychotic level cognitive distortions, thought form, and sensory perceptual experiences does appear to be a real occurrence, aligning with the larger role of cognitive regulation over emotional and behavioral processes. Impairment or damage to these cognitive regulatory processes produces the psychotic manifestations of schizophrenia and other illnesses. It is likely that a key reason for psychosis in mania, is that the disease state's impact on regulation over the conversion of mostly adaptive hypomania to largely maladaptive mania, also quite likely damages or impairs the cognitive regulatory control processes normally blocking psychotic level cognitions from the conscious and awake state. These regulatory control processes can also be impaired in other mental illness, such as severe depression producing psychotic depression; when psychosis occurs in the context of depression there are severe depressive symptoms (Coryell, 1997).

There is flexibility in the regulation of extreme cognitive distortions, thought form variants, and sensory perceptual experiences, as is evident with the relaxation of them during sleep and dreaming, and also when creativity is expressed (Chrysikou & Thompson-Schill, 2011; Solms & Turnbill, 2002). Likewise, the cognitive regulatory control process over psychotic level cognitions can be relaxed for defensive purposes. One example of psychosis serving a defensive function consists of hallucinations of a deceased person during the grieving period. Olson et al (1995) evaluated 293 widowed people, and found that 14% experienced a visual hallucination of their deceased spouse, 13% an auditory hallucination, and 47% the general hallucinatory event of perceiving the presence of the person. The sample consisted of healthy people, so these hallucinations could not be explained by mental illness, and if due to stress we would logically expect psychosis to occur in a much more random fashion, with delusions and hallucinations of various types. Instead, what occurs is very specific hallucinations replacing the lost sensory and related emotional stimuli, thereby fitting very well with a defensive perspective.

Extremely stressful events such as being kidnapped and told one is to be executed can trigger defensive psychosis, such as the delusional belief that God will save one and strike down one's kidnappers (Bowins, 2011, 2012b). In these instances the cognitive regulatory controls blocking psychotic level cognitions are relaxed, and defensive psychotic experiences intrude into the conscious and awake state (Bowins, 2011, 2012b). This is perhaps one reason why psychosis in the otherwise healthy population often follows trauma. In some instances, fatigue and physiological impairments associated with severe stress, such as occurs with traumatic events, can weaken the cognitive regulatory control processes over psychotic level cognitions, producing psychosis independent of or in conjunction with psychological defensive needs. Psychological defense can also be associated with psychosis, on the basis of how the content of at least delusions can be influenced by self-esteem and other psychological processes (Bowins & Shugar, 1998). For example, paranoid individuals commonly elaborate their delusional system such that their own worth is enhanced and that of others diminished.

The cognitive regulatory control process occurs on a continuum, with tighter control in some people and looser in others, the former providing more resilience to psychotic experiences, and the latter more proneness to them, but also to creative insights. The cultural context also influences how tight the regulation over psychotic level cognitions and perceptual experiences is: In a very reality focused environment, such as our modern day industrial society, regulation required to fit in will be much tighter than in a more mystical society believing in the presence of nature spirits and the like. In the latter the cognitive regulatory controls can be relaxed to facilitate more extensive cognitive distortions and sensory perceptual experiences. It is likely that an increase in dopamine levels (and possibly a decrease in GABA levels) provide for these routine psychotic-like experiences in the conscious and awake state.

Cognitive Regulatory Control Therapy Techniques

Assuming that psychosis does result from impaired regulation over psychotic level cognitions, various psychotherapeutic techniques might improve this regulatory control or compensate for deficiencies (Bowins, 2013). Cognitive behavioral therapy (CBT) has been applied to psychosis, almost exclusively delusions. A guiding principle is the notion of normalization, based on the assumption that psychotic level thoughts are on the extreme end of a normal continuum, and therapy can help bring them back to a more moderate level (Kingdon & Turkington, 1994; Landa et al, 2006). The cognitive regulatory control model of psychosis presented aligns with this, in that psychotic level thoughts and sensory perceptual experiences represent an extreme of what is normal for the person (Bowins, 2012b). This occurrence is one reason why psychosis is ego syntonic: It represents an extension of the person (Bowins, 2012b).

Another principle of CBT therapy for psychosis is that delusions are not fixed, but demonstrate a continuum of adherence, allowing for psychotherapeutic intervention (Beck et al, 2009; Kuller & Bjorgvinsson, 2010; Landa et al, 2006). Techniques applied to weaken delusional ideation and normalize beliefs consist of requesting evidence, experimentation, and generating alternative perspectives (Beck et al, 2009; Kuller & Bjorgvinsson, 2010; Landa et al, 2006). The delusion is never directly challenged, but the person is instead requested to provide evidence. For example, if the person believes that all coworkers are plotting her demise, evidence is required, such as emails or written notes demonstrating intent to harm. Typically the person cannot provide any evidence. Experimentation regarding delusional ideas is also helpful. For example, if the person assumes that she is being followed by coworkers, have the person conduct an experiment to test this idea by walking a route that no one from work would take, stopping, and observing. Is there anyone from work following? If not, then the hypothesis has not been supported by research. The next step is to generate alternative hypotheses. For example, the work setting simply monitors the computer time of all employees to ensure they are working. The more alternatives the person can generate and see as potentially viable, the less convincing the delusional belief seems, and these alternatives normalize the perspective. For persecutory beliefs group CBT is most effective, because a person can see first hand how others adhere to their clearly incorrect beliefs, and the social support helps them generate alternative options (Landa et al, 2006). These techniques typically work better in conjunction with antipsychotic medication, but can work without it if the patient is motivated and has some insight.

A mechanism proposed for auditory hallucinations, consistent with psychosis being an extension of the person and arising from impaired cognitive regulatory control, is that most auditory hallucinations, at least voices, actually involve the person's inner speech being heard as coming from an external source (Ford & Mathalon, 2004). According to this model, regulatory processes must deactivate the auditory cortex to prevent inner speech from being perceived as arising from an external source, and when this regulation fails inner speech is perceived as being from someone else (Ford & Mathalon, 2004). Listening to the content of verbal auditory hallucinations makes it clear that the voices are often expressing the person's self-perspective, such as "You're worthless, you don't deserve to live." Psychotic illness impacts very negatively on a person's self-image over time, and inner speech can reflect this negativity. An advanced therapy technique for psychosis, best reserved for patients with insight, and even then preferably when on antipsychotic medication, is to point out how the content of auditory verbal hallucinations might actually be expressing their own thoughts and inner speech. Frequently, both the patient and therapist gain a great deal of insight into the person's self-image and self-esteem from this technique.

CBT techniques can also help a person with psychosis improve regulation over sexual and aggressive urges if this is a concern, such as by learning more adaptive ways to express these feelings. While CBT therapy for psychosis might not have been formulated to improve cognitive regulatory control or compensate for deficiencies, the techniques do seem to achieve this objective. The fact that cognitive regulatory control over psychotic level cognitions can be improved by psychotherapy aligns with how this regulation has flexibility, such as being relaxed during sleep and for certain defensive needs. Given that sustained dopamine levels in the PFC and other controlling regions of the brain impair regulation and coordination of functions, antipsychotics by blocking dopamine also likely help restore effective regulation of psychotic level cognitive distortions, thought form variants, and sensory perceptual experiences. A question that remains unanswered, though, is what impairs or damages these cognitive regulatory control processes in the first place to produce psychosis? The answer is to be found in negative symptoms.

References

Allen, P., Freeman, D., Johns, L., & McGuire, P. (2006). Misattribution of self-generated speech in relation to hallucinatory proneness and delusional ideation in healthy volunteers. *Schizophrenia Research, 84*(2-3), 281-288.

Arnsten, A. (2009). Stress signaling pathways that impair prefrontal cortex structure and function. *Nature Reviews Neuroscience, 10*, 410-422.

Arnsten, A. (2011). Prefrontal cortical network connections: Key sites of vulnerability in stress and schizophrenia. *International Journal of Developmental Neuroscience, 29*(3), 215-223.

Balestriere, L. (2007). The work of the psychoanalyst in the field of psychosis. *International Journal of Psychoanalysis, 88*, 407-421.

Balzan, R., Delfabbro, P., Galletly, C., & Woodward, T. (2012). Reasoning heuristics across the psychosis continuum: The contribution of hypersalient evidence-hypothesis matches. *Cognitive Neuropsychiatry, 17*(5), 431-450.

Balzan, R., Delfabbro, P., Galletly, C., & Woodward, T. (2013). Illusory correlations and control across the psychosis continuum: The contribution of hypersalient evidence-hypothesis matches. *Journal of Nervous & Mental Disease, 201*(4), 319-327.

Barkus, E., Stirling, J., Hopkins, R., & Lewis, S. (2006). The presence of neurological soft signs along the psychosis proneness continuum. *Schizophrenic Bulletin, 32*(3), 573-577.

Beavan, V., Read, J., & Cartwright, C. (2011). The prevalence of voice-hearers in the general population: A literature review. *Journal of Mental Health, 20*(3), 281-292.

Bebbington, P.E., McBride, O., Steel, C., Kuipers, E., Radovanovic, M., Brugha, T. et al (2013). The structure of paranoia in the general population. *British Journal of Psychiatry, 202*, 419-427.

Beck, A. (1991). Cognitive therapy: A 30-year retrospective. *American Psychologist, 46*(4), 368-375.

Beck, A., Rector, N., Stolar, N., & Grant, P. (2009). *Schizophrenia: Cognitive Theory, Research, and Therapy*. New York, NY: Guilford

Bell, V., Halligan, P.W., & Ellis, H.D. (2006). Explaining delusions: A cognitive perspective. *Trends in Cognitive Science, 10*(5), 219-226.

Bentall, R.P. (1990). The illusion of reality: A review and integration of psychological research on hallucinations. *Psychological Bulletin, 107*(1), 82-95.

Bentall, R.P., Kinderman, P., & Kaney, S. (1994). The self, attributional processes and abnormal beliefs: Towards a model of persecutory delusions. *Behavior Research & Therapy, 32*, 331-341.

Bernstein, E.M. & Putman, F.W. (1986). Development, reliability, and validity of a dissociation scale. *Journal of Nervous & Mental Disorders, 174*, 727-735.

Bowers, M. (1973). *Retreat from Sanity*. New York, NY: Behavioral Publications.

Bowins, B.E. (2004). Psychological defense mechanisms: A new perspective. *American Journal of Psychoanalysis, 64*, 1-26.

Bowins, B.E. (2006a). How psychiatric treatments can enhance psychological defense mechanisms. *American Journal of Psychoanalysis, 66*(2), 173-194.

Bowins, B.E (2011). A cognitive regulatory control model of schizophrenia. *Brain Research Bulletin, 85*, 36-41.

Bowins, B.E. (2012b). Psychosis: A synthesis of motivational and defect perspectives. *The American Journal of Psychoanalysis, 72*, 152-165.

Bowins, B.E. (2013). Cognitive regulatory control therapies. *American Journal of Psychotherapy, 67*(3), 215-236.

Bowins, B. & Shugar, G. (1998). Delusions and self-esteem. *Canadian Journal of Psychiatry, 43*, 154-158.

Brass, M., Ullsperger, M., Knoesche, T., Von Vramon, D., & Yves, P. (2005). Who comes first? The role of the prefrontal and parietal cortex in cognitive control. *Journal of Cognitive Neuroscience, 17*(9), 1367-1375.

Buckley, P. (1981). Mystical experience and schizophrenia. *Schizophrenia Bulletin, 7*(3), 516-521.

Carhart-Harris, R., Erritzoe, D., Williams, T., Stone, J., Reed, L., Colasanti, A. et al (2012). Neural correlates of the psychedelic state as determined by fMRI studies with psilocybin. *Proceedings of the National Academy of Sciences USA, 109*(6), 2138-2143.

Choong, C., Hunter, M.D., & Woodruff, P.W. (2007). Auditory hallucinations in those populations that do not suffer from schizophrenia. *Current Psychiatry Reports, 9*, 206-212.

Chrysikou, E. & Thompson-Schill, S. (2011). Dissociable brain states linked to common and creative object use. *Human Brain Mapping, 32*(4), 665-675.

Coryell, W. (1997). Do psychotic, minor, and intermittent depressive disorders exist on a continuum? *Journal of Affective Disorders, 45*(1-2), 75-83.

Coy, A.L., & Hutton, S.B. (2012). Misperceiving facial affect: Effects of laterality and individual differences in susceptibility to visual hallucinations. *Psychiatry Research, 196*(2-3), 225-229.

Dalman, K., Boks, M.P., Diederen, K.M., De Weijer, A.D., Blom, J.D., Kahn, R.S., & Sommer, I.E. (2011). The same or different? A phenomenological comparison of auditory verbal hallucinations in healthy and psychotic individuals. *Journal of Clinical Psychiatry, 72*(3), 320-325.

Diamond, A. (2011). Biological and social influences on cognitive control processes dependent on the prefrontal cortex. *Progress in Brain Research, 189*, 319-339.

Dietrich, A. (2003). Functional neuroanatomy of altered states of consciousness: The transient hypofrontality hypothesis. *Conscious & Cognition, 12*, 231-256.

Dumontheil, J., Gilbert, S., Frith, C., & Burgess, C. (2010). Recruitment of lateral rostral prefrontal cortex in spontaneous and task-related thoughts. *Quarterly Journal of Experimental Psychology, 63*(9), 1740-1756.

Escher, A., Morris, M., Buiks, A., Delespaul, P., Van Os, J., & Romme, M. (2004). Determinants of outcome in the pathways through care for children hearing voices. *International Journal of Social Welfare, 13*, 208-222.

Flegr, J. (2007). Effects of toxoplasma on human behavior. *Schizophrenia Bulletin, 33*(3), 757-760.

Ford, J.M. & Mathalon, D.H. (2004). Electrophysiological evidence of corollary discharge dysfunction in schizophrenia during talking and thinking. *Journal of Psychiatry Research, 38*, 37-46.

Freeman, D. & Garety, P.A. (2003). Connecting neurosis and psychosis: The direct influence of emotion on delusions and hallucinations. *Behavior Research & Therapy, 41*, 923-947.

Freeman, D., Pugh, K., & Garety, P. (2008). Jumping to conclusions and paranoid ideation in the general population. *Schizophrenia Research, 102*(1-3), 254-260.

Freud, S. (1900). *The Interpretation of Dreams*. S.E. IV/V. London: The Hogarth Press.

Frith, C.D. (1992). *The Cognitive Neuropsychology of Schizophrenia*. Hove, UK: Psychology Press.

Frosch, J. (1976). Psychoanalytic contributions to the relationship between dreams and psychosis: A critical survey. *International Journal of Psychoanalytic Psychotherapy, 5*, 39-63.

Fuster, J. (2001). The prefrontal cortex—an update: Time is of the essence. *Neuron, 30*, 319-333.

Gale, C.K., Wells, J.E., McGee, M.A., & Browne, M.A. (2011). A latent class analysis of psychosis-like experiences in the New Zealand mental health survey. *Acta Psychiatrica Scandinavia, 124*(3), 204-213.

Garety, P.A., Bebbington, P., Fowler, D., Freeman, D., & Kuipers, E. (2007). Implications for neurobiological research of cognitive models of psychosis: A theoretical paper. *Psychological Medicine, 37*(10), 1377-1391.

Garety, P.A. & Freeman, D. (1999). Cognitive approaches to delusions: A critical review of theories and evidence. *British Journal of Clinical Psychology, 38*, 113-154.

Hardy, A., Fowler, D., Freeman, D., Smith, B., Steel, C., & Evans, J. et al (2005). Trauma and hallucinatory experience in psychosis. *Journal of Nervous Mental Disease, 193*, 501-507.

Hobson, J., Pace-Schott, E., & Stickhold, R. (2000). Dreaming and the brain: Towards a cognitive neuroscience of conscious states. *Behavioral Brain Science, 23*, 793-866.

Houran, J., & Lange, R. (2004). Redefining delusion based on studies of subjective paranormal ideation. *Psychological Report, 94*(2), 501-513.

Jardi, R., Bartels-Velthuis, A.A., Debbane, M., Jenner, J.A., Kelleher, I., Dauvilliers, Y. et al (2014). From phenomenology to neurophysiological understanding of hallucinations in children and adolescents. *Schizophrenic Bulletin, 40*(Suppl 4), S221-232.

Johns, L.C., Cannon, M., Singleton, N., Murray, R.M., Farrell, M., Brugha, T. et al (2004). Prevalence and correlates of self-reported psychotic symptoms in the British population. *British Journal of Psychiatry, 185*, 298-305.

Johns, L.C. & Van Os, J. (2001). The continuity of psychotic experiences in the general population. *Clinical Psychology Review, 21*, 1125-1141.

Kaney, S. & Bentall, R.P. (1992). Persecutory delusions and the self-serving bias: Evidence from a contingency judgment task. *Journal of Nervous & Mental Disorders, 180*, 773-780.

Kelleher, I, Connor, D., Clarke, M.C., Devlin, N., Harley, M., & Cannon, M. (2012). Prevalence of psychotic symptoms in childhood and adolescence: A systematic review and meta-analysis of population-based studies. *Psychological Medicine, 42*, 1857-1863.

Kingdon, D. & Turkington, D. (1994). *Cognitive-Behavioural Therapy of Schizophrenia.* Hillsdale: Lawrence A. Erlbaum Associates.

Kline, E., Wilson, C., Ereshefsky, S., Nugent, K.L., Pitts, S., Reeves, G., & Schiffman, J. (2012). Schizotypy, psychotic-like experiences and distress: An interaction model. *Psychiatric Research, 200*(2-3), 647-651.

Knowles, R., McCarthy-Jones, S., & Rowse, G. (2011). Grandiose delusions: A review and theoretical integration of cognitive and affective perspectives. *Clinical Psychology Review, 31*(4), 684-696.

Krabbendam, L., Mynin-Germeys, I., Bak, M., & Van Os., J. (2005). Explaining transitions over the hypothesized spectrum. *Australia & New Zealand Journal of Psychiatry, 39*(3), 180-186.

Kuipers, E. & Bebbington, P. (2006). Cognitive behavior therapy for psychosis. *Epidemiological Psychiatry & Society, 15*(4), 267-275.

Kuipers, E., Garety, P., Fowler, D., Freeman, D., Dunn, G., & Bebbington, P. (2006). Cognitive, emotional, and social processes in psychosis: Refining cognitive behavioral therapy for persistent positive symptoms. *Schizophrenic Bulletin, 32*(Suppl 1), S24-31.

Kuller, A. & Bjorgvinsson, T. (2010). Cognitive behavioral therapy with a paranoid schizophrenic patient. *Clinical Case Studies, 9*(5), 311-327.

Landa, Y., Silverstein, S., Schwartz, F., & Savitz, A. (2006). Group cognitive behavioral therapy for delusions: Helping patients improve reality testing. *Journal of Contemporary Psychotherapy, 36*(1), 9-17.

Langdon, R. & Coltheart, C. (2000). The cognitive neuropsychology of delusions. In *Pathologies of Belief.* Oxford: Blackwell.

Langer, A.I., Cangras, A.J., & Serper, M. (2011). Analysis of the multidimensionality of hallucination-like experiences in clinical and non-clinical Spanish samples and their relationship to clinical symptoms: Implications for the model of continuity. *International Journal of Psychology, 46*(1), 46-54.

Lhermitte, F., Pillon, B., & Serdaru, M. (1986). Human autonomy and the frontal lobes. Part I: Imitation and utilization behavior: A neuropsychological study of 75 patients. *Annals of Neurology, 19*, 326-334.

Linscott, R.J. & Van Os, J. (2010). Systematic reviews of categorical versus continuum models in psychosis: Evidence for discontinuous subpopulations underlying a psychometric continuum. Implications for DSM-V, DSM-IV, and DSM-VII. *Annual Review of Clinical Psychology, 6*, 391-419.

Loch, A.A., Wang, Y.P., Rossler, W., Tofoli, L.F., Silveira, C.M., & Andrade, L.H. (2011). The psychosis continuum in the general population: Findings from the Sao Paulo epidemiologic catchment area study. *European Archives of Psychiatry & Clinical Neuroscience, 261*(7), 519-527.

Maher, B. (2005). Delusional thinking and cognitive disorder. *Integrative Physiology & Behavioral Science, 40*(3), 136-146.

Mawson, A., Cohen, K., & Berry, K. (2010). Reviewing evidence for the cognitive model of auditory hallucination: The relationship between cognitive voice appraisals and distress during psychosis. *Clinical Psychology Review, 30*(2), 248-258.

Molina, V., Sanz, J., Reig, S., Martinez, R., Sarramea, F., Luque, R. et al (2005). Hypofrontality in men with first-episode psychosis. *British Journal of Psychiatry, 186*, 203-208.

Morice, R. & Delahunty, A. (1996). Frontal/executive impairments in schizophrenia. *Schizophrenic Bulletin, 22*, 125-137.

Morsella, E., Krieger, S., & Bargh, J. (2010). Minimal neuroanatomy for a conscious brain: Homing in on the networks constituting consciousness. *Neural Networks, 23*, 14-15.

Nelson, R. & Craighead, W. (1977). Selective recall of positive and negative feedback, self-control behaviors, and depression. *Journal of Abnormal Psychology, 86*, 379-388.

Nuevo, R., Chatterji, S., Verdes, E., Naidoo, N., Arango, C., & Ayuso-Mateos, J.L. (2012). The continuum of psychotic symptoms in the general population: A cross-national study. *Schizophrenic Bulletin, 38*(3), 475-485.

Olson, P.R., Suddeth, J.A., & Peterson, P.J. (1985). Hallucinations of widowhood. *Journal of the American Geriatric Society, 33*, 543-547.

Pechey, R. & Halligan, P. (2011). The prevalence of delusion like beliefs relative to sociocultural beliefs in the general population. *Psychopathology, 44*(2), 106-115.

Peters, E., Day, S., McKenna, J., & Orbach, G. (1999). Delusional ideation in religious and psychotic populations. *British Journal of Clinical Psychology, 38*(1), 83-96.

Previc. F. (1999). Dopamine and the origins of human intelligence. *Brain and Cognition, 41*, 299-350.

Ragland, J., Laird, A., Ranganath, C., Blumenfeld, R., Gonzales, S., & Glahn, D. (2009). Prefrontal activation deficits during episodic memory in schizophrenia. *American Journal of Psychiatry, 166*, 863-874.

Robbins, M. (2008). Primary mental expression: Freud, Klein, and beyond. *Journal of the American Psychoanalytic Association, 56*(1), 177-202.

Romme, M.A. & Escher, A.D. (1989). Hearing voices. *Schizophrenic Bulletin, 15*, 209-216.

Savine, A. & Braver, T. (2010). Motivated cognitive control: Reward incentives modulate preparatory neural activity during task-switching. *Journal of Neuroscience, 30*(31), 10294-10305.

Sharifi, V., Sajjadifar, A., & Amini, H. (2008). Psychotic-like ideations among a group of young normal subjects in Iran. *International Journal of Social Psychology, 54*(5), 390-394.

Shevlin, M., Murphy, J., Dorahy, M.J., & Adamson, G. (2007). The distribution of positive psychosis-like symptoms in the population: A latent class analysis of the national comorbidity survey. *Schizophrenia Research, 89*(1-3), 101-109.

Shinn, A.K., Pfaff, D., Young, S., Lewandowski, K.E., Cohen, B.M., & Ongur, D. (2012). Auditory hallucinations in a cross-diagnostic sample of psychotic disorder patients: A descriptive, cross-sectional study. *Comprehensive Psychiatry, 53*(6), 718-726.

Sno, H.N. (1994). A continuum of misidentification symptoms. *Psychopathology, 27*(3-5), 144-147.

Solms, M. & Turnbill, O. (2002). *The Brain and the Inner World*. New York: Other Press.

Spauwen, J., Krabbendam, L., Lieb, R., Wittchen, H.U., & Van Os, J. (2004). Does urbanicity shift the population expression of psychosis? *Journal of Psychiatric Research, 38*(6), 613-618.

Stip, E. & Letourneau, G. (2009). Psychotic symptoms as a continuum between normality and pathology. *Canadian Journal of Psychiatry, 54*, 140-151.

Taylor, H.E., Stewart, S.L., Dunn, G., Parker, S., Fowler, D., & Morrison, A.P. (2013). Core schemas across the continuum of psychosis: A comparison of clinical and non-clinical groups. *Behavioural & Cognitive Psychotherapy, 7*(1-13), 718-730.

Tiger, L. (1979). *Optimism: The Biology of Hope*. New York: Simon & Schuster.

Van Os, J., Hanssen, M., Bijl, R.V., & Ravelli, A. (2000). Strauss (1969) revisited: A psychosis continuum in the general population? *Schizophrenia Research, 45*(1-2), 11-20.

Van Os, J., Linscott, R.J., Myin-Germeys, I., Delespaul, P., & Krabbendam, L. (2009). A systematic review and meta-analysis of the psychotic continuum: Evidence for a psychosis proneness-persistence-impairment model of psychotic disorder. *Psychological Medicine, 39*(2), 179-195.

Van Os, J., Verdoux, H., Maurice-Tison, S., Gay, B., Liraud, F., Salamon, R., & Bourgeois, M. (1999). Self-reported psychosis-like symptoms and the continuum of psychosis. *Social Psychiatry & Psychiatric Epidemiology, 34*(9), 459-463.

Volkow, N. (1998). Association between decline in brain dopamine activity with age and cognitive and motor impairment in healthy individuals. *American Journal of Psychiatry, 155*(3), 344-349.

Weinberger, D., Berman, K., & Zec, R. (1986). Physiological dysfunction of dorsolateral prefrontal cortex in schizophrenia I. Regional cerebral blood flow evidence. *Archives of General Psychiatry, 43*, 114-125.

Wobrock, T., Schneider, M., Kadovic, D., Schneider-Axmann, T., Ecker, U., Retz, W. et al (2008). Reduced cortical inhibition in first-episode schizophrenia. *Schizophrenia Research, 105*(1-3), 252-261.

Woo, T. & Crowell, A. (2005). Targeting synapses and myelin in the prevention of schizophrenia. *Schizophrenia Research, 73*, 193-207.

Yung, A.R., Nelson, B., Baker, K., Buckby, J.A., Baksheev, G., & Cosgrove, E.M. (2009). Psychotic-like experiences in a community sample of adolescents: Implications for the continuum model of psychosis and prediction of schizophrenia. *Australian & New Zealand Journal of Psychiatry, 43*(2), 118-128.

CHAPTER 6

Negative Symptoms

The division of symptoms associated with schizophrenia into positive and negative does appear to have merit. Positive symptoms involve distortions and typically added mental activity beyond what is normal, whereas negative symptoms entail something removed from what is normal, and usually reduced mental activity (Arango et al, 2004; Bowins, 2011; Langdon et al, 2014). In addition, differences in course of illness, symptoms, response to treatment, neurochemistry relevant to pharmacological intervention, neurobiology, neuropsychological functioning, family history, premorbid adjustment, and risk factors support such a distinction (Arango et al, 2004; Carpenter et al, 1999; Fanous et al, 2001; Fenton & McGlashan, 1994; Horan & Blanchard, 2003; Kirkpatrick et al, 2000; Kirkpatrick et al, 2001; Klemm et al, 2006; Lahti et al, 2001; Malaspina & Coleman, 2003; Pogue-Geile & Harrow, 1984; Vaiva et al, 2002). Psychosis (positive symptoms) tends to be episodic and responds very well to antipsychotic medications that work by blocking dopamine, while negative symptoms develop gradually in a long prodromal phase and are quite resilient to treatment, with extensive efforts such as cognitive remediation often producing limited gains that frequently do not generalize beyond the task (Addington & Addington, 2009; Amador et al, 1999; Arango et al, 2004; Buchanan et al, 1990; Dickinson et al, 2010; Galletly, 2009; McCullumsmith et al, 2004). Negative symptoms do not respond at all well to dopamine blockage, and if anything seem to involve alternative neurochemical receptors and transmitters, such as serotonin receptors (including 5HT-1A and 5HT-2A), glycine, and glutamate (NMDA receptor subtype) (Galletly, 2009; Goff & Coyle, 2001; Gupta & Kulhara, 2010; Heresco-Levy, 1999; Javitt, 2008; Lane et al, 2005; Uchida et al, 2011). Also of fundamental importance, cognitive impairments are much more strongly linked to negative than positive symptoms (Bilder et al, 2000; Daly et al, 2012; Helldin et al, 2006; Kimhy et al, 2005; Lucas et al, 2004; Rossi et al, 1997; Smith et al, 2009).

Another key issue is that if positive and negative symptoms are of the same type, they would be more tightly correlated in symptom presentations, with more extensive positive symptoms related to more intense negative symptoms. However, what transpires is a range of both, with so-called negative symptom (deficit) schizophrenia at one end of a continuum characterized by mainly negative symptoms and fewer positive symptoms, and positive symptom (non-deficit) schizophrenia involving predominately psychosis and fewer negative symptoms (Amador et al, 1999; Arango et al, 2004; Bowins, 2011; Galderisi et al, 2008; Kimhy et al, 2006; Kirkpatrick & Buchanan, 1990; Kirkpatrick et al, 2000; Peralta & Cuesta, 2004). Countering the possibility that positive and negative symptoms themselves occur along the same continuum, with negative and positive symptom extremes at opposite poles, this arrangement would mean that the symptom types trade off, more positive meaning less negative and vice versa, whereas a mixture of prominent negative and positive symptoms often transpires. Hence, there must be two separate continuums.

Part of the confusion over whether or not positive and negative symptoms are distinct is a failure to appreciate the range of negative symptoms and what they actually mean. In some instances researchers focus on a select symptom or type that might be linked to psychosis if taken in isolation. For example, over the last several years there has been somewhat of an emphasis on motivation as the primary negative symptom, at least by those conducting research on newer antipsychotics. This occurrence is quite likely due to the fact that, of all the negative symptoms, motivation might be one that could respond to antipsychotics, given how motivational issues arise from so many different sources including depression. An important distinction here is between primary and secondary negative symptoms, with the former arising from a disease process inherent to the illness, and secondary symptoms from other sources such as depression or side effects of certain medications (Kaiser et al, 2011). While it appears as if there is improvement in the primary negative symptom, what is often occurring is resolution of the secondary negative symptoms, such as a second-generation antipsychotic increasing motivation by resolving depression, or removal of the amotivation side effect of first-generation antipsychotics. Negative symptoms can be cherry picked to support certain agendas, with those having strong secondary causation often the focus, due to their greater likelihood of responding to interventions.

What negative symptoms actually mean and refer to, though, is much more extensive, essentially involving a lack of the cognitive abilities that make us human, or what might be referred to as human specific cognition (Bowins, 2011; Burns, 2009; Fiszdon et al, 2007). The term human specific cognition is not meant to imply characteristics entirely absent in other species or our ancestors during evolution, as traits are derived from preexisting templates due to the way natural selection conserves resources by building on what has come before (Darwin, 1858/1958). It instead refers to the compilation of cognitive abilities that distinguish us behaviorally from other species. To avoid the potential charge that negative symptoms are being cherry picked to satisfy an agenda, it is best to be expansive regarding what constitutes human specific cognition, and when absent or diminished, produce negative symptoms.

In line with a comprehensive coverage of human specific cognition, negative symptoms include deficits in basic cognition, social cognition, and motivational states (often referred to as absence symptoms). A stable and enduring subset of these negative symptoms referred to as the deficit state has been identified, including restricted affect, diminished emotional range, poverty of speech, reduced interests, diminished sense of purpose, and diminished social drive (Amador et al, 1999; Carpenter, 1988; Kirkpatrick et al, 1989; Kulhara & Chandiramani, 1990). In keeping with the notion of expanding the range to be fully inclusive, the focus will not be on this subset. Basic cognitive symptoms consist of deficits in executive functioning, with executive functions referring to the following (Ashby et al, 1999; Bilder et al, 2000; Elvevag & Goldberg, 2000; Fiszdon et al, 2007; Gross & Grossman, 2010; Keefe & Fenton, 2007; Morice & Delahunty, 1996; Reichenberg et al, 2010):

Working memory—The ability to hold information in short term memory, allowing time to process it as required for the given mental activity.

Initiation—The capacity to begin a task or activity, or independently generate ideas.

Inhibition—The ability to stop behavior including thoughts, actions, and impulses.

Cognitive Flexibility (set shifting)—Being able to flexibly shift from one thought or behavior to another, in line with the demands of the situation.

Task Completion—The ability to carry through with a task to its endpoint without distraction.

Attention—Being able to focus on a mental or physical task for long enough to complete it.

Planning—The capacity to anticipate future events and prepare accordingly.

Organization—The ability to arrange thoughts, items, and behavior in an orderly and logical fashion or sequence.

Monitoring—The ability to assess performance during and after a task to ensure completion.

Multitasking—The capacity to perform different functions during the same short time frame.

Some of the executive functions depend on others, such as cognitive flexibility or set shifting relying on the ability to inhibit prior actions and responses (Gross & Grossman, 2010). Multitasking is a higher-level executive function requiring several others such as inhibition, set shifting, attention, monitoring, organizing, and task completion (Gross & Grossman, 2010). Basic cognition can also be expanded to more extensive abilities including problem solving, the ability to generalize beyond past experience, and overall or fluid intelligence, so it is not fully synonymous with executive functions, although in most instances it refers to the latter (Fiszdon et al, 2007; Ivleva et al, 2012b). Capacities such as problem solving, the ability to generalize, and overall intelligence actually do rely on executive functions (Bilder et al, 2000; Elvevag & Goldberg, 2000; Fiszdon et al, 2007; Gross & Grossman, 2010; Ivleva et al, 2012b; Keefe & Fenton, 2007; Morice & Delahunty, 1996; Reichenberg et al, 2010). Working memory in particular appears to be crucial for a diverse range of cognitive abilities (Johnson et al, 2013).

Basic cognition is understandably reliant on intact neural functioning (Collette et al, 2005; Eisenberg & Berman, 2010; Gross & Grossman, 2010; Monchi et al, 2006; Smith & Jonides, 1997). Many of the underlying neural structures overlap but there is independence, as is evident during conditions such as frontotemporal degeneration, where difficulties with organizing material stands out (Gross & Grossman, 2010). Indeed, several disease processes involving distinct brain regions can produce impairments to certain executive functions independent of others (Godefroy et al, 1999; Gross & Grossman, 2010). Furthermore, correlations in performance across executive functions are quite low (Gross & Grossman, 2010; Miyake et al, 2000).

The topic of what brain regions are linked to specific executive functions is an extensive one, beyond the scope of what can reasonably be covered in this chapter. However, some all encompassing points will be made regarding this topic. Generally speaking, executive functions rely on both structures, and also specific and intact connections (connectivity) between different brain regions (Eisenberg & Berman, 2010; Gross & Grossman, 2010). Regarding structures the frontal lobes, and particularly the prefrontal cortex (PFC), are highly implicated (Gross & Grossman, 2010). Equally important, though, is connectivity between various cortical structures (cortical-cortical), and cortical and subcortical (cortical-subcortical) (Gross & Grossman, 2010). Functional neuroimaging studies for example have suggested that frontoparietal connections are critical to several executive functions, including working memory, set shifting (cognitive flexibility), and inhibition (Collette et al, 2005; Gross & Grossman, 2010; Smith & Jonides, 1997). Connections between cortical regions and the basal ganglia (subcortical) appear to be important for planning (Gross & Grossman, 2010; Monchi et al, 2006). Integrity of both gray and white matter is also crucial for executive functions, with white matter the platform for connectivity (Eisenberg & Berman, 2010). The linkages between gray matter and white matter (connectivity), instrumental for executive functions, can be viewed as neural networks or neural circuits, with particular patterns of structures and connections associated with each executive function (Eisenberg & Berman, 2010; Gross & Grossman, 2010). Damage or impairment to the neural networks associated with executive functions does impact negatively on executive functions, and in turn adaptive behavior (Eisenberg & Berman, 2010; Gross & Grossman, 2010; Mateer, 1999). This is a key reason why impaired neurocognition is tightly linked to negative symptoms (Bilder et al, 2000; Daly et al, 2012; Helldin et al, 2006; Kimhy et al, 2005; Lucas et al, 2004; Rossi et al, 1997).

Social cognitive symptoms, the second type of negative symptoms, include impairments in how people think about themselves, others, social situations and interactions (so-called Theory of Mind deficits), plus emotional information processing, understanding complex social-emotional scenarios such as irony and sarcasm, and social drive limitations (Bediou et al, 2007; Combs et al, 2013; De Jong et al, 2013; Fett et al, 2011; Fiszdon et al, 2007; Kirkpatrick & Buchanan, 1990; Rapp et al, 2014). Emotional information processing is crucial for social cognition, and a key component of emotional information processing is facial expression recognition, with deficits greatly impairing social cognition (Bediou et al, 2007). Connectivity between the amygdala and both the PFC and temporal cortex are necessary for facial expression recognition (Bediou et al, 2007), demonstrating how, as with basic cognition, both structures and connectivity between regions is crucial. Lesions to the neural circuits providing the capacity for social affiliation and other social behaviors result in diminished social drive, poverty of speech, and blunted affect, all involved in the deficit syndrome (Kirkpatrick & Buchanan, 1990).

Social complexity is linked to larger brain size in animals, and social isolation not only impairs social cognition but also basic cognition (Cacioppo & Cacioppo, 2012). Not surprisingly, social cognition impacts heavily on social outcomes in schizophrenia, accounting for 23% of the variance, based on the work of Fett et al (2011) who analyzed outcomes from 52 research projects. Neurocognitive deficits linked to basic cognition accounted for 15% of the variance in social outcomes (Fett et al, 2011). Social cognition links to emotional intelligence that predicts success not only socially, but occupationally, more than does general intelligence (Goleman, 1995). We are a social species and those lacking solid social cognition often fare quite poorly.

The third type of negative symptom, motivational or absence states, consist of apathy, avolition, anhedonia, alogia, motor retardation, affective flattening, poverty of speech, and absence of play and curiosity (Ballmaier et al, 2008; Bemporad, 1991; Mahurin et al, 1998). The importance of these motivational states to healthy functioning is found in how they are well represented in the deficit syndrome, with restricted affect, poverty of speech, reduced interests, and diminished sense of purpose (Amador et al, 1999; Carpenter et al, 1988; Kirkpatrick et al, 1989; Kulhara & Chandiramani, 1990). Amotivational symptoms appear to be present in the normal population as well as the clinical population, with much higher levels in those with schizophrenia (Ballmaier et al, 2008; Kaiser et al, 2011).

Human Specific Cognition to Negative Symptoms

As we have seen, basic cognition, social cognition, and motivational states comprise human specific cognition (Bowins, 2011; Burns, 2009; Fiszdon et al, 2007). Negative symptoms involve an absence or reduction in these cognitive abilities, but why does this type of impairment occur? Why is always a difficult question and there are undoubtedly a multitude of reasons general and specific, but a few general ones do stand out, such as entropy (Bowins, 2011). Entropy provides a measure of the disorder in a system, higher entropy equating with greater disorder, and low entropy lesser (Atkins, 2007; Deutsch, 1998). In the absence of any other activity in the universe, matter will progress from order to disorder due to entropy (Atkins, 2007; Deutsch, 1998). Highly ordered structures are very vulnerable to this natural shift from order to disorder, and one of the most highly ordered structures in the universe is probably human specific cognition, and equivalent cognition in other intelligent life forms (Bowins, 2011). Hence, the second law of thermodynamics (entropy) is acting in an ongoing fashion to break down the orderly structuring of human specific cognition.

Entropy is assisted in its erosion of human specific cognition by the nature of these capacities, in particular, their relatively recent evolutionary origin (Bowins, 2011). Human cognition arose approximately 200,000 years ago, and although relative to our own lifespan this seems long, it is a mere drop in the evolutionary bucket (Glantz & Pearce, 1989). Consequently, human specific cognition is less stable than processes that have been evolving over a much longer period, such as olfaction (Bowins, 2011). Entropy and the relative instability of human specific cognition interact, in that entropy is likely to have a greater impact on these less fixed and resilient highly ordered structures (Bowins, 2011). Worsening the situation is how human specific cognitive abilities mature over childhood and adolescence, leaving them highly vulnerable to the impact of entropy over a longer time period.

An additional general process that might help account for negative symptoms is a phenomenon derived from computer engineering known as the NP Complete Problem (Pavlus, 2012). Essentially, this refers to the process of getting to the endpoint, and how the finished state does not clearly detail the steps involved (Pavlus, 2012): For example, looking at a car does not tell you what steps were required to assemble it. Instead, an algorithm must suffice, but due to entropy and other issues there is an error rate of about 3% from start to endpoint, or in other words the algorithm can only be about 97% accurate (Pavlus, 2012). Applied to neural systems, this means there is likely a 3% error rate in their development (Pavlus, 2012). Now if that 3% impacts on the maturation of human specific cognition, which is highly probable in light of how prominent the development of these capacities is, and their very ordered nature leaving them more vulnerable to the entropy, then human specific cognition will suffer, producing negative symptoms. Due to random variation, some people will even end up with significantly greater than the 3% error rate to human specific cognition.

In terms of more specific adverse influences on human specific cognition, and hence the development of negative symptoms, there are countless possibilities both genetic and environmental, and also how environmental inputs can activate or deactivate genes (epigenetic). Undoubtedly, there are multiple genes involved in the development of human specific cognitive abilities, and problems with any of these genes in isolation or combination could result in negative symptoms, at least in the context of the more general influences mentioned. From an environmental perspective, numerous factors could play a role, such as obstetrical complications impacting on the early development of human specific cognitive abilities, or infections. Some of these factors could result in the unhealthy expression of genes linked to human specific cognition, and via this epigenetic process produce negative symptoms. Indeed, the multitude of genetic, environmental, and epigenetic factors might make each person unique in the constellation of inputs, which in combination with the generally influences mentioned above can result in impairments to human specific cognition and negative symptoms.

Given the diverse range of basic cognition, social cognition, and motivational states, deficits in these human specific cognitions would be expected to manifest in several different illnesses. However, negative symptoms are typically only associated with schizophrenia. In reality, several mental illnesses appear to be characterized by human specific cognitive deficits (Owen, 2012; Waltereit et al, 2014). Intellectual disability (formerly known as developmental delay and mental retardation) involves global deficits in basic cognition, and specific forms of learning impairments, such as for math or language, result from focal deficits in basic cognition related to the nature of the impairment (Owen, 2012; Waltereit et al, 2014). Autism spectrum disorders arise from global deficits in social cognition (Owen, 2012; Waltereit et al, 2014). Considering the extensive nature of the impairments to social cognition in this condition, and how critical this form of human specific cognition is to success, it is not surprising that barely 55% have any employment, including volunteer and part-time work, 6 years after leaving high school, with the rate of employment higher for those with intellectual disability (Volkmar & Wolf, 2013). Attention deficit hyperactivity disorder (ADHD) is another condition closely linked to negative symptoms, which appears to involve select deficits in basic cognition, such as attention, inhibition, set shifting, and also possibly some social cognition limitations related to emotional information processing (Oades, 1998; Owen, 2012; Purper-Ouakil & Franc, 2011).

Schizophrenia, the condition most closely associated with negative symptoms, entails deficits in basic cognition, social cognition, and motivational states, underscoring the severity of it and the extent to which it typically compromises adaptive functioning (Owen, 2012; Waltereit et al, 2014). Although bipolar disorder is not usually thought of in terms of negative symptoms, they are actually very prominent (Ancin et al, 2013; Blanchard et al, 1994; Brandt et al, 2014; Kuswanto et al, 2013; Nieto & Castellanous, 2011; Simonsen et al, 2008). The focus is on BPI consisting of depression and mania, because there is no clear association between hypomania, consistent with its 1-3 day expression, and negative symptoms independent of depression. Hypomania typically occurs in conjunction with depression probably as a defensive compensation (see the "Hypomania-Mania" chapter). Depression often entails secondary negative symptoms, such as amotivation and impairments in basic cognition, and also primary negative symptoms potentially confounding whether negative symptoms are linked to depression, hypomania, or both.

Research comparing negative symptoms in schizophrenia and bipolar disorder is important to consider. Overall the results indicate substantial negative symptoms in both conditions when BPI is focused on (Ancin et al, 2013; Blanchard et al, 1994; Brandt et al, 2014; Kuswanto et al, 2013; Nieto & Castellanous, 2011; Simonsen et al, 2008). Ancin et al (2013) compared 148 bipolar patients, 262 stable schizophrenics, and 108 healthy controls on a battery of neuropsychology tests. BPI and schizophrenia subjects showed equal and widespread deficits in executive functioning, but BPII subjects (based on the 4-day criterion) only showed select impairments on planning and inhibitory tasks. Kuswanto et al (2013) and Ivleva et al (2012a) found similar levels of impairments to basic cognition in schizophrenic and bipolar subjects, but did not examine hypomania. The hypomania result from the Ancin et al (2013) study demonstrates how limited negative features are in this condition, given that impairments were only related to two executive functions, even when the standard diagnostic criterion for BPII is applied (Ancin et al, 2013). The results of a study by Simonsen et al (2008) comparing neurocognitive profiles between BPI and BPII also found fewer impairments with BPII using the minimum 4-day criterion. Furthermore, some of the deficits with BPII are likely linked to depression (Harvey, 2011).

Examining early onset schizophrenia and pediatric bipolar disorder, Nieto and Castellanous (2011) found similar impairments in cognitive performance (verbal learning and memory, information processing speed, and executive control) in the two groups, but those in the pediatric bipolar group were milder. Comparing adults with schizophrenia, bipolar disorder, and neither condition on a working memory task, Brandt et al (2014) found functional magnetic resonance imaging (fMRI) evidence for greater deficits in the schizophrenia group than bipolar group, who showed more damage than the normal group. Executive functions generally seem to be impaired in bipolar disorder even when the individual is not experiencing a manic episode (Arts et al, 2008). Focusing on anhedonia, Blanchard et al (1994) found less capacity for pleasure in schizophrenia than bipolar disorder. Anhedonia appears to be increased even in euthymic bipolar individuals, as well as remitted depressive patients, compared to healthy controls (Di Nicola et al, 2013). Atre-Vaidya et al (1998) discovered that anhedonia was related to memory impairments in those with bipolar disorder.

Negative symptoms in a primary form are clearly associated with illnesses other than schizophrenia, and not just secondary to the illness. They are a marker of severity, as with their presence in BPI but only minimally in BPII. Even in depression, the presence of primary negative symptoms indicates a more severe illness, as expressed by psychosis (Coryell, 1997). At a proximal level, negative symptoms appear to arise from so-called dysconnectivity between various brain regions, both local and distal, because human specific cognition relies on the correct connections between different cortical regions, and also between cortical and subcortical structures (Gross & Grossman, 2010). This reliance is evident from the role of connectivity in executive functioning examined earlier in the chapter. Dysconnectivity between brain regions involving deficient or excessive connectedness is a common finding in mental illnesses involving negative symptoms (Adler et al, 2004; Anticevic et al, 2013; Argyelan et al, 2014; Baker et al, 2014; Bartfield et al, 2014; Collin et al, 2013; Guo et al, 2014; Hong et al, 2015; Knochel et al, 2014; Kumar et al, 2014; Mamah et al, 2013; Meda et al, 2012; Pettersson-Yeo et al, 2011; Sharma et al, 2013; Siebenhuhner et al, 2013; Skudlarski et al, 2013; Stekelenburg et al, 2013; Uhlhaas, 2013). The literature pertaining to just schizophrenia and bipolar disorder alone is enormous and growing rapidly each year, and hence only a selection of studies will be reviewed to provide examples of how pivotal dysconnectivity is.

There are several instances of dysconnectivity common to both schizophrenia and BPI. White matter tracts so crucial for linking brain regions demonstrate substantial dysconnectivity in both conditions (Kumar et al, 2014; Skudlarski et al, 2013). The PFC, important for human specific cognition and also regulation, shows a loss of white matter coherence (Adler et al, 2004). Frontoparietal control networks demonstrate reduced connectivity (Baker et al, 2014). Fronto/occipital connectivity to anterior default mode/PFC seems to be impaired in both conditions, but the same study also found differences such as meso/paralimbic to sensory-motor connectivity only altered in schizophrenia, and meso-paralimbic to fronto-temporal/paralimbic altered only in bipolar disorder (Meda et al, 2012). Mamah et al (2013) found decreased connectivity in both illnesses for cingulo-opercular to cerebellar neural networks, with a somewhat greater reduction in the schizophrenic group. Decreased cerebellar to salience network connectivity distinguished bipolar disorder patients, whereas decreased cingulo-opercular to salience network, cingulo-opercular to frontoparietal, and frontoparietal to cerebellar characterized schizophrenic subjects (Mamah et al, 2013). Inconsistent findings are common, such as with Baker et al (2014) mentioned above finding reduced connectivity with frontoparietal networks for both conditions, but the same pattern not found by Mamah et al (2013). Dysconnectivity frequently appears to be more intense in schizophrenia than bipolar disorder. For example, Argyelan et al (2014), comparing global connectivity in schizophrenics, bipolar disorder patients, and normal individuals, found least in the latter group, and greatest global dysconnectivity in the schizophrenic group. Likewise, reductions in functional connectivity within the hippocampal network seem to be present in both schizophrenia and bipolar disorder, but more extensively in the former (Knochel et al, 2014).

Most of the results reported involve reduced connectivity between or within regions, but increased connectivity also occurs, such as increased amygdala-medial PFC connectivity in bipolar disorder (Anticevic et al, 2013). Long-range connectivity in schizophrenia appears to be increased, a problem attributed to failure to prune unneeded connections during the neurodevelopmental phase of adolescence (Guo et al, 2014). However, Sharma et al (2013) found reduced fronto-posterior connectivity. Compared to healthy subjects, in schizophrenia gray matter connectivity is both increased (such as left temporal and bilateral subcortical) and decreased (as with left frontal and bilateral subcortical) (Collin et al, 2013). The full extent and complexity of dysconnectivity patterns in schizophrenia is beyond the scope of this chapter, but interested readers can consult reviews such as by Pettersson-Yeo et al (2011) and Uhlhaas (2013), the latter showing increased and decreased connectivity and how it impacts on overall neural synchrony. Dysconnectivity is also present in other conditions involving negative symptoms, such as ADHD, where reduced dorsal caudate functional connectivity with the superior and middle PFC, and reduced putamen connectivity with the parahippocampal cortex have been identified (Hong et al, 2015). In ADHD temporal variability of functional connections appears to be associated with executive function deficits, and intrinsic dysconnectivity is linked to hyperactivity, impulsivity, and depression (Bartfield et al, 2014). Beyond the contribution of dysconnectivity to negative symptoms, it also plays a role in regulation, as suggested by the ADHD results. To examine this role it is important to consider how negative symptoms relate to regulation.

Negative Symptoms and Regulation

As presented in the preceding chapters, regulation appears to be critical for healthy functioning, with deficient regulation resulting in for the most part adaptive hypomania progressing to mostly maladaptive mania, and also the persistent intrusion of extreme cognitive distortions, thought form alterations, and sensory perceptual experiences into the conscious and awake state (psychosis). In the case of depression and anxiety, impaired regulation of excessive limbic system activity appears to be involved, and it is plausible that negative symptoms might play a role in this impairment. Regulation itself seems to rely on adequate connectivity, as we noted in the "Anxiety" and "Depression" chapters. In schizophrenia and BPI there are numerous examples of dysconnectivity, as reviewed above in reference to negative symptoms. It is quite likely that patterns of dysconnectivity inherent in negative symptoms also impair or damage regulation pertaining to schizophrenia and BPI, particularly considering how extensive are the problems of connectivity involving cortical and subcortical structures, and both local and distal connections.

Research shows how dysconnectivity can impair regulation. A study by Yoon et al (2008) revealed that during a high cognitive control task, connectivity between the dorsolateral PFC and task relevant brain regions is impaired in those with schizophrenia, resulting in reduced performance. Pertaining to psychosis, those with a psychotic illness (schizophrenia spectrum or psychotic bipolar) experience disruptions across various brain networks, and in particular reduced functional connectivity within the frontoparietal control network (Baker et al, 2014). In first episode psychosis, top down (frontal, parietal, occipital) connectivity, and control of sensorimotor, basal ganglia, and limbic-visual systems is impaired, with a negative correlation apparent between efficiency of the sensorimotor system and severity of psychosis (lesser efficiency, more psychosis) (Zhang et al, 2014). In bipolar disorder with psychosis there is more severe dysconnectivity, particularly between the medial thalamic nucleus and prefrontal networks (Anticevic et al, 2014).

While it is apparent that dysconnectivity is associated with negative symptoms and regulation, the nature of the relationship between these events and psychosis needs clarification. One possibility is that negative symptoms themselves result in psychosis and mania. However, regarding psychosis and negative symptoms, as we learned at the start of this chapter, there are too many differences in course of illness, symptoms, response to treatment, neurochemistry relevant to pharmacological intervention, neurobiology, neuropsychological functioning, family history, premorbid adjustment, and risk factors to support this conjecture (Arango et al, 2004; Carpenter et al, 1999; Fanous et al, 2001; Fenton & McGlashan, 1994; Horan & Blanchard, 2003; Kirpatrick et al, 2000; Kirkpatrick et al, 2001; Klemm et al, 2006; Lahti et al, 2001; Malaspina & Coleman, 2003; Pogue-Geile & Harrow, 1984; Vaiva et al, 2002). In addition, if negative symptoms in and of themselves result in positive symptoms, there would be both a tighter correlation and response pattern to interventions. The extent of negative symptoms would largely predict the degree of positive symptoms, but that is not the case, with varying levels occurring in both schizophrenia and BPI, such as so-called positive (non-deficit) and negative (deficit) schizophrenia (Amador et al, 1999; Arango et al, 2004; Bowins, 2011; Galderisi et al, 2008; Kimhy et al, 2006; Kirkpatrick & Buchanan, 1990; Kirkpatrick et al, 2000; Peralta & Cuesta, 2004). Regarding executive function deficits, one study found that they did not actually predict jumping to conclusions distortions in psychosis, but did do so in the normal population (Langdon et al, 2014). If negative symptoms actually caused positive symptoms one would expect antipsychotics to work for negative symptoms, but the impact is minimal and involves neurochemical targets other than dopamine (Galletly, 2009; Goff & Coyle, 2001; Gupta & Kulhara, 2010; Heresco-Levy, 1999; Javitt, 2008; Lane et al, 2005; Uchida et al, 2011).

A couple of brief clinical case examples will help illustrate how negative and positive symptoms are not tightly related, and how intervention patterns differ. Jim is a middle-aged man who throughout his life has struggled with social relationships, both personal and at work. He described his parents as "nerdy" with few friends, who fit together well. In his childhood and teenage years he struggled to make friends, and was picked on for being "odd." During adolescence he thought it was fine to approach teenage girls and young women, slap them on the buttocks, and run away. In the present he touches female coworkers and casual contacts to give them a shoulder massage, without first asking for their permission. Despite his significant intelligence and only somewhat limited motivation, he has always worked below his capacity, largely because he was never able to navigate the social and political landscape on the job. Clearly social cognition is lacking, and if we were to directly link negative and positive symptoms, we would predict that Jim is psychotic and likely schizophrenic. However, we would be wrong, as he has never experienced psychosis, nor apparently have his parents.

Frank is a man in his late 20s who, like Jim, suffers from social cognitive deficits. Frank does not have any sense of how to approach women beyond everyday interactions. He has no close friends as he cannot decipher intentions and respond appropriately. Despite being quite intelligent, like Jim he works below his capacity, largely due to an inability to navigate the social and political landscape on the job. There are some definite cognitive and motivational limitations, but social cognition problems are most prominent. Given that he is quite psychologically minded, we have worked on his social cognition, going over appropriate responses to social scenarios during therapy sessions. He has also tested his emotion recognition online and found it to be impaired, leading him to practice recognizing facial expressions. Only very limited gains though have transpired from these interventions. Similar patterns are thus present in Frank and Jim, but Frank also has pronounced delusions of persecution and reference, that respond to antipsychotics, although the social cognitive problems fail to respond to medication treatment. These examples illustrate how, of two people with similar negative symptoms, one is psychotic and the other not, an occurrence that would not be expected if negative symptoms directly result in positive symptoms.

Instead of negative symptoms in and of themselves resulting in positive symptoms, it is more likely that the neural disease process or processes causing negative symptoms via dysconnectivity also damage or impair the cognitive regulatory control processes blocking psychotic level cognitions from entering the conscious and awake state, and the conversion of hypomania to mania (Bowins, 2008, 2011). This occurrence is in line with how the typical pattern in schizophrenia is a very long prodrome of negative symptoms, followed by the development of positive symptoms. The neural disease process/es producing negative symptoms at some point appears to damage the cognitive regulatory processes blocking extreme cognitive distortions, thought form variants, and sensory perceptual expression from the conscious and awake state (Addington & Addington, 2009; Amador et al, 1999; Arango et al, 2004; Buchanan et al, 1990; Dickinson et al, 2010; Galletly, 2009; McCullumsmith et al, 2004). Given the role of excessive dopamine in impaired cognitive regulatory control over psychotic level cognitions, covered in the "Psychosis" chapter, damage to this regulation likely transpires via the proximal mechanism of sustained dopamine elevations. This process might involve compensatory increases in dopamine in reaction to the extensive and severe decline in human specific cognition, based upon how dopamine can enhance cognitive flexibility and plasticity (see the "Psychosis" chapter).

Evidence supports the presence of major disruptions in control processes. For example, cognitive control problems pertaining to intrusive cognitions, source monitoring, and inhibitory control have been identified in auditory verbal hallucinations (Badcock & Hugdahl, 2012). Deficient regulation over emotional processes, involving aberrant modulation of neural response during the interaction between cognitive control and emotion processing, is also present in schizophrenia (Vercammen et al, 2012). Given that the cognitive regulatory control over psychotic level cognitions is likely continuously organized, being stronger in some people and weaker in others, there will be some range in vulnerability to the neural disease process/es underlying negative symptom damage. However, with sufficient impairment psychosis is highly likely. Regarding the possibility of psychosis causing negative symptoms, or the latter being some defensive response to psychosis as expressed by Rector et al (2005), the pattern of negative symptoms followed by positive symptoms in schizophrenia makes these perspectives untenable, and severe positive symptoms do not predict negative deficit symptoms (Kirkpatrick et al, 2001).

Negative symptoms help explain why schizophrenia emerges at different ages. Schizophrenia has been described as both a neurodevelopmental and neurodegenerative disease (Gupta & Kulhara, 2010). Human specific cognitive capacities are not fully present at birth, but instead mature over at least the first couple of decades, as likely do the cognitive regulatory control processes hypothesized to play a key role in psychosis, bipolar disorder, depression, and anxiety. Failure in the neurodevelopment of human specific cognition, and hence negative symptom onset, can thus develop over at least a couple of decades. Earlier failure might be expected to lead to worse outcomes, given the longer and more extensive impairment to human specific cognition. Supporting this possibility, brain damage in schizophrenia has been found to occur on a continuum from maximal with childhood onset, to moderate with adolescent onset, to least with adult onset (Biswas et al, 2006). When schizophrenia develops later in life it is likely the case that human specific cognitive capacities are slowly deteriorating (neurodegeneration), producing the gradual emergence of negative symptoms. Much more rapid declines are more consistent with a dementing illness (Palmer et al, 2010). Late onset schizophrenia appears to be characterized by fewer negative symptoms than early onset schizophrenia (Brodaty et al, 1999).

The proposed model also helps explain why mania and psychosis occur together, in that when significant negative symptoms are present in bipolar disorder, the cognitive regulatory control processes blocking both the conversion of mostly adaptive hypomania to mostly maladaptive mania, and the emergence of psychosis, can be impaired. Of course, if the hypomanic defensive response to depression is not present, then there is no issue of hypomania progressing to mania. Given that hypomania is an energetic response, with increased behavioral activation and reduced behavioral inhibition (Meyer et al, 1999; Meyer et al, 2001), it is feasible that if negative symptoms are extremely severe, such that they impede behavioral activation, then the capacity for a hypomanic response to depression might be difficult to produce (Bowins, 2013). In the case of schizophrenia the continuous distribution of positive and negative symptom profiles can be explained by the model presented: When the cognitive regulatory control processes are heavily impacted with relatively limited negative symptoms, positive symptom (non-deficit) schizophrenia occurs; when the cognitive regulatory control processes are relatively spared despite pronounced negative symptoms, negative symptom (deficit) schizophrenia transpires; approximately equal negative and positive symptoms occur when damage to the cognitive regulatory control processes are more in synch with negative symptoms (Bowins, 2011).

The model presented currently remains hypothetical, but it does explain several interesting phenomena, including:

- Why we seem to be prone to psychosis, but expressions in the conscious and awake state are quite rare.
- Defensive activation of psychosis in some instances as covered in the "Psychosis" chapter.
- Occurrence of both positive and negative symptom forms of schizophrenia.
- Why a long prodrome of negative symptoms precedes positive symptoms in schizophrenia.
- The failure to identify an ideal animal equivalent to schizophrenia—it requires human specific cognition.
- Why hypomania shifts to mania, and the role of negative symptoms in this process.
- Why psychosis often occurs when there is mania.
- How influences such as antidepressants and other psychoactive substances, not present during the vast majority of our evolution, can induce mania and psychosis in those who are prone to it—by impairing the cognitive regulatory control processes.

The theory also suggests new approaches to treating psychosis and mania as covered in the respective chapters. Regarding treatment of negative symptoms, considering the lengthy erosion of human specific cognition, truly effective treatment interventions will likely need to focus on halting or reversing early damage to preserve human specific cognition. From a perspective of psychotherapy, it is important to appreciate that anyone with deficits to human specific cognition might have difficulty working with the cognitive, social, and motivational demands of treatment. If there are impairments to executive functions, such as working memory, cognitive flexibility, and attention, the person will have challenges processing information, such as transference interpretations or even working hypotheses of mental illness issues. Consequently, information might have to be parsed out in smaller units, and kept in concrete terms with more examples provided. Language might also have to be kept very basic.

Social cognitive impairments can limit a person's ability to respond appropriately to the social interaction between therapist and client, and also transform any social learning into constructive improvements in social interactions with others. More extensive role-playing is often required, with assistance provided in identifying emotions in facial expressions (facial expression recognition). Regarding motivational states, a frequent frustration encountered by therapists is not seeing clients transform therapeutic interventions into behavioral advances away from therapy. Such frustration can be diminished through an understanding of how negative amotivational symptoms play a role in this outcome, even in those not suffering from schizophrenia or severe mood disorders. Targeting specific behavioral improvements, as opposed to more general motivation, can help a client progress with behaviors outside of psychotherapy. For instance, focus on having a person engage with coworkers at lunch, instead of trying to advance socialization in general. Identifying and working with negative symptoms entails conscious awareness, both for therapist and client, of the relevant human specific cognitions and deficits that exist.

Resolving Diagnostic Confusion

The perspective presented regarding negative symptoms and their linkage to psychosis and bipolar disorder can also help sort out the massive confusion that arises regarding the diagnosis of schizophrenia, schizoaffective and bipolar disorders, as well as other psychotic conditions. Every practicing clinician experiences difficulty in diagnosing schizophrenia and bipolar disorder in real life settings where mixtures of symptoms are the norm. Frequently, we just put down "schizoaffective disorder" hoping that this resolves the confusion, but it actually just adds to it, and represents a default category. What is schizoaffective? It might be a combination of both schizophrenia and bipolar disorder, or a mid-point on a continuum from schizophrenia to bipolar disorder (Malhi et al, 2008). There is evidence for all three lying on a continuum (Kendler et al, 1995), but also for schizophrenia and bipolar disorder being distinct, with no real room for schizoaffective, other than perhaps a combination (Winokur et al, 1996). Smith et al (2009) found similar levels of negative symptoms in schizophrenia, schizoaffective disorder, and bipolar disorder, suggesting that negative symptoms are a crucial focal point.

Bipolar disorder consists of depression, at least at some point, and the hypomanic-manic defensive response with actual mania, at least at some point. Given that there is no evidence for hypomania being maladaptive when viewed in line with a 1-3 day expression, the real concern is mania. Defective cognitive regulatory control processes, linked to negative symptoms and dysconnectivity, appear to facilitate the progression of hypomania to mania, as well as the emergence of psychosis in the context of mania. On the other hand, schizophrenia does not involve the hypomanic-manic defensive response to depression, or at least the progression to actual mania. Depression, though, can and frequently does occur in the context of schizophrenia, and hypomania not progressing to mania is feasible. Given that mania is not present, psychosis occurs in a non-manic context.

Negative symptoms, or more directly the neural disease process/es producing dysconnectivity that underlies these symptoms, play a key role in impairing or damaging the cognitive regulatory control processes related to psychosis, and also the conversion of hypomania to mania. In this framework the distinction between bipolar disorder and schizophrenia is clear, in line with the early work of Kraepelin (1919/1971), although based on a very different model. Schizoaffective disorder has no place and is non-sensible, because there can be no such thing as a continuum directly from bipolar disorder to schizophrenia, given that the former involves mania based on the hypomanic-manic defensive response to depression, and impaired regulation over this defense. There are however continuums, in terms of negative symptoms, positive symptoms, hypomania-mania, and cognitive regulatory control processes (although the latter are hypothesized to be distinct for the conversion of hypomania to mania and psychosis), explaining the overlap between these conditions. If a scenario arises where a person has psychosis in the context of mania, but at other times psychosis when there is absolutely no mania but significant negative symptoms, then both conditions can be diagnosed, but not schizoaffective disorder. By cleaning up diagnoses and dispensing with the confusing default diagnosis of schizoaffective disorder, both research and clinical efforts can be improved, and the discipline cleared of charges such as schizophrenia being a failed category (Bentall, 2003).

Concluding Note

Negative symptoms are often the sleeper, being far less visible than their dramatic counterpart, positive symptoms. However, despite their lower profile they are instrumental in many conditions, such as intellectual disability, specific learning disorders, autism, and ADHD. They play a prominent role in the symptoms associated with both schizophrenia and bipolar disorder. The neural disease process/es, and resulting dysconnectivity, that produces negative symptoms appears to damage or impair, first, cognitive regulatory processes blocking the expression of extreme cognitive distortions, thought form variants, and sensory perceptual expressions in the conscious and awake state, resulting in psychosis, and second, the conversion of mostly adaptive hypomania to mostly maladaptive mania, with both forms of damage common to bipolar disorder.

References

Addington, J. & Addington, D. (2009). Three-year outcome of treatment in an early psychosis program. *Canadian Journal of Psychiatry, 54*, 626-630.

Adler, C.M., Holland, S.K., Schmithorst, V., Wilke, M., Weiss, K.L., Pan, H., & Strakowski, S.M. (2004). Abnormal frontal white matter tracts in bipolar disorder: A diffusion tensor imaging study. *Bipolar Disorder, 6*(3), 197-203.

Amador, X.F., Kirkpatrick, B., Buchanon, R.W., Carpenter, W.T., Marcinko, L., & Yale, S.A. (1999). Stability of the diagnosis of deficit syndrome in schizophrenia. *American Journal of Psychiatry, 156*(4), 637-639.

Ancin, I., Cabranes, J.A., Santos, J.L., Sanchez-Moria, E., & Barabash, A. (2013). Executive deficits: A continuum schizophrenia-bipolar disorder or specific to schizophrenia? *Psychiatry Research, 47*(11), 1564-1571.

Anticevic, A., Brumbaugh, M.S., Winkler, A.M., Lombardo, L.E., Barett, J., & Corlett, P.R. (2013). Global prefrontal and fronto-amygdala dysconnectivity in bipolar I disorder with psychosis history. *Biological Psychiatry, 73*(6), 565-573.

Anticevic, A., Yang, G., Savic, A., Murray, J.D., Cole, M.W., Repovs, G. et al (2014). Mediodorsal and visual thalamic connectivity differ in schizophrenia and bipolar disorder with and without psychosis. *Schizophrenia Bulletin, 40*(6), 1227-1243.

Arango, C., Buchanan, R., Kirkpatrick, B., & Carpenter, W. (2004). The deficit syndrome in schizophrenia: Implications for the treatment of negative symptoms. *European Psychiatry, 19*, 21-26.

Argyelan, M., Ikuta, T., DeRosse, P., Braga, R.J., Burdick, K.E., John, M. et al (2014). Resting-state fMRI connectivity impairment in schizophrenia and bipolar disorder. *Schizophrenia Bulletin, 40*(1), 100-110.

Arts, B., Jabben, N., Krabbendam, L., & Van Os, J. (2008). Meta-analyses of cognitive functioning in euthymic bipolar disorder patients and their first-degree relatives. *Psychological Medicine, 38*(6), 771-785.

Ashby, F.G., Isen, A.M., & Turken, U. (1999). A neuropsychological theory of positive affect and its influence on cognition. *Psychological Review, 106*(3), 529-550.

Atkins, P. (2007). *Four Laws That Drive the Universe*. Oxford, UK: Oxford University Press.

Atre-Vaidya, N., Taylor, M.A., Seidenberg, M., Reed, R., Perrine, A., & Glick-Oberwise, F. (1998). Cognitive deficits, psychopathology, and psychosocial functioning in bipolar mood disorder. *Neuropsychiatry & Neuropsychology Behavioral Neurology, 11*(3), 120-126.

Badcock, J.C. & Hugdahl, K. (2012). Cognitive mechanisms of auditory verbal hallucinations in psychotic and non-psychotic groups. *Neuroscience & Biobehavioral Reviews, 36*, 431-438.

Baker, J.T., Holmes, A.J., Masters, G.A., Yeo, B.T., Krienen, F., Buckner, R.L., & Ongur, D. (2014). Disruption of cortical association networks in schizophrenia and psychotic bipolar disorder. *JAMA Psychiatry, 71*(2), 109-118.

Ballmaier, M., Schlagenhauf, F., Toga, A.W., Gallinat, J., Koslowski, M., Zoli, M. et al (2008). Regional patterns and clinical correlates of basal ganglia morphology in non-medicated schizophrenia. *Schizophrenia Research, 106*(2-3), 140-147.

Bartfield, P., Petroni, A., Baez, S., Urquina, H., Sigman, M., Cetkovich, M. et al (2014). Functional connectivity and temporal variability of brain connections in adults with attention deficit/hyperactivity disorder and bipolar disorder. *Neuropsychobiology, 69*(2), 65-75.

Bediou, B., Asri, F., Brunelin, J., Krolak-Salmon, P., D'Amato, T., Saoud, M., & Tazi, I. (2007). Emotion recognition and genetic vulnerability to schizophrenia. *British Journal of Psychiatry, 191*, 126-130.

Bemporad, J.R. (1991). Dementia praecox as a failure of neoteny. *Theoretical Medicine, 12*, 45-51.

Bentall, R.P. (2003). *Madness Explained: Psychosis and Human Nature*. London: Penguin.

Bilder, R.M., Goldman, R.S., Robinson, D., Reiter, G., Bell, L., Bates, J.A. et al (2000). Neuropsychology of first-episode schizophrenia: Initial characterization and clinical correlates. *American Journal of Psychiatry, 157*, 549-559.

Biswas, P., Malhorta, S., Malhotra, A., & Gupta, N. (2006). Comparative study of neuropsychological correlates in schizophrenia with onset in childhood, adolescence and adulthood. *European Child & Adolescent Psychiatry, 15*(6), 360-366.

Blanchard, J.J., Bellack, A.S., & Mueser, K.T. (1994). Affective and social-behavioral correlates of physical and social anhedonia in schizophrenia. *Journal of Abnormal Psychology, 103*(4), 719-728.

Bowins, B. (2008). Hypomania: A depressive inhibition override defense mechanism. *Journal of Affective Disorders, 109*, 221-232.

Bowins, B.E (2011). A cognitive regulatory control model of schizophrenia. *Brain Research Bulletin, 85*, 36-41.

Bowins, B.E. (2013). Cognitive regulatory control therapies. *American Journal of Psychotherapy, 67*(3), 215-236.

Brandt, C.L., Eichele, T., Melle, I., Sundet, K., Server, A., Agartz, I. et al (2014). Working memory networks and activation patterns in schizophrenia and bipolar disorder: Comparison with healthy controls. *British Journal of Psychiatry, 204*, 290-298.

Brodaty, H., Sachdev, P., Rose, N., Rylands, K., & Prenter, L. (1999). Schizophrenia with onset after age 50 years. I: Phenomenology and risk factors. *British Journal of Psychiatry, 175*, 410-415.

Buchanan, R.W., Kirkpatrick, B., Heinrichs, R.W., & Carpenter, W.T. (1990). Clinical correlates of the deficit syndrome in schizophrenia. *American Journal of Psychiatry, 147*, 290-294.

Burns, J.K. (2009). Reconciling "the new epidemiology" with an evolutionary genetic basis for schizophrenia. *Medical Hypothesis, 72*, 353-358.

Cacioppo, S. & Cacioppo, J.T. (2012). Decoding the invisible forces of social connections. *Frontiers in Integrative Neuroscience, 25*(6), 51-59.

Carpenter, W., Arango, C., Buchanan, R., & Kirkpatrick, B. (1999). Deficit psychopathology and a paradigm shift in schizophrenic research. *Biological Psychiatry, 46*, 352-360.

Carpenter, W.T., Heinrichs, D.W., & Wagman, A.M. (1988). Deficit and nondeficit forms of schizophrenia: The concept. *American Journal of Psychiatry, 145*, 578-583.

Collette, F., Van der Linden, M., & Laureys, S. (2005). Exploring the unity and diversity of the neural substrates of executive functioning. *Human Brain Mapping, 25*(4), 409-423.

Collin, D., De Reus, M.A., Cahn, W., Hulshoff-Pol, H.E., Kahn, R.S., & Van Den Heuvel, M.P. (2013). Disturbed grey matter coupling in schizophrenia. *European Neuropsychopharmacology, 23*(1), 46-54.

Combs, D.R., Finn, J.A., Wohlfahrt, W., Penn, D.L., & Basso, M.R. (2013). Social cognition and social functioning in nonclinical paranoia. *Cognitive Neuropsychiatry, 18*(6), 531-548.

Coryell, W. (1997). Do psychotic, minor, and intermittent depressive disorders exist on a continuum. *Journal of Affective Disorders, 45*(1-2), 75-83.

Daly, M.P., Afroz, S., & Walder, D.J. (2012). Schizotypal traits and neurocognitive functioning among nonclinical young adults. *Psychiatry Research, 30*, 635-640.

Darwin, C. (1858/1859). *On the Origin of Species*. New York: Signet Classic.

De Jong, J.J., De Gelder, B., & Hodiamont, P.P. (2013). Sensory processing, neurocognition, and social cognition in schizophrenia: Towards a cohesive cognitive model. *Schizophrenia Research, 146*(1-3), 209-216.

Deutsch, D. (1998). *The Fabric of Reality*. London, UK: Penguin Books.

Dickinson, D., Tenhula, W., Morris, S., Brown, C., Peer, J., Spencer, K. et al (2010). A randomized controlled trial of computer-assisted cognitive remediation for schizophrenia. *American Journal of Psychiatry, 167*, 170-180.

Di Nicola, M., De Risio, L., Battaglia, C., Camardese, G., Tedeschi, D, Mazza, M. et al (2013). Reduced hedonic capacity in euthymic bipolar subjects: A trait-like feature? *Journal of Affective Disorders, 147*(1-3), 446-450.

Eisenberg, D.P. & Berman, K.F. (2010). Executive function, neural circuitry, and genetic mechanisms in schizophrenia. *Neuropsychopharmacology, 35*(1), 258-277.

Elvevag, B. & Goldberg, T.E. (2000). Cognitive impairment in schizophrenia is the core of the disorder. *Critical Review of Neurobiology, 14*, 1-21.

Fanous, A., Gardner, C., Walsh, D., & Kendler, K. (2001). Relationship between positive and negative symptoms of schizophrenia and schizotypal symptoms in nonpsychotic relatives. *Archives of General Psychiatry, 58*(7), 669-673.

Fenton, W.S. & McGlashan, T.H. (1994). Antecedents, symptom progression, and long-term outcome in the deficit syndrome in schizophrenia. *American Journal of Psychiatry, 151*, 351-356.

Fett, A.K., Viechtbauer, W., Dominguez, M.D., Penn, D.L., Van Os, J., & Krabbendam, L. (2011). The relationship between neurocognition and social cognition with functional outcomes in schizophrenia: A meta-analysis. *Neuroscience & Biobehavioral Review, 35*(3), 573-588.

Fiszdon, J.M., Richardson, R., Greig, T., & Bell, M.D. (2007). A comparison of basic and social cognition between schizophrenia and schizoaffective disorder. *Schizophrenia Research, 91*, 117-121.

Galderisi, S., Quarantelli, M., Volpe, U., Mucci, A., Cassano, G., Invernizzi, G. et al (2008). Patterns of structural MRI abnormalities in deficit and nondeficit schizophrenia. *Schizophrenia Bulletin, 34*(2), 393-401.

Galletly, C. (2009). Recent advances in treating cognitive impairment in schizophrenia. *Psychopharmacology, 202*, 1302-1309.

Glantz, K. & Pearce, J. (1989). *Exiles from Eden: Psychotherapy from an Evolutionary Perspective*. New York: W.W. Norton & Company.

Godefroy, O., Cabaret, M., & Petit-Chenal, V. (1999). Control function of the frontal lobes. Modularity of the central-supervisory system? *Cortex, 121*(1), 65-94.

Goff, D.C. & Coyle, J.T. (2001). The emerging role of glutamate in the pathophysiology and treatment of schizophrenia. *American Journal of Psychiatry, 158*(9), 1367-1377.

Goleman, D. (1995). *Emotional Intelligence*. New York: Bantam Books.

Gross, R.G. & Grossman, M. (2010). Executive resources. *Continuum, 16*(4), 140-152.

Guo, S., Palaniyappan, L., Yang, B., Liu, Z., Xue, Z., & Feng, J. (2014). Anatomical distance affects functional connectivity in patients with schizophrenia and their siblings. *Schizophrenia Bulletin, 40*(2), 449-459.

Gupta, S. & Kulhara, P. (2010). What is schizophrenia: A neurodevelopmental or neurodegenerative disorder or combination of both? A critical analysis. *Indian Journal of Psychiatry, 52*(1), 21-27.

Harvey, P.D. (2011). Mood symptoms, cognition, and everyday functioning in major depression, bipolar disorder, and schizophrenia. *Innovations in Clinical Neuroscience, 8*(10), 14-18.

Helldin, L., Kane, J.M., Karilampi, U., Norlander, T., & Archer, T. (2006). Remission and cognitive ability in a cohort of patients with schizophrenia. *Journal of Psychiatry Research, 40*, 738-745.

Heresco-Levy, U., Javitt, D.C., Ermilov, M., Mordel, C., Silipo, G., & Lichenstein, M. (1999). Efficacy of high dose glycine in the treatment of enduring negative symptoms of schizophrenia. *Archives of General Psychiatry, 56*(1), 29-36.

Hong, S.B., Harrison, B.J., Fornito, A., Sohn, C.H., Song, I.C., & Kim, J.W. (2015). Functional dysconnectivity of corticostriatal circuitry and differential response to methylphenidate in youth with attention-deficit/hyperactivity disorder. *Journal of Psychiatry & Neuroscience, 40*(1), 46-57.

Horan, W.P. & Blanchard, J.J. (2003). Neurocognitive, social, and emotional dysfunction in deficit syndrome schizophrenia. *Schizophrenia Research, 65*, 125-137.

Ivleva, E.I., Morris, D.W., Osuji, J., Moates, A.F., Carmody, T.J., Thaker, G.K. et al (2012a). Cognitive endophenotypes of psychosis within dimension and diagnosis. *Psychiatry Research, 196*(1), 38-44.

Ivleva, E.I., Shohamy, D., Mihalakos, P., Morris, D.W., Carmody, T., & Tamminga, C.A. (2012b). Memory generalization is selectively altered in the psychosis dimension. *Schizophrenia Research, 138*(1), 74-80.

Javitt, D.C. (2008). Glycine transport inhibitors and the treatment of schizophrenia. *Biological Psychiatry, 63*, 6-8.

Johnson, M.K., McMahon, R.P., Robinson, B.M., Harvey, A.N., Hahn, B., Leonard, C.J. et al (2013). The relationship between working memory capacity and broad measures of cognitive ability in healthy adults and people with schizophrenia. *Neuropsychology, 27*(2), 220-229.

Kaiser, S., Heekeren, K., & Simon, J.J. (2011). The negative symptoms of schizophrenia: Category or continuum? *Psychopathology, 44*(6), 345-353.

Keefe, R.S. & Fenton, W.S. (2007). How should DSM-V criteria for schizophrenia include cognitive impairment? *Schizophrenia Bulletin, 33*, 912-920.

Kendler, K.S., Neale, M.C., & Walsh, D. (1995). Evaluating the spectrum concept of schizophrenia in the Roscommon family study. *American Journal of Psychiatry, 152*(5), 749-754.

Kimhy, D., Yale, S., Goetz, R., McFarr, L., & Malaspina, D. (2006). The factorial structure of the schedule for the deficit syndrome in schizophrenia. *Schizophrenia Bulletin, 32*(2), 274-278.

Kirkpatrick, B. & Buchanan, R.W. (1990). The neural basis of the deficit syndrome of schizophrenia. *The Journal of Nervous and Mental Disease, 178*, 545-555.

Kirkpatrick, B., Buchanan, R.W., McKenney, P.D., Alpha, L.D., & Carpenter, W.T. (1989). The schedule for the deficit syndrome: An instrument for research in schizophrenia. *Psychiatry Research, 30*(2), 119-123.

Kirkpatrick, B., Buchanan, R.W., Ross, D.E., & Carpenter, W.T. (2001). A separate disease within the syndrome of schizophrenia. *Archives of General Psychiatry, 58*, 165-171.

Kirkpatrick, B., Ross, D.E., Walsh, D., Karkowski, L., & Kendler, K.S. (2000). Family characteristics of deficit and nondeficit in schizophrenia in Roscommon family study. *Schizophrenia Research, 45*, 57-64.

Klemm, S., Schmidt, B., Knappe, S., & Blanz, B. (2006). Impaired working speed and executive functions as frontal lobe dysfunctions in young first-degree relatives of schizophrenic patients. *European Child & Adolescent Psychiatry, 15*, 400-408.

Knochel, C., Stablein, M., Storchak, H., Reinke, B., Jurcoane, A., Prvulovic, D. et al (2014). Multimodal assessments of the hippocampal formation in schizophrenia and bipolar disorder: Evidence from neurobehavioral measures and functional and structural MRI. *Neuroimaging Clinics, 23*(6), 134-144.

Kraepelin, E. (1919/1971). *Dementia Praecox and Paraphrenia*. New York: Krieger.

Kulhara, K. & Chandiramani, T. (1990). Positive and negative subtypes of schizophrenia: A follow-up study from India. *Schizophrenia Research, 3*(2), 107-116.

Kumar, J., Iwabucchi, S., Oowise, S., Balain, V., Palaniyappan, L., & Liddle, P.F. (2014). Shared white-matter dysconnectivity in schizophrenia and bipolar disorder with psychosis. *Psychological Medicine, 4*, 1-12.

Kuswanto, C.N., Sum, M.Y., & Sim, K. (2013). Neurocognitive functioning in schizophrenia and bipolar disorder: Clarifying concepts of diagnostic dichotomy vs. continuum. *Frontiers in Psychiatry, 5*(4), 162-169.

Lahti, A.C., Holocomb, H.H., Medoff, D.R., Weiler, M.A., Tamminga, C.A., & Carpenter, W.T. (2001). Abnormal patterns of regional cerebral blood flow in schizophrenia with primary negative symptoms during an auditory recognition task. *American Journal of Psychiatry, 158*, 1797-1808.

Lane, H., Chang, Y., Liu, Y., Chiu, C., & Guochan, T. (2005). Sarcosine or d-serine add-on treatment for acute exacerbation of schizophrenia. *Archives of General Psychiatry, 62*(11), 1196-1204.

Langdon, R., Still, M., Connors, M., Ward, P., & Catts, S. (2014). Jumping to delusions in early psychosis. *Cognitive Neuropsychiatry, 19*(3), 241-256.

Lucas, S., Fitzgerald, D., Redoblado-Hodge, A., Anderson, J., Sanbrook, M., Harris, A. et al (2004). Neuropsychological correlates of symptom profiles in first episode schizophrenia. *Schizophrenia Research, 71*, 323-330.

Mahurin, R.K., Velligan, D.I., & Miller, A.L. (1998). Executive-frontal lobe cognitive dysfunction in schizophrenia: A symptom subtype analysis. *Psychiatry Research, 79*, 139-149.

Malaspina, D. & Coleman, D. (2003). Olfaction and social drive in schizophrenia. *Archives of General Psychiatry, 60*, 578-584.

Malhi, G.S., Green, M., Fagiolini, A., Peselow, E.D., & Kumari, V. (2008). Schizoaffective disorder: Diagnostic issues and future recommendations. *Bipolar Disorder, 10*(1-2), 215-230.

Mamah, D., Barch, D.M., & Repovs, G. (2013). Resting state functional connectivity of five neural networks in bipolar disorder and schizophrenia. *Journal of Affective Disorders, 150*(2), 601-609.

Mateer, C.A. (1999). Executive function disorders: Rehabilitation challenges and strategies. *Seminars in Clinical Neuropsychiatry, 4*(1), 50-59.

McCullumsmith, R.E., Clinton, S.M., & Meador-Woodruff, J.H. (2004). Schizophrenia as a disorder of neuroplasticity. *International Review of Neurobiology, 59*, 19-45.

Meda, S.A., Gill, A., Stevens, M.C., Lorenzoni, R.P., Glahn, D.C., Calhoun, V.D., Sweeney, J.A. et al (2012). Differences in resting-state functional magnetic resonance imaging functional network connectivity between schizophrenia and psychotic bipolar probands and their unaffected first-degree relatives. *Biological Psychiatry, 71*(1), 881-889.

Meyer, B., Johnson, S.L., & Carver, C.S. (1999). Exploring behavioral activation and inhibition sensitivities among college students at risk for bipolar spectrum symptomatology. *Journal of Psychopathology & Behavioral Assessment, 21*, 275-292.

Meyer, B., Johnson, S.L., & Winters, R. (2001). Responsiveness to threat and incentive in bipolar disorder: Relations of the BIS/BAS scales with symptoms. *Journal of Psychopathology & Behavioral Assessment, 23*, 133-143.

Miyake, A., Friedman, N.P., & Emerson, M.J. (2000). The unity and diversity of executive functions and their contributions to complex "frontal lobe" tasks: A latent variable analysis. *Cognitive Psychology, 41*(1), 49-100.

Monchi, O., Petrides, M., & Strafella, A.P. (2006). Functional role of the basal ganglia in the planning and execution of actions. *Annuals of Neurology, 59*(2), 257-264.

Morice, R. & Delahunty, A. (1996). Frontal/executive impairments in schizophrenia. *Schizophrenia Bulletin, 22*, 125-137.

Nieto, R.G. & Castellanous, F.X. (2011). A meta-analysis of neuropsychological functioning in patients with early onset schizophrenia and bipolar disorder. *Journal of Clinical Child & Adolescence Psychology, 40*(2), 266-280.

Oades, R.D. (1998). Frontal, temporal and lateralized brain function in children with attention-deficit hyperactivity disorder: A psychophysiological and neuropsychological viewpoint on development. *Behavioral Brain Research, 94*(1), 83-95.

Owen, M.J. (2012). Intellectual disability and major psychiatric disorders: A continuum of neurodevelopmental causality. *British Journal of Psychiatry, 200*(4), 268-269.

Palmer, B.W., Loughran. C.I., & Meeks, T.W. (2010). Cognitive impairment among older adults with late-life schizophrenia or bipolar disorder. *Continuum, 16*(2), 135-152.

Pavlus, J. (2012). Machines of the infinite. *Scientific American*, September, 67-71.

Peralta, V. & Cuesta, M.J. (2004). The deficit syndrome of the psychotic illness: A clinical and nosological study. *European Archives of Psychiatry & Clinical Neuroscience, 254*, 165-171.

Pettersson-Yeo, W., Allen, P., Benetti, S., McGuire, P., & Mechelli, A. (2011). Dysconnectivity in schizophrenia: Where are we now? *Neuroscience & Biobehavioral Reviews, 35*(5), 1110-1124.

Pogue-Geile, M. & Harrow, M. (1984). Negative and positive symptoms in schizophrenia and depression: A follow-up. *Schizophrenia Bulletin, 10*(3), 371-387.

Purper-Ouakil, D. & Franc, N. (2011). Emotional dysfunction in attention deficit hyperactivity disorder. *Archives De Pediatrie, 18*(6), 679-685.

Rapp, A.M., Langohr, K., Mutschler, D.E., & Wild, B. (2014). Irony and proverb comprehension in schizophrenia: Do female patients "dislike" ironic remarks? *Schizophrenia Research & Treatment, 84*, 10-18.

Rector, N.A., Beck, A.T., & Stolar, N. (2005). The negative symptoms of schizophrenia: A cognitive perspective. *Canadian Journal of Psychiatry, 50*(5), 247-255.

Reichenberg, A., Caspi, A., Harrington, H., Houts, R., Keefe, R., Murray, R. et al (2010). Static and dynamic cognitive deficits in childhood preceding adult schizophrenia: A 30-year study. *American Journal of Psychiatry, 167*, 160-169.

Rossi, A., Daneluzzo, E., Mattei, P., Bustini, M., Casacchia, M., & Stratta, P. (1997). Wisconsin card sorting test and Stroop test performances in schizophrenia: A shared construct. *Neuroscience Letters, 226*, 87-90.

Sharma, A., Weisbrod, M., & Bender, S. (2013). Connectivity and local activity within the fronto-posterior brain network in schizophrenia. *Supplement Clinical Neurophysiology, 62*, 181-196.

Siebenhuhner, F., Weiss, S.A., Coppola, R., Weinberger, D.R., & Bassett, D.S. (2013). Intra- and inter-frequency brain network structure in health and schizophrenia. *Plos One, 8*(8), e72351.

Simonsen, C., Sundet, K., & Vaskinn, A. (2008). Neurocognitive profiles in bipolar I and bipolar II disorder: Differences in pattern and magnitude of dysfunction. *Bipolar Disorder, 10*, 245-255.

Skudlarski, P., Schretlen, D.J., Thaker, G.K., Stevens, M.C., Keshavan, M.S., Sweeney, J.A. et al (2013). Diffusion tensor imaging white matter endophenotypes in patients with schizophrenia or psychotic bipolar disorder and their relatives. *American Journal of Psychiatry, 170*(8), 886-898.

Smith, M.J., Barch, D.M., & Csernansky, J.G. (2009). Bridging the gap between schizophrenia and psychotic mood disorders: Relating neurocognitive deficits to psychopathology. *Schizophrenia Research, 107*(1), 69-75.

Smith, E.E. & Jonides, J. (1997). Working memory: A view from neuroimaging. *Cognitive Psychology, 33*(1), 5-42.

Stekelenburg, J.J., Maes, J.P., Van Gool, A.R., Sitskoorn, M., & Vroomen, J. (2013). Deficient multisensory integration in schizophrenia: An event-related potential study. *Schizophrenia Research, 147*(2-3), 253-261.

Uchida, H., Takeuchi, H., Graff-Guerrero, A., Suzuki, T., Watanabe, K., & Mamo, D.C. (2011). Dopamine D2 receptor occupancy and clinical effects: A systematic review and pooled analysis. *Journal of Clinical Psychopharmacology, 31*(4), 497-502.

Uhlhaas, P.J. (2013). Dysconnectivity, large-scale networks and neuronal dynamics in schizophrenia. *Current Opinions in Neurobiology, 23*(2), 283-290.

Vaiva, G., Cottencin, O., & Llorca, P.M. (2002). Regional cerebral blood flow in deficit/ nondeficit types of schizophrenia according to SDS criteria. *Progress in Neuro-psychophathology, 26*, 481-485.

Vercammen, A., Morris, R., Green, M.J., Lenroot, R., Kulkarni, J., Carr, V.J. et al (2012). Reduced neural activity of the prefrontal cognitive control circuitry during response inhibition to negative words in people with schizophrenia. *Journal of Psychiatry & Neuroscience, 37*(6), 379-388.

Volkmar, F.R. & Wolf, J.M. (2013). When children with autism become adults. *World Psychiatry, 12*(1), 78-80.

Waltereit, R., Banaschewski, T., Meyer-Lindenberg, A., & Poustka, L. (2014). Interaction of neurodevelopmental pathways and synaptic plasticity in mental retardation, autistic spectrum disorder and schizophrenia: Implication for psychiatry. *World Journal of Biological Psychiatry, 15*(7), 507-516.

Winokur, G., Monahan, P., Coryell, W., & Zimmerman, M. (1996). Schizophrenia and affective disorder—distinct entities or continuum? An analysis based on a prospective 6-year follow-up. *Comprehensive Psychiatry, 37*(2), 77-87.

Yoon, J.H., Minzenberg, M.J., Ursu, S., Ryan-Walter, B.S., Wendelken, C., Ragland, J.D., & Carter, C.S. (2008). Association of dorsolateral prefrontal cortex dysfunction with disrupted coordinated brain activity in schizophrenia: Relationship with impaired cognition, behavioral disorganization, and global function. *American Journal of Psychiatry, 165*(8), 1006-1014.

Zhang, R., Wei, Q., Kang, Z., Zalesky, A., Li, M., Xu, Y. et al (2014). Disrupted brain anatomical connectivity in medication-naïve patients with first-episode schizophrenia. *Brain Structure & Function, 22*, 50-57.

CHAPTER 7

Dissociation

Dissociation as a concept generates enormous confusion and controversy, in part due to a lack of focus on the underlying issue, stress and the stress response system. Stress is unavoidable for every organism, and evolution has equipped any species that has managed to survive with capacities facilitating resilience to stressors. The topic of stress response and resilience in organisms is beyond the scope of this chapter, but for humans it entails several components, including:

- Executive functions such as working memory to process the stressor (see the "Negative Symptoms" chapter).
- Emotional information processing as covered in the "Depression" and "Anxiety" chapters, to identify the nature of the stressor, such as a threat eliciting a fear response.
- An overlay of human intelligence often amplifying the emotional and perceptual components, but also capable of overriding automatic responses.
- Activation of neurotransmitters and neural structures, such as norepinephrine and the amygdala once threat or danger is perceived.
- Involvement of the hypothalamic-pituitary-adrenal (HPA) axis to initiate physiological stress responses, with the release of cortisol being critical.
- Wide-ranging physiological changes, such as activation of the sympathetic nervous system and deactivation of the parasympathetic nervous system to prepare for fight/flight/freeze responses.
- Mechanisms designed to deactivate the stress response once the stressor/s and distress have passed.

(Bovin & Marx, 2011; DeCarvalho et al, 2010; Dresler et al, 2013; Goel et al, 2014; Herman, 2012; Holzschneider & Mulert, 2011; Linares et al, 2012; Mathew & Ho, 2006; Stankiewicz et al, 2013; Weiss, 2007)

The stress response system requires synchronicity of these diverse components involving patterns of connectivity (Bovin & Marx, 2011; DeCarvalho et al, 2010; Dresler et al, 2013; Goel et al, 2014; Herman, 2012; Holzschneider & Mulert, 2011; Linares et al, 2012; Mathew & Ho, 2006; Stankiewicz et al, 2013; Weiss, 2007). Dissociation occurs when there is some alteration in the connectivity involved in stress responses. A key reason why it is important to frame the stress response and dissociation in terms of connectivity is that, at a neural and physiological level, both processes must entail connections between various components of the stress response system. Connectivity hence places the topic on a more scientific foundation, rather than attempting to decipher diverse theories from different perspectives. Given that every organism requires stress responses that are vulnerable to alterations in the underlying connectivity, dissociation represents a naturally occurring entity. Altered connectivity in the stress response system appears to be due to defensive functioning or dysregulation. The chapter will examine psychological and somatic dissociation in separate sections, and posttraumatic stress disorder (PTSD) as dissociation occurring in response to severe stress. Regarding continuums, there is a range of stressors from mild to extreme, with corresponding patterns of stress response and dissociation. The main patterns of dissociation appear to lie on somewhat separated although overlapping continuums, much as thought content, thought form, and sensory perceptual experiences do in regards to psychosis.

Psychological Dissociation

Emotional numbing, absorption with or without imaginative involvement, compartmentalization, depersonalization and derealization, amnesia, and identity fragmentation comprise the various forms of psychological dissociation (Allen & Lolafaye, 1995; Bowins, 2012c; Bernstein & Putman, 1986; Brown, 2006, 1986; Holmes et al, 2005; Ross et al, 1990, 1991; Waller et al, 1996). They represent progressively intense degrees of dissociation, although there is a range of each, resulting in overlap (Allen & Lolafaye, 1995; Bowins, 2004; Bowins, 2006a; Brown, 2006; Fischer & Elnitsky, 1990; Holmes et al, 2005; Ross et al, 1990, 1991). Emotional numbing diminishes the intensity of negative emotions occurring in response to stressful situations that a person must attend to (Bowins, 2004, 2006a). For example, emergency personnel such as paramedics encounter disturbing scenarios that they must focus on, but to cope with these, negative emotions such as fear, anger, and disgust are often automatically diminished.

Absorption consists of disconnecting from one's current circumstances, both external and psychological, and becoming immersed in another focus, with imaginative involvement frequently elaborating the pleasing aspects of the altered focus (Bowins, 2004, 2006a; Ross et al, 1990, 1991; Waller et al, 1996). For instance, during a boring drawn out presentation your mind tunes out, and you engage in fantasy about the date you are about to go on that evening. Ross et al (1991) have done extensive work on absorption, identifying several different forms: Missing part of a conversation, remembering past events so vividly one seems to be reliving them, uncertainty whether a remembered event happened or was a dream, absorption in a television program or a movie, being so involved in a fantasy that it seemed real, being able to ignore pain, staring into space, talking out loud to oneself when alone, not sure whether one has done something or only thought about it, finding evidence of having done things one can't remember doing.

These absorptive experiences are extremely common, being utilized by virtually everyone from time to time, when circumstances are unpleasant but do not have to be closely attended to (Ross et al, 1990, 1991). Anyone doubting this must observe how, when one presents a dry and/or complex point in a conversation, the other person's eyes often seem to glaze over and their mind briefly drifts off. As an interesting and humorous anecdote, I have noted this very reaction when I discuss the more mundane details of dissociation with dissociation doubters. Frequently, when I point out that they have just experienced a brief episode of dissociation as an escape from the boredom of the subject matter, they deny this occurred. However, absorption is not indicative of pathological dissociation even when displayed at high levels (Bowins, 2012c; Hymer, 1984; Kihlstrom et al, 1994; Kwekkeboom et al, 1998; Ross et al, 1990, 1991). It represents more of a psychological safety valve, an occurrence reflected in how the Dissociative Experiences Scale (DES) short form version for pathological dissociation (DES-T) does not include any absorption items (Nijenhuis et al, 1996). Highlighting its adaptive nature, absorption is likely instrumental in the various forms of meditation, producing a comfortable detachment from stress (Bowins, 2012c). Related to absorption is auto-hypnosis, such as so-called highway hypnosis occurring when a person cannot recall driving along a section of road that is monotonous. Trance states also involve absorptive dissociation, and cultural specific forms occur worldwide (Castillo, 2003; Ferracuti et al, 1996; Ross et al, 2013).

Compartmentalization involves segmenting different components of experience (Bowins, 2004, 2012c). Virtually everyone who is able to cope with intense and diverse sources of stress has learned to compartmentalize, so that problems in one area do not spill over into others and compromise performance. One of the fascinating aspects of milder forms of dissociation is that they can be learned and practiced to foster greater resilience to stress (Bowins, 2004, 2012c). Both compartmentalization and absorption (elaborated with imaginative involvement) can be applied therapeutically to produce a comfortable detachment from adverse emotional states, thereby reducing stress (Bowins, 2012c). These therapeutic dissociation techniques are easily learned relative to cognitive reappraisal and other cognitive behavioral strategies (Bowins, 2012c). With compartmentalization are generated mental divisions, frequently elaborated with visual imagery. For example, work is separated from non-work, and a building representing work visualized and locked down when in the non-work sphere (Bowins, 2012c). The numerous computer based modes of communication currently available make compartmentalization more challenging, but people can learn to shut off these devices to detach. Subdivisions can be created, such as work meetings with coworkers, a person's manager/s, and clients.

Absorption simply involves immersing oneself in a pleasing mental or behavioral focus, and often elaborating it with imagination (Bowins, 2012c): For instance, thinking about the upcoming ski season and imagining a trip, or in regards to behavioral foci, knitting, gardening, and an endless wide range of other activities pleasing to the individual. Additional dissociation based psychotherapy techniques include willful detachment, suppression therapy, and attention shifts as with metacognitive therapy (Bowins, 2013). Suppression therapy defensively blocks adverse memories associated with traumatic occurrences (Anderson & Levy, 2009), dissociating the sufferer from the event. Traumatic memories then lose their ability to elicit anxiety. Willful detachment relies on attention shifts to dissociate a person from stressful input (Schardt et al, 2010). These techniques are often a prelude to absorption, facilitating the shift to a pleasing absorptive focus. The capacity to acquire milder forms of dissociation aligns with how they can be invoked voluntarily (Farb et al, 2007; Leonard et al, 1999).

It appears that milder forms of psychological dissociation, including brief emotional numbing, absorption, and compartmentalization, are evolved or evolving defensive processes, thereby representing a natural part of our stress response system (Bowins, 2004). Indeed, dissociation represents a key defense mechanism template that, along with positive cognitive distortions (see the "Psychosis" chapter), forms the basis of many specific defenses, including traditional psychoanalytic ones (Bowins, 2004). Major forms of psychiatric treatment (antidepressants and psychotherapy) foster a healthy dissociation from adverse emotional states, by shifting emotional information processing in a positive direction (Bowins, 2006a). In addition, the universal predilection for mind-altering substances likely arises from the way they facilitate dissociation and/or positive cognitive distortions (Bowins, 2006a). For example, marijuana routinely produces dissociation (Hurlimann et al, 2012).

The notion that dissociation, even milder forms, can be adaptive, defensive, and learned, frequently evokes negative reactions from clinicians and researchers. To a large extend this reaction appears to be due to how the focus is typically on more moderate to extreme, seemingly discrete, forms of psychological dissociation, such as depersonalization/derealization, amnesia and identity fragmentation (Hall, 2003). More benign adaptive forms pass beneath the radar of most clinicians trained to detect and treat dysfunctional states. Conceptualizing dissociation as a spectrum from mild everyday occurrences to extreme, quite rare events helps clarify the situation.

Depersonalization and derealization represent intermediate forms along the dissociation spectrum, consisting of altered connections with the self and external world, respectively (Bowins, 2004, 2006a). Research provides support for the notion that depersonalization and derealization are common, and at least in a more limited expression can be adaptive. Transient symptoms of depersonalization and derealization have a lifetime prevalence of 26%-75%, and 31%-66% at the time of trauma (Hunter et al, 2004). Depersonalization involves deactivation or dampening of limbic system activity by the prefrontal cortex (PFC), likely as an evolutionary derived mechanism to manage excessive adverse emotional stimulation (Reutens et al, 2010; Sierra & David, 2011; Simeon, 2004; Stein & Simeon, 2009). Regions of the PFC that experience increased activity are those involved in the contextualization and appraisal of emotionally salient information, particularly relevant for stressful inputs (Phillips & Sierra, 2003). Depersonalization and derealization have also been linked to the evolved defensive process of freeze/immobility, aiding animals in not being detected by predators (Scaer, 2001). Dissociation in animals and humans occurs in response to traumatic situations where defensive responses are required (Fikretoglu et al, 2006; Scaer, 2001). While depersonalization and derealization can be defensive, in other instance they appear to arise from dysregulation of more synchronized stress responses, as suggested by the way these experiences can be common in organic conditions, such as epilepsy and migraines (Lambert et al, 2002; Van Dijke et al, 2010). Supporting this perspective, depersonalization can involve dysregulation of the HPA axis (Simeon, 2004).

Amnesia constitutes a more extreme form of psychological dissociation than depersonalization and derealization, although there can be substantial overlap in intensity, with milder amnesia, such as in alcohol induced blackouts, being less intense than extensive and prolonged depersonalization and derealization (Bowins, 2004, 2006a; Van der Hart & Nijenhuis, 2001). Memory loss pertains to personal information, as well as semantic and procedural memories (Van der Hart & Nijenhuis, 2001). Fugue is a form of psychological dissociation that appears to be a more intense and prolonged variant of amnesia (Spiegel et al, 2013). At the most extreme end of the psychological dissociation spectrum is identity fragmentation, characteristic of dissociative identity disorder (DID), formerly multiple personality disorder. The notion of multiple personalities is not correct, as this form of dissociation involves the separation of different components of one's personality into what are often referred to as alters. These alters are more than mere metaphors for emotional states, and represent fragmented self-representations (Forrest, 2001; Merckelbach et al, 2002), commonly demonstrating unique physiological expressions, such as ocular results that are impossible to voluntarily control (Birnbaum & Thomann, 1996). Unfortunately, questionable assessment procedures by certain investigators over time have undermined the acceptability of DID as a valid entity according to Boysen (2011). Furthermore, skepticism as to the authenticity of the condition occurs due to various cognitive errors identified by Ross (1990), including the notion that more than one personality exists, people with DID are only suffering from borderline personality disorder, it is an iatrogenic artifact, abuse histories are confabulated, and these individuals are trying to please the therapist. Ross (1990) indicates that in contrast to these false perceptions, it is a real condition that can be reliably diagnosed and has stable features.

Consistent with how amnesia and identity fragmentation comprise the most extreme forms of psychological dissociation, very severe stress is typically involved, usually transpiring in early life (Dorahy et al, 2014; Ellason et al, 1996). Due to their less developed cognitive structures, global undifferentiated thinking, and greater dependence on parental figures, children are more sensitive to trauma (Levy, 2000). Amnesia and identity fragmentation can arise from dysregulated stress responses due to the overwhelming nature of the stressors, and also defensive processes (Brenner, 1994). Supporting the role of impaired regulation, it has been found that avoidant and disorganized patterns of attachment in early life are strong predictors of dissociation (Ogawa et al, 1997). Countering the perspective that dissociative "disorders" always represent dysfunction, it has been found that those with dissociative disorders have an advantage when it comes to dividing attention, working memory maintenance and updating, and set shifting in the presence of negative emotions (Chiu et al, 2009). A couple of case examples will illustrate the defensive function of more extreme dissociation.

Pat, as she will be referred to, experienced physical, sexual, and psychological abuse from her older brother during her childhood. Her parents were very busy and consumed with their own lives, paying little attention to the children. Pat's brother began to sexually abuse her when he was about 14, and she around 8 years of age. He threatened to hurt her if she told on him, and often tormented her when she resisted, such as pushing her into the doghouse without a coat when it was cold. She "forgot" many of these experiences, and only gradually recovered them without prompting during long-term psychotherapy. As an adult Pat often experiences amnesia when aggressive encounters transpire. She typically walks away and loses track of the time frame for several hours. Actual identity fragmentation does not appear to occur, based on a review of purchases made during the amnestic periods, showing that she bought the same items she normally would have; if in a different alter state the purchases would likely have been more distinct. Due to early life trauma Pat is very sensitive to aggressive encounters, and amnesia for such events protects her psychologically.

A middle aged female patient who will here be referred to as Cathy was diagnosed with dissociative identity disorder. As a child Cathy was physically and verbally abused by her mother. Her oldest brother was forced into the role of primary caregiver for Cathy and her sisters. He beat them daily and would only waive the daily beating if the given sister made money for him. Each of the sisters, other than for Cathy, developed severe alcohol/drug abuse problems and were largely dysfunctional, two of them eventually succumbing to hepatic complications. Cathy was (apparently) the only one to have developed a dissociative disorder, and the only one to avoid alcohol/drug abuse problems. A young girl alter took all the abuse and remained silent, while several other alters fulfilled important roles, such as organizing and cleaning. She functioned well in secretarial jobs with the specialized alters managing tasks, married, and had a child. From these case examples, the adaptive value of extreme dissociation is evident. Both women were able to lead fairly normal lives in terms of functioning despite the severe trauma, although they suffer from pronounced emotional fluctuations and inner turmoil requiring therapeutic intervention.

Many aspects of psychological dissociation are contentious, and the issue of dissociation types and whether they are organized continuously or discretely is no exception. The continuous organization presented above is logical and consistent with much of the data. For example, there is no evidence that absorption even when displayed at high levels is maladaptive (Bowins, 2012c; Hymer, 1984; Kihlstrom et al, 1994; Kwekkeboom et al, 1998; Nijenhuis et al, 1996; Ross et al, 1990, 1991). Depersonalization and derealization occur on a continuum from transient episodes in psychologically healthy individuals, to persistent and severe forms compromising adaptive functioning, but generally tend to be less intense than amnesia and identity fragmentation (Mula et al, 2007; Hunter et al, 2003). Identity fragmentation due to extreme abuse during childhood is understandably on the severe end of the dissociative spectrum (Ellason et al, 1996). Dissociative symptoms of varying types and severity levels can be found in children as well as adults (Silberg, 2000). While the various forms of psychological dissociation appear to occur on a continuum of severity, there is a discrete aspect provided by the different forms themselves.

Taking a more dichotomous perspective Brown (2006) and Holmes et al (2005) suggest that detachment and compartmentalization subtypes of dissociation occur. Detachment is proposed as a separation from everyday aspects of experience including emotional numbing, depersonalization/derealization, and somatization disorder (Brown, 2006; Holmes et al, 2005). Compartmentalization is seen as a deficit in the control of processes or actions and includes absorptive states, hypnotic phenomena, amnesia, and dissociative identity disorder (Holmes et al, 2005; Brown, 2006). A problem with this perspective is that the dichotomy might not stand up well to close scrutiny, as overlap frequently occurs. For example, absorption is a detachment from everyday experiences, much like emotional numbing. Dissociative states have also been separated into negative involving a loss like amnesia, and positive consisting of added activity as with absorption (Nijenhuis et al, 1996). This separation dates back to Janet (1901) who believed that functional losses resulted in negative dissociation, while intrusions produced positive dissociation. However, the distinction is hard to maintain given that defensive functions to any form of dissociation can be seen as positive, thereby adding something, and each form of dissociation can involve both the removal and addition of psychological and somatic functioning.

Psychological dissociation then occurs in various forms that can be considered discrete to some extent, although dimensionality occurs both within the type, such as a range of depersonalization and derealization, and also how there is a continuum of severity from emotional numbing and absorption to identity fragmentation. Alteration of connectivity within the stress response system transpires, due to defensive functioning or dysregulation. Milder versions of psychological dissociation, such as emotional numbing and absorption, are more likely to be adaptive and defensive. More severe versions, such as amnesia and identity fragmentation, often involve dysregulation in the stress response system and can be maladaptive, although as we have seen they frequently have a defensive value in the midst of at least severe and extended trauma. Intermediate forms of psychological dissociation—depersonalization and derealization—likely occur due to a mix of defensive and dysregulation sources. Closely linked to psychological dissociation is somatic dissociation.

Somatic Dissociation

Currently, psychological and somatic dissociation are seen as being distinct entities, with somatoform disorders not even linked to dissociation (American Psychiatric Association, 2013; World Health Organization, 1992). This arrangement represents a significant departure from historical perspectives that typically included psychological and somatic versions. The term hysteria tended to be used instead of dissociation. Briquet (1859, cited in Nijenhuis et al, 1999) indicated that hysteria is a general disease modifying the whole organism. Disturbances of perception and control are integral to hysteria, according to Charcot (1887, cited in Nijenhuis et al, 1999). Janet (1901) viewed hysteria as a collection of disorders involving dissociation, induced by psychological trauma or physical stressors such as fatigue. Those with hysteria fail to integrate experiences and reactions to these occurrences, resulting in dissociated systems of ideas and functions, including somatic.

Breur and Freud (1895, cited in Nijenhuis et al, 1999) also believed that hysteria involves dissociation, but viewed it as a consequence of childhood sexual trauma. Sexual fantasy and forbidden wish fulfillment later became the key causal elements for Freud (1908, cited in Nijenhuis et al, 1999). Freud also identified conversion (the transformation of unacceptable mental contents into somatic symptoms) as a key process in the generation of somatoform hysterical symptoms. The notion of conversion underlying somatoform dissociation has largely persisted (Nijenhuis et al, 1999). However, diagnostic systems have struggled with the categorization of dissociative conditions, with more recent versions completely rejecting psychoanalytic formulations (Nijenhuis et al, 1999). Each version of major diagnostic systems categorizes conversion, somatization, and dissociation differently (Nijenhuis et al, 1999). The most recent ones (DSM-5 and ICD-10) separate dissociative disorders from somatoform disorders (American Psychiatric Association, 2013; World Health Organization, 1992). ICD-10 also confuses dissociation and conversion listing dissociative (conversion) disorders and somatoform disorders, when conversion applies more to somatoform conditions. Why the confusion?

At least two reasons stand out regarding why there is so much confusion regarding the classification of dissociation, and in particular the relationship between dissociation and somatoform conditions. The first is a blanket rejection of psychoanalytic concepts and other theoretical formulations in the current atheoretical era. Present day psychiatry and clinical psychology are still feeling the impact of the overthrow of psychoanalysis, the dominant force until the 1960s (Shorter, 1997). As psychoanalysis was heavily theoretical, and light on the empirical side, we now have the reverse, with little or no value given to theoretical contributions, unlike in physics, the so-called ultimate science, where a balance of theoretical and empirical approaches powers the discipline. Consequently, we lack unifying theoretical frameworks for conditions, and in the case of complex entities such as dissociation, such a contribution is essential if we are to advance our understanding. Empirical studies can test predictions from these theories, but cannot on their own generate a comprehensive unifying framework.

The second reason, and one very much linked to the de-emphasis on (or complete rejection of) theoretical approaches, is a deficient appreciation and understanding of the mind-body relationship, and our natural predilection for separating mind and body. Research indicates that intuitively we are mind-body dualists, separation being a default strategy (Anglin, 2014; Forstmann & Burgmer, 2015). Various thought experiments were employed by Forstmann and Burgmer (2015) to assess how we cognitively process the mind and body. Physical properties were consistently seen as being retained compared to mental properties, and under conditions that taxed cognitive resources or primed them with an intuitive thinking style, mind-body dualistic beliefs were intensified (Forstmann & Burgmer, 2015). The authors indicate that despite scientific advances in understanding the neurological origins of mental life, we are still essentially mind-body dualists. Anglin (2014) found that subjects tend to locate the self and mind in the head, whereas the soul or essence of a person is in the chest, reflecting our propensity to see discreteness in entities such as mind, body, and soul.

In contrast to perceptions of mind-body dualism, there is actually synchrony between the mind and body (Kumar & Yeragani, 2010; Leitan & Murray, 2014). Kumar and Yeragani (2010) describe how the central and autonomic nervous systems, endocrine system, immune system, and stress system all interact at multiple levels. For example, cells of the immune system have receptors for neurotransmitters (Kumar & Yeragani, 2010). Leitan and Murray (2014) point out how cognition is "embodied," being derived from interactions with the world via the body. Medicine is said to be dominated by the notion of mind-body dualism, derived from Cartesian dualism, and the effort of many 19th century physician-scientists to base the medical curriculum on a fully materialistic approach to body functions (Mehta, 2011; Panksepp, 2011). A fundamental flaw at the heart of much of the dualistic mind-body approach is not seeing that mind is body too! The mind is brain, and not some free-floating entity, and the brain is part of the body. The linkage of the central and peripheral nervous systems, and also neurotransmitters within and outside of the brain in diverse tissues, demonstrate this connection (Kumar & Yeragani, 2010). Somatic expressions of emotional states are actually very common, as with anxiety manifesting in symptoms such as palpitations, shortness of breath, sweating, tremor, and the like. Countering our default mind-body dualism opens the way to understanding how somatic conditions are also a form of dissociation, derived from mental activity, based upon connections and synchronization of the mind and body in the stress response. This enlightened approach aligns with mindfulness based therapies that are demonstrating success across a range of conditions (Leitan & Murray, 2014; Schmidt, 2004).

Highlighting how dissociation can take both a psychological and somatic form, in line with the tight mind-body connection, is research evidence demonstrating the overlap. Spitzer et al (1999) found significantly more dissociative symptoms in patients with conversion disorder than in controls, and expressed that similar psychological processes underlie conversion and dissociative disorders, despite descriptive differences. Brown et al (2007) also believe that the evidence supports the existence of shared underlying processes, based on a review of relevant issues such as reported correlations between pseudoneurological (conversion) and dissociated symptoms, and rates of trauma linked to both. Nijenhuis et al (1999) found that somatoform dissociation is extreme in dissociative identity disorder, high in dissociative disorder (both being forms of psychological dissociation), and increased in somatoform disorders. Attributions for somatic symptoms are both somatic and psychological in nature, countering the notion that they are strictly somatic (Douzenis & Seretis, 2013). Now that we have seen how dissociation can take both a psychological and somatic form, and how these forms are not fully separate as suggested by current diagnostic systems, we can look at the variety of expressions that somatic dissociation takes and the overlap between them.

Essentially, somatic dissociation expresses itself in as many forms as there are body systems. The more recognized expressions are covered starting with neurologically based forms. Psychogenic nonepileptic seizures (PNES) are a more extreme variant that has the unique feature of being diagnosed with near certainty, unlike many other forms of somatic dissociation (Benbadis, 2005). Goldstein et al (2000) evaluated 20 patients with established pseudoseizures, and found that they demonstrated high levels of dissociation and escape-avoidance coping strategies. Other nervous system forms of somatic dissociation occur, such as psychogenic movement disorders (PMDs), including tremor, dystonia, Parkinsonism, gait disorders, and dyskinesias (Thomas & Jankovic, 2004). PMDs cannot be attributed to a lesion of the nervous system (Thomas & Jankovic, 2004). Functional weakness or paralysis is quite a common form of neurological somatic dissociation, demonstrating comorbidity with depression and anxiety, despite those experiencing it tending not to relate their neurological symptoms to emotional states (Stone et al, 2010). Neurological forms of somatic dissociation have traditionally been referred to as conversion disorders. Virtually any neurological function, including sensation and sensory perceptions, can be impacted (Vuilleumier, 2005). Neuroimaging shows selective decreases in brain activity pertaining to the region involved, such as frontal and subcortical circuit activity for motor control during hysterical paralysis, somatosensory cortices during hysterical anesthesia, and the visual cortex when hysterical blindness occurs (Vuilleumier, 2005). Activity in many other brain regions is altered, including that involved in emotional functioning, cognitive control, motor inhibition, motor planning, coordination, self-referential processing, and perceptual awareness (Perez et al, 2014). These results demonstrate how neurological dissociation manifests at a structural level.

Turning to another major body system, irritable bowel syndrome (IBS) is a very prevalent form of somatic dissociation, representing one of the most common conditions seen by gastroenterologists. Salmon et al (2003) compared 64 outpatients with IBS to 61 patients with bowel symptoms explained by physical disease. Those with IBS experienced more anxiety, depression, dissociation, and other forms of somatization, and recalled more physical, sexual, and psychological abuse (Salmon et al, 2003). Investigating the latent structure of IBS, Jasper et al (2015) found a strong general somatization factor and three symptom specific factors consisting of diarrhea, constipation, and pain (likely secondary to diarrhea and constipation). They conclude that IBS is a continuous and multidimensional construct (Jasper et al, 2015). Highlighting the difficulty of separating symptoms due to somatic dissociation from those linked to actual physical disease, Mearin (2011) believes that many patients with new onset IBS suffered from a bowel infection just prior to the "somatic" symptoms. It appears that transitory inflammation of the bowel due to infections can lead to permanent changes in the structure and function of the digestive system inducing IBS symptoms (Mearin, 2011).

Distinguishing symptoms due to actual disease from those with no organic basis is a major issue with most somatic conditions. Many patients have heard the "It's in your head" explanation, with some manifesting a biological cause later on. This problem frequently occurs with localized pain syndromes. One condition where this has been noted is with post-vasectomy pain syndrome (PVPS), which is frequently ascribed to psychological problems, an occurrence linked to how vasectomy is incorrectly seen as a "safe and simple procedure" (Bowins, 2006b). Approximately 5%-15% of vasectomies produce pain, often of an enduring and extreme nature, arising from vasectomy-induced physiological complications (Bowins, 2006b). PVPS is often attributed to psychogenic causes, as with so-called complex regional pain syndrome mostly involving the limbs, which Hill et al (2012) indicate is due to newly discovered neuro-inflammatory processes, and not the psychogenic pain model usually favored by physicians and mental health professionals.

One of the most frequently encountered localized pain syndromes usually attributed to somatic dissociation is chronic pelvic pain in females. Nijenhuis et al (2003) assessed 52 women experiencing chronic pelvic pain for dissociative symptoms. Actual dissociative disorders (based on DSM-IV criteria) were very low, but both somatoform and psychological dissociation were common and positively correlated (Nijenhuis et al, 2003). Somatization, psychological dissociation, and distress are common in women experiencing chronic pelvic pain, with an apparent linkage to sexual and/or physical abuse (Badura et al, 1997; Walker et al, 1992). Caution has to be applied when attributing localized pain conditions to somatization, as PVPS demonstrates. In the case of chronic pelvic pain physiological damage and inflammation might even be induced by sexual and/or physical trauma. In localized pain syndromes a more reasonable application of dissociative attributions is that the level of pain and impact on the person's life might be influenced by somatization, but unless absolutely proven otherwise (rarely the case) a physiological source of localized pain should be assumed to be present.

Most somatic dissociation does not entail pain, as is evident with functional respiratory conditions including paroxysmal sneezing, sighing, dypsnea, habit cough, and vocal cord dysfunction (Butani & O'Connell, 1997; Fochtmann,

1995). These conditions are most common in children, adolescents, and young adults, and are frequently accompanied by other psychiatric disorders (Butani & O'Connell, 1997; Fochtmann, 1995). Given its major role in sensation and contact with the external environment, it is not surprising that the skin is another organ highly linked to somatic dissociation (Gupta, 2006; Harth et al, 2006). A heterogeneous group of somatic conditions occur, including pruritis, paresthesia, urticaria, angioedema, flushing reactions, profuse perspiration, numbness, "body memories," disfiguration, eco-syndromes, erythrophobia, and psychogenic pseudoeffluvium, as well as exacerbations of dermatological conditions such as psoriasis and eczema (Gupta, 2006; Harth et al, 2006). Harth et al (2006) indicate that these conditions lack a medical basis and can be differentiated variably as somatizaton disorders, hypochondriachal disorders, or somatoform disorders.

To this point the forms of somatic dissociation covered pertain to a particular physiological system, such as neurological, gastrointestinal, gynecological, respiratory, or dermatological. There are also a number of general syndromes not clearly linked to particular physiological systems. These conditions include chronic fatigue syndrome, fibromyalgia, multiple chemical sensitivities, reactive hypoglycemia, mass psychogenic illness, and sick building syndrome (Ford, 1997; Kanaan et al, 2007). These conditions are described by Ford (1997) as "fashionable diagnoses," based on the way the acceptable version shifts over time. Reactive hypoglycemia was popular in the 1960s and 1970s, particularly in the United States, accounting for a wide range of vague symptoms (Ford, 1997). During the middle ages there was mass psychogenic illness, described as "dancing manias," having the common ingredient of a closed social unit experiencing substantial anxiety/tension, with a vague illness starting in one person and spreading, particularly if the index case was a leader (Ford, 1997). Currently, fibromyalgia and chronic fatigue syndrome are very "fashionable," and those suffering from them often gain a great deal of medical attention and support, providing reinforcement (Ford, 1997). Fibromyalgia involves diffuse and often shifting pain. The non-localized nature of the pain in fibromyalgia aligns with it being more somatic in origin, perhaps related to sustained muscle tension and fatigue arising from persistent anxiety and/or depression.

Two characteristics strongly suggest that these conditions represent somatic dissociation and not primarily organic pathology: First, symptom overlap, and second, how a diagnosis of one typically entails a diagnosis of at least one other (Ford, 1997; Kanaan et al, 2007). Buchwald and Garrity (1994) compared patients with chronic fatigue syndrome, fibromyalgia, and multiple chemical sensitivities. They found tremendous overlap of physical and psychological symptoms, as well as demographic characteristics (Buchwald & Garrity, 1994). A comparison of chronic fatigue syndrome to fibromyalgia shows overlap of key symptoms: Fatigue in 86% of those with fibromyalgia, and arthralgia in 88% of those with chronic fatigue syndrome (Aaron et al, 2000). Regarding diagnostic overlap, 70% of those with fibromyalgia, and 30% with multiple chemical sensitivities, meet the criteria for chronic fatigue syndrome (Buchwald & Garrity, 1994). Reviewing 53 studies where patients with one of these conditions were assessed for others, Aaron and Buchwald (2001) ascertained that between 35% and 70% of those with chronic fatigue syndrome also meet criteria for fibromyalgia, and 53%-67% satisfy the criteria for multiple chemical sensitivity. Interestingly, they also found that 58%-92% meet the criteria for IBS (Aaron & Buchwald, 2001). Demonstrating the "changing faces" of somatization, Stewart (1990) found that 90% of those diagnosed with multiple chemical sensitivities had also been diagnosed with another general somatic illness. These results demonstrate that symptoms are shared between "illnesses," and consistent with this occurrence a diagnosis of one also often qualifies a person for a diagnosis of another (Ford, 1997).

Ford (1997) points to several features of the "fashionable diagnoses" that demonstrate that they are psychosomatic in origin:

- Symptoms are nonspecific and subjective, such as fatigue.
- No definitive physical signs or confirmatory laboratory findings are present.
- Biological explanations are lacking, although superficially appealing.
- A majority of patients meet diagnostic criteria, past or present, for anxiety and/or depression, indicating emotional distress.
- Somatization disorder is present in a significant minority of these patients.
- Psychological explanations are rejected.
- Despite exhaustive evaluations medical or psychiatric explanations are often lacking.

Ford (1997) cautions that some of these patients do have unrecognized underlying organic disease. However, taking all factors into account these conditions do appear to be primarily a form of somatic dissociation that can shift over time (Ford, 1997; Kanaan et al, 2007).

Framing expressions of somatic dissociation in terms of both particular physiological systems, and general systems not clearly linked to any physiological system, is scientifically accurate, but distinct from the typical framing in terms of categories such as somatization or somatoform disorder, conversion, psychogenic pain, and hypochondriasis. These categories provide an inaccurate picture of what somatic dissociation entails (Kirmayer & Looper, 2006). Somatization is a general description that applies more to symptoms than actual diseases (Oyama et al, 2007). Conversion typically refers to functional neurological symptoms, but these really only represent one of several physiological systems expressing somatic dissociation (Oyama et al, 2007). Psychogenic pain is probably for the most part entirely inaccurate, at least when applied to localized pain, and is largely based on our very limited understanding of pain mechanisms, as complex regional pain syndrome highlights (Hill et al, 2012). Perhaps there can be amplification of pain due to distress or stress, but it is unlikely that localized pain syndromes are entirely due to somatic dissociation (Fishbain et al, 2009; Hill et al, 2012). As an example, many women with chronic pelvic pain actually have ovarian cysts or other organic reasons for the pain, although there can be a psychological overlay related to stress or trauma

(Nijenhuis et al, 2003). Amplification also applies to hypochondriasis, where in addition to the somatic symptoms, attribution to a physical illness occurs (Avia, 1999; Oyama et al, 2007)—for example, believing that the symptom of shortness of breath indicates lung cancer. Another form of somatic dissociation involving amplification is body dysmorphic disorder, occurring when altered self-perceptions are attributed to a physical condition, such as being overweight, slim, or asymmetrical (Oyama et al, 2007).

A major issue perpetuating our current inaccurate framing of somatic dissociation is a misunderstanding of the statistic often involved in studies framing it in terms of somatization, somatoform disorder, conversion, psychogenic pain, and hypochondriasis: Factor analysis and related techniques. When factor analytic results are presented the understanding appears to be that this is the right outcome, as evidenced by few researchers presenting the limitation of the statistical technique. Factor analysis does not provide for one correct answer, and indeed an infinite number of potentially accurate solutions can arise from a given data set (Marsh et al, 2014; Wetzel, 2012). Factor analysis can only produce reasonably valid solutions when many studies using a variety of descriptors, with numerous diverse samples, are applied over time, as has been the case with normal personality research. In this instance solutions gravitated to a very limited number of factors that appear to describe normal personality (see the chapter “Personality Disorders”). Even then the results cannot be said to be fully certain. This level of rigor does not even remotely apply to research pertaining to somatic dissociation. Hence, conceptualizing somatic dissociation in terms of particular physiological systems, and also general systems not clearly linked to any physiological system, gives a more accurate picture of somatic dissociation not distorted by unrealistic interpretations of factor analytic type studies. Another aspect of conceptualizing somatic dissociation is whether or not there is a continuum from normal health.

Somatic dissociation pertaining to particular physiological systems does occur on a continuum from mild to extreme, aligning quite well with the level of distress or anxiety experienced (Escobar & Gureje, 2007; Gupta & Gupta, 2006). Gupta and Gupta (2006) evaluated 360 participants, assessing nine unexplained cutaneous symptoms and dissociation, the latter based on Dissociative Experiences Scale (DES) scores. Dermatological dissociative symptom intensity correlated very well with dissociation scores (Gupta & Gupta, 2006), the authors suggesting that even mild dissociation in the nonclinical range may play a role in the genesis of unexplained cutaneous symptoms. Reviewing international research pertaining to somatic complaints and syndromes, Escobar and Gureje (2007) found that they are closely related to stress and other conditions indicating distress, including depression.

Health anxiety, such as a concern about what slight shortness of breath might mean in terms of medical illness, appears to exist on a continuum with hypochondriasis, suggesting that hypochondriasis is just the most extreme end of the health anxiety continuum (Braddock & Abramowitz, 2006; Hart & Bjorgvinsson, 2010; Oyama et al, 2007). Hypochondriachal level health anxiety appears to arise from intense levels of fear/anxiety, with an erroneous perception of threat amplifying the concern (Abramowitz & Braddock, 2006). As pertains to both hypochondriasis and medically unexplained symptoms in general, the number and intensity of symptoms at baseline influences the course of the condition (Olde-Hartman et al, 2009). Regarding somatic dissociation involving general systems not clearly linked to any physiological system, a range of expressions can occur, such as mild to severe fatigue with chronic fatigue syndrome, indicating a continuum of expressions (Ford, 1997; Kanaan et al, 2007). In addition, the nature of these more vague somatic expressions is highly dependent on cultural and historical factors, resulting in a range of expressions (Ford, 1997; Kanaan et al, 2007; Mayou, 1975; Zaroff et al, 2012).

So far we have looked at how somatic dissociation is expressed, but not why it occurs. In this regard, both dysregulation and psychological defense appear to play a role. Somatic dissociation involves alterations in several aspects of regulation, such as pertaining to emotions, cognitive control, self-referential information processing, perceptual awareness, and motor planning, coordination, and inhibition (Kirmayer & Looper, 2006; Perez et al, 2014; Van Der Kruijs et al, 2014). Overwhelming emotions and psychological distress seem to be linked to both the intensity of somatic dissociation and alterations in regulatory functioning (Roberts & Reuber, 2014; Simon & VonKorff, 1991). Kirmayer and Looper (2006) believe that disturbances in the regulation of physiological systems account for many unexplained symptoms and sickness behavior. Amplification, such as occurs with catastrophizing, can intensify disturbances in regulation (Avia, 1999).

The defensive function of somatic dissociation is not as clear as for psychological dissociation, but might transpire in certain ways. It has been suggested (Kozlowska, 2007; Kozlowska & Williams, 2009) that conversion symptoms in general are derived from two evolutionary based responses to threat. The first links to the freeze response, expressed in humans as emotional inhibition to avoid punishment, including in children an inhibitory attachment style. This component relates to the disconnection from the emotional component of distress seen in somatic dissociation (Kozlowska, 2007; Kozlowska & Williams, 2009). The second is excitatory, including in children an excitatory attachment style, facilitating the organization of appeasement strategies. This second component ties in with the conversion to somatic symptoms (Kozlowska, 2007; Kozlowska & Williams, 2009). Their explanation appears to have merit, because with somatic dissociation there does seem to be a disconnect from negative emotional states, and transfer to a somatic expression that is often better acknowledged by others than emotional distress, as evidenced by the attention somatic dissociation receives from heath care providers and those close to the person. Somatic dissociation might even simply reduce tension and distress (Farley & Barkan, 1997), perhaps in part via the concerned and caring attention these symptoms often bring.

The origin of somatic (and psychological) dissociation also relates to trauma and reactions to it (Badura et al, 1997; Gupta, 2006; Nijenhuis et al, 2003;

Roelofs & Spinhoven, 2007; Salmon et al, 2003). Trauma is associated with medically unexplained symptoms (Badura et al, 1997; Gupta, 2006; Nijenhuis et al, 2003; Roelofs & Spinhoven, 2007; Salmon et al, 2003). Nijenhuis et al (2003) found that somatoform dissociation is more strongly linked to trauma than psychological dissociation. This might arise from the mechanism proposed above for somatic dissociation as a defense (Kozlowska, 2007; Kozlowska & Williams, 2009), because the emotional distress associated with trauma is often difficult for medical practitioners to acknowledge and attend to relative to somatic symptoms, resulting in somatic symptoms being heavily reinforced. The link between trauma and both somatic and psychological dissociation now brings us to posttraumatic stress disorder (PTSD).

Posttraumatic Stress Disorder (PTSD)

Dissociation is linked to trauma and PTSD, but the nature of the relationship is unclear (Van Der Hart et al, 2005). Of crucial significance is whether dissociation is central or peripheral to PTSD, and the related matter of whether there is a dissociative subtype for PTSD. Dissociation involves some alteration in the stress response system, and since this system is activated with trauma, it logically follows that dissociation would arise in at least some instances of trauma. Van Der Hart et al (2005) argue that dissociation is central to PTSD, representing a division of psychobiological systems that constitute personality into a part avoiding traumatic elements and functioning, and another part that is fixated on traumatic experiences and defensive actions. This implies that those with PTSD have preserved functioning that is actually uncommon, consistent with PTSD being such a disabling condition lacking ideal treatments. Lanius et al (2010) believe that there is a dissociative subtype of PTSD consisting of emotional over-modulation, and a non-dissociative version consisting of re-experiencing and hyper-vigilance. In practice this separation is difficult because re-experiencing symptoms, increased arousal and alertness, and avoidance commonly mix together in varying degrees. Dissociation in PTSD is often conceptualized based on actual psychological dissociation categories, such as depersonalization and derealization (Lanius et al, 2012). However, what might be occurring is a traumatic form of dissociation distinct from more standard forms, such as depersonalization and derealization. To appreciate this process it is necessary to examine PTSD as a form of repetition compulsion (Bowins, 2010a).

For at least 100 years the tendency to repeat maladaptive behavior has been noted. Freud (1914) proposed that a propensity to repeat past experiences is a fundamental human characteristic. Schur (1966) argued that repetitiveness is a ubiquitous phenomenon transmitted in every living organism by the genetic code. Inderbitzin and Levy (1998) suggest that the question is not why we repeat but what stops us from repeating. Repetitious behavior can include thoughts, images, flashbacks, dreams, emotions, somatic sensations, and behavioral re-enactments. Regarding repetition compulsion, it appears that there are traumatic and non-traumatic forms (Bowins, 2010a).

The non-traumatic form of repetition compulsion represents an evolutionary based mechanism assisting, during the early years of life, in the acquisition of beneficial patterns of interacting with the social and physical environments (Bowins, 2010a). Patterns demonstrated by caregivers that align with a young individual's temperament and developing personality tend to be adopted and repeated as a path of least resistance. For example, if caregivers demonstrate an avoidance pattern, and the person has a temperament consisting of low openness to experience and high harm avoidance, the pattern will almost certainly be adopted. If the person has a temperament consisting of high openness to experience and high novelty seeking, then a pattern of avoidance is less likely to be acquired, but an approach-oriented pattern will be readily adopted. Assisting in this process is the fact that, during 95% of our evolution in a hunting-gathering context, children were exposed to a wide range of behavioral patterns adaptive for the group (Bowins, 2010a; Glantz & Pearce, 1989). Although the mechanism typically facilitates the adoption of adaptive patterns of behavior for the particular social and environmental circumstances, maladaptive patterns can also be acquired, such as abusive behavior (Bowins, 2010a). The adoption of maladaptive patterns might even be intensified outside of a hunting-gathering context, because children are typically exposed to more limited number of individuals, even as few as one in the case of single parents, allowing for the impact of any maladaptive pattern demonstrated by caregivers to be unopposed by more adaptive patterns (Bowins, 2010a).

The traumatic form of repetition compulsion arises from the way traumatic experiences are processed (Bowins, 2010a). Cognitive and emotional aspects of experience are automatically and unconsciously forged into a psychological program, based on a biologically based learning process (Bowlby, 1988; Kutz, 1989; Van Der Kolk, 1987). Given the evolutionary fitness reducing implications of traumatic experiences, the cognitive and emotional aspects have to enter consciousness and achieve awareness in order to prevent a recurrence (Bowins, 2010a). However, due to how painful this awareness is, fusion of the cognitive and emotional aspects of experience is often avoided via dissociation (Bowins, 2010a). Consequently, the various components of experience repeat endlessly as dissociated elements. This perspective aligns with Janet's (1901) belief that those with hysteria fail to integrate experiences and reactions to these occurrences, resulting in dissociated systems of ideas and functions including somatic. Consistent with the model presented, trauma can disrupt the normal integration sequence of parallel processes of the self during childhood (Manning & Manning, 2009). It has been suggested that PTSD arises from insufficient encoding of trauma memory, with persistent dissociation blocking memory elaboration (Brewin & Holmes, 2003). However, this hypothesis did not hold up when trait dissociation and rater-coded or computer-generated measures of fragmentation were applied (Bedard-Gilligan & Zoellner, 2012). An important cautionary note relevant to PTSD symptoms is that in some instances involving blast effects and concussions, many of the symptoms experienced can be physiological, and not strictly due to trauma induced dissociation. However, the vast majority of traumatic experiences producing PTSD do not involve blast effects and concussions.

PTSD is characterized largely by disconnected cognitive, emotional, somatic, and behavioral experiences that intrude into conscious awareness (Bovin & Marx, 2011; Gupta, 2006; Van Der Kolk & Fisler, 1995). Gupta (2006) indicates that the traumatic memories of PTSD are often experienced on a sensory level as "body memories," including local or generalized pruritic states, urticaria, angioedema, flushing reactions, and profuse perspiration. Van Der Kolk and Fisler (1995) in evaluating 46 patients with PTSD found that traumatic memories were retrieved, at least initially, as "dissociated mental imprints" of sensory and affective elements of the traumatic experience, consisting of visual, olfactory, auditory, and kinesthetic experiences. The trauma effect can be maintained or intensified by amplification of the fear components, derived from threat amplifying cognitions (Gershuny & Thayer, 1999; Punamaki et al, 2005). In addition to dissociated elements, PTSD is characterized by avoidance of trauma related stimuli and heightened arousal/hyper-vigilance. These symptoms are understandable within an evolutionary context, based on the defensive value of avoiding agents, and anything associated with them, that have proven highly damaging, plus being hyper-vigilant for threats (Bowins, 2010a). The largely dissociated repetition of traumatic elements almost certainly perpetuates these additional PTSD symptoms (Bowins, 2010a).

Dissociation is then central to PTSD, representing a traumatic form of repetition compulsion (Bowins, 2010a). A prevailing notion in psychoanalytic writings is that repetition compulsion serves to achieve mastery (Bibring, 1943; Cohen, 1980; Freud, 1920, 1926; Horowitz, 1976; Janet, 1925). However, mastery never actually occurs, as is demonstrated by the endless repetition of dissociated elements seen in PTSD (Inderbitzin & Levy, 1998; Keane, 1985; Kriegman & Slavin, 1989). From a common sense perspective, if repetition compulsion in and of itself actually succeeded in achieving mastery, then the suffering would frequently resolve without the need for therapeutic intervention, a possibility that never seems to transpire. The dissociation so integral to PTSD can be viewed as a form of dysregulation of the normal healthy stress response system, due to the overwhelming nature of the experience. However, it more likely constitutes a defensive processing safeguarding conscious system functioning in the moment of trauma (Bowins, 2010a). What works in the moment as a defense can produce problems later on, as with the endless repetition compulsion seen with PTSD dissociation preventing healthy functioning in various areas of a person's life.

In contrast to the endless repetition occurring with PTSD, the grieving process appears to resolve negative experiences by achieving a healthy fusion of the cognitive and emotional components (Bowins, 2010a). Traumatic experiences always entail a loss of some form, such as a loss of control, freedom, mental or physical wellbeing, relationship, trust, or a valued object (Bowins, 2004, 2010a). Grieving appears to have evolved as a defensive process to help us cope with losses, and the loss involved in trauma contributes greatly to an event being experienced as traumatic (Bowins, 2010a). By extension the grieving process might well be designed to enable us to cope with, and master, trauma. If it engages and progresses unimpeded immediately after a traumatic occurrence, then disturbing emotions are consciously linked to the cognitive components of the trauma, and healing occurs. When the grieving process fails to engage, due to the painfulness of the fusion of the emotional and cognitive elements of the trauma, the dissociated elements repeat endlessly. In support of this notion therapeutic experiences that help to merge the disconnected components of trauma, such as art therapy, appear to have success in treating PTSD (Avrahami, 2005). A unique therapeutic intervention consists of attempting to reactivate the grieving process, allowing this natural defense mechanism to fuse the disconnected elements, an occurrence that is feasible in the safe environment of psychotherapy (Bowins, 2010a). Focusing the person on losses associated with the trauma can help reactivate the grieving process (Bowins, 2010a).

Dissociation is thus very central to PTSD, occurring when the stress response system is overwhelmed. It represents a defensive process (although dysregulation might play a role in some instances), blocking fusion of the cognitive and emotional components of a traumatic experience to protect conscious system functioning in the moment, resulting in endless repetition of traumatic elements. Conceptualizing PTSD, or at least the dissociation component, as a form of repetition compulsion advances therapeutic options, because it shifts treatment to strategies that can help fuse the dissociated elements, namely ones such as reactivating the grieving process and art therapy. By fusing these elements, the other components of PTSD—avoidance of traumatic stimuli and hyper-vigilance—are more likely to diminish or resolve.

Dissociation Summary

Dissociation is a complex entity, but is more understandable when conceived of as some alteration in stress response system connectivity, involving psychological and/or somatic functioning. Somatic dissociation is very closely linked to psychological dissociation given that mind is body too, related to how mind is brain and brain is body. Mind-body fusion is how nature works, and this occurrence is reflected in the synchronization evident with healthy stress response system functioning. Alterations of the synchronized connectivity of the stress response can be due to defensive functioning and/or dysregulation. Milder forms of psychological dissociation, such as absorption, are almost universally defensive and adaptive. More extreme forms, including amnesia and identity fragmentation, arise from intense negative circumstances and tend to only be adaptive in the moment of trauma, with dysfunctional behavior emerging over time.

Somatic dissociation can also be due to dysregulation or defense, the latter involving a disconnection from disturbing emotional states, and then conversion to a bodily form that is often easier for others to acknowledge and attend to, resulting in reinforcement and tension reduction. Psychological and somatic dissociation occur on a spectrum in terms of the intensity of their expression, linked to the degree of distress/anxiety experienced. Somatic dissociation is best conceived of as, first, that related to particular physiological systems, and second that comprising general syndromes not directly linked to any particular physiological system, as opposed to categories such as somatization. Extreme distress in the form of trauma commonly results in PTSD, with dissociation defensively blocking the fusion of the emotional and cognitive aspects of the traumatic experience to protect conscious system functioning in the moment, resulting in endless repetition of dissociated elements cognitive, emotional, somatic, and behavioral.

References

Aaron, L.A. & Buchwald, D. (2001). A review of the evidence for overlap among unexplained clinical conditions. *Annals of Internal Medicine, 134*, 868-881.

Aaron, L.A., Burke, M.M., & Buchwald, D. (2000). Overlapping conditions among patients with chronic fatigue syndrome. *Archives of Internal Medicine, 160*, 221-227.

Abramowitz, J.S. & Braddock, A.E. (2006). Hypochondriasis: Conceptualization, treatment, and relationship to obsessive-compulsive disorder. *Psychiatry Clinics of North America, 29*(2), 503-519.

Allen, J. & Lolafaye, C. (1995). Dissociation and vulnerability to psychotic experience: The dissociative experiences scale and the MMPI-2. *The Journal of Nervous and Mental Disease, 183*(10), 615-622.

American Psychiatric Association (2013). *Diagnostic & Statistical Manual 5*. Washington, DC: American Psychiatric Publishing.

Anderson, M. & Levy, B. (2009). Suppressing unwanted memories. *Current Directions in Psychological Science, 18*(4), 189-194.

Anglin, S.M. (2014). I think, therefore I am? Examining conceptions of the self, soul, and mind. *Consciousness & Cognition, 29*, 105-116.

Avia, M.D. (1999). The development of illness beliefs. *Journal of Psychosomatic Research, 47*(3), 199-204.

Avrahami, D. (2005). Visual art therapy's unique contribution in the treatment of post-traumatic stress disorders. *Journal of Trauma & Dissociation, 6*(4), 5-38.

Badura, A.S., Reiter, R.C., Altmaier, E.M., Rhomberg, A., & Elas, D. (1997). Dissociation, somatization, substance abuse, and coping with women with chronic pelvic pain. *Obstetrics & Gynecology, 90*(3), 405-410.

Bedard-Gilligan, M. & Zoellner, L.A. (2012). Dissociation and memory fragmentation in post-traumatic stress disorder: An evaluation of the dissociative encoding hypothesis. *Memory, 20*(3), 277-299.

Benbadis, S.R. (2005). The problem of psychogenic symptoms: Is the psychiatric community in denial? *Epilepsy & Behavior, 6*(1), 9-14.

Bernstein, E.M. & Putman, F.W. (1986). Development, reliability and validity of a dissociation scale. *Journal of Nervous and Mental Disease, 174*, 727-735.

Bibring, E. (1943). The conception of the repetition compulsion. *Psychoanalytic Quarterly, 12*, 486-519.

Birnbaum, M.H. & Thomann, K. (1996). Visual function in multiple personality disorder. *Journal of the American Optomologists Association, 67*(6), 327-334.

Bovin, M.J. & Marx, B.P. (2011). The importance of peritraumatic experience in defining traumatic stress. *Psychological Bulletin, 137*(1), 47-67.

Bowins, B. (2004). Psychological defense mechanisms: A new perspective. *American Journal of Psychoanalysis, 64*, 1-26.

Bowins, B.E. (2006a). How psychiatric treatments can enhance psychological defense mechanisms. *American Journal of Psychoanalysis, 66*, 173-194.

Bowins, B.E. (2006b). *The Cruelest Cut of All: The Modern Medical Nightmare of Post-Vasectomy Pain Syndrome*. West Conshohocken, PA: Infinity Publishing.

Bowins, B.E. (2010a). Repetitive maladaptive behavior: Beyond repetition compulsion. *The American Journal of Psychoanalysis, 70*, 282-298.

Bowins, B.E. (2012c). Therapeutic dissociation: Compartmentalization and absorption. *Counselling Psychology Quarterly, 25*(1), 307-317.

Bowlby, J. (1988). Developmental psychiatry comes of age. *American Journal of Psychiatry, 145*, 1-10.

Boysen, G.A. (2011). The scientific status of childhood dissociative identity disorder: A review of published research. *Psychotherapy & Psychosomatics, 80*(6), 329-334.

Braddock, A.E. & Abramowitz, J.S. (2006). Listening to hypochondriasis and hearing health anxiety. *Expert Review of Neurotherapeutics, 6*(9), 1307-1312.

Brenner, I. (1994). The dissociative character: A reconsideration of "multiple personality." *Journal of the American Psychoanalytic Association, 42*(3), 819-846.

Brewin, C.R. & Holmes, E.A. (2003). Psychological theories of posttraumatic stress disorder. *Clinical Psychology Review, 23*, 339-376.

Brown, R.J. (2006). Different types of "dissociation" have different psychological mechanisms. *Journal of Trauma & Dissociation, 7*(4), 7-28.

Brown, R.J., Cardena, E., Nijenhuis, E., Sar, V., & Van Der Hart, O. (2007). Should conversion disorder be reclassified as a dissociative disorder in DSM V? *Psychosomatics, 48*(5), 369-378.

Buchwald, D. & Garrity, D. (1994). Comparison of patients with chronic fatigue syndrome, fibromyalgia, and multiple chemical sensitivities. *Archives of Internal Medicine, 154*, 2049-2053.

Butani, L. & O'Connell, E.J. (1997). Functional respiratory disorders. *Annals of Allergy & Asthma Immunology, 79*(2), 91-99.

Castillo, R.J. (2003). Trance, functional psychosis, and culture. *Psychiatry, 66*(1), 9-21.

Chiu, C.D., Yeh, Y.Y., Huang, Y.M., Wu, Y.C., & Chiu, Y.C. (2009). The set switching function of nonclinical dissociators under negative emotion. *Journal of Abnormal Psychology, 118*(1), 214-222.

Cohen, J. (1980). Structural consequences of psychic trauma: A new look at "beyond the pleasure principle." *International Journal of Psychoanalysis, 61*, 421-432.

DeCarvalho, M.R., Dias, G.P., Cosci, F., De-Melo-Neto, V.L., Bevilaqua, M.C., Gardino, P.F., & Nardi, A.E. (2010). Current findings of fMRI in panic disorder: Contributions for the fear neurocircuitry and CBT effects. *Expert Reviews Neurotherapeutics, 10*(2), 291-303.

Dorahy, M.J., Brand, B.L., Sar, V., Kruger, C., Stavropoulos, P., Martinez-Taboas, A. et al (2014). Dissociative identity disorder: An empirical review. *Australian & New Zealand Journal of Psychiatry, 48*(5), 402-417.

Douzenis, A. & Seretis, D. (2013). Descriptive and predictive validity of somatic attributions in patients with somatoform disorders: A systematic review of quantitative research. *Journal of Psychosomatic Research, 75*(3), 199-210.

Dresler, T., Guhn, A., Tupak, S.V., Ehlis, A.C., Hermann, M.J., Fallgatter, A.J. et al (2013). Revise the revised? New dimensions of the neuroanatomical hypothesis of panic disorder. *Journal of Neural Transmission, 120*(1), 3-29.

Ellason, J.W., Ross, C.A., & Fuchs, D.L. (1996). Lifetime axis I and II comorbidity and childhood trauma history in dissociative identity disorder. *Psychiatry, 59*(3), 255-266.

Escobar, J.I. & Gureje, O. (2007). Influence of cultural and social factors on the epidemiology of idiopathic somatic complaints and syndromes. *Psychosomatic Medicine, 69*(9), 841-845.

Farb, N.A., Segal, Z.V., Mayberg, H., Bean, J., McKeon, D., Fatima, Z., & Anderson, A.K. (2007). Attending to the present: Mindfulness meditation reveals distinct neural modes of self-reference. *Social Cognitive & Affective Neuroscience, 2*(4), 313-322.

Farley, M. & Barkan, H. (1997). Somatization, dissociation, and tension-reducing behaviors in psychiatric outpatients. *Psychotherapy & Psychosomatics, 66*(3), 133-140.

Ferracuti, S., Sacco, R., & Lazzari, R. (1996). Dissociative trance disorder: Clinical and Rorschach findings in 10 persons reporting demon possession and treated by exorcism. *Journal of Personality Assessment, 66*(3), 525-539.

Fikretoglu, D., Brunet, A., Best, S., Metzler, T., Delucchi, K., Weiss, D.S. et al (2006). The relationship between peritraumatic distress and peritraumatic dissociation: An examination of two competing models. *Journal of Nervous & Mental Disease, 194*(11), 853-858.

Fischer, D.G. & Elnitsky, S. (1990). A factor analytic study of two scales measuring dissociation. *American Journal of Clinical Hypnosis, 32*, 201-207.

Fishbain, D.A., Lewis, J.E., Gao, J., Cole, B., & Steele-Rosomoff, R. (2009). Is chronic pain associated with somatization/hypochondriasis? An evidence-based structured review. *Pain Practice, 9*(6), 449-467.

Fochtmann, L.J. (1995). Intractable sneezing as a conversion symptom. *Psychosomatics, 36*(2), 103-112.

Ford, C.V. (1997). Somatization and fashionable diagnoses: Illness as a way of life. *Scandinavian Journal of Work & Environmental Health, 23*(Suppl 3), 7-16.

Forrest, K.A. (2001). Toward an etiology of dissociative identity disorder: A neurodevelopmental approach. *Consciousness & Cognition, 10*(3), 259-293.

Forstmann, M. & Burgmer, P. (2015). Adults are intuitive mind-body dualists. *Journal of Experimental Psychology General, 144*(1), 222-235.

Freud, S. (1914). *Remembering, Repeating and Working-Through (Further Recommendations on the Technique of Psycho-Analysis II)*. S.E. XII. London: The Hogarth Press.

Freud, S. (1920). *Beyond the Pleasure Principle*. S.E. XIIX. London: The Hogarth Press.

Freud, S. (1926). *Inhibitions, Symptoms and Anxiety*. S.E. XX. London: The Hogarth Press.

Gershuny, B.S. & Thayer, J.F. (1999). Relations among psychological trauma, dissociative phenomena, and trauma-related distress: A review and integration. *Clinical Psychology Review, 19*(5), 631-657.

Glantz, K. & Pearce, J. (1989). *Exiles from Eden: Psychotherapy from an Evolutionary Perspective*. New York: W.W. Norton & Company.

Goel, N., Workman, J.L., Lee, T.T., Innala, L., & Viau, V. (2014). Sex differences in the HPA axis. *Comprehensive Psychiatry, 4*(3), 1121-1125.

Goldstein, L.H., Drew, C., Mellers, J., Mitchell-O'Malley, S., & Oakley, D.A. (2000). Dissociation, hypnotizability, coping styles and health locus of control: Characteristics of pseudoseizure patients. *Seizure, 9*(5), 314-322.

Gupta, M.A. (2006). Somatization disorders in dermatology. *International Review of Psychiatry, 18*(1), 41-47.

Gupta, M.A. & Gupta, A.K. (2006). Medically unexplained cutaneous sensory symptoms may represent somatoform dissociation: An empirical study. *Journal of Psychosomatic Research, 60*(2), 131-136.

Hall, J.M. (2003). Dissociative experiences of women child abuse survivors: A selective constructivist review. *Trauma Violence Abuse, 4*(4), 283-308.

Hart, J. & Bjorgvinsson, T. (2010). Health anxiety and hypochondriasis: Description and treatment issues highlighted through a case illustration. *Bulletin of the Menninger Clinic, 74*(2), 122-140.

Harth, W., Hermes, B., Niemeier, V., & Gieler, U. (2006). Clinical pictures and classification of somatoform disorders in dermatology. *European Journal of Dermatology, 16*(6), 607-614.

Herman, J.P. (2012). Neural pathways of stress integration: Relevance to alcohol abuse. *Alcohol Research, 34*(4), 441-447.

Hill, R.J., Chopra, P., & Richardi, T. (2012). Rethinking the psychogenic model of complex regional pain syndrome: Somatoform disorders and complex regional pain syndromes. *Anesthesia & Pain Medicine, 2*(2), 54-59.

Holmes, E.A., Brown, R.J., Mansell, W., Fearon, R.P., Hunter, E.C., Frasquilho, F., & Oakley, D.A. (2005). Are there two qualitatively distinct forms of dissociation? A review and some clinical implications. *Clinical Psychology Review, 25*, 1-23.

Holzschneider, K. & Mulert, C. (2011). Neuroimaging in anxiety disorders. *Dialogues Of Clinical Neuroscience, 13*(4), 453-461.

Horowitz, M.J. (1976). *Stress Response Syndrome*. New York: Jason Aronson.

Hunter, E.C., Phillips, M.L., Chadler, T., Sierra, M., & Davis, A.S. (2003). Depersonalisation disorder: A cognitive-behavioural conceptualisation. *Behavior Research & Therapy, 41*(12), 1451-1467.

Hunter, E.C., Sierra, M., & Davis, A.S. (2004). The epidemiology of depersonalization and derealisation: A systematic review. *Social Psychiatry & Psychiatric Epidemiology, 39*(1), 9-18.

Hurlimann, F., Kupferschmid, S., & Simon, A.E. (2012). Cannabis-induced depersonalization disorder in adolescence. *Neuropsychobiology, 65*(3), 141-146.

Hymer, S. (1984). Absorption as a therapeutic agent. *Journal of Contemporary Psychotherapy, 14*(2), 93-198.

Inderbitzin, L. & Levy S. (1998). Repetition compulsion revisited: Implications for technique. *Psychoanalytic Quarterly, LXVII*, 32-53.

Janet, P. (1901). *The Mental State of Hystericals: A Study of Mental Stigmata and Mental Accidents*. New York: Putman.

Janet, P. (1925). *Psychological Healing* (Vol. 1). New York: Macmillan.

Jasper, F., Egloff, B., Roalfe, A., & Witthoft, M. (2015). Latent structure of irritable bowel syndrome symptom severity. *World Journal of Gastroenterology, 21*(1), 292-300.

Kanaan, R.A., Lepine, J.P., & Wessely, S.C. (2007). The association or otherwise of the functional somatic syndromes. *Psychosomatic Medicine, 69*(9), 855-859.

Keane, T. (1985). A behavioral approach to assessing and treating post-traumatic stress disorders in Vietnam veterans. In *Trauma and Its Wake*. New York: Brunner Mazel.

Kihlstrom, J., Glisky, M., & Angiulo, M. (1994). Dissociative tendencies and dissociative disorders. *Journal of Abnormal Psychology, 103*(1), 117-124.

Kirmayer, L.J. & Looper, K.J. (2006). Abnormal illness behavior: Physiological, psychological and social dimensions of coping with distress. *Current Opinion in Psychiatry, 19*(1), 54-60.

Kozlowska, K. (2007). The developmental origins of conversion disorders. *Clinical Child Psychology & Psychiatry, 12*(4), 487-510.

Kozlowska, K. & Williams, L.M. (2009). Self-protective organization in children with conversion and somatoform disorders. *Journal of Psychosomatic Research, 67*(3), 223-233.

Kriegman, D. & Slavin, M.O. (1989). The myth of the repetition compulsion and the negative therapeutic reaction: An evolutionary biological analysis. *Progress in Self Psychology, 5*, 209-253.

Kumar, R. & Yeragani, V.K. (2010). Psyche and soma: New insights into the connection. *Indian Journal of Psychiatry, 52*(Suppl 1), S233-239.

Kutz, I. (1989). Samson's complex: The compulsion to re-enact betrayal and rage. *British Journal of Medical Psychology, 62*, 123-134.

Kwekkeboom, K, Huseby-Moore, K., & Ward, S. (1998). Imagining ability and effective use of guided imagery. *Research in Nursing & Health, 21*(3), 189-198.

Lambert, M.V., Sierra, M., Phillips, M.L., & David, A.S. (2002). The spectrum of organic depersonalization: A review plus four new cases. *Journal of Neuropsychiatry & Clinical Neuroscience, 14*(2), 141-154.

Lanius, R.A., Brand, B., Vermetten, E., Frewen, P.A., & Spiegel, D. (2012). The dissociative subtype of posttraumatic stress disorder: Rationale, clinical and neurobiological evidence, and implications. *Depression & Anxiety, 29*(8), 701-708.

Lanius, R.A., Vermetten, E., Loewenstein, R.J., Brand, B., Schmahl, C., Bremner, J.D., & Spiegel, D. (2010). Emotion modulation in PTSD: Clinical and neurobiological evidence for a dissociative subtype. *American Journal of Psychiatry, 167*(6), 640-647.

Leitan, N.D. & Murray, G. (2014). The mind-body relationship in psychotherapy: Grounded cognition as an explanatory framework. *Frontiers in Psychology, 20*(5), 472-479.

Leonard, K., Telch, M., & Harrington, P. (1999). Dissociation in the laboratory: A comparison of strategies. *Behavior Research and Therapy, 37*(1), 49-61.

Levy, M. (2000). A conceptualization of the repetition compulsion. *Psychiatry, 63*, 45-53.

Linares, I.M., Trzesniak, C., Chagas, M.H., Hallak, J.E., Nardi, A.E., & Crippa, J.A. (2012). Neuroimaging in specific phobia disorder: A systematic review of the literature. *Review Brasil Psiquiatry, 34*(1), 101-111.

Manning, M.L. & Manning, R.L. (2009). Convergent paradigms for visual neuroscience and dissociative identity disorder. *Journal of Trauma & Dissociation, 10*(4), 405-419.

Marsh, H.W., Morin, A.J., Parker, P.D., & Kaur, G. (2014). Exploratory structural equation modeling: An integration of the best features of exploratory and confirmatory factor analysis. *Annual Review of Clinical Psychology, 10*, 85-110.

Mathew, S.J. & Ho, S. (2006). Etiology and neurobiology of social anxiety disorder. *Journal of Clinical Psychiatry, 67*(Suppl 12), 9-13.

Mayou, R. (1975). The social setting of hysteria. *British Journal of Psychiatry, 127*, 466-469.

Mearin, F. (2011). Postinfectious functional gastrointestinal disorders. *Journal of Clinical Gastroenterology, 45*(Suppl), S102-105.

Mehta, N. (2011). Mind-body dualism: A critique from a health perspective. *Mens Sana Monographs, 9*(1), 202-209.

Merckelbach, H., Devilly, G.J., & Rassin, E. (2002). Alters in dissociative disorder: Metaphors or genuine entities? *Clinical Psychology Review, 22*(4), 481-497.

Mula, M., Pini, S., & Cassano, G.B. (2007). The neurobiology and clinical significance of depersonalization in mood and anxiety disorders: A critical reappraisal. *Journal of Affective Disorders, 99*(1-3), 91-99.

Nijenhuis, E.R., Spinhoven, P., Dyck, R.V., Van Der Hart, O., & Vanderlinden, J. (1996). The development and psychometric characteristics of the somatoform dissociation questionanaire (SDQ-20). *The Journal of Nervous and Mental Disease, 184*, 688-694.

Nijenhuis, E.R., Van Dyck, R., Spinhoven, P., Van Der Hart, O., Chatrou, M., Vanderlinden, J., & Moene, F. (1999). Somatoform dissociation discriminates among diagnostic categories over and above general psychopathology. *Australian & New Zealand Journal of Psychiatry, 33*, 511-520.

Nijenhuis, E.R., Van Dyke, R., Ter Kuile, M.M., Mouritis, M.J., Spinhoven, P., & Van Der Hart, O. (2003). Evidence for associations among somatoform dissociation, psychological dissociation and reported trauma in patients with chronic pelvic pain. *Journal of Psychosomatic Obstetrics & Gynaecology, 24*(2), 87-98.

Ogawa, J.R., Sroufe, L.A., Weinfield, N.S., Carlson, E.A., & Egeland, B. (1997). Development and the fragmented self: Longitudinal study of dissociative symptomatology in a nonclinical sample. *Developmental Psychopathology, 9*(4), 855-879.

Olde-Hartman, T.C., Borghuis, M.S., Lucassen, P.L., Van De Laar, F.A., Speckens, A.E., & Van Weel, C. (2009). Medically unexplained symptoms, somatisation disorder and hypochondriasis: Course and prognosis. A systematic review. *Journal of Psychosomatic Research, 66*(5), 363-377.

Oyama, O., Paltoo, C., & Greengold, J. (2007). Somatoform disorders. *American Family Physician, 76*(9), 1333-1338.

Panksepp, J. (2011). Toward a cross-species neuroscientific understanding of the affective mind: Do animals have emotional feelings? *American Journal of Primatology, 73*(6), 545-561.

Perez, D.L., Dworetzky, B.A., Dickerson, B.C., Leung, L., Cohn, R., Baslet, G., & Silbersweig, D.A. (2014). An integrative neurocircuit perspective on psychogenic nonepileptic seizures and functional movement disorders: Neural functional unawareness. *Clinics in EEG & Neuroscience, 27*, 35-41.

Phillips, M.L. & Sierra, M. (2003). Depersonalization disorder: A functional neuroanatomical perspective. *Stress, 6*(3), 157-165.

Punamaki, R.L., Komproe, I.H., Qouta, S., Elmasri, M., & DeJong, J. (2005). The role of peritraumatic dissociation and gender in the association between trauma and mental health in a Palestinian community sample. *American Journal of Psychiatry, 162*, 545-551.

Reutens, S., Nielsen, O., & Sachdev, P. (2010). Depersonalization disorder. *Current Opinion in Psychiatry, 23*(3), 278-283.

Roberts, N.A. & Reuber, M. (2014). Alterations of consciousness in psychogenic nonepileptic seizures: Emotion, emotion regulation and dissociation. *Epilepsy & Behavior, 30*, 43-49.

Roelofs, K. & Spinhoven, P. (2007). Trauma and medically unexplained symptoms: Towards an integration of cognitive and neuro-biological accounts. *Clinical Psychology Review, 27*(7), 798-820.

Ross, C.A. (1990). Twelve cognitive errors about multiple personality disorder. *American Journal of Psychotherapy, 44*(3), 348-356.

Ross, C., Joshi, S., & Currie, R. (1990). Dissociative experiences in the general population. *American Journal of Psychiatry, 147*(11), 1547-1552.

Ross, C., Joshi, S., & Currie, R. (1991). Dissociative experiences in the general population: A factor analysis. *Hospital and Community Psychiatry, 42*(3), 297-301.

Ross, C.A., Schroeder, E., & Ness, L. (2013). Dissociation and symptoms of culture-bound syndromes in North America: A preliminary study. *Journal of Trauma & Dissociation, 14*(2), 224-235.

Salmon, P., Skaife, K., & Rhodes, J. (2003). Abuse, dissociation, and somatization in irritable bowel syndrome: Towards an explanatory model. *Journal of Behavioral Medicine, 26*(1), 1-18.

Scaer, R.C. (2001). The neurophysiology of dissociation and chronic disease. *Applied Psychophysiological Biofeedback, 26*(1), 73-91.

Schardt, D., Erk, S, Nusser, C., Nothen, M., Cichon, S., Rietschel, M. et al (2010). Volition diminishes genetically mediated amygdala hyperreactivity. *Neuroimage, 53*(3), 943-951.

Schmidt, S. (2004). Mindfulness and healing intention: Concepts, practice, and research evaluation. *Journal of Alternative and Complementary Medicine, 10*(Suppl 1), S7-14.

Schur, M. (1966). *The Id and the Regulatory Principles of Mental Functioning*. New York: International University Press.

Shorter, E. (1997). *A History of Psychiatry*. Toronto: John Wiley & Sons.

Sierra, M. & David, A.S. (2011). Depersonalization: A selective impairment of self-awareness. *Consciousness & Cognition, 20*(1), 99-108.

Silberg, J.L. (2000). Fifteen years of dissociation in maltreated children: Where do we go from here? *Child Maltreatment, 5*(2), 119-136.

Simeon, D. (2004). Depersonalisation disorder: A contemporary overview. *CNS Drugs, 18*(6), 343-354.

Simon, G.E. & VonKorff, M. (1991). Somatization and psychiatric disorder in the NIMH epidemiologic catchment area study. *American Journal of Psychiatry, 148*(11), 1494-1500.

Spiegel, D., Lewis-Fernandez, R., Lanius, R., Vermetten, E., Simeon, D., & Friedman, M. (2013). Dissociative disorders in DSM-5. *Annual Review of Clinical Psychology, 9*, 299-326.

Spitzer, C., Spelsberg, B., Grabe, H.J., Mundt, B., & Freyberger, H.J. (1999). Dissociative experiences and psychopathology in conversion disorders. *Journal of Psychosomatic Research, 46*(3), 291-294.

Stankiewicz, A.M., Swiergiel, A.H., & Lisowski, P. (2013). Epigenetics of stress adaptations in the brain. *Brain Research Bulletin, 98*, 76-92.

Stein, D.J. & Simeon, D. (2009). Cognitive-affective neuroscience of depersonalization. *CNS Spectrum, 14*(9), 467-471.

Stewart, D.E. (1990). The changing faces of somatization. *Psychosomatics, 31*, 153-158.

Stone, J., Warlow, C., & Sharpe, M. (2010). The symptom of functional weakness: A controlled study of 107 patients. *Brain, 111*(5), 1537-1551.

Thomas, M. & Jankovic, J. (2004). Psychogenic movement disorders: Diagnosis and management. *CNS Drugs, 18*(7), 437-452.

Van Der Hart, O., & Nijenhuis, E.R. (2001). Generalized dissociative amnesia: Episodic, semantic and procedural memories lost and found. *Australian & New Zealand Journal of Psychiatry, 35*(5), 589-600.

Van Der Hart, O., Nijenhuis, E.R., & Steele, K. (2005). Dissociation: An insufficiently recognized major feature of complex posttraumatic stress disorder. *Journal of Trauma & Stress, 18*(5), 413-423.

Van Der Kolk, B.A. (1987). *The Separation Cry and the Trauma Response: Developmental Issues in the Psychology of Attachment and Separation in Psychological Trauma*. Washington, DC: American Psychological Press.

Van Der Kolk, B.A. & Fisler, R. (1995). Dissociation and the fragmentary nature of traumatic memories: Overview and exploratory study. *Journal of Trauma & Stress, 8*(4), 505-525.

Van Der Kruijs, S.J., Bodde, N.M., Carrette, E., Lazeron, R.H., Vonck, K.E., Boon, P.A. et al (2014). Neurophysiological correlates of dissociative symptoms. *Journal of Neurosurgery & Psychiatry, 85*(2), 174-179.

Van Dijke, A., Van Der Hart, O., Ford, J.D., Van Son, M., Van Der Heijden, P., & Buhring, M. (2010). Affect dysregulation and dissociation in borderline personality disorder and somatoform disorder: Differentiating inhibitory and excitatory experiencing states. *Journal of Trauma & Dissociation, 11*(4), 424-443.

Vuilleumier, P. (2005). Hysterical conversion and brain function. *Progress in Brain Research, 150*, 309-329.

Walker, E.A., Katon, W.J., Neraas, K., Jemelka, R.P., & Massoth, D. (1992). Dissociation in women with chronic pelvic pain. *American Journal of Psychiatry, 149*(4), 534-537.

Waller, N., Putnam, F.W., & Carlson, E.B. (1996). Types of dissociation and dissociative types: A taxometric analysis of dissociative experiences. *Psychological Methods, 1*, 300-321.

Weiss, S.J. (2007). Neurobiological alterations associated with traumatic stress. *Perspectives in Psychiatric Care, 43*(3), 114-122.

Wetzel, A.P. (2012). Factor analysis methods and validity evidence: A review of instrument development across the medical education continuum. *Academic Medicine, 87*(8), 1060-1069.

World Health Organization (1992). *The ICD-10 Classification of Mental and Behavioral Disorders: Clinical Descriptions and Diagnostic Guidelines*. Geneva: World Health Organization.

Zaroff, C.M., Davis, J.M., Chio, P.H., & Madhavan, D. (2012). Somatic presentations of distress in China. *Australian & New Zealand Journal of Psychiatry, 46*(11), 1053-1057.

CHAPTER 8

Eating Disorders

Due to how profoundly food consumption, and related reproductive strategies, impact evolutionary fitness, it is understandable that eating behavior and disorders comprise a naturally occurring entity. Anorexia nervosa, bulimia nervosa, and binge eating disorder (BED) represent the current eating disorders, based on DSM-5 (American Psychiatric Association, 2013) and ICD-10 focusing on anorexia and bulimia (World Health Organization, 1992). Interestingly, the most common "eating" disorder, obesity, is not even included, although ICD-10 does list overeating associated with other psychological disturbances (World Health Organization, 1992). Obesity is present in about 1 in 3 Americans and 1 in 4 Canadians, and about half the population in these countries is overweight (Ogden et al, 2006; Taubes, 2011; Taylor, 2012). Excessive weight applies to children as well, with 1 in 10 Canadian children suffering from obesity, and at least this many in America (Ogden et al, 2006; Taubes, 2011; Taylor, 2012). Obesity is defined as a Body Mass Index (BMI) of 30 and over (Maskarinec et al, 2006; Taubes, 2011). BMI is weight in kilograms divided by the square of height in meters; in essence it evaluates weight relative to height (Maskarinec et al, 2006; Taubes, 2011). BMI does not directly measure the percent of body fat, but higher values mean more weight for the given height. Unless a person is extremely muscular, higher values indicate a weight and fat problem. A BMI of 25-29.9 means that a person is overweight, and many more people tend to be overweight than obese, with upwards of half the population in the developed world being somewhat overweight (Maskarinec et al, 2006; Ogden et al, 2006; Taubes, 2011).

Considering how common excessive weight and obesity is, the role of psychological factors in its initiation and maintenance, and psychological problems arising from it, this occurrence represents one of the most common mental health problems there is. In addition, several psychiatric medications (predominately the second generation antipsychotics) increase weight, and even worse promote the metabolic syndrome, consisting of various abnormalities of metabolism, such as raised bad cholesterol, reduced good cholesterol, elevated glucose levels in the blood, insulin resistance (an inability to store the raised blood sugar), and increased blood pressure (Aronne, 2003; Bessesen et al, 2008;

Kraschnewski et al, 2010; Taylor, 2012). Metabolic syndrome greatly increases the risk of several related diseases including diabetes, heart attacks, hypertension, and stroke (Aronne, 2003; Bessesen et al, 2008; Kraschnewski et al, 2010). Hence, the omission or lack of emphasis on obesity under eating disorders in psychiatric diagnostic systems is striking. Excessive food intake and weight, not just associated with binging, will be considered in the current chapter.

Continuums, Regulation, and Defense

The key issues of continuums, regulation, and defense blend together very smoothly when it comes to eating disorders, although there are very few definitive conclusions. Many eating disorder behaviors can be viewed as an expression of dysregulation, or alternatively as a defensive reaction, or both processes applying to different individuals in various settings.

Continuums

When continuums are considered it is useful to conceptualize them in terms of, first, eating disorder categories such as anorexia and bulimia, and second, potential dimensions underlying these. To address the first issue, taxometric research is informative. Taxometric studies indicate that categories of eating disorders do occur (Gleaves et al, 2004; Hilbert et al, 2011; Mitchell et al, 2007; Williamson et al, 2005). Williamson et al (2005), in reviewing several taxometric studies, conclude that binge eating (and possibly purging) and anorexia nervosa, at least the restrictive type, are distinct. Gleaves et al (2004), reviewing 30 years of research, found support for the position that binge eating is distinct from anorexia, in line with the results of Williamson et al (2005).

Based on a sample of 687 patients being evaluated for eating disorders, Mitchell et al (2007) also found support for the distinction between anorexia and bulimia. However, they found that there is much more variation and mixing than is often considered, with for example overweight individuals with little traditional eating disorder symptoms (Mitchell et al, 2007), supporting the inclusion of obesity as a separate eating disorder. Of the 687 patients evaluated, 403 received the catchall diagnosis of eating disorder not otherwise specified, with latent profile analysis revealing that these patients actually fit into dimensions of anorexia, bulimia, and BED, being on the lower range, a result indicating that the "not otherwise specified" designation can be replaced with a continuous profile of the three eating disorder categories (Mitchell et al, 2007). Binge eating disorder is the least solid diagnosis as it can be seen as part of the bulimia continuum, representing a milder version with no purging. Hilbert et al (2011) found evidence that BED is a distinct taxon from affective and anxiety disorders, but the issue of whether it is truly distinct from bulimia was not addressed. Mitchell et al (2007) noted that some individuals have higher rates of vomiting than binge eating and vice versa, suggesting more of a continuum within bulimia.

Non-taxometric research is also informative regarding the number of distinct eating disorder dimensions. Hay and Fairburn (1998) examining a population of 250 young women with recurrent binge eating could not distinguish BED from non-purging bulimia, based on present state features, but the outcome of BED was better at one year. The researchers conclude that there is a continuum from BED (mildest) to bulimia non-purging (moderate) to bulimia purging (Hay & Fairburn, 1998). Comparing the quantity and quality of binge eating between BED and bulimia, Fitzgibbon and Blackman (2000) concluded that there is no difference in quantity, but bulimics consumed more calories and sugar overall. These results suggest that BED is really on a spectrum, with bulimia representing the milder portion of the range, a conclusion that intuitively makes sense given that binging is less extreme and damaging than purging, and the combination (full bulimia) is most severe. A study by Stice et al (1998) comparing normal, subthreshold bulimics, and bulimic women concluded that there is a continuum, at least based on weight concern and psychopathology. Hence, regarding the issue of distinct eating disorder dimensions, it appears that anorexia and bulimia qualify, with BED being a milder variant on the bulimic spectrum. Obesity/overweight also appear to be a distinct continuum ranging from thin (but not anorexic) to obese, based on the lack of traditional eating disorder symptoms (Mitchell et al, 2007), and distinct pathology in anorexia, although it is possible that excessive weight is on a continuum with anorexia.

Regarding the number of dimensions underlying the primary ones, there are a large number of potential candidates, including drive for thinness, calorie restriction, weight preoccupation, drive for muscle mass, body dissatisfaction, body image cognitive distortions, impulsivity, compulsivity, perfectionism, and exercise addiction (Wildes & Marcus, 2013). Drive for thinness is frequently noted in the literature as well as popular conceptualizations of anorexia, and is tightly linked to calorie restriction, weight preoccupation, and drive for muscle mass (Wildes & Marcus, 2013). It is also extensively influenced by social and cultural norms (Wildes & Marcus, 2013; Williamson, 1998). Drive for thinness and drive for muscularity are related, overlapping in 65.4% of female and male college students in one study (Kelley et al, 2010). The presence of both drives predicts body compulsivity and body anxiety in females, and body self-esteem in males (Kelley et al, 2010).

Compulsivity, perfectionism, and impulsivity represent dimensions commonly linked to eating disorders, with compulsivity and perfectionism tied to anorexia, and impulsivity to bulimia and binge eating. Bardone-Cone et al (2010) examined perfectionism and recovery from eating disorders, finding that fully recovered and healthy young women had significantly lower levels of perfectionism than partially recovered and active eating disorder individuals. They cite perfectionism as an impediment to recovery (Bardone-Cone et al, 2010). High negative perfectionism (concern over not meeting personal standards) is present in a range of mental health conditions, and appears to be something that is difficult to change given the perceived value to the individual

(Egan et al, 2013). Compulsivity is often noted in anorexia, and has been linked to "over-control" characterized by rigidity, compulsivity, inhibition, and avoidance (Wildes & Marcus, 2013). Both perfectionism and compulsivity qualify as defensive responses to stress, providing the anorexic individual with a sense of control not present in other areas of their life. Even the stress of body dissatisfaction has been found to increase perfectionism (Jones et al, 2007). Perhaps based on the defensive role of compulsive and perfectionistic behavior, it is often maintained despite the impediment it can present to recovery (Bardone-Cone et al, 2010).

Impulsivity is an under-controlled reaction to stress linked with bulimia and BED (Wildes & Marcus, 2013), although impulsivity is not present in all bulimic individuals (Tseng & Hu, 2012). Impaired regulation is typically associated with impulsive behavior, and this seems to apply to binge and purge symptoms given their under-controlled nature (Wildes & Marcus, 2013). Conceptualizing eating disorders as over-controlled, under-controlled, and also low psychopathology (as applies frequently to obesity) does seem to have some merit based upon the ability of this scheme to predict outcome, recovery, and associated characteristics (Bardone-Cone et al, 2010; Wildes & Marcus, 2013), although overlap occurs such as with more compulsive over-controlled bulemics.

Exercise adherence or addiction is another potential dimension underlying eating disorder categories. Elbourne and Chen (2007) applied structural equation modeling to longitudinal data on female triathletes, finding support for the continuum model of obligatory exercise. In addition to obligatory exercise behavior, weight and shape preoccupation also played a role in the range of eating disorder behavior amongst these athletes (Elbourne & Chen, 2007). Exploring the reasons given by women regarding why they exercise excessively, Johnston et al (2011) found that the need to control their body was paramount, with exercise being viewed as superior to disturbed eating, suggesting a defensive function to excessive exercise. Based on a review of eating behavior in elite athletes, Sundgot-Borgen and Torstveit (2010) found that disordered eating was most likely in sports emphasizing a thin body size/shape, a high power-to-weight ratio, and weight categories, highlighting the role of social influence and other external forces in their eating behavior.

A very internal dimension that seems to play a key role in eating disorder behavior is cognitive distortions related to body image. Konstantakopoulos et al (2012) applied the Brown Assessment of Beliefs Scale (BABS) to assess delusionality of body image beliefs in 39 anorexic and 33 bulimic participants. Only anorexics (29%) experienced delusional level body image beliefs, but less extreme over-valued ideas were common with anorexic and bulimic subjects (Konstantakopoulos et al, 2012). The researchers suggest that their results support a continuum with the extreme end of delusional beliefs impairing insight in some anorexics (Konstantakopoulos et al, 2012). Recall the discussion regarding the spectrum of cognitive distortions in the "Psychosis" chapter, with delusional beliefs on the extreme end. Cognitive distortions of varying levels of intensity apply to body image in eating disorder subjects.

Highlighting how body image distortions are crucial to eating disorder pathology, and certainly in the case of anorexia, Castellini et al (2013) induced body image distortions in anorexic women and evaluated neural responses using fMRI, comparing the results to those found in healthy controls. Anorexic subjects showed increased activation in the dorsolateral PFC in response to distortions of their own body in the overweight direction, whereas healthy subjects had the same response to distortions in the overly thin direction (Castellini et al, 2013). The greater the activation with anorexic subjects the worse their eating disorder pathology (Castellini et al, 2013). Perpina et al (2011) examined intrusive thoughts related to eating in a large non-clinical sample of women, and found that a continuum of such thoughts occur pertaining to appearance-dieting, need to exercise, and thought-impulse links related to eating. The high dietary restraint subjects showed the most intense eating related intrusive thoughts (Perpina et al, 2011). Cognitions in eating disorder subjects are biased in favor of selectively processed information related to fatness/thinness, dieting, and control of food intake or body weight, all relevant to body image (Williamson et al, 1999).

The continuums of drive for thinness (and related calorie restriction, weight preoccupation, and drive for muscle mass), compulsivity/perfectionism, and impulsivity, exercise adherence, and body image cognitive distortions can contribute to the dimensions of anorexia and bulimia (including binge eating) in several ways. Anorexia links to the continuums of a greater drive for thinness, compulsivity/perfectionism, exercise addiction, and body image cognitive distortions favoring weight reduction. Bulimia links to impulsivity and a lesser drive for thinness, more limited exercise addiction, and body image distortions involving body dissatisfaction but not favoring thinness. This is not to say that these continuums cause anorexia and bulimia, but rather that they support these eating disorder continuums, and in turn the presence of anorexia and bulimia reinforce the dimensions underlying them. For example, a person suffering from anorexia is motivated to remain thin, with excessive exercise often helping maintain lower weight, and lower weight (at least to a certain point) makes it easier to exercise. To better understand why anorexia and bulimia occur we also have to consider regulation, defense, and ultimate causation in contrast to proximal causation.

Regulation

Perhaps the key aspect of regulation implicated in eating disorders is emotional dysregulation. Several processes mitigating, intensifying, and maintaining a given emotion pertain to emotional regulation (Fiore et al, 2014; Racine & Wildes, 2013). To clarify the nature of emotional dysregulation and facilitate its evaluation, Gratz and Roemer (2004) developed the Difficulties in Emotion Regulation Scale (DERS). Various aspects of emotional dysregulation are assessed in six subscales: Lack of awareness of emotional responses, lack of clarity of emotional responses, non-acceptance of emotional responses, limited access to emotion regulation strategies perceived as effective, difficulties controlling impulses when experiencing negative emotions, and difficulties engaging in goal-directed behaviors when experiencing negative emotions (Gratz & Roemer, 2004). The DERS has been applied in many studies of eating disorders, demonstrating how emotional dysregulation plays a prominent role in anorexia and bulimia.

Focusing on anorexia, Racine and Wildes (2013) discovered that while the various forms of emotional dysregulation are associated with eating disorder cognitive distortions, only lack of emotional awareness is independently so. Binge eating and recurrent purging in anorexia are linked to difficulties controlling impulses when experiencing negative emotions, consistent with the impulsive under-controlled aspect of binging and purging observed with bulimia (Racine and Wildes, 2013). Highlighting the importance of cognitions, no significant relationship emerged between actual BMI and emotional dysregulation (Racine & Wildes, 2013). In a follow-up study, Racine and Wildes (2014) found that emotional dysregulation predicted change in anorexia symptom severity, but not the reverse. Other research has also found a relationship between anorexia and emotional dysregulation. Alexythymia, associated with a lack of awareness of emotional responses, is present in anorexia to a greater extent than in controls (Gilboa-Schechtman et al, 2006). Anorexics also have difficulty recognizing emotions in others, making it difficult to regulate their own emotional reactions (Harrison et al, 2009). Hypersensitivity, at least self-perceived sensory, is associated with greater emotional dysregulation, and this hypersensitivity persists even with recovery from anorexia and improved emotional regulation (Merwin et al, 2013).

Emotional dysregulation is also present in bulimia. Lavender et al (2014) administered the DERS to 80 adults (90% women) with bulimia, and found that the global DERS score correlated significantly with eating disorder behavior. Specifically, the difficulties engaging in goal-directed behaviors when experiencing negative emotions subscale was associated with the frequency of purging and driven exercise, although none of the subscales was linked to binging (Lavender et al, 2014). The difficulties controlling impulses when experiencing negative emotions aspect of emotional dysregulation was associated with bulimia, as it was to anorexic binging and recurrent purging in the Racine and Wildes (2013) study. For example, negative urgency, defined as the tendency to act impulsively in response to negative affect, is increased when there is binging and purging (Fischer et al, 2008). Despite the apparent role of impulse control in binge and purging, it only accounts for about 9% of the variance in objective binge episodes and 3% of the variance in purging, highlighting how many other influences must apply (Racine & Wildes, 2013). An interesting contributor to emotional dysregulation might be the Amplification Effect discussed in the chapters pertaining to depression and anxiety, given how negative emotions and associated cognitions interact to reinforce each other, to the point where emotions can become overwhelming and difficult to regulate (Bowins, 2004). Behaviors following from the unregulated emotions can produce further emotional responses, fueling the negative emotion-cognitive cycle (Bowins, 2004).

Acting both independently and via their influence on emotional dysregulation are other factors pertinent to psychological regulation, including personality traits, abuse, attachment, the stress response system, neural alterations, and executive functioning. As pertains to personality, Podar et al (1999), comparing eating disorder patients to both a weight-reduction training group and control group, found that neuroticism is the main personality dimension linked to eating disorders, although openness to experience and conscientiousness also contribute. Neuroticism involves excessive emotional reactivity, and hence likely contributes to emotional dysregulation. High harm avoidance was found to be associated with eating disorders in another study (Fassino et al, 2004). High harm avoidance often implies excessive anxiety, and this can contribute to emotional dysregulation problems.

Trauma appears to play a role in eating disorders, with childhood abuse being particularly noteworthy. Studies have attempted to discern the path from childhood abuse to eating disorders. Focusing on a sample of adults seeking treatment for eating disorders, Tasca et al (2013) applied structural equation models to questionnaire responses regarding variables related to abuse. Their results suggest that attachment insecurity involving emotional dysregulation likely mediates the relationship between childhood abuse and eating disorders (Tasca et al, 2013). In a similar study also applying a cross sectional design and mediation models, emotional dysregulation and dissociation emerged as intervening variables between childhood abuse and eating disorders (Moulton et al, 2015). Of course, cross sectional designs cannot demonstrate causation, only possible associations.

Highly connected to childhood abuse issues are attachment problems, although the nature of the relationship between childhood trauma, attachment, and eating disorders is not entirely clear. Ringer and Crittenden (2007) assessed attachment in young women with anorexia, bulimia, and bulimic anorexia, finding that anxious attachment primarily occurred, characterized by coercive strategies or coercive plus dismissing strategies. Delvecchio et al (2014) examined attachment style in anorexic patients, finding a high rate of unresolved attachment (60%) and pathological mourning (64.4%). The authors indicate that many of their subjects experienced loss or perceived loss of an attachment figure, resulting in pathological mourning that accounts for symptoms such as yearning for the lost object and fear of abandonment (Delvecchio et al, 2014). In another study, Patton (1992) discovered that in a sample of women with eating disorders abandonment stimuli triggered increased food consumption, compared to a control group. Hence, loss of attachment figures in early life appears to contribute to eating disorders.

Considering how neurologically based attachment is, and also the impact of childhood trauma on the maturing nervous system, it is understandable that neural and related hormonal changes that occur are capable of impairing regulation over healthy adaptive functioning, including that pertaining to eating behavior. Research evidence suggests dysregulation of the stress response system in eating disorders. Ginty et al (2012) compared 12 women with disordered eating to 12 healthy controls, before and after a stressful mental arithmetic task, measuring indicators of the stress response system, such as salivary cortisol and cardiovascular parameters. They found that the eating disorder group experienced blunted cortisol and altered heart rate, cardiac output, and stroke volume, supporting the position that eating disorders are characterized by dysregulation of the autonomic stress response system (Ginty et al, 2012). A key component of the stress response system—the hypothalamic-pituitary-adrenal axis (HPA)—also appears to be impaired (Birketvedt et al, 2006). The issue of brain changes associated with eating disorders is complex and beyond the scope of this chapter, but evidence indicates dysregulation of frontal cortical neural networks and regional reward systems (Stefano et al, 2013). One of the difficulties in establishing neural changes linked to eating disorders is uncertainty as to whether the neural changes contribute to the eating disorder or are a result, such as with anorexia inducing many neural and neuroendocrine changes due to chronic starvation (Miller, 2013).

Some of the neural changes associated with eating disorders relate to executive functions (Spinella & Lyke, 2004). Fagundo et al (2012) compared anorexic and obese subjects to healthy controls on measures of executive functioning, with the finding that anorexic and obese individuals were impaired on cognitive flexibility and decision-making compared to controls, and obese individuals further showing significantly impaired response inhibition relative to anorexics. In another study obese individuals with binge eating demonstrated reduced response inhibition and attention compared to obese individuals without binge eating, but cognitive flexibility was not impaired (Mobbs et al, 2011).

The various forces impacting on regulation of eating behavior—emotional dysregulation, personality traits, abuse, attachment, the stress response system, neural alterations, and executive functioning—can in total have a profoundly negative impact on this regulation, thereby contributing to eating disorder pathology. Even on its own, emotional dysregulation appears to impair the regulation of eating behavior, and is intensified by some of the other influences. Although psychological defense might appear to be dwarfed by these regulatory issues, in at least some instances eating disorder behavior appears to serve a defensive or compensatory function.

Defense

While more research has examined the role of emotional dysregulation and other influences impacting on the regulation of eating behavior, some research has been directed to defense. Several studies have investigated classical psychological defenses present in eating disorders, applying the Defense Style Questionnaire. Blaase and Elklit (2001) found that women with eating disorders use immature defenses compared to women without eating disorders, and related to this defense profile, perceive themselves as more exposed to stress and have less efficient ways of coping. Hay and Williams (2013) also found that immature defenses are associated with eating disorders, but an early study by Sullivan et al (1994) failed to identify any consistent pattern of psychological defense in eating disorders, based on qualitative, univariate, and multivariate analyses.

More pertinent to the issue of whether eating disorder behavior itself provides a defensive or compensatory function, Fiore et al (2014) investigated the interaction of emotional dysregulation, anxiety control, and drive for thinness. Their evidence supports emotional dysregulation as the distal factor, with anxiety control a mediating variable influencing the drive for thinness, suggesting that drive for thinness is a compensatory response to emotional dysregulation (Fiore et al, 2014). Perfection and compulsivity producing over-control, particularly in anorexia, can be conceptualized as a defensive response to perceived lack of control, accounting for why such behavior is often maintained even when it hinders recovery (Bardone-Cone et al, 2010; Wildes & Marcus, 2013). Supporting this supposition is Johnston et al's (2011) finding that excessive exercise is often viewed as an adaptive way to control one's body.

Ultimate Causation

The various issues discussed above represent proximal reasons for eating disorders. Left open are the questions of why eating disorders arise in the first place, and why they are far more common in females. To provide an example of the limitations of proximal causation explanations, emotional dysregulation applies to both males and females, and could conceivably produce anxiety instead of eating disorders, so this problem cannot account for eating disorders or explain the very clear preponderance of females. Even when eating disorders occur in males, they often have an excess of feminine traits (Fichter et al, 1985). For ultimate causation we must look at our evolutionary past and examine evolved continuums relevant to energy status.

Feeding behavior is directly linked to evolutionary success given the need of all animals for adequate calories, and also indirectly due to its impact on reproductive success, as evidenced by how a woman suffering from malnutrition is less likely to conceive, carry a pregnancy to term, deliver a healthy baby capable of surviving and reproducing, and successfully nurse and care for that child. Consequently, it appears that continuums related to energy have evolved in humans, although this is speculative. There are various possibilities, with the most likely being food consumption style (quality of food intake), quantity of food consumed, and activity level.

Food Consumption Style

Casual observation of people reveals that there is a range of preferred consumptions styles, from grazers who nibble food throughout the day, to those who take in all their calories in one sitting. Social-cultural influences, such as prescribed meal times, can partially or fully override these natural proclivities, but free of these external influences people gravitate to what feels right for them. These consumption styles almost certainly have their origin in herbivore and carnivore eating patterns, the former favoring grazing due to the low calorie content of the required food, and the latter how meals might be infrequent but extremely high in calorie content when they occur. It follows that "grazers" such as herd animals eat throughout the day, whereas major predators such as tigers do so much less frequently.

Being omnivores we appear to have evolved a continuum of food consumption styles, providing the capacity to adapt to different environments. In an environment with a great deal of low calorie vegetation and a scarcity of prey animals, the ideal food consumption style is grazing. In a cold environment with no vegetation and large prey animals that are difficult to take down, an infrequent, calorie rich style is most adaptive. At the level of each individual, a preference or motivation for a particular consumption style appears to be inherited and/or acquired that expresses itself in the individual's natural eating preference. When the environment aligns with the individual's natural consumption style, the person is likely to do well, but face adaptive challenges when the environment does not align at all. For example, a person who prefers to eat one time per day must learn to adapt to nearly constant nibbling of low calorie food if they are to survive, whereas a grazer adapts easily. For our purposes the key point is that a continuum of food consumption styles seems to have evolved in humans.

Quantity of Food Consumed

Once again casual observation of people reveals, even in children, a wide variation in the quantity of food ingested. Some people seem to eat everything in sight or beyond, whereas others eat very little and have to be encouraged to eat. Social-cultural influences, as with food consumption style, can partially or fully override these natural proclivities, but free of these external influences people will eat the amount that feels right. Each person seems to inherit and/or acquire a preference or motivation level pertaining to the quantity of food consumed. The most adaptive scenario is when the environment matches the person's level of motivation. For example, if high calorie food is readily available, a lower motivation for quantity of food consumed prevents excessive weight that impedes activities such as hunting and evading predators. In our modern developed societies, and increasingly in developing societies too, a high level of motivation for quantity of food consumed contributes to the epidemic of obesity. If an environment is such that food is scarce but abundant at select times, a high motivation can aid an individual in packing on calories required to survive periods of food scarcity. Given the relationship between quantity of food ingested and weight, the higher a person is on the quantity of food consumed continuum the more likely they are to be overweight, and the lower they are on the continuum the more likely they are to be thin, everything else being equal, although the dimension of activity level must also be considered in this regard.

Activity Level

As with the other two energy dimensions, people naturally vary in their activity level. Patterns emerge in childhood, with a range from sloth like to perpetually on. The activity level continuum can be observed in animals both as a species and individually, and the preferred pattern relates to food consumption and evolutionary fitness. Hummingbirds are always on the go because they must consume a large amount of nectar to sustain their high-energy requirements, whereas lions well fed with a large prey animal do as little as possible, aside from mating behavior. People seem to inherit and/or acquire a preference or motivation for activity level. During our evolution a match between environmental circumstances and activity level would favor greater success. For example, in an environment where the hunting-gathering group had to be constantly moving, with elusive prey and isolated pockets of vegetation, a high activity level is most adaptive. If food is concentrated in a local area, and dangerous predators abundant, then staying put and minimizing activity increases the chances of survival.

Interactions between Energy Continuums

In presenting the evolved energy continuums of food consumption style (quality), quantity of food consumed, and activity level, they appear completely independent. As continuums they are hypothesized to be separate, but they interact in multiple ways and hence are not fully independent. Different environmental circumstances can favor various combinations and interactions. For example, in an environment such as our modern day one where high calorie and often low quality food is readily available, a combination of a grazing style to cherry pick high quality items, low motivation for quantity of food consumed, and high activity level is most adaptive, providing for a healthy physique and resistance to diseases such as diabetes. In an environment where predators are abundant and prey animals hard to find, a combination of a food consumption style leaning towards infrequent eating, high motivation pertaining to quantity of food consumed when it is available, and high activity is most adaptive. The continuums directly interact as well, because motivation in one can influence the expression of the others. For example, a high activity level will require a greater quantity of food, extending an individual's level of motivation on this dimension, and will also motivate more frequent food consumption unless high calorie food sources are available.

Relationship between Energy Continuums and Eating Disorders

In following this discussion of evolved energy continuums and their interaction, the relevance to eating disorders might have dawned on readers. Essentially, certain profiles on these dimensions favor particular eating disorders, whereas others are protective. As an obvious example, those who are on the infrequent eating end of the food consumption style continuum will be vulnerable to binge eating and bulimia, whereas those on the grazing end will be resilient to this eating behavior problem. People with a high motivation on the quantity of food consumed dimension, and low motivation on the activity level continuum, are highly vulnerable to obesity, whereas the reverse profile protects against obesity. A very low motivation for quantity of food consumed and high activity level predisposes to anorexia. If this profile is combined with a preference for infrequent food consumption, then binging is more likely to occur in the context of anorexia.

The ultimate causation energy continuums described in this section link to the proximal causation continuums (drive for thinness, calorie restriction, weight preoccupation, drive for muscle mass, body dissatisfaction, body image cognitive distortions, impulsivity, compulsivity, perfectionism, and exercise addiction) underlying eating disorder categories. Impaired regulation due to emotional dysregulation, personality traits, abuse, attachment issues, impeded stress response, neural alterations, and executive functioning problems reduces or removes blocks to extremes on these underlying continuums, resulting in eating disorder behavior. In some instances, such as with over-control (perfectionism and compulsivity), defense functioning can also remove barriers to extremes of select underlying continuums favoring anorexia. When a person's profile on both the proximal underlying continuums and ultimate causation energy continuums align, favoring a given form of disordered eating, an additive effect occurs, resulting in a full-fledged eating disorder. For example, due to emotional dysregulation and compensatory over-control a person's eating behavior shifts to an anorexic pattern; if that person's profile regarding the energy continuums favors anorexia as well (low quantity of food consumed and high activity level), then the profiles are additive, resulting in anorexia. Likewise, if due to emotional dysregulation a person experiences more impulsive eating, and the energy continuum profile also favors binges (infrequent feeding preference and high quantity of food), then bulimia ensues from the additive profiles.

Consistent with their ultimate causation role, energy continuum profiles also slant proximal behavior in a certain direction. For example, if a person has a profile on the energy continuums favoring binge eating, then with childhood abuse and emotional dysregulation, impulsive behavior compatible with binge eating is more likely to occur. If a person has a profile on the energy continuums favoring excessive weight (frequent feeding, high quantity, and low activity level), then under stress, reduced activity and high food intake is more likely to transpire, resulting in obesity. One major issue however remains unanswered, namely why are females so vulnerable to eating disorders?

Female Sex and Eating Disorders

Eating behavior and sexual reproductive success are tightly linked (Abed, 1998; Schneider et al, 2012). Metabolic energy is the most important factor controlling reproductive biology, and food consumption is directly linked to metabolic energy (Schneider et al, 2012). When we consider the relationship between the proposed energy continuums and reproduction, it is crucial to take male/female sex into account. For males the emphasis is on the individual, and how their eating behavior links to their own survival and reproductive success, whereas with females at least two individuals apply, the woman and her offspring. During the 95% of our evolution in nomadic hunting-gathering groups with survival topping out at 30-40 years, reproductive aged women would typically have been pregnant and/or caring for a child. What this means is that the impact of the energy continuums would have been greatly amplified. If too large or too thin, or too active/inactive, relative to environmental circumstances, the evolutionary fitness of a female and her offspring would be severely compromised. For example, if food scarcity was common, then extra weight would aid in her own survival and that of her offspring, whereas if food was quite abundant and widely spaced, and predators numerous, excess weight might well mean a quick end. Males, only having to carry their own mass, would be less impacted by environmental circumstances pertaining to eating and weight, although by no means immune to it.

The relationship between female sex, energy continuums, and the environment extends to the need for women to be attuned to environmental cues pertaining to eating behavior. The social milieu would often communicate preferences related to eating behavior. For example, in the food scarcity environment mentioned above, the social group would value some extra weight, and particularly in females having to carry two individuals. In an abundant food environment with dangerous predators, the social group would value lesser weight, and more so in females. The survival and reproductive success of women would likely have relied on how attuned they were to these social and physical environmental cues, motivating them to adjust their eating behavior and activity level to adapt, a process that would be facilitated by having a level of motivation on the energy continuums compatible with environmental circumstances.

Attunement to these cues ties into mate selection preferences, with the most sought after females being those most likely to successfully bear and raise a child. Abed (1998) believes that eating disorders originated in human female mate attraction and retention strategies, with "archaic female strategies" becoming over-activated or disrupted in the modern environment. At the very least, females appear to be much more sensitive to social cues pertaining to energy related behavior, being more prone to excessive thinness if the culture emphasizes the value of thinness, or excess weight if culturally prescribed, and male attraction patterns link to the social-cultural prescription. For instance, when the culture values thinness most males are attracted to thinner females, but if the culture emphasizes more weight males of that culture are more drawn to overweight females, an occurrence that the females of the particular culture are highly attuned to, given the influence of environmental cues on the weight status of women. Males are also attuned to the social and environmental cues pertaining to the energy continuums, but the process is amplified in females given how in our evolutionary context they were frequently carrying two individuals.

A justifiable critique that has often been leveled at evolutionary theories is that any behavior can be seen as being evolutionarily based if the researcher is creative and convincing enough. Due to this very real problem it is crucial to apply a high bar of credibility for acceptance, and ensure that the proposed mechanism is consistent with established principles, and is also intrinsically logical. The proposed ultimate causation model appears to meet this standard, given how energy related behavior is tightly linked to reproductive success, and the logic of why such behavior is likely amplified in females. Unquestionably, both sexes are attuned to social and environmental cues to reproductive success, and these cues influence mate selection preferences and strategies. The proposed energy continuums of food consumption style, quantity of food consumed, and activity level are not necessarily exclusive, as other continuums might apply, but these three appear to be valid given the range of expressions evident in people, and they have a clear role to play in our evolutionary hunting-gathering context. Furthermore, the proposed model does provide a viable reason for eating disorders being far more common in females.

Eating Disorder Summary

Examining eating disorders from the perspective of proximal and ultimate causation yields a comprehensive understanding. Regarding proximal causation various continuums apply, both in terms of eating disorder categories and underlying processes. Research supports anorexic, bulimic (including binge eating disorder), and also overweight-obesity continuums, although the latter is mysteriously absent from eating disorder classification systems, despite it being the most common eating problem. Overweight-obesity might be part of the anorexic continuum, but with the absence of traditional eating disorder symptoms in many overweight and obese individuals, and the distinct pathology in anorexics, it appears to be a separate continuum ranging from thin (but not anorexic) to obese.

Potential continuums underlying actual eating disorders include drive for thinness, calorie restriction, weight preoccupation, drive for muscle mass, body dissatisfaction, body image cognitive distortions, impulsivity, compulsivity, perfectionism, and exercise addiction. Impaired regulation, due to emotional dysregulation, personality traits, abuse, attachment issues, an impeded stress response system, neural alterations, and executive functioning problems, appears to greatly influence eating behavior and disorders. Defense plays a role in eating disorders, particularly perfectionism and compulsivity, or over-control, in anorexics compensating for a lack of actual or perceived control. Despite the importance of these proximal mechanisms, they largely leave unanswered the related questions of why eating disorders occur, and why they are far more common in females.

The ultimate causation model proposed answers both questions and meets a high bar for an evolutionary explanation, and also has solid intrinsic validity. Energy continuums consisting of food consumption style (quality), quantity of food consumed, and activity level appear to have evolved from our omnivorous evolutionary nomadic hunting-gathering past, in turn based on evolved mechanisms in herbivores and carnivores. These continuums interact with environmental circumstances, and with each other, to influence energy related behavior for both males and females. Given how during our evolutionary past women frequently had to carry both themselves and a child, the impact of these continuums and their interactions are amplified for females. Relevant to this amplification, females are more sensitive to social and physical environmental cues (the former typically expressing the latter), pertaining to energy and eating behavior. One aspect of this is male mate selection preferences for females of a physical profile fostering greater evolutionary success. Consequently, females are more prone to extremes of energy related behavior, and hence to eating disorders. The ultimate and proximal causation continuums interact, both in terms of the former influencing patterns on the proximal continuums, and additive effects, to produce full-fledged eating disorders.

References

Abed, R.T. (1998). The sexual competition hypothesis for eating disorders. *British Journal of Medical Psychology, 71*(4), 525-547.

American Psychiatric Association (2013). *Diagnostic & Statistical Manual 5*. Washington, DC: American Psychiatric Publishing.

Aronne, L. (2003). The neurological and endocrine components of weight gain and obesity. *Advanced Studies in Medicine, 3*(6A), S477-S482.

Bardone-Cone, A.M., Sturm, K., Lawson, M.A., Robinson, D.P., & Smith, R. (2010). Perfectionism across stages of recovery from eating disorders. *International Journal of Eating Disorders, 43*(2), 139-148.

Bessesen, D., Bull, S., & Cornier, M. (2008). Trafficking of dietary fat and resistance to obesity. *Physiology & Behavior, 94*(5), 681-688.

Birketvedt, G.S., Drivenes, E., Agledahl, I., Sundsfjord, J., Olstad, R., & Florholmen, J.R. (2006). Bulimia nervosa—a primary defect in the hypothalamic-pituitary-adrenal axis? *Appetite, 46*(2), 164-167.

Blaase, H. & Elklit, A. (2001). Psychological characteristics of women with eating disorders: Permanent or transient features? *Scandinavian Journal of Psychology, 42*(5), 467-478.

Bowins, B.E. (2004). Psychological defense mechanisms: A new perspective. *American Journal of Psychoanalysis, 64*, 1-26.

Castellini, G., Polito, C., Bolognesi, E., D'Argenio, A., Ginestroni, A., Mascalchi, M. et al (2013). Looking at my body: Similarities and differences between anorexia nervosa patients and controls in body image visual processing. *European Psychiatry, 28*(7), 427-435.

Delvecchio, E., DiRiso, D., Salcuni, S., Lis, A., & George, C. (2014). Anorexia and attachment: Dysregulated defense and pathological mourning. *Frontiers of Psychology*, 10.3389/ppsyg.2014.01218.

Egan, S.J., Piek, J.P., Dyck, M.J., Rees, C.S., & Hagger, M.S. (2013). A clinical investigation of motivation to change standards and cognitions about perfectionism. *Behavioral & Cognitive Psychotherapy, 41*(5), 565-578.

Elbourne, K.E. & Chen, J. (2007). The continuum model of obligatory exercise: A preliminary investigation. *Journal of Psychosomatic Research, 62*(1), 73-80.

Fagundo, A.B., De la Torre, R., Jimenez-Murcia, S., Aguera, Z., Granero, R., Tarrega, S. et al (2012). Executive functions profile in extreme eating/weight conditions: From anorexia nervosa to obesity. *Plos One, 7*(8), e43383.

Fassino, S., Amianto, F., Gramaglia, C., Facchini, F., & Abbate-Daga, G. (2004). Temperament and character in eating disorders: Ten years of studies. *Eating & Weight Disorders, 9*(2), 81-90.

Fichter, M.M., Daser, C., & Postpischi, F. (1985). Anorexic symptoms in the male. *Journal of Psychiatry Research, 19*(2-3), 305-313.

Fiore, F., Ruggiero, G.M., & Sassaroli, S. (2014). Emotional dysregulation and anxiety control in the psychopathological mechanism underlying drive for thinness. *Frontiers in Psychiatry, 5*, 43-49.

Fischer, S., Smith, G.T., & Cyders, M.A. (2008). Another look at impulsivity: A meta-analytic review comparing specific dispositions to rash action in their relationship to bulimic symptoms. *Clinical Psychology Review, 28*, 1413-1425.

Fitzgibbon, M.L. & Blackman, L.R. (2000). Binge eating disorder and bulimia nervosa: Differences in the quality and quantity of binge eating episodes. *International Journal of Eating Disorders, 27*(2), 238-243.

Gilboa-Schechtman, E., Avnon, L., Zubery, E., & Jeczmien, P. (2006). Emotional processing in eating disorders: Specific impairment or general distress related deficiency? *Depression & Anxiety, 23*, 331-339.

Ginty, A.T., Phillips, A.C., Higgs, S., Heaney, J.L., & Carroll, D. (2012). Disordered eating behavior is associated with blunted cortisol and cardiovascular reactions to acute psychological stress. *Psychoneuroendocrinology, 37*(5), 715-724.

Gleaves, D.H., Brown, J.D., & Warren, C.S. (2004). The continuity/discontinuity models of eating disorders: A review of the literature and implications for assessment, treatment, and prevention. *Behavior Modification, 28*(6), 739-762.

Gratz, K.L. & Roemer, L. (2004). Multidimensional assessment of emotion regulation and dysregulation: Development, factor structure, and initial validation of the difficulties in emotion regulation scale. *Journal of Psychopathology and Behavioral Assessment, 26*, 41-54.

Harrison, A., Sullivan, S., Tchanturia, K., & Treasure, J. (2009). Emotion recognition and regulation in anorexia nervosa. *Clinical Psychology & Psychotherapy, 16*, 348-356.

Hay, P. & Fairburn, C. (1998). The validity of the DSM-IV scheme for classifying bulimic eating disorders. *International Journal of Eating Disorders, 23*(1), 7-15.

Hay, P. & Williams, S.E. (2013). Exploring relationships over time between psychological distress, perceived stress, life events and immature defense style on disordered eating pathology. *BMC Psychology, 1*(1), 1-27.

Hilbert, A., Pike, K.M., Wilfley, D.E., Fairburn, C.G., Dohm, F.A., & Striegel-Moore, R.H. (2011). Clarifying boundaries of binge eating disorder and psychiatric comorbidity: A latent structure analysis. *Behavior Research & Therapy, 49*(3), 202-211.

Johnston, O., Reilly, J., & Kremer, J. (2011). Excessive exercise: From quantitative categorization to a qualitative continuum approach. *European Eating Disorders Review, 19*(3), 237-248.

Jones, C.J., Harris, G., Leung, N., Bissett, J., & Meyer, C. (2007). The effect of induced stress on the relationship between perfectionism and unhealthy eating attitudes. *Eating & Weight Disorders, 12*(2), 339-343.

Kelley, C.C., Neufeld, J.M., & Musher-Eizenman, D.R. (2010). Drive for thinness and drive for muscularity: Opposite ends of the continuum or separate constructs? *Body Image, 7*(1), 74-77.

Konstantakopoulos, G., Varsou, E., Dikeos, D., Ionnidi, N., Gonidakis, F., Papadimitriou, G., & Oulis, P. (2012). Delusionality of body image beliefs in eating disorders. *Psychiatry Research, 200*(2-3), 482-428.

Kraschnewski, J., Boan, J., Esposito, J., Sherwood, N., Lehman, E., Kephart, D. et al (2010). Long-term weight loss maintenance in the United States. *International Journal of Obesity*, 34, 1644-1654.

Lavender, J.M., Wonderlich, S.A., Peterson, C.B., Crosby, R.D., Engel, S.G., Mitchell, J.E. et al (2014). Dimensions of emotion dysregulation in bulimia nervosa. *European Eating Disorders Review, 22*(3), 212-216.

Maskarinec, G., Takata, Y., Pagano, J., Carlin, L., Goodman, M., LeMarchand, L. et al (2006). Trends and dietary determinants of overweight and obesity in a multiethnic population. *Obesity, 14*(4), 717-726.

Merwin, R.M., Moskovitch, A.A., Wagner, H.R., Ritschel, L.A., Craighead, L.W., & Zucker, N.L. (2013). Emotion regulation difficulties in anorexia nervosa: Relationship to self-perceived sensitivity. *Cognition & Emotion, 27*(3), 441-442.

Miller, K.K. (2013). Endocrine effects of anorexia nervosa. *Endocrinology & Metabolism Clinics of North America, 42*(3), 515-528.

Mitchell, J.E., Crosby, R.D., Wonderlich, S.A., Hill, L., Le Grange, D., Powers, P., & Eddy, K. (2007). Latent profile analysis of a cohort of patients with eating disorders not otherwise specified. *International Journal of Eating Disorders, 40*(Suppl), S95-98.

Mobbs, O., Iglesias, K., Golay, A., & Van Der Linden, M. (2011). Cognitive deficits in obese persons with and without binge eating disorders. Investigation using a mental flexibility task. *Appetite, 57*(1), 263-271.

Moulton, S.J., Newman, E., Power, K., Swanson, V., & Day, K. (2015). Childhood trauma and eating psychopathology: A mediating role for dissociation and emotion dysregulation? *Child Abuse & Neglect, 39*, 167-174.

Ogden, C., Carroll, M., Curtin, L., McDowell, M., Tabak, C., & Flegal, K. (2006). Prevalence of overweight and obesity in the United States, 1999-2004. *Journal of the American Medical Association, 295*, 1549-1555.

Patton, C.J. (1992). Fear of abandonment and binge eating: A subliminal psychodynamic activation investigation. *Journal of Nervous & Mental Disease, 180*(8), 484-490.

Perpina, C., Roncero, M., Belloch, A., & Sanchez-Reales, S. (2011). Eating-related intrusive thoughts inventory: Exploring the dimensionality of eating disorder symptoms. *Psychological Reports, 109*(1), 108-126.

Podar, I., Hannus, A., & Alik, J. (1999). Personality and affectivity characteristics associated with eating disorders: A comparison of eating disordered, weight-preoccupied, and normal samples. *Journal of Personality Assessment, 73*(1), 133-147.

Racine, S.E. & Wildes, J.E. (2013). Emotion dysregulation and symptoms of anorexia nervosa: The unique roles of lack of emotional awareness and impulse control difficulties when upset. *International Journal of Eating Disorders, 46*(7), 713-720.

Racine, S.E. & Wildes, J.E. (2014). Dynamic longitudinal relations between emotion regulation difficulties and anorexia nervosa symptoms over the year following intensive treatment. *Journal of Consulting & Clinical Psychology, 83*(4), 785-795.

Ringer, F. & Crittenden, P.M. (2007). Eating disorders and attachment: The effects of hidden family processes on eating disorders. *European Eating Disorders Review, 15*(2), 119-130.

Schneider, J.E., Klingerman, C.M., & Abdulhay, A. (2012). Sense and nonsense in metabolic control of reproduction. *Frontiers of Endocrinology (Lausanne), 5*, 3-26.

Spinella, M. & Lyke, J. (2004). Executive personality traits and eating behavior. *International Journal of Neuroscience, 114*(1), 83-93.

Stefano, G.B., Ptacek, R., Kuzelova, H., Mantione, K.J., Raboch, J., Papezova, H., & Kream, R.M. (2013). Convergent dysregulation of frontal cortical cognitive and reward systems in eating disorders. *Medical Science Monitor, 19*, 353-358.

Stice, E., Killen, J.D., Hayward, C., & Taylor, C.B. (1998). Support for the continuity hypothesis of bulimic pathology. *Journal of Consulting & Clinical Psychology, 66*(5), 784-790.

Sundgot-Borgen, J. & Torstveit, M.K. (2010). Aspects of disordered eating continuum in elite high-intensity sports. *Scandinavian Journal of Medical Science & Sports, 20*(Suppl 2), 112-120.

Sullivan, P.F., Bulik, C.M., Hall, S., Weltzin, T.E., & Kaye, W.H. (1994). Defense style in women with eating disorders. *International Journal of Eating Disorders, 16*(3), 251-256.

Tasca, G.A., Ritchie, K., Zachariades, F., Proulx, A., Trinneer, A., Balfour, L. et al (2013). Attachment insecurity mediates the relationship between childhood trauma and eating disorder psychopathology in a clinical sample: A structural equation model. *Child Abuse & Neglect, 37*(11), 926-933.

Taubes, G. (2011). *Why We Get Fat*. New York: Anchor Books.

Taylor, V., McIntyre, R., Remington, G., Levitan, R., Stonehocker, B., & Sharma, A. (2012). Beyond pharmacotherapy: Understanding the links between obesity and chronic mental illness. *Canadian Journal of Psychiatry, 57*(1), 5-12.

Tseng, M.C. & Hu, F.C. (2012). Latent class analysis of eating and impulsive behavioral symptoms in Taiwanese women with bulimia nervosa. *Journal of Psychosomatic Research, 72*(1), 65-72.

Wildes, J.E. & Marcus, M.D. (2013). Incorporating dimensions into the classification of eating disorders: Three models and their implications for research and clinical practice. *International Journal of Eating Disorders, 46*(5), 396-403.

Williamson, L. (1998). Eating disorders and the cultural forces behind the drive for thinness: Are African American women really protected? *Social Work & Health Care, 28*(1), 61-73.

Williamson, D.A., Gleaves, D.H., & Stewart, T.M. (2005). Categorical versus dimensional models of eating disorders: An examination of the evidence. *International Journal of Eating Disorders, 37*(1), 1-10.

Williamson, D.A, Muller, S.L., Reas, D.L., & Thaw, J.M. (1999). Cognitive bias in eating disorders: Implications for theory and treatment. *Behavior Modification, 23*(4), 556-577.

World Health Organization (1992). *The ICD-10 Classification of Mental and Behavioral Disorders: Clinical Descriptions and Diagnostic Guidelines*. Geneva: World Health Organization.

CHAPTER 9

Reinforcement Based Disorders

Many disorders fall under the headings of addiction, impulse control, and compulsion. The list is extensive and ever shifting, but includes multiple substance abuse problems, sexual excesses, and numerous excesses of other behaviors, such as intermittent explosive disorder, kleptomania, trichotillomania, onychophagia, psychogenic excoriation, pyromania, compulsive shopping, pathological gambling, internet gaming, and binge watching (TV shows). In line with our natural tendency to categorize, diagnostic systems have established divisions into various addictions, impulse control disorders, and compulsions (American Psychiatric Association, 2013; First et al, 2002; World Health Organization, 1992). Despite how appealing such a scheme sounds, it is plagued by weaknesses taking the form of conceptual-practical overlap and common mechanisms, requiring an entirely different way of formulating these conditions.

This chapter will examine the weaknesses of the way these conditions are currently structured, and then propose a new way of formulating them that is flexible, allowing for any behavior that appears excessive and dysfunctional to be evaluated. Such flexibility is crucial because, as things currently stand, for a behavioral problem to be treated as a mental health condition, it first has to gain the attention of researchers and policy makers; then be tested over several research studies to determine if it meets the criteria for an addiction, impulse control disorder, or compulsion; and finally research must validate the proposed criteria. For each condition this process requires at least a decade or two, and when computer/internet related issues are the focus, technology can change more quickly than the establishment of a formal mental health condition. In addition, there are numerous behaviors that can be problematic, with no real way of conceptualizing them as a mental health issue. For example, countless sexual behaviors as extensive as the human imagination allows for reveal addictive/impulsive/compulsive manifestations. Even behaviors considered more "normal" can be dysfunctional, such as a golfer who persists despite the behavior worsening cervical spine problems. It is difficult to evaluate these problems within the current framework, and often leaves those with such issues lacking treatment, particularly in health care systems requiring a diagnostic code for treatment reimbursement. Revising how we approach such problems is preferable, and will be explored in the current chapter. The title "Reinforcement Based Disorders" has been selected because, as will be shown, the common element is reinforcement.

Weaknesses: Addictions, Impulse Control, and Compulsions

Conceptual and Practical Overlap

At a superficial level the terms addiction, impulse control problems, and compulsions appear distinct, but on closer examination it becomes very difficult to clearly distinguish them, as much overlap occurs. Decades ago addictions were applied to substances of abuse showing patterns of tolerance, cravings, and withdrawal, but it became apparent that behaviors such as gambling demonstrate addictive qualities. Often a person requires more intense stimulation over time (tolerance), misses and thinks about the behavior when not partaking (craving-like), and seems to suffer if the behavior is stopped (withdrawal). At that point a flexible way to describe behavioral excesses free of labels such as addictions, impulse control, and compulsions could have been designed. However, in keeping with our desire for discreteness, efforts were directed at determining the qualities of behavioral excesses qualifying them as an addiction, impulse control problem, or compulsion. Now we have the ludicrous scenario of gambling being shifted from an impulse control disorder in DSM-IV to an addiction in DSM-5, while gambling clearly shows impulse control problems, at least for some gamblers (American Psychiatric Association, 2013; First et al, 2002). The notion seems to be that somehow an addiction is superior to a lowly impulse control problem, and gambling has made the grade. Apparently, we are gambling with our manner of conceptualizing these conditions.

So far the discussion has attempted to describe the pattern of addiction/impulse control/compulsive classification without reference to the literature, but it is important to back up the assertions made with research results. Research often does not consider the conscious reason why people abuse substances, but Newton et al (2009) looked at this issue with methamphetamine users. They found that the most common reason was pleasure seeking (56%), followed by impulsivity (27%) and habits (25%). These results are interesting because for an addictive substance, impulsivity and habits (compulsive like) were key reasons for using it (Newton et al, 2009). In another study examining amphetamine use, Kelly et al (2006) ascertained that high impulsive sensation seekers have increased subjective experiences associated with drug abuse potential. Papachristou et al (2012) found that heavy drinkers scored higher on trait impulsivity than light drinkers, and in heavy drinkers impaired response inhibition influenced cravings. Other studies show that increased impulsivity is linked to substance abuse risk (Hommer et al, 2011; Woicik et al, 2009). Lubman et al (2004) point to neuroscience evidence indicating that inhibitory control over reward related behavior is impaired in addicted individuals, resulting in compulsive patterns of abuse. Top-down control is impaired in many "addictions" contributing to impulsive and compulsive behavior, particularly when decision-making is distorted, such as with delay discounting consisting of over-valuing short-term immediate rewards (Adinoff et al, 2007). Indeed, "addiction" often entails impulsivity and compulsivity related to impaired regulation (Clark, 2014; Grant et al, 2010; Grant & Chamberlain, 2014; Koob & Kreek, 2007; Lubman et al, 2004).

Addiction, impulsivity, and compulsivity overlap in research because the concepts overlap, and impulsivity and compulsivity often underlie addiction (Clark, 2014; Grant et al, 2010). Impulsivity consisting of unplanned responding and hasty decisions is a key shared marker of addictions (Clark, 2014). Various processes contribute to addictive behavior such as reward deficiency, salience attributions, and impaired inhibition (Berridge et al, 2009; Clark, 2014; Grant et al, 2010). With reward deficiency natural rewards lose their potency and additional stimulation is required (Grant et al, 2010). Salience attribution highlights the role of cues and triggers in addictive behavior as signals of reward (Berridge et al, 2009; Grant et al, 2010). Impaired response inhibition makes it difficult to prevent addictive responses or compulsive enactments (Clark, 2014; Grant et al, 2010). These processes contribute to the overlap between concepts, because if there is a deficiency as pertains to natural rewards, enhanced sensitivity to signals of reward (largely due to reward deficiency), and difficulties inhibiting responses and compulsive behavior related to reward cues, how can the concepts be fully separated? Impulsivity does refer to more reactive behavior and compulsivity more persistent habit behavior, but what if a person reacts to multiple cues of reward resulting in ongoing addictive behavior, and the compulsive actions arise from a failure to inhibit responses? It is difficult, conceptually and practically, to separate addiction, impulsivity, and compulsivity.

Highlighting the high degree of overlap it has been proposed that what might actually be occurring is a spectrum of conditions along one dimension, often referred to as obsessive-compulsive spectrum conditions (Hollander & Evers, 2004; Hollander & Wong, 1995; Stein & Hollander, 1993). However, the name is incorrect, as if anything it should be the impulsive-compulsive spectrum, given how impulsivity and compulsivity underlie addictions. Multiple conditions have been suggested to be part of this spectrum including obsessive-compulsive disorder (OCD) and eating disorders, in addition to those listed at the start of the chapter. Various elements of compulsiveness, impulse control, and addiction seem to apply to many conditions. Hollander and Wong (1995) proposed arranging applicable conditions on a spectrum from impulsive to compulsive, based on low to high harm avoidance. Although this arrangement has its appeal, there are many problems with it. For example, OCD seems to be characterized by anxiety and harm avoidance, while impulse issues have novelty seeking as a central feature (Potenza, 2007; Potenza et al, 2009). The relationship between impulsivity and compulsivity is also quite complex, as demonstrated by how those with OCD have higher levels of cognitive impulsiveness than those without OCD, suggesting more of an overlap of concepts than a single spectrum (Ettelt et al, 2007).

Another problem is how the various conditions might be placed on the spectrum. For example, how would sexual excesses be placed on a continuum given that there are addictive, impulsive, and compulsive aspects? It has been suggested that obsessive-compulsive spectrum conditions be described orthogonally based on relative degree of factors such as impulsivity, compulsivity, and addictiveness characterizing the specific condition (Lochner & Stein, 2006). However, the degree of overlap between addiction, impulsivity, and compulsivity prevents them from being separated as distinct points on an orthogonal scheme. Furthermore, even if this arrangement could be worked out, positioning of a given condition does not explain why this occurred in the first place. An important note at this point is that OCD must be distinguished from compulsive behavior itself. As the name implies, OCD entails both obsessions and compulsions in a relationship with one another, for reasons we will explore in the "Personality Disorders" chapter. Compulsivity is a pattern of behavior applicable to many conditions (including obsessions), such as anorexia as we covered in the "Eating Disorders" chapter, and the conditions addressed in the current chapter.

Common Mechanisms

Ultimately, substance and behavioral excesses are likely based on an aberration of evolved systems designed to foster the acquisition of natural rewards (Blum et al, 2012; Durrant et al, 2009). Natural rewards such as water, food, shelter, social support, and sexual contact were and still are critical to survival and reproductive success. Neural substrates designed to facilitate approach behavior ensure that these important resources are strived for and acquired if at all possible. The problem arises when these natural reward systems interact with modern day settings offering a variety of more potent rewards, such as chemical substances, and activities not available during our evolution, such as internet gaming (Blum et al, 2012; Durrant et al, 2009). Consistent with an evolved natural reward system, it follows that there are common and prominent neural substrates providing for this capacity. Although different chemical substances and non-chemical sources of reward do entail some differences in neural response (Berridge et al, 2009; Clark et al, 2012; Lajtha, 2008; Peters et al, 2013), there is enormous overlap of these mechanisms.

Central to the reward system is the neurotransmitter dopamine. The mesocorticolimbic dopaminegic system is even integral to the establishment of pair bonding, demonstrating the range of adaptive rewards it applies to (Curtis et al, 2006). This system seems to play a key role in substance addictions and reward deficiency involving reduced reward responsiveness, leading to compensatory overindulgence in substances or behaviors that stimulate this system (Bowirrat & Oscar-Berman, 2005). The critical role of dopamine is evident in Parkinson's disease arising from a deficiency of this neurotransmitter: Replacement therapy with dopamine agonists can result in a variety of impulsive, compulsive, and addictive behaviors, a condition known as dopamine dysregulation syndrome (Kondo, 2008; O'Sullivan et al, 2009).

However, dopamine is only one part of a complex interconnected reward system activated by substances and behavioral excesses. The extent and complexities are such that it is not feasible to cover it fully in the current chapter, but some of the key findings and patterns will be described.

Numerous substances of abuse including opioids, nicotine, cocaine, alcohol, cannabis, and amphetamines such as MDMA (ecstasy), and natural rewards such as food and sexual activity, increase extracellular concentrations of dopamine in a ventral striatal structure known as the nucleus accumbens (Gianoulakis, 2009; Lajtha & Sershen, 2010). The nucleus accumbens mediates the reinforcing effect of natural rewards, drugs of abuse, and behavioral excesses (Blum et al, 2012). Stimulation of opioid receptors in the nucleus accumbens or ventral tegmental area, either by endogenous or external opioids, appears to augment extracellular dopamine in the former structure, demonstrating how chemical systems act in concert (Gianoulakis, 2009). Dopamine signal-receiving neurons in the nucleus accumbens, in turn, synthesize endogenous opioids, and send projections to numerous reward areas (Dackis & O'Brien, 2001). Opioid receptors and endogenous opioids are recruited in response to both natural rewards and drugs of abuse (Le Merrer et al, 2009). Cannabinoids and opioids also demonstrate reciprocal interaction, stimulation of one system triggering a release of endogenous forms of the other substance (Parolaro et al, 2010; Spano et al, 2010). Cannabinoid reward involves the same brain mechanisms as other drugs of abuse, and natural rewards (Viachou & Panagis, 2014).

In addition to dopamine, opioid, and cannabinoid systems, serotonin, oxytocin, GABA, and glutamate play an important role (Berrendero et al, 2010; Clapp et al, 2008; McGregor et al, 2008). Furthermore, multiple brain regions, receptors, neurons, neurotransmitters, transporters, circuits, peptides, and proteins are involved in reward mechanisms, with some distinct to the substance or type of reward, but many overlapping (Gianoulakis, 2009; Lajtha & Sershen, 2010). Serotonin, via its various receptor subtypes spread throughout the brain, has a generalized impact on reward related behaviors (Hayes & Greenshaw, 2011). Oxytocin interacts with mesolimbic dopamine to promote sexual and social behaviors, and also appears to play a role in addictions to substances (McGregor et al, 2008). GABA and glutamate as the major inhibitory and excitatory neurotransmitters, respectively, seem to modulate the actions of dopamine and endogenous opioids (Ting-A-Kee & Van Der Kooy, 2012). For example, GABA receptors in the ventral tegmental area influence the interaction of dopamine and opioids (Ting-A-Kee & Van Der Kooy, 2012). Ventral tegmental area GABA interneurons are the primary inhibitory neurons of dopamine neurons, and alterations impair the modulation of anxiety and stress responses (Enoch, 2008). All drugs of abuse seem to modulate glutamatergic transmission, resulting in long-lasting neuroplastic changes perpetuating drug-seeking behavior (Glass & Olive, 2008).

Beyond the neural structures listed above, various stressors such as early life abuse impact on components and regulation of the stress response system, including corticotropin releasing factor influencing multiple neural systems, the hypothalamic-pituitary-adrenal (HPA) axis, autonomic arousal, and central noradrenergic systems (Martin-Fardon et al, 2010; Sinha, 2008). These changes in turn impact on corticostriatal-limbic motivational, learning, and adaptation systems, such as mesolimbic dopamine, opioids, glutamate, and GABA (Koob, 2004; Sinha, 2008). Endogenous opioids feed back to and regulate the HPA axis (Kreek et al, 2012). Exposure to various substances, and even behavioral experiences, can influence gene expression, adding a very complex layer of epigenetic regulation to the picture (Bilinski et al, 2012). Some of the neural, hormonal, and genetic changes are specific to a given input, such as type of substance, and some do not seem to cross over from substance abuse to behavioral excesses (Berridge et al, 2009; Clark et al, 2012; Peters et al, 2013). However, on the whole the commonalities are far greater than the differences (Berridge et al, 2009; Clark et al, 2012; Peters et al, 2013), as would be expected given how both substances of abuse and behavioral excesses tap into evolved reward circuits and systems. These common mechanisms, and the conceptual-practical overlap described in the above section, make it virtually impossible to separate substance abuse and behavioral excess conditions into discrete categories of addiction, impulse control problems, and compulsions. This reality opens the way to a new and more flexible system.

A Reinforcement Based Model

The proposed model affords flexibility in describing any behavior that has addictive, impulsive, and compulsive aspects, and provides a rich description of the behavior. Continuums of positive and negative reinforcement, frequency of the behavior, intensity of the behavior, and cost/benefit valuation are each to be assessed. It is suggested that they be rated on scales.

Reinforcement

Addictive, impulsive, and compulsive behaviors involve reinforcement, both positive and negative. Reinforcement increases the frequency of a behavior, as opposed to punishment that at least theoretically decreases the frequency. Positive reinforcement occurs when a behavior leads to a positive outcome comprising a reward, whereas negative reinforcement transpires when a behavior reduces or eliminates an aversive state. For example, by drinking alcohol, anxiety (the aversive state) is eliminated or diminished. Traditionally, addiction has been viewed as consisting of positive and negative reinforcement, the behavior producing a reward and also reduction of a negative state. However, only one type of reinforcement might apply to a given behavior at a particular time, or for a certain person. For instance, some people drink alcohol excessively because they like the initial stimulant effect, while others drink to reduce anxiety or boredom—positive and negative reinforcement respectively. Given that only one form of reinforcement can apply, addiction cannot simply be characterized as involving both forms. Impulsive behavior is often viewed as only providing positive reinforcement, the person acting impulsively to acquire a reward. In some instances, though, a person will act impulsively to relieve a negative state, such as a person spontaneously deciding to drink in order to relieve boredom. At times impulsive actions can be adaptive, as when a person who feels lonely impulsively calls an old friend and enjoys the conversation. Compulsive behavior typically is seen as a form of negatively reinforced behavior, with the compulsion relieving distress in the moment, as in the case of obsessive-compulsive states. However, compulsive behavior can be positively reinforcing, as with a golfer who feels compelled to indulge every day but enjoys it.

Hence, both positive and negative reinforcement occur with addictions, impulsivity, and compulsivity, making it untenable to simply link certain patterns of reinforcement to these types of behavior. Research backs up this perspective, demonstrating how various types of reinforcement apply to addictions, impulsivity, and compulsivity (Robinson & Berridge, 2013; Saunders & Robinson, 2013). Linking addiction to compulsive behavior, it has been found that cues for reward (positive reinforcement) create desires and cravings that in addicts can become compulsive (Robinson & Berridge, 2013). Some people seem to be sensitive to cues for positive reinforcement, with Pavlovian (classical conditioned) cues eliciting strong and persistent desires, making the person vulnerable to impulsive or compulsive behavior (Saunders & Robinson, 2013).

Positive and negative reinforcement can apply at different phases of an "addiction," positive reinforcement often being more prominent at the start, but negative reinforcement more potent later on, although negative reinforcement is also powerful early on as well (Gilpin & Koob, 2008; Koob, 2013). Negative reinforcement often increases due to tolerance and withdrawal effects of substances, whereby a person requires increased amounts of the substance to experience the same effect (tolerance), and then experiences more intense withdrawal: The adverse physiological and psychological sensations of withdrawal constitute an adverse state, and using the substance to end withdrawal is potently negatively reinforcing. This form of reinforcement can also play a prominent role with ongoing substance use, because some substances such as alcohol tend to induce negative affective states over time, which can be relieved in the short-term by consuming the substance, setting up a negative cycle of excessive ongoing use-negative affect-negative reinforcement-increasing use and negative affect (Helig & Koob, 2007; Leventhal et al, 2013). Stress alone can serve as an aversive state negatively reinforcing behaviors that relieve it, a process found for nicotine addiction (Bruijnzeel, 2012; McKee et al, 2011). Pain is another common adverse state, and substances such as opioids that relieve it are negatively reinforcing (Becker et al, 2012; Ewan & Martin, 2013; Garland et al, 2013). Reinforcement, particularly positive, can and has been applied to treating addictions. One example is the Community Reinforcement Approach, helping people with substance abuse disorders restructure their lifestyle to acquire rewards, such as pleasant social activities (Meyers et al, 2011).

So far the discussion has focused on substances of abuse, but behaviors not involving substances also share reinforcement properties. In the case of excessive gambling early large wins seem to increase the likelihood of a person becoming addicted, due to the intense positive reinforcement (Clark, 2014). Although substances of abuse are often viewed as providing the most intense reinforcement, animals actually prefer natural rewards, such as sugar or sex, to drugs of abuse, highlighting how intensely reinforcing behaviors not involving substances can be (Clark, 2014). Cognitive distortions favoring the behavior seem to ramp up the reinforcement value of "addictions" in general, and certainly for those not involving substances of abuse (Johansson et al, 2009). For example, in the case of excessive gambling, cognitive distortions such as "I can beat the house" and "I've figured out a system to win" maintain the addiction, and it is crucial to address these in treatment (Johansson et al, 2009). Despite potential differences given the electronic media, internet gambling appears to be like other forms of gambling (Braverman et al, 2011). Gambling can be a way of escaping negative emotions and also seeking attention and recognition, indicating negative and positive reinforcement respectively (Ledgerwood & Petry, 2006).

Internet gaming "addiction" is an increasingly common problem, particularly among young males, that like other behavioral excesses involves impulsive and compulsive aspects (Floros et al, 2014). Numerous behavioral excesses, including but certainly not restricted to compulsive shopping, excessive tanning, skin picking, binge watching, and sexual excesses, are characterized by positive and negative reinforcement, showing addictive, impulsive, and compulsive aspects (Grant et al, 2010). Even motion sickness likely arises from a reinforcement process, in this instance the highly aversive motion sickness sensation negatively reinforcing motion stabilizing behavior that reduces or removes the sensation, based on how aberrant motion increases the risk of injury or predation in an evolutionary context, thereby reducing evolutionary fitness (Bowins, 2010c).

Sexual excesses deserve special mention, given that sex is a major source of natural reinforcement, and also the wide range of behaviors that show addictive, impulsive, and compulsive aspects. Attempting to establish one as a formal condition, and refining criteria as per the current system, is a dubious prospect considering the number and variety of such behaviors. For example, what about excessive masturbation, pornography, bondage, "water sports," cuckolding, sounding, and a host of others? In addition, cultures vary enormously in behaviors viewed as "sex-positive" and "sex-negative," making it difficult to establish criteria that apply to all (Bhugra et al, 2010). Furthermore, there can be multiple reasons why a sexual behavior is indulged in. For example, a study of bondage found numerous motivations, including exchange of power, intensified sexual pleasure, and tactile stimulation and bodily sensations, amongst others (Ernulf & Innala, 1995). Hence, even if viewed as excessive it might not represent a problem. Hypersexuality has been put forward as a formal condition, but "hyper" behavior is equally divided between conventional and unconventional (Kafka, 1997; Kafka & Prentky, 1992; Reid et al, 2012). Paraphilias—fetishism, frotteurism, transvestic fetishism, exhibitionism, and sadomasochism—arise in part from operant and classical conditioning, and are reinforced by the arousal (Bhugra et al, 2010). Sadomasochism is a complex entity, and for the most part is probably not a disorder. For example, Richters et al (2008) found that it is a sexual interest, and not pathology related to past abuse or sexual problems. More severe paraphilic disorders and sexual deviance seems to involve self-regulatory defects blocking response inhibition (Stinson et al, 2008). Dopamine dysregulation likely applies to these extreme variations, as evidenced by the occurrence of paraphilias in some Parkinson's disease patients treated with dopamine agonists (Solla et al, 2015).

Positive and negative reinforcement are clearly involved in all the substance abuse and behavioral conditions described. According to the model proposed, each behavior that is suspected of being problematic is first rated separately for positive and negative reinforcement, given that they are distinct forms of reinforcement. These ratings are to be based on the person's experience (self-rated), and it is suggested that these rating utilize 10-point scales to provide a more extensive range. Positive reinforcement rates the extent to which the substance/behavior induces positive feelings, and negative reinforcement the extent to which it reduces negative feelings. Frequently there will be elevated levels on both, but sometimes only on one, and as we have seen addictive, impulsive, and compulsive influences can align with both positive and negative reinforcement. From a treatment perspective, the difference between positive and negative reinforcement is important, because if positive reinforcement dominates, then substituting non-problematic rewards can reduce reliance on the substance or behavior. If negative reinforcement dominates, strategies to reduce or eliminate the negative state are crucial. For example, if anxiety constitutes the negative state, then psychotherapy and/or anti-anxiety medication can help, while if boredom constitutes the aversive state, then introducing and building on more stimulating activities can be effective, in addition to techniques designed to help the person tolerate periods of boredom. Beyond reinforcement, it is important to rate the frequency, intensity, and costs/benefits of the behavior.

Frequency of the Behavior

In considering how problematic any behavior is, the frequency is crucial to consider, with greater frequency typically meaning more of a problem. Frequency also helps to determine if the behavior is of an ongoing or binge type, with these two patterns characterizing many "addictions," such as to alcohol. The distinction is critical for at least two reasons, the first being that in the case of the binge type, cues or triggers are often more significant, and working with those triggers can produce major gains. For example, if a drinking binge is triggered by a couple of days of intense work stress, then awareness of the pattern, and interventions such as toning down the stress and more healthy outlets for it, can dramatically reduce or eliminate problem drinking. However, if consumption occurs daily triggers are often less relevant. The same applies to smoking cigarettes, because if a person chain smokes throughout the day triggers are usually not relevant, but if the person smokes at select times, such as when driving to work, managing the cued urge to smoke at such times is very helpful. The second reason why identifying the usage pattern is helpful relates to acceptance that the behavior is a problem: When usage is infrequent in the form of binges people are better able to rationalize their usage, deceiving themselves and others that there is no concern. Cognitive distortions designed to rationalize or deny substance abuse and behavioral excesses are to be expected, but more creativity is often required for highly frequent use, and the narrative is less convincing even to the user.

It is suggested that a single continuum, perhaps on a 10-point scale, be applied to a given substance of abuse or behavioral excess, ranging from extremely infrequent to extremely frequent. It might be commented that the time frame as pertains to frequency will vary somewhat for different substances or behaviors: Smoking cigarettes many times a day is common, in contrast to cocaine where similar usage seemingly represents a much more severe problem. While there is a point to such a comment, in an attempt to make the process as user friendly as possible, frequency rating should not involve an attempt to discern different levels for various substances and behaviors. One reason for this is that extremely frequent patterns do translate into worse outcomes, such as with increased risk of emphysema and lung cancer with chain smoking.

Intensity

In contrast to frequency, with a single dimension, intensity must necessarily consist of sub-dimensions given the number of inputs influencing it. Research will have to establish those dimensions that are most pertinent, but likely ones will include tolerance, withdrawal effects, cravings, conscious focus and attention to the substance or behavior, resistance to alteration as evidenced by the extent of rationalizing cognitive distortions, and capacity to inhibit the behavior. These sub-dimensions cover the range of cognitive, emotional, physiological, and behavioral factors influencing intensity. Some might argue that certain ones apply better to particular types of "addictions," such as tolerance, withdrawal, and cravings applying more to substances of abuse. However, if a behavior is truly excessive then these occurrences also apply. For example, with pornography it is common for a person (almost always a male) who indulges to habituate to a given level of stimulation, and progressively seek out more extreme forms (tolerance). If pornography is not available, the person often experiences a negative emotional reaction (withdrawal), and strongly desires it (cravings).

While the various sub-dimensions might apply less to one "addiction" and more to another, the inclusion of several intensity components will result in an averaging out of applicability. Basing intensity on several components also has the advantage of providing a richer description of this crucial aspect of any substance or behavioral "addiction." It is suggested that the sub-dimensions be rated on separate scales, perhaps 10-point to maintain consistency, and then averaged to provide an overall 10-point intensity score. More intense instances of substance abuse or behavioral excess require more intense therapeutic interventions. In addition, information from the sub-dimension scales can be applied to target more effective interventions. For example, if a person rates at the most intense level for resistance to alterations based on rationalizing cognitive distortions, then focused cognitive-behavioral intervention designed to modify these cognitive distortions will prove very helpful. Likewise, if there is a very high conscious focus on the substance or behavioral excess, absorption in other pleasurable activities can be applied (see the "Dissociation" chapter for absorption).

Costs/Benefits

It would be a mistake to assume that only costs apply to substance abuse or behavioral excesses, and the benefits are often crucial when it comes to the initiation and maintenance of the behavior. For example, it is possible that nicotine provides some neural stimulation capable of compensating for deficiencies in schizophrenia (Nees, 2014). This action of nicotine, if true, constitutes a benefit of smoking cigarettes for those with schizophrenia that undoubtedly helps maintain the behavior. Internet games, and in particular first person shooter ones, seem very popular with teenagers suffering from ADHD, perhaps in part because these games might compensate for executive functioning deficits by improving information processing speed and focus, representing a benefit, although this is not proven. Tension/stress reduction is a very common benefit for any substance or behavioral excess. Defensive motivation is a benefit that in many ways follows from negative reinforcement, such as providing relief from stress. More specifically, "addictive" behavior can defensively compensate for self-perceived lack of control in some instances, such as with gambling and cigarette smoking (Friedland et al, 1992; Heckman et al, 2012).

Benefit should not directly include positive and negative reinforcement as this is rated separately, and constitutes a more profound motivational influence central to any substance or behavioral excess. Benefits and costs should cover a wide range considering social, personal, emotional, occupational, and school functioning. Take for example internet games for a teenage boy with ADHD. On the benefit side might be stimulation and less hyperactive behavior. On the cost side could be staying up too late, and hence not being able to get up in the morning resulting in lateness to school, lack of exercise due to the excessive time spent gaming, and neglect of in person friendships. It is suggested that all the costs and benefits be carefully listed, and a ratio be created, perhaps from 1 to 10 to maintain consistency, with 10 = costs >> benefits, and 1 = costs << benefits. Obviously, if benefits far exceed costs the behavior in question is not a problem to treat.

Combining Components of the Model

Reinforcement (positive and negative), frequency, intensity, and costs/benefits combined provide an extensive and insightful picture of substance abuse or behavioral excess. The information can be utilized to guide more effective interventions. Although this approach might seem laborious with ratings of positive and negative reinforcement, frequency, the sub-dimensions of intensity, and costs/benefits, the advantages outweigh the negatives considering improved understanding and targeted therapeutic interventions. In addition, the process is actually a formalization of what every clinician experienced with these problems intuitively does: Consider the frequency, intensity, and costs/benefits, with an implicit understanding that the behavior is reinforcing to the person.

A key advantage to the model is that is enables any behavior suspected of being problematic to be rapidly evaluated, and in a way that guides effective interventions. This capacity is far superior to the current approach of a behavior or substance having to achieve a critical level of awareness among scientists and policy makers for it to be researched, then years of expensive empirical investigations to establish it as an addictive, impulsive, or compulsive condition, followed by additional years of costly studies to provide diagnostic criteria. In our current era of rapidly changing technology, potential "addictions" might come and go even before this process is complete. For example, in a few short years we have shifted from separate still and video cameras, iPods, phones, and internet access devices, to just a "smart" phone that many people seem "addicted" to. Conceivably, in a few more years devices connected to the body might replace these phones. In other words, the pace of technological change, with the behavioral excess potential of many devices, is outstripping the development of the current system of establishing conditions that qualify as addictions, impulse control disorders, and compulsions.

Summary

At the heart of the various substance abuse and behavioral excess problems discussed is reinforcement, with overlapping addictive, impulsive, and compulsive aspects. The current approach of attempting to classify each as either an addiction, impulse control disorder, or compulsion is untenable and inefficient, due to the conceptual and practical overlap of these concepts, and the common underlying mechanisms. Related to the inefficiency of this approach, it takes decades for a problem to be established as a condition, with numerous problems of behavioral excess excluded, and either under-treated or denied treatment at all in some medical systems. The model proposed allows for the immediate evaluation of any potential instance of behavioral or substance excess, regardless of the source. Furthermore, by taking into account continuums of positive and negative reinforcement, frequency, intensity, and costs/benefits, the model provides an extensive understanding of the problem for a given individual, providing for more focused treatment interventions.

References

Adinoff, B., Rilling, L.M., Williams, M.J., Schreffler, E., Schepis, T.S., Rosvall, T. et al. (2007). Impulsivity, neural deficits, and the addictions: The "oops" factor in relapse. *Journal of Addictive Disorders, 26*(Suppl 1), 25-39.

American Psychiatric Association (2013). *Diagnostic & Statistical Manual 5*. Washington, DC: American Psychiatric Publishing.

Becker, S., Gandhi, W., & Schweinhardt, P. (2012). Cerebral interactions of pain and reward and their relevance for chronic pain. *Neuroscience Letters, 520*(2), 182-187.

Berrendero, F., Robledo, P., Trigo, J.M., Martin-Garcia, E., & Maldonado, R. (2010). Neurobiological mechanisms involved in nicotine dependence and reward: Participation of the endogenous opioid system. *Neuroscience Biobehavioral Review, 35*(2), 220-231.

Berridge, K.C., Robinson, T.E., & Aldridge, J.W. (2009). Dissecting components of reward: "Liking," "wanting," and learning. *Current Opinion in Pharmacology, 9*(1), 65-73.

Bhugra, D., Popelyuk, D., & McMullen, I. (2010). Paraphilias across cultures: Contexts and controversies. *The Journal of Sex Research, 47*(2-3), 242-262.

Bilinski, P., Wojtyla, A., Kapka-Skrzypczak, L., Chwedorowicz, R., Cyranka, M., & Studzinski, T. (2012). Epigenetic regulation in drug addiction. *Annals of Agriculture & Environmental Medicine, 19*(3), 491-496.

Blum, K., Werner, T., Carnes, S., Carnes, P., Bowirrat, A., Giordana, J. et al (2012). Sex, drugs, and rock 'n' roll: Hypothesizing common mesolimbic activation as a function of reward gene polymorphisms. *Journal of Psychoactive Drugs, 44*(1), 38-55.

Bowins, B.E. (2010c). Motion sickness: A negative reinforcement model. *Brain Research Bulletin, 81*, 7-11.

Bowirrat, A. & Oscar-Berman, M. (2005). Relationship between dopaminergic neurotransmission, alcoholism, and reward deficiency syndrome. *American Journal of Medical Genetic B Neuropsychiatric Genetics, 132B*(1), 29-37.

Braverman, J., LaBrie, R.A., & Shaffer, H.J. (2011). A taxometric analysis of actual internet sports gambling behavior. *Psychological Assessment, 23*(1), 234-244.

Bruijnzeel, A.W. (2012). Tobacco addiction and the dysregulation of brain stress systems. *Neuroscience Biobehavioral Reviews, 36*(5), 1418-1441.

Clapp, P., Bhave, S.V., & Hoffman, P.L. (2008). How adaptation of the brain to alcohol leads to dependence: A pharmacological perspective. *Alcohol Research & Health, 31*(4), 310-339.

Clark, L. (2014). Disordered gambling: The evolving concept of behavioral addiction. *Annals of the New York Academy of Science, 1327*, 46-61.

Clark, L., Stokes, P.R., Wu, K., Michalczuk, R., Benecke, A., Watson, B.J. et al (2012). Striatal dopamine D2/D3 receptor binding in pathological gambling is correlated with mood-related impulsivity. *Neuroimage, 63*(1), 40-46.

Curtis, J.T., Liu, Y., Aragona, B.J., & Wang, Z. (2006). Dopamine and monogamy. *Brain Research, 1126*(1), 76-90.

Dackis, C.A. & O'Brien, C.P. (2001). Cocaine dependence: A disease of the brain's reward centers. *Journal of Substance Abuse Treatment, 21*(3), 111-117.

Durrant, R., Adamson, S., Todd, F., & Sellman, D. (2009). Drug use and addiction: Evolutionary perspective. *Australian & New Zealand Journal of Psychiatry, 43*(11), 1049-1056.

Enoch, M.A. (2008). The role of GABA(A) receptors in the development of alcoholism. *Pharmacological Biochemical Behavior, 90*(1), 95-104.

Ernulf, K.E. & Innala, S.M. (1995). Sexual bondage: A review and unobtrusive investigation. *Archives of Sexual Behavior, 24*(6), 631-654.

Ettelt, S., Ruhrmann, S., Barnow, S., Buthz, F., Hochrein, A., Meyer, K. et al (2007). Impulsiveness in obsessive-compulsive disorder: Results from a family study. *Acta Psychiatrica Scandinavica, 115*, 41-47.

Ewan, E.E. & Martin, T.J. (2013). Analgesics as reinforcers with chronic pain: Evidence from operant studies. *Neuroscience Letters, 557*(Pt A), 60-64.

First, M.B., Frances, A., & Pincus, H.A. (2002). *DSM-IV-TR Handbook of Differential Diagnosis*. Washington, DC: American Psychiatric Publishing.

Floros, G., Siomos, K., Stogiannidou, A., Giozepas, I., & Garyfallos, G. (2014). The relationship between personality, defense styles, internet addiction disorder, and psychopathology in college students. *Cyberpsychology Behavioral Social Network, 17*(10), 672-676.

Friedland, N., Keinan, G., & Regev, Y. (1992). Controlling the uncontrollable: Effects of stress on illusory perceptions of controllability. *Journal of Personality and Social Psychology, 63*(6), 923-931.

Garland, E.L., Froeliger, B., Zeidan, F., Partin, K., & Howard, M.O. (2013). The downward spiral of chronic pain, prescription opioid misuse, and addiction: Cognitive, affective, and neuropsychopharmacologic pathways. *Neuroscience Biobehavioral Reviews, 37*(10 Pt 2), 2597-2607.

Gianoulakis, C. (2009). Endogenous opioids and addiction to alcohol and other drugs of abuse. *Current Topics in Medical Chemistry, 9*(11), 999-1015.

Gilpin, N.W. & Koob, G.F. (2008). Neurobiology of alcohol dependence: Focus on motivational mechanisms. *Alcohol Research & Health, 31*(3), 185-195.

Glass, J.T. & Olive, M.F. (2008). Glutamatergic substrates of drug addiction and alcoholism. *Biochemical Pharmacology, 75*(1), 218-265.

Grant, J.E. & Chamberlain, S.R. (2014). Impulsive action and impulsive choice across substance and behavioral addictions: Cause or consequence? *Addiction Behavior, 39*(11), 1632-1639.

Grant, J.E., Potenza, M.N., Weinstein, A., & Gorelick, D.A. (2010). Introduction to behavioral addictions. *American Journal of Drug & Alcohol Abuse, 36*(5), 233-241.

Hayes, D.J. & Greenshaw, A.J. (2011). 5-HT receptors and reward-related behaviour: A review. *Neuroscience Biobehavioral Review, 35*(6), 1419-1449.

Heckman, B.W., Ditre, J.W., & Brandon, T.H. (2012). The restorative effects of smoking upon self-control resources: A negative reinforcement pathway. *Journal of Abnormal Psychology, 121*(1), 244-249.

Helig, M. & Koob, G.F. (2007). A key role for corticotropin-releasing factor in alcohol dependence. *Trends in Neuroscience, 30*(8), 399-406.

Hollander, E. & Evers, M. (2004). Review of obsessive-compulsive spectrum disorders: What do we know? Where are we going? *Clinical Neuropsychiatry, 1*, 32-51.

Hollander, E. & Wong, C.M. (1995). Obsessive-compulsive spectrum disorders. *Journal of Clinical Psychiatry, 56*(Suppl 4), 3-6.

Hommer, D.W., Bjork, J.M., & Gilman, J.M. (2011). Imaging brain response to reward in addictive disorders. *Annals of the New York Academy of Science, 1216*, 50-61.

Johansson, A., Grant, J.E., Kim, S.W., Odlaug, B.L., & Gotestam, K.G. (2009). Risk factors for problematic gambling: A critical literature review. *Journal of Gambling Studies, 25*(1), 67-92.

Kafka, M.P. (1997). Hypersexual desire in males: An operational definition and clinical implications for males with paraphilias ad paraphilia-related disorders. *Archives of Sexual Behavior, 26*(5), 505-526.

Kafka, M.P. & Prentky, R. (1992). A comparative study of nonparaphilic sexual addictions and paraphilias in men. *Journal of Clinical Psychiatry, 53*(10), 345-350.

Kelly, T.H., Robbins, G., Martin, C.A., Fillmore, M.T., Lane, S.D., Harrington, N.G., & Rush, C.R. (2006). Individual differences in drug abuse vulnerability: D-amphetamine and sensation-seeking status. *Psychopharmacology (Berl), 189*(1), 17-25.

Kondo, T. (2008). Dopamine dysregulation syndrome. Hypothetical application of reward system stimulation for the treatment of anhedonia in Parkinson's disease patients. *Journal of Neurology, 255*(suppl 4), 14-18.

Koob, G.F. (2004). A role for GABA mechanisms in the motivational effects of alcohol. *Biochemical Pharmacology, 68*(8), 1515-1525.

Koob, G.F. (2013). Theoretical frameworks and mechanistic aspects of alcohol addiction: Alcohol addiction as a reward deficit disorder. *Current Topics Behavioral Neuroscience, 13*, 3-30.

Koob, G. & Kreek, M.J. (2007). Stress, dysregulation of drug reward pathways, and the transition to drug dependence. *American Journal of Psychiatry, 164*(8), 1149-1159.

Kreek, M.J., Levran, O., Reed, B., Schlussman, S.D., Zhou, Y., & Butelman, E.R. (2012). Opiate addiction and cocaine addiction: Underlying molecular neurobiology and genetics. *Journal of Clinical Investigations, 122*(10), 3387-3393.

Lajtha, A. (2008). Interrelated mechanisms in reward and learning. *Neurochemical International, 52*(1-2), 73-79.

Lajtha, A. & Sershen, H. (2010). Heterogeneity of reward mechanisms. *Neurochemistry Research, 35*(6), 851-867.

Ledgerwood, D.M. & Petry, N.M. (2006). Psychological experience of gambling and subtypes of pathological gamblers. *Psychiatry Research, 144*(1), 17-27.

Le Merrer, J., Becker, J.A., Befort, K., & Kieffer, B.L. (2009). Reward processing by the opioid system in the brain. *Physiology Review, 89*(4), 1379-1412.

Leventhal, A.M., Greenberg, J.B., Trujillo, M.A., Ameringer, K.J., Lisha, N.E., Pang, R.D., & Monterosso, J. (2013). Positive and negative affect as predictors of urge to smoke: Temporal factors and meditational pathways. *Psychology of Addictive Behavior, 27*(1), 262-267.

Lochner, C. & Stein, D. (2006). Does work on obsessive-compulsive spectrum disorders contribute to understanding the heterogeneity of obsessive-compulsive disorder? *Progress in Neuro-Psychopharmacology & Biological Psychiatry, 30*, 353-361.

Lubman, D.I., Yucel, M., & Pantelis, C. (2004). Addiction, a condition of compulsive behaviour? Neuroimaging and neuropsychological evidence of inhibitory dysregulation. *Addiction, 99*(12), 1491-1502.

Martin-Fardon, R., Zorrilla, E.P., Ciccocioppo, R., & Weiss, F. (2010). Role of innate and drug-induced dysregulation of brain stress and arousal systems in addiction: Focus on corticotropin-releasing factor, nociceptin/orphanin FQ, and orexin/hypocretin. *Brain Research, 1314*, 165-161.

McGregor, I.S., Callaghan, P.D., & Hunt, G.E. (2008). From ultrasocial to antisocial: A role for oxytocin in the acute reinforcing effects and long-term adverse consequences of drug use? *British Journal of Pharmacology, 154*(2), 358-368.

McKee, S.A., Sinha, R., Weinberger, A.H., Sofuoglu, M., Harrison, E.L., Lavery, M., & Wanzer, J. (2011). Stress decrease and the ability to resist smoking and potentiates smoking intensity and reward. *Journal of Psychopharmacology, 25*(4), 490-502.

Meyers, R.J., Roozen, H.G., & Smith, J.E. (2011). The community reinforcement approach: An update of the evidence. *Alcohol Research & Health, 33*(4), 380-388.

Nees, F. (2015). The nicotinic cholinergic system function in the human brain. *Neuropharmacology, 289-301*(14), 396-397.

Newton, T.F., De La Garza, R., Kalechstein, A.D., Tziortzis, D., & Jacobsen, C.A. (2009). Theories of addiction: Methamphetamine users' explanations for continuing drug use and relapse. *American Journal of Addiction, 18*(4), 294-300.

O'Sullivan, S.S., Evans, A.H., & Lees, A.J. (2009). Dopamine dysregulation syndrome: An overview of its epidemiology, mechanisms and management. *CNS Drugs, 23*(2), 157-170.

Papachristou, H., Nederkoorn, C., Havermans, R., Van Der Horst, M., & Jansen, A. (2012). Can't stop the craving: The effect of impulsivity on cue-elicited cravings for alcohol in heavy and light drinkers. *Psychopharmacology (Berl), 219*(2), 511-518.

Parolaro, D., Rubino, T., Vigano, D., Massi, P., Guidali, C., & Realini, N. (2010). Cellular mechanisms underlying the interaction between cannabinoid and opioid system. *Current Drug Targets, 11*(4), 393-405.

Peters, J., Pattji, T., & De Vries, T.J. (2013). Targeting cocaine versus heroin memories: Divergent roles within ventromedial prefrontal cortex. *Trends in Pharmacological Science, 34*(12), 689-695.

Potenza, M.N. (2007). Impulse control disorders and co-occurring disorders: Dual diagnosis considerations. *Journal of Dual Diagnosis, 3*, 47-57.

Potenza, M.N., Koran, L.M., & Pallanti, S. (2009). The relationship between impulse-control disorders and obsessive-compulsive disorder: A current understanding and future research directions. *Psychiatry Research, 170*, 22-31.

Reid, R.C., Carpenter, B.N., Hook, J.N., Garos, S., Manning, R., Gilliland, R. et al (2012). Report of findings in a DSM-5 field trial for hypersexual disorder. *Journal of Sexual Medicine, 9*(11), 2868-2877.

Richters, J., De Visser, R.O., Rissel, C.E., Grulich, A.E., & Smith, A. (2008). Demographics and psychosocial features of participants in bondage and discipline, "sadomasochism" or dominance and submission (BDSM): Data from a national survey. *The Journal of Sexual Medicine, 5*(7), 1660-1668.

Robinson, M.J. & Berridge, K.C. (2013). Instant transformation of learned repulsion into motivational "wanting." *Current Biology, 23*(4), 282-289.

Saunders, B.T. & Robinson, T.E. (2013). Individual variation in resisting temptation: Implications for addiction. *Neuroscience Biobehavioral Reviews, 37*(p Pt A), 1955-1975.

Sinha, R. (2008). Chronic stress, drug use, and vulnerability to addiction. *Annals of the New York Academy of Science, 1141*, 105-130.

Solla, P., Bortolato, M., Cannas, A., Mulas, C.S., & Marrosu, F. (2015). Paraphilias and paraphilic disorders in Parkinson's disease: A systematic review of the literature. *Movement Disorders, 30*(15), 604-613.

Spano, M.S., Fadda, P., Fratta, W., & Fattore, L. (2010). Cannabinoid-opioid interactions in drug discrimination and self-administration: Effect of maternal, postnatal, adolescent and adult exposure to the drugs. *Current Drug Targets, 11*(4), 450-461.

Stein, D.J. & Hollander, E. (1993). Impulsive aggression and obsessive-compulsive disorder. *Psychiatric Annals, 23*, 389-395.

Stinson, J.D., Becker, J.V., & Sales, B.D. (2008). Self-regulation and the etiology of sexual deviance: Evaluating causal theory. *Violence & Victimization, 23*(1), 35-51.

Ting-A-Kee, R. & Van Der Kooy, D. (2012). The neurobiology of opiate motivation. *Cold Spring Harbor Perspectives in Medicine, 2*(10), 100-109.

Viachou, S. & Panagis, G. (2014). Regulation of brain reward by the endocannabinoid system: A critical review of behavioral studies in animals. *Current Pharmacological Desertations, 20*(13), 2072-2088.

Woicik, P.A., Stewart, S.H., Pihl, R.O., & Conrod, P.J. (2009). The substance use risk profile scale: A scale measuring traits linked to reinforcement-specific substance use profiles. *Addiction Behavior, 34*(12), 1042-1055.

World Health Organization (1992). *The ICD-10 Classification of Mental and Behavioral Disorders: Clinical Descriptions and Diagnostic Guidelines.* Geneva: World Health Organization.

CHAPTER 10

Personality Disorders

As enduring and characteristic ways of acting and reacting, there is a very extensive range of behaviors comprising personality. Some of these behaviors can potentially be viewed as discrete, others continuous, and some both, so it is not surprising that a diverse range of personality models have been proposed. The Greek philosopher Theophrastus (c 371-287 BC) in *The Characters* listed 30 descriptions organized along one structure, with each character type named and illustrated via examples (cited in Crocq, 2013). Gerald Heymans (1857-1930) proposed three bipolar dimensions (activity level, emotionality, and primary versus secondary functioning) yielding eight personality types on a cube consisting of amorphous, sanguine, nervous, choleric, apathetic, phlegmatic, sentimental, and passionate (cited in Crocq, 2013). Some of these personality types hint at modern day abnormal personality designations.

Emil Kraepelin (1856-1926) brought personality types into the psychiatric realm, referring to "psychopathic personalities" (cited in Crocq, 2013). By the eighth edition of his textbook seven types were listed: Excitable, irresolute, instinct followers (impulsive), eccentrics, pathological liars and swindlers, enemies of society, and quarrelsome (cited in Crocq, 2013). Some of these types relate to modern day categories, such as excitable with borderline personality disorder, and pathological liars and swindlers antisocial personality disorder. Clarifying the notion of disordered personality, Kurt Schneider (1887-1967) defined "psychopathic" personality as those individuals who suffer, or cause society to suffer, because of their personality traits (cited in Crocq, 2013). Of equal or greater significance, he argued that it would be artificial and meaningless to derive clinically relevant abnormal types from exaggerations of normal personality dimensions (cited in Crocq, 2013). This is a point that we will return to.

As pertains to normal personality, what has come to dominate over time is the trait approach. The basic technique underlying the trait approach is to assemble adjectives used to describe personality, and subject them to the statistical technique of factor analysis (Crocq, 2013). Factors theoretically representing normal personality emerge from the data. An important restraint resides in limits to factor analysis, in that an infinite number of solutions can follow from any data set (Marsh et al, 2014; Wetzel, 2012). In other words, there is no one correct solution, a limitation often not spelled out in research studies utilizing factor analytic techniques. The first of these approaches to gain widespread recognition was Raymond Cattell's (1905-1998) 16-factor system listing bipolar dimensions, referenced by letters to reduce the risk of erroneous interpretations (cited in Crocq, 2013). What has transpired with personality trait research is that over time and many studies, certain dimensions have repeated, with these best embodied in models devised by Cloninger (Cloninger, 1987; Cloninger et al, 1993) and Costa and McCrae (1992).

Cloninger's Seven-Factor Model (Cloninger, 1987; Cloninger et al, 1993) provides four temperamental dimensions (novelty-seeking, harm avoidance, reward dependence, and persistence), and three dimensions of character (self-directedness, cooperativeness, and self-transcendence) (Cloninger, 1987; Cloninger et al, 1993). Costa and McCrae (1992) proposed a five-factor model (FFM) of temperament/personality that has come to be known as the "Big Five." The five bipolar dimensions consist of extraversion-introversion, neurotic-emotionally stable, open-closed to experience, agreeable-antagonism, and conscientious-negligence (Costa & McCrae, 1992). Costa and McCrae's (1992) model has tended to dominate in part because it seems to capture the essence of "normal" personality, and in a fashion much easier to understand than that of Cloninger's Seven-Factor Model (Cloninger, 1987; Cloninger et al, 1993), the division into temperaments and character types creating confusion. It is important to keep in mind, though, that there is no one correct solution, and other options are viable.

In contrast to the intensive and comprehensive trait approach to "normal" personality, efforts to determine "abnormal" personality have been less robust. The radically different psychoanalytic approach led by Freud postulated that personality disorders result from unsuccessful resolution of conflicts emerging with psychosexual stages of development, such as obsessive-compulsive problems related to unresolved conflict from the anal stage (Freud, 1959). The DSM and ICD classification systems of personality disorders eventually came to be based on the views of Kraepelin, embodying his notion of discrete personality disorder types (American Psychiatric Association, 2013; First et al, 2002; World Health Organization, 1992). These types are both separate from others, and present/absent in the sense that a person has to have a certain number and form of symptoms to meet the diagnosis; if not, then the personality disorder does not characterize the person. This approach also relies on a model by Gunderson (1988) providing levels of severity: Psychotic type most severe; "self-disorders" including narcissistic, antisocial, and borderline mid-level; and avoidant, dependent, histrionic, and obsessive-compulsive closest to normality.

Although the notion of distinct present/absent categories of disordered personality is appealing, there are a number of problems with this approach, including excessive co-occurrence of symptoms that should distinguish types, insufficient coverage such that "not otherwise specified" is often the most common diagnosis, arbitrary and shifting boundaries between conditions, inability to manage diverse presentations of a given type, and no real scientific basis (Trull & Durrett, 2005; Widiger & Trull, 2007). These problems combined with the apparent success of the trait approach for normal personality raise the possibility that abnormal personality might be dimensional in nature like normal personality. Furthermore, it seems highly unlikely that abnormal personality is completely removed from normal personality, as is implied by the discrete condition approach.

Perhaps the simplest way of incorporating a continuous element is to transform existing DSM and ICD categories into dimensions, as opposed to having to meet a threshold number of criteria for a diagnosis. Oldham and Skodol (2000) proposed a model rating the extent to which a person matches DSM-IV-TR prototypes, derived from all the criteria of a particular personality disorder. Shedler and Westen (2004) proposed a similar system, but based on narrative descriptions of a prototypical disordered personality type. Although these approaches each address some of the weaknesses of the categorical system, they do not adequately address all of the problems, and do not assist in linking normal and abnormal personality (Trull & Durrett, 2005; Widiger & Trull, 2007). A cognitive approach to personality disorders has been proposed linking types of beliefs to categorical disorders (Beck et al, 2001), but it is more likely that the disorder entails certain thought patterns than it is that the thought patterns cause the disorder. For example, with borderline personality disorder various self-critical thoughts arise, but it is hard to conceive of how these cause the personality disorder.

Given the success of the trait approach for normal personality, it is not surprising that is has been extended to DSM categories (Clark et al, 1996; Livesley, 1998; Livesley & Jackson, 1986). These trait approaches involve the application of factor analysis to various aspects of DSM personality disorders. Although these approaches utilize factor analytic methods found to be useful for normal personality, they are based on what is provided by the DSM personality disorder categories, and hence map onto this system too well (Trull & Durrett, 2005). A different trait approach involves extending normal personality, such as Cloninger's seven-factor and Costa and McCrae's Big Five models, to abnormal forms. Regarding Cloninger's Seven-Factor Model, research has shown that the profiles can map onto categorical personality disorders, such as low reward dependence, high novelty-seeking, and high harm avoidance characterizing the odd/eccentric personality disorders (Svrakic et al, 1993). However, relationships between Cloninger's temperament and character dimensions, and both individual and clusters of personality disorders, have demonstrated mixed results overall (Trull & Burrett, 2005). Regarding Costa and McCrae's FFM, research has tended to show that the five dimensions and six facets under each can be mapped onto abnormal personality categories (Trull & Burrett, 2005). However, at the level of the five main factors the linkage is not ideal, with most personality disorders involving elevated neuroticism, introversion, antagonism, and negligence, but the 30 facets do provide a linkage to personality disorder categories (Trull & Burrett, 2005).

Considering the application of the trait approach to abnormal personality there are two major problems, the first being that the approach really just involves linking or mapping normal trait dimensions to existing abnormal personality disorder categories. With Cloninger's Seven-factor and Costa and McCrae's FFM models the main dimensions do not map on well, requiring a focus on underlying facets. However, a quick look at the 30 facets of the FFM (too extensive to reproduce here) reveals that they could map onto virtually any aspect of human behavior, due to how broad the coverage is. The early assertion by Kurt Schneider that it is artificial and meaningless to derive clinically relevant abnormal types from exaggerations of normal personality dimensions is worth noting here (cited in Crocq, 2013).

One option is to apply a trait approach to normal and abnormal populations, based on adjectives describing abnormal personality as well. However, in designing the factor analytic studies of "normal" personality all possible adjectives for personality were applied, with no exclusion because they might be negative or dysfunctional. For example, a study by Ashton et al (2004) utilized 1,710 adjectives that included both positive and negative descriptors, their results largely replicating the Big Five dimensions. The term "normal" personality does not mean that those with negative personality aspects were excluded, but instead refers to broad samples of adjectives and people. Hence, focusing on strictly abnormal populations is not likely to reveal radically different personality dimensions, and particularly if abnormal personality is an extension of normal personality.

At the heart of this problem is that normal personality dimensions derived from the trait approach, even in an extreme form, do not actually yield personality disorders, at least not those we are familiar with. For example, extreme introversion and extroversion do not produce personality disorders, other than some aspects of histrionic related to extreme extroversion. However, histrionic behavior can also arise from mania and other sources. Likewise, extremes of conscientiousness, openness to experience, and agreeableness do not give rise to personality disorders. An important comment at this point is that the neurotic-emotionally unstable dimension is probably misnamed, because in an evolutionary context the real issue is reactivity. Organisms vary in the strength of their response to challenges, high reactivity equating with neuroticism. Presumably, normal personality dimensions arose from evolutionary selection pressures, with core dimensions having an impact on fitness. For example, reactivity would undoubtedly have influenced evolutionary fitness, the adaptive value of a given level fluctuating with environmental circumstances. In an environment with many lethal threats, such as crocodiles at watering holes, a high degree of reactivity would be very adaptive. However, in a much more benign setting, such as our modern day one, high reactivity only impairs social relationships. In a setting where rigorous planning and implementation fostered survival, such as with difficult to hunt prey, a high level of conscientiousness would be highly adaptive, but in a setting where preparation did not matter, conscientiousness would just waste resources. If an environment offers novel and valuable rewards, such as patches of highly nutritious food, then high openness to experience is adaptive, while in an environment with few novel rewards and dangerous predators, being closed to experience and harm avoidant is adaptive.

The social setting, so crucial to our hunting-gathering evolution, probably influenced the value of agreeableness and extroversion. Reciprocity was crucial to our success, and being agreeable would facilitate reciprocity. Deceit was also common, enabling a person to acquire more resources. If there were many "cheaters" then being disagreeable might preserve resources. In the case of a non-threatening social environment, being extroverted would help a person acquire social support and mates, but in a hierarchical and threatening context introversion would be best, except for the most socially dominant individuals. Each of these personality dimensions then had relevance to our evolution, and since circumstances varied the most adaptive placement on the dimension would vary. Those individuals whose personality profile most closely matched physical and social environmental circumstances would likely have adapted more easily, while those fully mismatched would struggle to adapt.

The second problem encountered with the trait approach and abnormal personality is one that opens up an entirely different option: The trait approach is based on the assumption, to the best of my knowledge never raised, that personality can be fully derived from conscious experience. Adjectives are the basis of the trait approach, and they are part of language that is fully conscious, at least at the level of the words applied. What about unconscious contributions to personality? Other than the largely discredited psychoanalytic approach of linking supposed psychosexual stage conflicts to abnormal personality, this is largely unexplored territory. The energy consumed by unconscious active messaging, referred to as the default mode network, occurring during sleep, daydreaming, anesthesia and other states, is 20 times greater than the energy used to respond consciously (Fox & Raichle, 2007; Zhang & Raichle, 2010). Consistent with this energy imbalance, many aspects of mental life, including motivation, and cognitive and emotional information processing, appear to be largely unconscious (Morsella et al, 2010). With so much more energy utilization for unconscious thought, and the number and diversity of processes influencing behavior, it follows that much of personality is derived from unconscious experience. It might be opined that trait derived dimensions are largely unconscious, but the number of available adjectives to describe this aspect of personality in so many languages suggests that much of it is conscious, such as openness and conscientiousness.

Consciousness in contrast seems to play a more restricted, although critical role, involving awareness of the very brief now where reality transpires (see the "Hypomania-Mania" chapter for a discussion of time distinctions), thereby providing the evolutionary fitness enhancing capacity to adaptively adjust behavior in the moment. For example, conscious awareness of a ripple on the surface of a watering hole enables a person to rapidly retreat before the crocodile attacks. This capacity likely accounts for why it has evolved in so many different species (Butler et al, 2005; Fabbro et al, 2015). According to Fabbro et al (2015) there are five lines of evidence supporting the presence of consciousness in a wide range of animal species: First, a pattern of EEG activity in the range of 20-70 Hz, typically linked to wakefulness and REM sleep; second, thalamo-cortical activity; third, widespread brain activity during processing of sensory stimuli; fourth, selective synchronization at cortical and brainstem levels of dynamically formed neural networks involved in binding sensory stimuli; fifth, the presence of egocentric maps for localizing an individual in a given space. Fish, amphibians, reptiles, birds, mammals, and primates demonstrate some form of consciousness based on these parameters (Butler et al, 2005; Fabbro et al, 2015). Indeed, it seems that once a minimal level of cognitive sophistication is achieved an organism becomes conscious. Interestingly, the role of time distinctions in the evolution of consciousness might provide a logical proof for time distinctions: Natural selection is an established scientific process, and since consciousness has largely evolved based on time distinctions, these distinctions must be real.

Regarding personality and the unconscious, although there are a number of different candidates for unconscious contributors to normal and abnormal personality, a viable option consists of psychological defense mechanisms in an expanded framework (Bowins, 2010b). Upon discovering and elucidating classical psychological defense mechanisms Freud commented, "I have the distinct feeling that I have touched on one of the greatest secrets of nature" (1899, cited in Masson, 1985: 45). This statement appears to be accurate, because compared to most other psychoanalytic concepts psychological defense mechanisms have stood the test of time very robustly. Psychological defense mechanisms characterize many personality disorders, such as projection with paranoid personality disorder, schizoid fantasy with schizoid personality disorder, and a host of immature ones with borderline personality disorder, including acting out, splitting, idealization-devaluation, and projective identification (Bond & Perry, 2004; Perry, 2001; Van Wijk-Herbrink et al, 2011). Furthermore, improvement in borderline personality disorder, and other personality disorders for that matter, is largely defined by a shift from immature to mature defenses (Bond & Perry, 2004; Perry, 2001; Van Wijk-Herbrink et al, 2011).

Psychological defense mechanisms, including the templates of positive cognitive distortions and dissociation subsuming the classical psychoanalytic defenses, appear to have evolved in response to amplified negative emotions, derived from the evolution of human intelligence (Bowins, 2004, 2006a). They moderate the intensity of negative emotions in the moment, tending to be very adaptive when expressed in a milder form, and more dysfunctional in a severe and enduring form (Bowins, 2004, 2006a). When expressed in the latter form several defensive styles produce the personality disorder categories that we are familiar with (Bowins, 2010b). Under chronic stress, and likely impaired capacity to regulate stress responses, the intensity and persistence of the defensive style advances such that a formal personality disorder arises. This model of abnormal personality disorders is based on unconscious system functioning, and is hybrid in that categories clinicians are familiar with can be retained, as well as dimensional in that the defensive responses range from normal and healthy to severe and maladaptive along a continuum (Bowins, 2010b). One advantage of the model is that it is flexible, allowing for the addition of new personality disorders, based on extremes of milder defenses. At this point the model will be demonstrated for each personality disorder in current diagnostic systems.

Avoidant Personality Disorder (Anxious Personality Disorder ICD-10)

One of the most basic defenses consists of avoiding threats (Bowins, 2010b). For example, if when walking along a street you notice a person shouting and waving a knife, what is your natural reaction? Approaching and encountering the person could well result in injury or death, impeding evolutionary fitness. The natural reaction is to avoid the person, perhaps by withdrawing. Avoiding real and potent threats comprises mild avoidance, because there is a high threshold for eliciting the response. If a person avoids challenges that are not objectively threatening and offer reward, then the threshold if very low and the response maladaptive. Adult romantic involvement, while a challenge, is not objectively threatening, and to most people offers substantial reward potential. Hence, avoiding such contact is usually maladaptive. Those with avoidant personality disorder avoid challenges that are not objectively threatening, and offer the potential for reward. Although often considered in the milder realm of personality pathology, avoidance can actually be devastating, because there is no personal growth, and frequently a decline in functioning. A typical scenario is for a person with this problem to be pushed by others to seek help, as they naturally avoid the challenge of psychotherapy. Frequently the person is not employed or well below their potential, or not attending school or failing to complete assignments. If psychotherapy is mostly supportive the person will often persist, but if the therapist attempts to get the person to face challenges, even in a graded fashion, they commonly avoid therapy.

At the core of avoidant personality disorder is anxiety, and linked to this excessive behavioral inhibition. Essentially, the person demonstrates inhibited behavior, and certainly not approach behavior associated with behavioral activation (Alden et al, 2002; Bowins, 2010b). Behavioral inhibition regulates sensitivity to threat and non-reward cues, and guides inhibition and avoidance responses (Gray, 1987; Fowles, 1988). Frequently, those with avoidant personality disorder have rejecting and isolating experiences in their early life, contributing to a cognitive style of perceiving threats (Alden et al, 2002). The more they avoid, the more anxious they tend to be, resulting in the perception of more intense threats, leading to more avoidance, and so on and so forth (Meyer, 2002).

Conceptualizing avoidant personality disorder dimensionally, with behavioral inhibition and anxiety central, retains the category clinicians are familiar with, while placing the condition on an evolutionary based and hence scientific foundation. It also affords an effective way to intervene psychotherapeutically, initially by getting the person to distinguish the landscape. Have the person list all threats in their life, and then divide them into those that are objectively threatening such as a knife wielding person, and those that are not objectively threatening. Given the person's high behavioral inhibition and anxiety, many agents are perceived to be threatening. A helpful cognitive technique at this point is the 100-juror scenario: Have them imagine a hundred objective jurors deliberating on whether the threat is real. If a high percentage say that it is real then there is an objective threat, but if only a minority say it is real then the threat is subjective. For real threats simply avoid them as the person is inclined to. For subjective threats further divide them into those that offer the potential for reward, and those that do not. Focus the person on approaching those that offer reward, in a graded fashion starting with the least threatening. As the person acquires the reward and masters the challenge, avoidance can shift to approach behavior. Eventually, the person will become "normal" avoiding threatening agents, while approaching sources of reward.

Narcissistic Personality Disorder

Compensating for weaknesses and insecurities with strengths is a natural defense utilized by everyone (Bowins, 2010b). If your one arm is sore, you will do more with the other. In attempting to acquire a partner, those who are attractive but not well spoken will let their appearance talk, whereas those with the reverse profile will talk to impress. In narcissistic personality disorder there are very significant insecurities and weaknesses, and intense overcompensation relying on strengths. The former limit the person from growing, and the latter alienates others due to the intensity and pronounced sense of entitlement. Fenichel (1945) noted this compensatory relationship, suggesting that excessive achievement striving derives from defective self-esteem. More specific weaknesses and insecurities are usually involved rather than global self-esteem. Strengths in some areas are important because without them the narcissistic defense is not workable. Research has supported the presence of vulnerable and grandiose aspects (Dickinson & Pincus, 2003; Rovik, 2001). In addition, grandiosity might involve over-control in response to under-controlled aspects, perhaps related to excessive control by parents (Horton & Tritch, 2014).

Insecurities/weaknesses and grandiosity can be viewed either as separate aspects dividing the condition, or grandiose aspects compensating for vulnerabilities. Given the limitation of discrete subdivision approaches applied to other conditions, as discussed throughout the book, it is unlikely that the division of narcissism into distinct insecure and grandiose types will hold out. A more robust proposal is varying degrees of insecurities/weaknesses and grandiosity, with the latter defensively compensating for the former. It is often commented that many people feel entitled; does this mean that everyone has narcissistic personality disorder (possibly linked to the notion of a grandiose type of narcissism)? Entitlement can arise from many sources, such as social prescription, with kings and queens for example being entitled to special privileges and rewards. In a sense we live in an entitled era where everyone seems to feel entitled to unlimited consumer goods and rewards, contributing to all the problems associated with hyper-consumption (Bowins, 2014, pp. 142-161). Hence, although entitlement is widespread, narcissism as a personality disorder is much more restricted.

As with avoidant personality disorder, a defense conceptualization of narcissism retains a category that clinicians are familiar with and find valuable, while structuring it dimensionally in a way that places it on a scientific foundation. Regarding the notion of categories that clinicians are familiar with, several of the personality disorders have merit because they are commonly encountered in clinical practice. They are not fictitious entities, but constitute real occurrences. The problem resides not in their presence, but in their framing as discrete categories representing present/absent diagnoses with no connection to the normal population.

An additional advantage of the defense model of narcissism is that it affords a more effective way to intervene therapeutically. A common finding among clinicians experienced with personality disorder patients is that those with narcissistic personality disorder are as, or more, challenging to treat than those with borderline personality disorder. Any comment perceived as a slight can lead the person to exit therapy. The defense conceptualization is very humanistic in that it links normal personality to abnormal, and in a very parsimonious fashion, facilitating the bond between patient and therapist. The starting point is to explain how we all compensate for weaknesses and insecurities with strengths, and the more intense the former are the more powerful the compensation tends to be. Those with narcissism can relate to this explanation because it fits with their experience, even unconscious. The explanation also accurately acknowledges that the person has strengths. Building on the therapeutic bond the next step is to explore strengths and insecurities/weaknesses, and see how the former might compensate for the latter. Therapy next proceeds to bolstering the insecurities via various techniques applicable to a given person and instance, such as a more dynamic approach for early life issues, and cognitive restructuring for distorted perspectives. As the insecurities and weaknesses are bolstered, the overcompensation tends to moderate, particularly with supportive interventions designed to help the person gradually relinquish such behaviors. Over time the person settles to a level of narcissism more within the normal range.

Histrionic Personality Disorder

Histrionic personality disorder is one of the weakest personality disorders as it is rarely found in a pure form, and much more frequently as traits consistent with it. These traits can arise from diverse sources, such as excessive extroversion, reinforcement of dramatic behavior, manic presentations, or manipulation related to antisocial personality disorder (Bowins, 2010b). It almost certainly does not constitute a personality disorder in its own right, and might well represent narcissistic personality disorder with the dramatic behavior overcompensating for insecurities (Bowins, 2010b).

Dependent Personality Disorder

Humans are a social species due to our evolution in hunting-gathering groups (Glantz & Pearce, 1989). Lacking the body weaponry of other species we relied on this form of social organization. In addition, reciprocity was critical, as for example if your hunt went well and you shared, then those you shared with would reciprocate when your efforts failed (Glantz & Pearce, 1989). Hence, to rely on others is natural and defensive in that we turn to people when threatened or suffering. Even simple emotional support from others can impact greatly on how a person adapts to stressors. However, it is a matter of degree, with mild dependence being very adaptive, and intense reliance, such that a person cannot function independently, constituting a maladaptive scenario (Bowins, 2010b). The latter degree of intensity tends to greatly limit what a person can do, and alienate those depended on, with the exception of select very insecure people who form a co-dependent relationship with the individual. Excessive dependency impairs physical health, and increases both health care utilization and the risk of violence to self or others (Bornstein, 2012). Anxiety often motivates dependency, although modeling influences and reinforcement can also contribute to such behavior. Anxiety fostering dependency can arise from overprotective, controlling, and authoritarian parenting (Bornstein, 1992; Head et al, 1991).

Regarding treatment, the most optimal approach is to moderate the dependent behavior, a goal that is more understandable when such behavior is conceptualized in terms of a dimension from normal healthy dependency to extreme and maladaptive (Bowins, 2010b). Modeling of independent behavior and structuring of therapy, such as to limit calls between sessions, can assist in reducing dependency on others. Cognitive restructuring of thoughts and schemata maintaining anxiety and limiting independent actions is also very helpful. As the person starts acting independently successes occur that positively reinforce independence, reducing anxiety and improving confidence, further lowering dependency needs. Gradually, the person shifts to a level of dependency that is within the normal range.

Obsessive-Compulsive Personality Disorder (Anankastic ICD-10)

In the "Reinforcement Based Disorders" chapter it was mentioned that compulsivity must be distinguished from obsessive-compulsive. Compulsive behavior is present in many conditions overlapping with impulsive behavior and addictions. Compulsivity refers to persistent behavior that is motivated by reinforcement. For example, repetitive hand washing reduces anxiety, and hence is negatively reinforced. Obsessions refer to anxiety producing thoughts. When linked to obsessions, compulsions represent a defense that reduces anxiety, at least in the moment (Bowins, 2010b). For instance, anxiety pertaining to contamination by germs (an obsession) is relieved in the moment by compulsive hand washing behavior. The defensive function is often far more extensive, because diverse sources of anxiety can be funneled into a particular obsession, and relieved by a compulsive action, whether physical or mental. Anxiety about illness and death for instance can be funneled into an obsession about germs, and then hand washing reduces the anxiety. Likewise, anxiety pertaining to the messiness and disorder of life might be funneled into an obsession about maintaining order, relieved by compulsive mental lists of things to do. Compulsive ritualistic behavior has been found to maintain tension at a manageable level (Rachman & Hodgson, 1980). From an analytic perspective, guilt-related anxiety is managed and contained by obsessive-compulsive behavior, via excessive application of the undoing defense mechanism (Fenichel, 1945). From an evolutionary perspective, obsessive-compulsive type behavior serves the defensive function of minimizing risk by maintaining order (Brune, 2006), or managing various other threats such as contamination or resource depletion (Polimeni et al, 2005).

On a milder scale, emotional discomfort and anxiety can be managed and contained by ritualistic behavior. Numerous examples are available, such as routine prayer at the end of the day to manage anxieties arising from daily stressors. Exercise and cleaning can also serve this function, helping to contain anxieties, in part by absorption in the activity (Bowins, 2012c). Rigorous note taking and documentation help clinicians manage anxiety arising from the ever-present risk of patient complaints and litigation. Consistent with a dimensional obsessive-compulsive defense, 90% of healthy adults and children demonstrate such behavior (Boyer & Lienard, 2006). While milder forms of obsessive-compulsive behavior are adaptive, more extensive variants impair a person's flexibility and capacity to cope, frequently drawing too much of a person's mental and physical energy. Given that obsessive-compulsiveness is a defensive process, the prospect of eliminating all such behavior is unrealistic, and often frightening to a person. Instead of attempting to eliminate all such behavior, therapy such as exposure and response prevention should aim to diminish it to more normal levels (Bowins, 2010b). Obsessions have been found to vary in how strongly a person adheres to them, as occurs with delusions, indicating a spectrum of intensity and the feasibility of moderating them (Veale, 2002).

One critique of the defensive interpretation of obsessive-compulsive behavior is that, if true, then symptom substitution will always occur. In many instances it does with diminishing of one focus resulting in intensification of another. A young patient who will be referred to as Susan experienced intense anxiety, with two main obsessive-compulsive foci, although others occurred from time to time. The first was bed bugs and the second sexually transmitted diseases. Her anxiety focus was almost always on disease, in part triggered by the death of her father from cancer at an early age. She greatly feared illness in her mother and self. Both bed bugs and sexually transmitted diseases have an illness/contamination and physical vulnerability theme. When not in a romantic relationship the bed bug obsession dominated, and while in a romance the sexually transmitted disease one dominated. By engaging in the compulsions of checking her bed and pubic region meticulously, she relieved the anxiety in the moment, but yet when anxiety peaked from stress, the intensity of the compulsion significantly interfered with her functioning. When both obsessive-compulsive foci were present and one targeted in treatment, the other would intensify, and when both were targeted other less dominant ones grew. In some instances symptom substitution does not transpire, largely because the treatment can substantially diminish the anxiety that motivates the obsessive-compulsive defensive response.

Another critique is that the model fails to distinguish obsessive-compulsive disorder (OCD) from obsessive-compulsive personality disorder. Given the dimensional nature of the obsessive-compulsive defensive response, there is a range of expressions, and when such behavior characterizes a person's actions on a daily basis, it is referred to as a personality disorder. When it does not characterize daily behavior, but is still expressed in a strong form, it tends to be referred to as OCD. However, this is a completely artificial distinction, as the underlying cognitive and physical behaviors tend to persist, at least without treatment, and worsen under stress due to intensified anxiety. Given its primarily defensive role obsessive-compulsive behavior best fits under the personality disorder umbrella.

Antisocial Personality Disorder (Dissocial ICD-10)

Several aspects of antisocial personality disorder are contentious, such as whether it is dimensional, and if so does it run continuous with the normal population, is it strictly dysfunctional perhaps due to brain damage, and can it be improved? Regarding dimensionality, more recent studies employing rigorous taxometric procedures tend to support a continuous distribution. Studies of prison inmates suggest that it is dimensional within these populations (Coid & Ullrich, 2010; Marcus et al, 2004), and also when court-ordered substance abusers are considered (Edens et al, 2006; Marcus et al, 2006). Regarding specific elements of the disorder, both callousness/unemotionality and impulsivity/antisocial behavior are dimensional in convicted offenders (Guay et al, 2007). Studying both male and female forensic psychiatric and jail/prisoner inmates, Walters et al (2007) found that overall antisocial and facets (interpersonal, affective, impulsive lifestyle, and antisocial behavior) demonstrate a continuous organization. Among youth psychopathy like personality features are organized dimensionally in non-forensic populations (Edens et al, 2011; Murrie et al, 2007). A dimensional organization also applies to male delinquent youth (Walters, 2014). Applying a longitudinal study design (in contrast to a cross-sectional approach adopted in all the previously mentioned studies), Walters and Ruscio (2013) followed 1,708 youth, assessing them for antisocial behavior, based on scale ratings by mothers, every 2 years starting at 6 years of age and ending at 14. The data revealed solid evidence for antisocial behavior having a continuous latent structure (Walters & Ruscio, 2013). The results for youth support psychopathic behavior being on a continuum with the normal population, as opposed to a clear separation of normal and psychopathic.

Considering how antisocial behavior is structured continuously, it appears unlikely that it is strictly dysfunctional. Studies of antisocial personality disorder have commonly focused on convicted offenders, and often more violent ones at that, helping to reinforce the perspective that it is completely maladaptive. In contrast to this perspective is the notion of an evolved deceit strategy (Bowins, 2010b; Harpending & Sobus, 1987). Deceit is part of human nature (and that of most other social species, for that matter), based on how deception can enhance the acquisition of important resources. Children demonstrate the capacity for deceit from as young as 2 years old, well before there is any conscious understanding of what their actions entail (Chandler et al, 1989). With maturity deceit can become increasingly sophisticated. A major limitation to deceitful behavior is that if caught the consequences are often severe, and during our evolution would have meant ostracism involving rejection from the social group if extensive, and exclusion from receiving important resources if milder. Emotional expressions of the deceitful person often inform the potential victim of the deception, as with brief expressions of fear, shame, or guilt. Due to this limitation it appears that evolution has favored more advanced deceit strategies in the form of psychopathic capacities (Harpending & Sobus, 1987). These capacities include emotional detachment from the victim's experience, although perceptions of their reactions are typically very acute to facilitate the deception. For example, successful con artists readily catch victims' reactions informing of whether or not the con is working, and adjust their pitch accordingly, but are emotionally detached from the other person's experience.

Consistent with this interpretation of psychopathic behavior, emotional detachment and antisocial behavior emerge as the two main components, based on factor analyses of the Psychopathy Checklist-Revised, the primary scale for assessing sociopathic behavior (Patrick et al, 1994). The emotional detachment factor includes emotional and interpersonal items, such as superficial charm, grandiosity, lying and manipulation, affective shallowness, and the absence of remorse or empathy. It has been noted that emotional detachment from, and indifference to, the feelings and welfare of others is a hallmark of the condition (Intrator, 1997). Psychopathic behavior has also been described as a "mask of sanity" in which language and conceptual reasoning are intact but are dissociated from affect (Patrick et al, 1994). Dissociation as one of the classical defense mechanisms involving an actual separation of mental processes is only secondary to acting out as a defensive style demonstrated by sociopaths (Vaillant, 1994). Quite likely it is the main defense mechanism for non-violent "white-collar" antisocial individuals.

The major psychological defense mechanism template of psychological dissociation (see the "Dissociation" chapter) appears to provide the capacity for the emotional detachment ability of psychopaths, representing a more extreme variant of dissociation compatible with advanced deception (Bowins, 2004). Such emotional detachment also reduces or removes emotional impediments to behaviors such as raping and pillaging during times of war, thereby fostering further resource acquisition such as enhanced mating opportunities (Bowins, 2004). In support of this supposition, it has been found that contract killers have an exceptional ability to encapsulate emotions, enabling them to commit their violent crimes and continue to function adaptively (Schlesinger, 2001). Interestingly, given how the capacity to dissociate can be advanced via practice (see the "Dissociation" chapter), such as with compartmentalization, people who are not inherently antisocial can learn to detach emotionally and appear to be antisocial. For example, if a person who is not inherently antisocial ends up in a violent gang, he or she can learn to emotionally detach from the experience of those being violated, making it appear that they are antisocial. The difference, however, is that after leaving this type of culture the person might well experience remorse, whereas the true antisocial individual will not.

Several interesting conjectures, all supported by research, follow from the perspective that antisocial personality disorder is an evolved deceit strategy, representing an advanced level on the deceit continuum. One obvious one is that there must be a solid genetic basis. Ferguson (2010) conducted a meta-analysis of behavioral genetic studies, finding that 56% of the variance in antisocial personality disorder is explained by genetic influences. Another prediction is that social cognitive abilities should be relatively intact in those with antisocial personality disorder to facilitate deceitful actions. Dolan and Fullam (2004) compared males with antisocial personality disorder to controls, matched for age and general IQ, on tests of theory of mind. They found that the antisocial group performed just as well as controls, but showed an indifference to the impact of their actions, an adaptive function maintaining antisocial behavior (Dolan & Fullam, 2004).

The evolutionary deceit model also predicts that frequency of occurrence is an issue, in that when those with advanced deception ability become too numerous, detection will be easier, resulting in attacks diminishing their numbers. An evolutionary game model by Colman and Wilson (1997) demonstrates that a stable equilibrium evolves in a population, whereby if too common they are removed, dropping the number down. Antisocial personality disorder thus represents a rare example of frequency dependent selection (Colman & Wilson, 1997). The underlying dimensions of deceit and dissociation, though, do persist in the population. A further prediction is that as an evolved deception strategy it should not respond well to interventions, and if anything the person will attempt to deceive those providing the treatment. Of all the personality disorders, antisocial is one that shows virtually no response to treatment, and a frequent experience of therapists is to feel manipulated. In some instances those with antisocial personality disorder are capable of using their higher cognitive functioning to restrain behavior, when made aware of the advanced deceit process, but in most cases will simply encapsulate the knowledge and be more careful in deceptions.

The evolutionary deceit model does not predict excessive aggression, as this often works against deceit. For example, an antisocial investor with good social cognition and charm can steal far more than a violent person, and is far less likely to be caught and punished. Antisocial males often demonstrate "spectacular promiscuity" not because they are raping women (typically), but due to their charm and the lack of anxiety often experienced by non-antisocial males, aiding in the antisocial seduction. Antisocial women not uncommonly use their charm to convince a good provider that the child she is carrying is his, when the pregnancy arose from a more antisocial type male. The question then arises as to how aggression/violence links to an antisocial nature? Although there is no definitive answer, a few mutually compatible options exist.

One scenario is that aggression occurs on a continuum like other natural processes, and by random chance some antisocial individuals place on the higher end of the aggression continuum, increasing the chances that they will commit violent crimes (for more information regarding aggression as a continuum see the chapter "Diagnostic Considerations"). Another possibility is that the presence of circumstances facilitating aggression, such as war or street gang membership, might reinforce violence, with an antisocial individual having fewer inhibitions due to their emotional detachment. Reduced inhibitions can also arise from concussions, modeling of aggression by caregivers, or physical abuse occurring during youth, resulting in criminal violence if the person is antisocial. Hence, violence in some antisocial individuals could transpire from the confluence of psychopathic deception capacity and aggression, the person rating to the higher end of both dimensions. Combining the various sources of evidence, the case is strong that antisocial personality disorder arises from evolutionary selection pressures favoring advanced deceit, with aggression an added component in some individuals. Neuroscience data finding "defects" might be targeting the more aggressive ones, and tapping into neurological changes associated with violence in some instances. In other instances the "defects" might actually be substrates underscoring emotional detachment, such as reduced amygdala responsiveness (Halty et al, 2011). Aggression then is not an integral part of antisocial personality disorder. At the core this personality disorder consists of intense levels of two continuums—deception and dissociation—fostering enhanced resource acquisition.

Borderline Personality Disorder (Emotionally Unstable ICD-10):

Several components seem to play a role in borderline personality disorder (BPD), including emotional dysregulation, attachment, defense mechanisms, and trauma. Affective instability is common with rapid shifts in emotions, even from elation to anger in seconds, strongly implicating emotional dysregulation (Cheavens, et al, 2012; Ebner-Priemer et al, 2015; Herr et al, 2013; Scott et al, 2014; Stepp et al, 2014; Tragesser & Robinson, 2009). Ebner-Priemer et al (2015) examined electronic diary entries of those with BPD and normal subjects, finding that those with BPD have a more negative emotional baseline and greater variability. As part of emotional variability, anger/aggression can transpire, and it has been found that emotional dysregulation, rather than impulsivity per se, accounts for this occurrence (Scott et al, 2014). Comparing emotional regulation dysfunction, problematic relations, and nonintegrated self, Cheavans et al (2012) discovered that the former had the strongest relationship to BPD symptoms. Herr et al (2013) studying a BPD adult sample ascertained that emotional regulation mediates the relationship between BPD symptom severity and interpersonal dysfunction. It has been suggested that ruminations over emotional stimuli intensify emotions, resulting in emotional dysregulation, but it is not clear why the ruminations would occur in the first place (Selby & Joiner, 2009). As with depression and anxiety it appears that prefrontal cortex control of limbic system emotional responses is impaired (Herpertz et al, 2014). A longitudinal study over a year examining the influence of emotional dysregulation on BPD symptoms, and vice versa, concluded that the interaction is reciprocal with the data supporting the position that emotional dysregulation primarily maintains BPD symptoms (Stepp et al, 2014). Regarding symptom severity there is a range from mild to severe, with the most intense level often characterized by brief psychotic episodes (Balaratnasingam & Janca, 2015).

Attachment relationships early in life influence stability and success in future relationships, with attachment problems being common in BPD (Choi-Kain et al, 2009; Levy et al, 2011). Choi-Kain et al (2009) compared attachment style in BPD, depression, and a control group, finding that preoccupied and fearful styles are 3-30 times more common in BPD. In a cross-sectional study, mentalization, self-other boundaries, and identity diffusion mediated the relationship between attachment style and BPD (Beeney et al, 2015). One of the most consistent findings in BPD research, aligning well with clinical experience, is the way immature defense mechanisms, such as acting out, splitting, idealization-devaluation, and projective identification, dominate (Bond et al, 1994; Bond & Perry, 2004; Landecker, 1992; Perry, 2001; Van Wijk-Herbrink et al, 2011). Kernberg (1976) was one of the first to identify how more maladaptive and image distorting defense mechanisms characterize BPD. Bond et al (1994) suggest that intense and long-term use of immature defenses contributes to the development of BPD symptoms. Furthermore, improvement with therapy (almost always long term) involves a shift from immature defenses to mature ones, such as sublimation, suppression, altruism, and humor (Bond & Perry, 2004; Perry, 2001; Van Wijk-Herbrink et al, 2011).

Trauma is another component of BPD, although there is debate. Interestingly, the volatility of BPD symptoms is expressed in the volatility of the debate regarding many aspects of BPD, including trauma. Research evidence supports the role of trauma in BPD, as does the experience of most clinicians treating this condition (Bandelow et al, 2005; Landecker, 1992). However, some researchers such as Gunderson (2009) do not believe that it is necessary, nor that it accounts for much of the etiological variance. A very critical issue here is what constitutes trauma. Is it what researchers or clinicians decide should be objectively traumatic, as with physical or sexual abuse, or what the person subjectively experiences as traumatic? The latter appears to be more relevant as trauma is a subjective experience (Bowins, 2010b). Trauma is highly subjective in that an experience devastating one person might be negligible in its impact on another, depending on an individual's constitution, environmental circumstances, and available support (Bowins, 2010b). For example, to one researcher being denied promotion might be experienced as traumatic, but to another it will just be a sign to work harder. Indeed, only focusing on objective trauma misses much of what can be experienced as traumatic (Levy, 2000).

Due to their less developed cognitive structures, global undifferentiated thinking, and great dependence on parental figures, children are particularly vulnerable to traumatic reactions (Anguyal, 1965; Levy, 2000). "Even objectively harmless events can become major traumas in the absence of ways to cope with them. Traumatization depends so much on the child's view of the event" (Anguyal, 1965: 65). If a child/teenager's temperament/personality is such that they rate high on neuroticism (reactivity), then the impact of any negative experience will be vastly amplified, increasing the likelihood that it will be traumatic (Bowins, 2010b). Although subjective trauma is highly relevant, it even appears that objective trauma applies in most instances of BPD. Bandelow et al (2005) found that only 6.1% of their BPD sample did not report any severe traumatic occurrence, compared to 61.5% of the normal control group. Interestingly, Gunderson (2009) referenced this study to support the perspective that trauma is not necessary for the development of BPD. One of the other two studies referenced—Fossati et al (1999)—only focused on sexual abuse. Hence, the evidence is compelling that trauma, objective and subjective, is present with BPD, and much more so than with other personality disorders.

An interesting interaction appears to occur between trauma and defense mechanisms: Trauma "freezes" defense mechanism development and regulation (Bowins, 2010b; Cramer & Block, 1998; Finzi-Dottan & Karu, 2006). When a person is under stress, available defense mechanisms are overused to cope, and with the severe stress of trauma and intense repetition of the defenses, they become fixed in personality (Cramer & Block, 1998; Finzi-Dottan & Karu, 2006). The defenses available during childhood and adolescence are for the most part immature ones. Vaillant (1977, 1994) placed classical defense mechanisms on a continuum from least to most mature, the level of maturity referring to the adaptive value of the defense and the age when it is most commonly expressed. For example, acting out is a grossly inadequate defense mechanism when applied in adulthood, and is most commonly expressed in childhood. To protect against the effects of trauma, a child or teenager over-applies age appropriate immature defense mechanisms, to such an extent that these defenses come to characterize the personality (Cramer & Block, 1998; Finzi-Dottan & Karu, 2006). Regulation of psychological defenses occurs unconsciously, as pertains to the selection of a defense, when it is activated, and then deactivated. This regulation also appears to be arrested at the stage of development when the trauma occurred (Bowins, 2010b). This model of BPD is consistent with the finding that traumatic experiences encountered in the earlier years of life often in effect "freeze" personality development at the stage at which the traumatic event occurred (Massie & Szajnberg, 2006; Spates et al, 2003).

The question remains as to how emotional dysregulation and attachment play a role in BPD. Regarding emotional dysregulation, the overuse and reliance on immature defense mechanism will invariably contribute to dysregulated emotions. For example, acting out, splitting those involved, idealizing one moment and devaluating the next, and inducing a negative state in another person to identify with it (projective identification) all contribute to tremendous emotional volatility. Compare this defense mechanism profile to sublimating negative emotions into constructive pursuits, suppressing negative reactions in the moment, and placing a humorous, lighter spin on events. This mature defense mechanism profile fosters emotional stability, while the immature one breeds emotional instability. Regulation of emotions might also be "frozen" with trauma in a similar fashion to defense mechanisms and other aspects of personality. Consequently, the person's capacity to regulate emotions remains largely at the level of development at which the trauma transpired.

Attachment appears to be a moderating, rather than causal, variable in BPD. Many individuals with BPD seem to have solid attachment to caregivers, and yet develop the condition due to trauma during their teenage years. Conversely, many people who have disordered attachment do not develop BPD. Solid attachment can moderate the impact of abuse, as when a child has supportive parents to involve in the trauma. Discrediting parental reactions, indicative of poor attachment, can be as traumatic as the initial insult. Research results suggest that both attachment and emotional dysregulation are intervening variables between trauma and mental illness manifestations. Tasca et al (2013) found that attachment insecurity involving emotional dysregulation likely mediates the relationship between childhood abuse and eating disorders. In a similar study, emotional dysregulation and dissociation emerged as intervening variables between childhood abuse and eating disorders (Moulton et al, 2015).

Trauma beyond leading to BPD can induce posttraumatic stress disorder (PTSD) as covered in the "Dissociation" chapter. Those with BPD show many features of PTSD, such as the endless repetition of traumatic elements, and indeed seem to recapitulate the trauma, as when an abused woman dates abusive men, and angers them via projective identification. The question arises as to why PTSD does not involve BPD in most instances. The answer has to do with the age of the victim and consequent level of defense maturity, defense regulation, and emotional regulation. When a person is young and has an immature profile regarding these functional parameters, trauma can lead to both PTSD and BPD. However, if a person is older and has progressed to mature defenses, defense mechanism regulation, and emotional regulation, then BPD does not arise, except possibly in the instance where there is significant personality regression over time. This occurrence has been noted in various conditions, such as bipolar disorder, where a previously high functioning person showing mature defenses and emotional regulation regresses with the illness and develops borderline-like features, including the use of immature psychological defense mechanisms, the illness severity potentially constituting a traumatic occurrence.

The pivotal role of classical defense mechanisms and their regulation in BPD affords a unique therapeutic opportunity. Since progress in therapy entails the shift from immature to mature defenses (Bond & Perry, 2004; Perry, 2001; Van Wijk-Herbrink et al, 2011), then directly targeting these defenses in therapy sessions can potentially foster faster and more rounded progress (Bowins, 2010b). Examples of issues arising both in the person's life outside of therapy and with the therapist provide material demonstrating the use of the various immature defenses. The therapist explains the nature of mature defenses, and shows how they could have been applied in the examples available. The person is then coached and supported in applying these more mature defenses in interactions, both within and outside of therapy. The therapist can also assist by modeling mature defenses, the regulation of these defense mechanisms, and regulation of emotional responses. A treatment provider who in sessions shifts radically in terms of emotional reactions, and also use of defenses, does not assist those with BPD in achieving mature regulation over defenses and emotions. A solid, stable, and professional stance, with clear limits and boundary setting, is much more helpful in this regard.

Schizophrenic Spectrum "Personality Disorders"

Schizotypal, paranoid, and schizoid have been grouped together because they appear to be part of the schizophrenic spectrum rather than personality disorders. A key issue to cover is that persistence of a psychiatric condition does not qualify it as a personality disorder. For instance, persistent depression or anxiety do not make for depressive personality disorder and anxious personality disorder, respectively. Likewise, persistence of schizophrenia is not schizophrenic personality disorder. Given that personality is any enduring and characteristic way of acting and reacting, essentially any condition that persists comes to comprise an aspect of personality, but should not be considered a personality disorder if it arises from an already established process. Adhering to this "non-redundancy principle" can reduce much of the confusion arising around the notion of proposed conditions such as "depressive personality disorder" and also the schizophrenic spectrum "personality disorders." Furthermore, it reduces double diagnosing, whereby the same condition is cited in more than one context.

With this non-redundancy principle in mind let us take a look at research evidence for schizotypal, paranoid, and schizoid personality disorders. Schizotypal consists of milder positive and negative symptoms (see the "Psychosis" and "Negative Symptoms" chapters) than typically occur with schizophrenia. The milder nature of the symptoms does not mean that schizotypal represents a unique diagnosis, just that it indicates a more moderate point on a continuum of cognitive distortions, thought form alterations, sensory perceptual experiences, and the various negative symptoms. Taxometric research generally supports schizotypal and schizophrenia as being continuous with one another (Cochrane et al, 2012; Tyrka et al, 1995). In addition, schizotypal appears to be the midpoint on a continuum between the normal population and schizophrenia (Ahmed et al, 2013; Hazlett et al, 2015). Hazlett et al (2015) measured evoked potentials in healthy controls, schizotypal personality disorder, and schizophrenic subjects, finding that those with schizotypal personality disorder are mid-way between the other two groups on a continuous distribution.

Taxometric research findings pertaining to schizotypy can be complex and not entirely straightforward in regards to their interpretation, and the outcome can depend on the measures used (Horan et al, 2004; Linscott, 2013). In part the complexity arises from the diversity of symptom types in schizophrenic spectrum conditions, with each on a continuum: Psychotic continuums of cognitive distortions, thought form, sensory perceptual experiences, and negative symptom continuums with basic cognition, social cognition, and motivational states. If delusions and hallucinations per se are the criteria, then there is a distinction between the normal population and schizotypal/schizophrenia, and perhaps even schizotypal and schizophrenia, because not everyone has delusions or hallucinations. However, there is a continuum as pertains to the underlying processes, such as cognitive distortions, thought form variants, and sensory perceptual experiences. There can be variation within a normal and functional range, and then a level that becomes increasingly dysfunctional. Underlying the dysfunctional range are neural alterations that are also progressive in their extent, making it appear that schizotypal and schizophrenia are distinct from each other and the normal population (Fervaha & Remington, 2013; Grant et al, 2014).

Paranoid personality disorder clearly makes reference to delusions being the dominant symptom, and in particular persecutory delusions. It is interesting that persecutory delusions have been transformed into a distinct personality disorder, because other delusional types can persist, such as somatic, although we do not consider other expressions to represent personality disorders. Perhaps it is the colorfulness of persecutory delusions, and how antagonistic these individuals are, as with litigation, that raises their profile. Contrasting the notion that persecutory delusions and paranoid personality disorder are distinct, both appear to occur on a continuum with normality (Ahmed et al, 2012; Edens et al, 2009; Green et al, 2011). Studying normal subjects, Green et al (2011) found that 15.5% generated paranoid explanations for experimental manipulations, such as hearing laughter outside the test room. Interpersonal sensitivity and attribution style, both demonstrating a range of expressions, were more intense in those producing paranoid explanations (Green et al, 2011). Triebwasser et al (2013) in a review of paranoid personality disorder studies argue that there is insufficient evidence to support it being a distinct condition.

One issue that seems to contribute to the apparent uniqueness of paranoid personality disorder is the cognitive biases underlying it. Haselton and Nettle (2006) suggest that in line with error management theory, judgments under uncertain conditions should favor the least costly error, which in an evolutionary context would be heightened suspicion. According to this perspective, erring on the side of trust would be more costly. However, given the role of both reciprocity and deceit in our hunting-gathering evolutionary background, it seems that a balance of trust and suspicion is most optimal, not one or the other. The error management perspective does highlight how there is a range of suspicion that has an adaptive value. Relying on projection as a psychological defense, paranoid individuals project their own negative qualities onto others, seeing them as the source of their problems, generating suspiciousness and also ensuring resistance to treatment. Motivating the suspicious and hostile perspective might be underlying insecurities and fears, demonstrating a narcissistic defensive structure (Akhtar, 1990).

Overall, then, there is insufficient evidence for paranoid "personality disorder" being distinct, and solid evidence that it resides on the higher end of a continuum of cognitive distortions, with psychological defenses of projection and narcissism playing an important role. This interpretation is supported by the way the paranoid ideation fades with antipsychotic medication, although since these individuals do not see any personal fault they rarely take or adhere to medication. Interestingly, the notion of the narcissistic defensive structure playing a role does open up the possibility of trying to intervene using the techniques discussed under this personality disorder, although the psychotic level of their cognitive distortions and the projection defense casts doubt on the effectiveness of such an approach.

Schizoid mostly consists of social cognitive type negative symptoms, including diminished motivation for socializing, resulting in withdrawal. There can be psychotic elements such as schizoid fantasy, referring to the highly distorted fantasies that some schizoid individuals have, and how full-fledged psychosis can emerge with significant stress. These occurrences support schizoid being part of the schizophrenic spectrum. The failure of antipsychotic medication to produce much, or any, improvement beyond psychotic elements, supports it being due to social cognition negative symptoms. Schizoid must be distinguished from avoidant features, as the latter are largely a defensive response to anxiety, as covered earlier in the chapter. Researchers examining data for schizoid personality disorder have found too little evidence supporting it as a personality disorder (Ahmed et al, 2012; Triebwasser et al, 2012).

Schizotypal, paranoid, and schizoid are thus not personality disorders, but instead occur on the schizophrenic spectrum. Schizotypal refers to a milder variant of positive and negative symptoms, paranoid to positive symptoms consisting of delusions based on the psychological defenses of projection and likely narcissism, and schizoid derived from social cognition negative symptoms. This arrangement upholds the crucial non-redundancy principle of not presenting persistent expressions of other conditions as personality disorders, to prevent double diagnosing and diagnostic confusion.

Summary

The model of personality disorders based on extreme and persistent expressions of defensive dimensions is highly parsimonious. It clearly identifies the aspect of normal personality that is overextended in personality disorders. There is no need to extend normal personality as traits to abnormal personality, something that does not work for the primary traits, and only somewhat for the underlying facets. Even then, due to the extensiveness of the facets they can be applied to almost any aspect of human functioning, and really only amount to links drawn between normal personality traits and personality disorders. There is no understanding of why the personality disorders occur in the first place. The defense mechanism approach does not require clinicians to apply normal personality scales and transform the results to abnormal personality. The use of any scales in busy clinical practice has to be straightforward and yield important information, as with the proposed scales for reinforcement based conditions (see the "Reinforcement Based Disorders" chapter). The proposals in the lead up to DSM-5 were so convoluted that they were difficult to follow, even by those familiar with both trait approaches and personality disorders.

Clear and effective treatment strategies also follow from the defense mechanism approach to personality disorders, generally conceptualized as moderating extreme and enduring expressions of normal defensive structures (Bowins, 2010b). In the case of BPD immature defenses, defense regulation, and related emotional regulation comprise the focus. With antisocial personality disorder, an understanding that it represents an evolved deceit mechanism derived from deceit and dissociation continuums underscores why treatment is not a reasonable goal. An additional aspect of treatment following from the model is the humanistic approach: Instead of the us/them or in-group/out-group framework that normally characterizes treatment, viewing those with personality disorders as for the most part having more extreme and persistent expressions of defensive styles we all rely on bridges the divide. The person is not seen as being so radically different, almost alien, thus fostering a better therapeutic alliance. In the case of BPD we all have relied on immature defenses early in life, and with antisocial personality disorder we all display deceit and dissociation, despite how many doubt these occurrences.

While the defense mechanism approach to personality disorders does not depend on the extension of normal personality traits to abnormal personality, normal trait profiles influence the defensive styles, and hence personality disorders derived from them (Bowins, 2010b). For example, a person who is high in conscientiousness is more likely to adopt an obsessive-compulsive defense style. A person high on harm avoidance and introversion, and low on openness to experience, is very likely to adopt an avoidant defensive style, whereas the reverse profile on these traits is unlikely to lead to avoidance. Hence, trait approaches serve a secondary role in the proposed model, influencing the defensive styles that manifest for a given person and that, under chronic stress and likely impaired capacity to regulate stress responses, advance to a formal personality disorder.

Another advantage of the proposed model is that additional personality disorders can be added, as several normal defenses expressed in an extreme and persistent form will constitute a personality disorder (Bowins, 2010b). For example, extensive and ongoing aggression might comprise an "aggressive personality disorder" (see the section on antisocial personality disorder and also the "Diagnostic Considerations" chapter), given that aggression is a key defensive strategy relied on throughout our evolution to safeguard the self, offspring, the hunting-gathering group, and key resources. "Difficult personality disorder" is another option, based on how a persistent and extreme expression of a defensive process to individuate personality from caregivers, expressed during childhood and the teenage years, can result in a person being contrary, antagonistic, and generally difficult (Bowins, 2010b). Finally, the defense mechanism approach is the only one that relies on unconscious processes in the formation of personality disorders, a very likely possibility considering that the energy for unconscious mental activity, simply at rest, is 20 times greater than that required for conscious mental activity. Indeed, many of the processes covered in this book actually transpire at an unconscious level, increasing the probability of an unconscious origin for personality disorders.

References

Ahmed, A.O., Green, B.A., Buckley, P.F., & McFarland, M.E. (2012). Taxometric analyses of paranoid and schizoid personality disorders. *Psychiatry Research, 196*(1), 123-132.

Ahmed, A.O., Green, B.A., Goodrum, N.M., Doane, N.J., Birgenheir, D., & Buckley, P.F. (2013). Does a latent class underlie schizotypal personality disorder? Implications for schizophrenia. *Journal of Abnormal Psychology, 122*(2), 475-491.

Akhtar, S. (1990). Paranoid personality disorder: A synthesis of developmental, dynamic, and descriptive features. *American Journal of Psychotherapy, 44*(1), 5-25.

Alden, L.E., Laposa, J.M., Taylor, C.T., & Ryder, A.G. (2002). Avoidant personality disorder: Current status and future directions. *Journal of Personality Disorders, 16*(1), 1-29.

American Psychiatric Association (2013). *Diagnostic & Statistical Manual 5*. Washington, DC: American Psychiatric Publishing.

Anguyal, A. (1965). *Neurosis and Treatment: A Holistic Theory*. New York: Wiley.

Ashton, M.C., Lee, K., & Goldberg, L.R. (2004). A hierarchical analysis of 1,710 English personality-descriptive adjectives. *Journal of Personality & Social Psychology, 87*(5), 707-721.

Balaratnasingam, S. & Janca, A. (2015). Normal personality, personality disorder and psychosis: Current views and future perspectives. *Current Opinion in Psychiatry, 28*(1), 30-34.

Bandelow, B., Krause, J., Wedekind, D., Broocks, A., Hajak, E., & Ruther, E. (2005). Early traumatic life events, parental attitudes, family history, and birth risk factors in patients with borderline personality disorder and healthy controls. *Psychiatry Research, 134*, 169-179.

Beck, A.T., Butler, A.C., Brown, G.K., Dahlsgaard, K.K., Newman, C.F., & Beck, J.S. (2001). Dysfunctional beliefs discriminate personality disorders. *Behaviour Research and Therapy, 39*, 1213-1225.

Beeney, J.E., Stepp, S.D., Hallquist, M.N., Scott, L.N., Wright, A.G., Ellison, W.D. et al (2015). Attachment and social cognition in borderline personality disorder: Specificity in relation to antisocial and avoidant personality disorders. *Personality Disorders, 6*(3), 207-215.

Bond, M., Paris, J., & Zweig-Frank, H. (1994). The Defense Style Questionnaire in borderline personality disorder. *Journal of Personality Disorder, 8*, 28-31.

Bond, M. & Perry, J.C. (2004). Long-term changes in defense styles with psychodynamic psychotherapy for depressive, anxiety, and personality disorders. *American Journal of Psychiatry, 161*(9), 1665-1671.

Bornstein, R.F. (1992). The dependent personality: Development, social, and clinical perspectives. *Psychological Bulletin, 112*(1), 3-23.

Bornstein, R.F. (2012). Illuminating a neglected clinical issue: Societal costs of interpersonal dependency and dependent personality disorder. *Journal of Clinical Psychology, 68*(7), 766-781.

Bowins, B. (2004). Psychological defense mechanisms: A new perspective. *American Journal of Psychoanalysis, 64*, 1-26.

Bowins, B.E. (2006a). How psychiatric treatments can enhance psychological defense mechanisms. *American Journal of Psychoanalysis, 66*, 173-194.

Bowins, B.E. (2010b). Personality disorders: A dimensional defense mechanism approach. *American Journal of Psychotherapy, 64*(2), 153-169.

Bowins, B.E. (2012c). Therapeutic dissociation: Compartmentalization and absorption. *Counselling Psychology Quarterly, 25*(1), 307-317.

Bowins, B.E. (2014). *At the Tipping Point: How to Save Us from Self-Destruction.* West Conshohocken, PA: Infinity Publishing.

Boyer, P. & Lienard, P. (2006). Why ritualized behavior? Precaution systems and action parsing in developmental, pathological and cultural rituals. *Behavioural and Brain Sciences, 29*, 595-613.

Brune, M. (2006). The evolutionary psychology of obsessive-compulsive disorder. *Perspectives in Biology and Medicine, 49*(3), 317-329.

Butler, A.B., Manger, P.R., Lindahl, B.I., & Arhem, P. (2005). Evolution of the neural basis of consciousness: A bird-mammal comparison. *Bioessays, 27*(9), 923-936.

Chandler, M., Fritz, A., & Hala, S. (1989). Small-scale deceit: Deception as a marker of two, three, and four-year-olds' early theories of mind. *Child Development, 60*, 1263-1277.

Cheavens, J.S., Strunk, D.R., & Chriki, L. (2012). A comparison of three theoretically important constructs: What accounts for symptoms of borderline personality disorder? *Journal of Clinical Psychology, 68*(4), 477-486.

Choi-Kain, L.W., Fitzmaurice, G.M., Zanarini, M.C., Laverdiere, O., & Gunderson, J.G. (2009). The relationship between self-reported attachment styles, interpersonal dysfunction, and borderline personality disorder. *Journal of Nervous and Mental Disease, 197*(11), 816-821.

Clark, L.A., Livesley, W.J., Schroeder, M.L., & Irish, S. (1996). The structure of maladaptive personality traits: Convergent validity between two systems. *Psychological Assessment, 8*, 294-303.

Cloninger, C.R. (1987). A systematic method for clinical description and classification of personality variants. *Archives of General Psychiatry, 44*, 573-588.

Cloninger, C.R., Svrakic, D.M., & Przybeck, T.R. (1993). A psychobiological model of temperament and character. *Archives of General Psychiatry, 50*, 975-990.

Cochrane, M., Petch, I., & Pickering, A.D. (2012). Aspects of cognitive functioning in schizotypy and schizophrenia: Evidence for a continuum model. *Psychiatry Research, 196*(2-3), 230-234.

Coid, J. & Ullrich, S. (2010). Antisocial personality disorder is on a continuum with psychopathy. *Comprehensive Psychiatry, 51*(4), 426-433.

Colman, A.M. & Wilson, J.C. (1997). Antisocial personality disorder: An evolutionary game theory analysis. *Legal and Criminological Psychology, 2*(1), 23-34.

Costa, P.T. & McCrae, R.R. (1992). *Revised NEO Personality (NEO-PI-R) and NEO Five Factor Inventory (NEO-FFI) Professional Journal Manual.* Odessa, FL: Psychological Assessment Resources.

Cramer, P. & Block, J. (1998). Preschool antecedents of defense mechanism use in young adults: A longitudinal study. *Journal of Personality & Social Psychology, 74*, 159-169.

Crocq, M.A. (2013). Milestones in the history of personality disorders. *Dialogues Clinical Neuroscience, 15*(2), 147-153.

Dickinson, K.A. & Pincus, A.L. (2003). Interpersonal analysis of grandiose and vulnerable narcissism. *Journal of Personality Disorders, 17*, 188-207.

Dolan, M. & Fullam, R. (2004). Theory of mind and mentalizing ability in antisocial personality disorders with and without psychopathy. *Psychological Medicine, 34*(6), 1093-1102.

Ebner-Priemer, U.W., Houben, M., Santangelo, P., Kleindienst, N., Tuerlinckx, F., Oravecz, Z. et al (2015). Unraveling affective dysregulation in borderline personality disorder: A theoretical model and empirical evidence. *Journal of Abnormal Psychology, 124*(1), 186-198.

Edens, J.F., Marcus, D.K., Lilienfeld, S.O., & Poythress, N.G. Jr. (2006). Psychopathic, not psychopath: Taxometric evidence for the dimensional structure of psychopathy. *Journal of Abnormal Psychology, 115*(1), 131-144.

Edens, J.F., Marcus, D.K., & Morey, L.C. (2009). Paranoid personality has a dimensional latent structure: Taxometric analyses of community and clinical samples. *Journal of Abnormal Psychology, 118*(3), 545-553.

Edens, J.F., Marcus, D.K., & Vaughn, M.G. (2011). Exploring the taxometric status of psychopathy among youthful offenders: Is there a juvenile psychopath taxon? *Law & Human Behavior, 35*(1), 13-24.

Fabbro, F., Aglioti, S.M., Bergamasco, M., Clarici, A., & Panksepp, J. (2015). Evolutionary aspects of self- and world consciousness in vertebrates. *Frontiers in Human Neuroscience, 26*(9), 10.3389/fnhum.2015.00157.

Fenichel, O. (1945). *The Psychoanalytic Theory of Neurosis.* New York: Norton & Company.

Ferguson, C.J. (2010). Genetic contributions to antisocial personality and behavior: A meta-analytic review from an evolutionary perspective. *The Journal of Social Psychology, 150*(2), 160-180.

Fervaha, G. & Remington, G. (2013). Neuroimaging findings in schizotypal personality disorder: A systematic review. *Progress in Neuropsychopharmacology & Biological Psychiatry, 43*, 96-107.

Finzi-Dottan, R. & Karu, T. (2006). From emotional abuse in childhood to psychopathology in adulthood: A path mediated by immature defense mechanisms and self-esteem. *The Journal of Nervous and Mental Disease, 194*(8), 616-620.

First, M.B., Frances, A., & Pincus, H.A. (2002). *DSM-IV-TR Handbook of Differential Diagnosis.* Washington, DC: American Psychiatric Publishing.

Fossati, A., Madeddu, F., & Maffei, C. (1999). Borderline personality disorder and childhood sexual abuse. *Journal of Personality Disorders, 13*(3), 268-280.

Fowles, D.C., (1988). Psychophysiology and psychopathology: A motivational approach. *Psychophysiology, 25*, 373-391.

Fox, M.D. & Raichle, M.E. (2007). Spontaneous fluctuations in brain activity with functional magnetic resonance imaging. *Nature Reviews Neuroscience, 8*, 700-711.

Freud, S. (1959). Character and anal erotic. S.E. IX, pp. 1691-1675. London: The Hogarth Press.

Glantz, K. & Pearce, J. (1989). *Exiles from Eden: Psychotherapy from an Evolutionary Perspective.* New York: W.W. Norton & Company.

Grant, P., Gabriel, F., Kuepper, Y., Wielpuetz, C., & Hennig, J. (2014). Psychosis-proneness correlates with expression levels of dopaminergic genes. *European Psychiatry, 29*(5), 304-306.

Gray, J.A., (1987). Perspectives on anxiety and impulsivity: A commentary. *Journal of Research in Personality, 21*, 493-509.

Green, C.E., Freeman, D., Kuipers, E., Bebbington, P., Fowler, D., Dunn, G., & Garety, P.A. (2011). Paranoid explanations of experience: A novel experimental study. *Behavioural and Cognitive Psychotherapy, 39*(1), 21-34.

Guay, J.P., Ruscio, J., Knight, R.A., & Hare, R.D. (2007). A taxometric analysis of the latent structure of psychopathy: Evidence for dimensionality. *Journal of Abnormal Psychology, 116*(4), 701-716.

Gunderson, J.G. (1988). Personality disorders. In *The New Harvard Guide to Psychiatry*. Cambridge, MA: Harvard University Press.

Gunderson, J.G. (2009). Borderline personality disorder: Ontogeny of a diagnosis. *American Journal of Psychiatry, 166*(5), 530-539.

Halty, L., Martinez, A., Requena, C., Santos, J.M., & Ortiz, T. (2011). Psychopathy in children and teenagers: Models, theories, and the latest research. *Review of Neurology, 52*(Suppl 1), S19-27.

Harpending, H. & Sobus, J. (1987). Sociopathy as an adaptation. *Ethology and Sociobiology, 8*, 63S-72S.

Haselton, M.G. & Nettle, D. (2006). The paranoid optimist: An integrative evolutionary model of cognitive biases. *Personality & Social Psychology Review, 10*(1), 47-66.

Hazlett, E.A., Rothstein, E.G., Ferreira, R., Silverman, J.M., Siever, L.J., & Olincy, A. (2015). Sensory gating disturbances in the spectrum: Similarities and differences in schizotypal personality disorder and schizophrenia. *Schizophrenia Research, 161*(2-3), 283-290.

Head, S.B., Baker, J.D., & Williamson, D.A. (1991). Family environment characteristics and dependent personality disorder. *Journal of Personality Disorders, 5*(3), 256-263.

Herpertz, S.C., Jeung, H., Mancke, F., & Bertsch, K. (2014). Social dysfunctioning and brain in borderline personality disorder. *Psychopathology, 47*(6), 417-424.

Herr, N.R., Rosenthal, M.Z., Geiger, P.J., & Erikson, K. (2013). Difficulties with emotional regulation mediate the relationship between borderline personality disorder symptom severity and interpersonal problems. *Personality & Mental Health, 7*(3), 191-202.

Horan, W.P., Blanchard, J.J., Gangestad, S.W., & Kwapil, T.R. (2004). The psychometric detection of schizotypy: Do putative schizoptypy indicators identify the same latent class? *Journal of Abnormal Psychology, 113*(3), 339-357.

Horton, R.S. & Tritch, T. (2014). Clarifying the links between grandiose narcissism and parenting. *Journal of Psychology, 148*(2), 133-143.

Intrator, J. (1997). A brain imaging (single photon emission computerized tomography) study of semantic and affective processing in psychopaths. *Biological Psychiatry, 42*, 96-103.

Kernberg, O.F. (1976). *Borderline Conditions and Pathological Narcissism*. New York: Jason Aronson.

Landecker, H. (1992). The role of childhood sexual trauma in the etiology of borderline personality disorder: Considerations for diagnosis and treatment. *Psychotherapy, 29*(2), 234-242.

Levy, K.N., Beeney, J.E., & Temes, C.M. (2011). Attachment and its vicissitudes in borderline personality disorder. *Current Psychiatry Reports, 13*(1), 50-59.

Levy, M. (2000). A conceptualization of the repetition compulsion. *Psychiatry, 63*, 45-53.

Linscott, R.J. (2013). The taxonicity of schizotypy: Does the same taxonic class structure emerge from analyses of different attributes of schizotypy and from fundamentally different statistical methods? *Psychiatry Research, 210*(2), 414-421.

Livesley, W.J. (1998). Suggestions for a framework for an empirically based classification of personality disorder. *Canadian Journal of Psychiatry, 43*, 137-147.

Livesley, W.J. & Jackson, D.N. (1986). The internal consistency and factorial structure of behaviors judged to be associated with DSM-III personality disorders. *American Journal of Psychiatry, 143*, 1473-1474.

Marcus, D.K., John, S.L., & Edens, J.F. (2004). A taxometric analysis of psychopathic personality. *Journal of Abnormal Psychology, 113*(4), 626-635.

Marcus, D.K., Lilienfeld, S.O., Edens, J.F., & Poythress, N.G. (2006). Is antisocial personality disorder continuous or categorical? A taxometric analysis. *Psychological Medicine, 36*(11), 1571-1581.

Marsh, H.W., Morin, A.J., Parker, P.D., & Kaur, G. (2014). Exploratory structural equation modeling: An integration of the best features of exploratory and confirmatory factor analysis. *Annual Review of Clinical Psychology, 10*, 85-110.

Massie, H. & Szajnberg, N. (2006). My life is a longing: Child abuse and its adult sequelae. Results of the Brody longitudinal study from birth to age 30. *International Journal of Psychoanalysis, 87*(2), 471-496.

Masson, J.M. (1985) *The Complete Letters of Sigmund Freud to Wilhelm Fliess, 1887-1904*. Cambridge, MA: Harvard University Press.

Meyer, B. (2002). Personality and mood correlates of avoidant personality disorder. *Journal of Personality Disorders, 16*(2), 174-188.

Morsella, E., Krieger, S.C., & Bargh, J.A. (2010). Minimal neuroanatomy for a conscious brain: Homing in on the networks constituting consciousness. *Neural Networks, 23*, 14-15.

Moulton, S.J., Newman, E., Power, K., Swanson, V., & Day, K. (2015). Childhood trauma and eating psychopathology: A mediating role for dissociation and emotion dysregulation? *Child Abuse & Neglect, 39*, 167-174.

Murrie, D.C., Marcus, D.K., Douglas, K.S., Lee, Z., Salekin, R.T., & Vincent, G. (2007). Youth with psychopathy features are not a discrete class: A taxometric analysis. *Journal of Child Psychology & Psychiatry, 48*(7), 714-723.

Oldham, J.M. & Skodol, A.E. (2000). Charting the future of axis II. *Journal of Personality Disorders, 14*, 17-29.

Patrick, C., Cuthbert, B., & Lang, P. (1994). Emotion in the criminal psychopath: Fear image processing. *Journal of Abnormal Psychology, 103*(3), 523-534.

Perry, C. (2001). A pilot study of defenses in adults with personality disorders entering psychotherapy. *The Journal of Nervous and Mental Disease, 189*, 651-660.

Polimeni, J., Reiss, J.P., & Sareen, J. (2005). Could obsessive-compulsive disorder have originated as a group-selected adaptive trait in traditional societies? *Medical Hypothesis, 65*, 655-664.

Rachman, S. & Hodgson, R. (1980). *Obsessions and Compulsions*. Englewood Cliffs: Prentice-Hall.

Rovik, J.O. (2001). Overt and covert narcissism: Turning points and mutative elements in two psychotherapies. *British Journal of Psychotherapy, 17*, 435-447.

Schlesinger, L.B. (2001). The contract murderer: Patterns, characteristics, and dynamics. *Journal of Forensic Sciences, 46*(5), 1119-1123.

Scott, L.N., Stepp, S.D., & Pilkonis, P.A., (2014). Prospective associations between features of borderline personality disorder, emotion dysregulation, and aggression. *Personality Disorders, 5*(3), 278-288.

Selby, E.A. & Joiner, T.E. Jr. (2009). Cascades of emotion: The emergence of borderline personality disorder from emotional and behavioral dysregulation. *Review of General Psychology, 13*(3), 219-228.

Shedler, J. & Westen, D. (2004). Refining DSM-IV personality disorder diagnosis: Integrating science and practice. *American Journal of Psychiatry, 161*, 1350-1365.

Spates, C.R., Waller, S., Samaraweera, N., & Plaisier, B. (2003). Behavioral aspects of trauma in children and youth. *Pediatric Clinics of North America, 50*(4), 901-918.

Stepp, S.D., Scott, L.N., Morse, J.Q., Nolf, K.A., Hallquist, M.N., & Pilkonis, P.A. (2014). Emotion dysregulation as a maintenance factor of borderline personality disorder features. *Comprehensive Psychiatry, 55*(3), 657-666.

Svrakic, D.M., Whitehead, C., Przybeck, T.R., & Cloninger, C.R. (1993). Differential diagnosis of personality disorders by the seven factor model of temperament and character. *Archives of General Psychiatry, 50*, 991-1000.

Tasca, G.A., Ritchie, K., Zachariades, F., Proulx, A., Trinneer, A., Balfour, L. et al (2013). Attachment insecurity mediates the relationship between childhood trauma and eating disorder psychopathology in a clinical sample: A structural equation model. *Child Abuse & Neglect, 37*(11), 926-933.

Tragesser, S.L. & Robinson, R.J. (2009). The role of affective instability and UPPS impulsivity in borderline personality disorder features. *Journal of Personality Disorders, 23*(4), 370-383.

Triebwasser, J., Chemerinski, E., Roussos, P., & Siever, L.J. (2013). Paranoid personality disorder. *Journal of Personality Disorders, 27*(6), 795-805.

Trull, T.J. & Durrett, C.A. (2005). Categorical and dimensional models of personality disorder. *Annual Review of Clinical Psychology, 1*, 355-380.

Tyrka, A.R., Cannon, T.D., Haslam, N., Mednick, S.A., Schulsinger, F., Schulsinger, H., & Parnas, J. (1995). The latent structure of schizotypy: 1. Premorbid indicators of a taxon of individuals at risk for schizophrenia-spectrum disorders. *Journal of Abnormal Psychology, 104*(1), 173-183.

Vaillant, G. (1977). *Adaptation to Life*. Boston: Little, Brown & Company.

Vaillant, G. (1994). Ego mechanisms of defense and personality psychopathology. *Journal of Abnormal Psychology, 103*(1), 44-50.

Van Wijk-Herbrink, M., Andrea, H., & Verheul, R. (2011). Cognitive coping and defense styles in patients with personality disorders. *Journal of Personality Disorders, 25*(5), 634-644.

Veale, D. (2002). Over-valued ideas: A conceptual analysis. *Behavioural Research & Therapy, 40*(4), 383-400.

Walters, G.D. (2014). The latent structure of psychopathy in male adjudicated delinquents: A cross-domain taxometric analysis. *Personality Disorders, 5*(4), 348-355.

Walters, G.D., Gray, N.S., Jackson, R.L., Sewell, K.W., Rogers, R., Taylor, J., & Snowden, R.J. (2007). A taxometric analysis of the psychopathy checklist: Screening version (PCL: SV): Further evidence of dimensionality. *Psychological Assessment, 19*(3), 330-339.

Walters, G.D. & Ruscio, J. (2013). Trajectories of youthful antisocial behavior: Categories or continua? *Journal of Abnormal Child Psychology, 41*(4), 653-666.

Wetzel, A.P. (2012). Factor analysis methods and validity evidence: A review of instrument development across the medical education continuum. *Academic Medicine, 87*(8), 1060-1069.

Widiger, T.A. & Trull, T.J. (2007). Plate tectonics in the classification of personality disorder: Shifting to a dimensional model. *American Psychologist, 62*(2), 71-83.

World Health Organization (1992). *The ICD-10 Classification of Mental and Behavioral Disorders: Clinical Descriptions and Diagnostic Guidelines*. Geneva: World Health Organization.

Zhang, D. & Raichle, M.E. (2010). Disease and the brain's dark energy. *Nature Reviews Neurology, 6*, 15-18.

CHAPTER 11

Diagnostic Considerations

The current chapter examines specific issues related to diagnoses, not yet presented or developed fully.

Comorbidity

Comorbidity refers to one or more additional disorders co-occurring with the primary one, or the effect of these additional disorders. The term, or at least the latter part, suggests a worse scenario than if only the primary disorder is present. Based on what has been covered in this book, mental illness (and health) is comprised of several continuums (see the section on number of diagnoses of the current chapter), and as indicated in the "Depression" chapter, these dimensions can and often do interface with one another. Indeed, the interfacing is integral to how mental illness presents for at least three reasons. First, some dimensions are more likely to interface because of common elements, such as the anxiety and depression continuums sharing emotional information processing features: Circumstances indicating threat or danger producing fear frequently also entail loss resulting in sadness, with fear and sadness the root emotions of anxiety and depression, respectively. Due to the evolution of human intelligence, emotional information processing has been amplified (the Amplification Effect), setting the stage for anxiety and depression as disorders (Bowins, 2004).

The second reason is that the interfacing of certain continuums results in mental illness, or more accurately, impairs regulation of one, shifting the expressed level into the maladaptive and dysfunctional range. An example of this occurrence is with the negative symptom continuum: When basic cognition (executive functions), social cognition, and motivational states are substantially impaired (negative symptoms), the cognitive regulatory control processes blocking psychotic level cognitions from the conscious and awake state are compromised, producing psychosis, and if hypomania is present regulation over its progression is damaged, resulting in mania. The third reason why the interfacing of continuums is integral to how mental illness presents consists of defensive functioning. For instance, the hypomania-mania continuum appears to interface with the depression continuum, to provide the defensive benefits of hypomania for depression, namely restoring adaptive functioning in the present moment, thereby optimizing evolutionary fitness. Certain personality disorder continuums can interface with other continuums to provide a defensive function, such as the avoidant, dependent, and obsessive-compulsive continuums for anxiety issues.

Regarding the most appropriate terminology, it is suggested that the term interfacing continuums or interfacing dimensions be applied, because interfacing suggests an interaction but does not prejudge the nature of it, as with the term comorbidity that strongly implies a negative outcome. Continuum, or dimension, emphasizes that a continuous expression exists. Co-occurring is a possible term, but could suggest a random process when in most instances both dimensions are interacting. Interfacing continuums really reflects how everything in nature is interconnected, despite how we tend to see discrete elements in line with our motivation to simplify information processing. As pertains to world issues, such as global warming and the hyper-exploitation of resources, a major reason why motivation to deal with them is so limited is that we see nature as consisting of disconnected elements, and hence perceive these issues as not having an impact on us. Unfortunately, given that everything in nature is interconnected these changes will impact us, and even now are doing so. The term interfacing continuums (or dimensions) then aligns with the structure and functioning of natural phenomena helping to place mental illness on a more scientific foundation.

Number of Diagnoses

The current version of DSM (DSM-5) has been criticized in several regards, with one of the most prominent consisting of the number of diagnoses. DSM-I in 1952 listed 106 conditions, increasing to 265 diagnoses by DSM-III in 1980, and 297 in DSM-IV. The number of diagnosable conditions in DSM-5 has been a source of controversy with some reporting over 300, and the American Psychiatric Association officially citing 157 (American Psychiatric Association, 2013). These arguments, while entertaining, miss the point that the entire enterprise of setting discrete conditions is bound to fail, given how nature is organized dimensionally. In line with the Continuum Principle (Bowins, 2015), evidence for discreteness must be unassailable in quality before we conclude that a condition is fully discrete. As pertains to mental illness, the evidence falls far below this standard, and only highlights potentially viable dimensions. However, the number of viable dimensions is far less than 157, not even close in fact. Current diagnostic systems for mental illness are more consensus based, dependent on politics. Establishing a system aligning with how nature is organized into dimensions is much more scientific.

Defenders of current diagnostic systems will point to research supporting these discrete entities, but a sobering reality is that about 80% of medical research results, even top tier, are false! These results have emerged from studies conducted by the pharmaceutical industry itself, attempting to understand why so many results, even from top labs throughout the world, completely fail (Begley & Ellis, 2012; Prinz et al, 2011). Bayer's Health-Care's drug discovery researchers, Prinz et al (2011), looked at their own experiences and came up with some quantitative data. They found that, "With reasonable efforts (sometimes the equivalent of 3-4 fulltime employees over 6-12 months), we have frequently been unable to reconfirm published data." To measure the extent of the problem they conducted an analysis of research and development on early stage in-house projects (target identification and target validation) for Bayer's three main strategic research fields of oncology, women's health, and cardiovascular disease. Amazingly they found that published data aligned with in-house findings for only 14/67 (21%) of projects. Of the 14 projects only one perfectly reproduced the data, while 12 could be adapted, and one was not applicable (Prinz et al, 2011).

These striking revelations from Bayer prompted Glenn Begley, head of Hematology and Oncology Research at Amgen, to conduct an investigation focusing on cancer. Begley and Ellis (2012) identified 53 "landmark" publications (papers in top journals from reputable labs) over the prior decade that his team checked on. These studies, according to Begley and Ellis, were ones that the pharmaceutical industry relies on to identify new targets for cancer drug development. Of the 53, only 6 (11%) could be confirmed. A full 47/53 or 89% failed! They expressed, "Even knowing the limitations of preclinical research, this was a shocking result!" Equally shocking, confidentiality agreements between the authors and Amgen bar any disclosure of the 47 studies that failed, meaning that "the world will never know" that these often highly cited papers are false (Begley & Ellis, 2012).

If about 80% of medical research results are false, and this is for conditions such as cancer and cardiovascular disease with relatively hard endpoints, imagine what the true figure is for mental health research involving soft endpoints, such as points on a self-rating scale! Hence, it cannot be assumed that the results in support of discrete diagnoses are accurate, and indeed it is almost certain that most are invalid. More likely to be valid are continuums (dimensions) aligning with natural occurrences. Based on what has been covered in this book, it is suggested that diagnoses be based on continuums. Within these continuums there are often sub-dimensions, and even dimensions within these sub-dimensions. What follows is a summary of this occurrence for the various conditions.

Depression and anxiety represent distinct continuums, with quantitative variation yielding qualitative variation as an emergent property, creating the impression of discreteness. Furthermore, various circumstances that are now the basis of discrete types really comprise eliciting mechanisms activating the depression and anxiety continuums. Both depression and anxiety are best described by combining the sub-dimensions of duration and severity. Hypomania-mania is a single continuum, with mania hypothesized to arise from impaired cognitive regulatory control over mostly functional defensive hypomania. Psychosis involves sub-dimensions consisting of cognitive distortions (thought content), thought form, and sensory perceptual experiences. Negative symptoms also involve sub-dimensions comprised of basic cognition (executive functions), social cognition, and motivational states, with further dimensions underlying these, such as the various executive functions.

Dissociation is an even more complex entity in several ways starting with sub-dimensions of psychological and somatic. This conjecture might appear to support mind-body dualism, so instrumental in separating dissociation and somatic conditions in current diagnostic systems, but as sub-dimensions the division is warranted, given that with psychological dissociation physical manifestations are not primary, and with somatic dissociation psychological expressions are limited. Psychological dissociation occurs on a spectrum from benign and highly defensive absorption, with or without imaginative involvement, to personality fragmentation. There is a range demonstrating dimensionality within each form, but the variation is limited. For example, even the most intense level of absorption does not come close to personality fragmentation, although intense depersonalization and derealization can be more severe than milder amnesia. Somatic dissociation is further divided into dimensions based on the physical system involved, such as neurological, cardiac, dermatological, and also general conditions including chronic fatigue syndrome and fibromyalgia. The enormous symptom and diagnostic overlap between the generalized forms of somatic dissociation suggest that one underlying process is organized dimensionally in terms of severity. Dissociation is also primary to PTSD, and hence PTSD represents a sub-dimension of dissociation.

Eating disorders appear to consist of bulimic, anorexic, and obesity continuums, although anorexic and obesity might be on the same continuum. Underlying these major dimensions are several viable supporting continuums consisting of drive for thinness, calorie restriction, weight preoccupation, drive for muscle mass, body dissatisfaction, body image cognitive distortions, impulsivity, compulsivity, perfectionism, and exercise addiction. The dimension of emotional regulation also plays a key role. Shifting from proximal to ultimate causation we have the proposed evolutionary based energy continuums of food consumption style (quality of food intake), quantity of food consumed, and activity level. These ultimate causation dimensions interact with each other, and the proximal ones underlying the main eating disorder dimensions, to produce the diverse manifestations of eating disorders.

Reinforcement based conditions are currently understood as addictive, impulsive, or compulsive, but as we learned this distinction does not work, largely due to the conceptual and practical overlap of these entities, and common mechanisms. The discrete conditions that they are based on then often lack validity. For any instance of substance use or behavior suspected of being excessive, a model is proposed encompassing the contributing dimensions of positive and negative reinforcement, frequency, intensity, and costs/benefits. If separate diagnoses are provided for every instance of possible substance or behavioral excess, the total number of dimensions could swell into the tens or even hundreds, a ludicrous scenario (although in line with current diagnostic systems) given how they are all reinforcement based. Hence, each instance of substance or behavioral excess is best conceived of as a sub-dimension.

Personality disorders are conceptualized in the model proposed as excessive expressions, in terms of intensity and duration, of normal defensive dimensions. Separate dimensions include avoidant, narcissistic, dependent, obsessive-compulsive, antisocial, and borderline. The psychotic "personality disorders" are actually part of the schizophrenic spectrum, including positive and negative symptoms. A key benefit of the proposed system is flexibility in adding personality disorders, based on extremes of normal defensive styles, with "aggressive personality disorder" (see the next section) and "difficult personality disorder" leading contenders.

As pertains to the exact number of diagnoses in the proposed model, it is suggested that we move away from "diagnosis" implying discrete entities, to continuums more in keeping with nature. I will refrain from adding up the exact number of "diagnoses" in the proposed model to emphasize this point, but it will certainly be a fraction of those in current discrete diagnostic systems. It has been suggested that a value of discrete diagnoses is ease of application, perhaps in line with our proclivity to see discrete entities. However, science is about capturing true results, and not generating a distortion that fits with our perceptual and cognitive processes. Regarding ease of use, the present day discrete approach to classification with its multiple diagnoses is burdensome, and even more when it is appreciated how often "not otherwise specified" is applied as a diagnosis. The dimensional model proposed here retains the notion of key diagnoses that have stood the test of time, such as depression, anxiety, hypomania-mania, psychosis, dissociation, eating disorders, and personality disorders. In addition, it raises negative symptoms to the prominent level warranted, and brings clarity to the confusing realm of addictive, impulsive, and compulsive conditions, by bringing them under the umbrella of reinforcement based disorders.

Aggression Continuum

Arguably the greatest omission in current diagnostic systems is the lack of a comprehensive aggression category. Aggression is an integral part of human nature, due to how essential it was during our evolution. Attacks by predators and competing hunting-gathering groups had to be repelled, as did attempts by same-group members to take an individual's resources, providing a clear defensive function. In addition, aggression enabled our ancestors to acquire important resources, such as by attacking dangerous prey, another hunting-gathering group to secure their resources, or launched against an individual as when a person attempted to rise up the ranks, yielding an offensive role for aggression. Given the defensive and offensive functions it appears that there might be two variants, but in line with nature being dimensional, the most likely scenario is that there is one dimension of aggression, with defensive and offensive eliciting circumstances. Furthermore, consistent with quantitative variation producing qualitative variation as an emergent property, a higher quantitative level of aggression probably provides for offensive (instrumental) aggression. For instance, a person who rates low in aggression is highly unlikely to be aggressive unless strongly provoked, such as by an attack. On the other hand, a person who rates high in aggression requires much lower stimulation to act aggressively, as with an opportunity to acquire an item from someone else, resulting in offensive aggression. Hence, quantitative variation in level of aggression produces qualitative variation (offensive aggression) as an emergent property.

Regulation over aggression is another key aspect determining the level of aggression. Much as with depression and anxiety, the prefrontal cortex (and frontal cortices more generally) regulates limbic system based anger and aggression. Anger occurs when violation or damage is detected by the emotional information processing system (Rozin et al, 1999; Shaver et al, 1987), and aggression is a key response following from this perception to improve the situation. The safety of expressing reactive aggression is a primary issue in regards to regulation, as indicated by road rage where people feel safe inside their metal protection, the same level of aggression being far less likely outside the car face to face. A study asking people about road rage reveals that the majority of drivers experience it, demonstrating how prone we can be to aggression when a violation is perceived, and we feel safe expressing our feelings (Vanlaar et al, 2008).

Offensive aggression is triggered by the perception of an opportunity to acquire an important resource, and as with defensive aggression is regulated. If the regulation is impaired then expressed aggression can be extreme. This occurrence has been noted for those with damage to the frontal lobes, and also when there is poor self-control as with ADHD (Haller & Kruk, 2006; Retz & Rosler, 2009; Struber et al, 2008; Turgay, 2004; Wood & Thomas, 2013). Impaired regulation effectively lowers the threshold for reactive and instrumental aggression. Perhaps this is one reason why anger and aggression can arise with mood disorders (Weisbrot & Ettinger, 2002), in that these disorders involve compromised regulation over emotions. It is also feasible that certain conditions intensify limbic system responses. Alcohol intoxication, for instance, might ramp up limbic system activity during the initial stimulant action, and also impair frontal cortical regulation.

Considering our capacity for aggression and the potential for damage, it qualifies as a continuum relevant to mental illness and health. Low levels, as with reactive aggression appropriate to the circumstance, are on the adaptive healthy level of the range, while high levels not appropriate for the circumstance constitute a maladaptive scenario. Problematic levels of aggression can result from genetic influences combined with experiences, such as modeling of aggressive actions and abuse, and also compromised regulation. In childhood the circumstances eliciting it will typically be different as will the expression, but have the same theme involving perception of violation or damage for defensive reactive aggression, and an opportunity for resource acquisition for offensive instrumental aggression, as with bullying to steal a cell phone. Deficient emotional regulation also plays a role in childhood aggression (Green & Doyle, 1999).

Excessive reactive and proactive offensive forms of aggression have been identified in both boys and girls, expressed in the form of conduct disorder and oppositional defiant disorder (Fite et al, 2006; Kempes et al, 2005; Keenan et al, 1999). Research does not clearly separate these two disorders, other than for oppositional defiant disorder occurring in younger children, and conduct disorder later, a distinction that makes sense insofar as in early childhood the focus is more on parents and teachers, but shifts to behaviors later on (Hofvander et al, 2009; Loeber et al, 1991). Loeber et al (1991) found that almost every youth with conduct disorder had oppositional defiant disorder, but not everyone with the latter progresses to the former. Conduct disorder is said to be a child version of antisocial personality disorder, or at least the aggressive variant, placing it on a continuum with excess adult aggression (Eme, 2007; Frick & Dickens, 2006; Hofvander et al, 2009). Hofvander et al (2009) argue that research does not distinguish and find "zones of rarity" for disruptive behavior disorders from childhood to adulthood.

The evidence therefore supports a continuum of aggression in the population. Those with a high level of aggression demonstrate offensive instrumental aggression, and excessive reactive aggression out of keeping with circumstances. The early childhood version of excessive aggression is given the discrete label of oppositional defiant disorder, and its expression in later childhood and adolescence, conduct disorder. Given that oppositional defiant disorder and conduct disorder are on the aggressive continuum they do not represent discrete entities, although due to differences in the circumstances eliciting them, and expressions related largely to age, research can find differences suggesting or supporting their distinction. These disorders also encompass an antisocial element with callous-unemotional expressions indicating reduced emotional reactivity (Viding et al, 2012). The question at this point is what excessive aggression looks like in adulthood.

Excessive aggression in adulthood, much like that in youth, can arise from impaired regulation manifesting as impulsive aggression, such as with intermittent explosive disorder, although given the continuous nature of aggression a discrete diagnosis is not warranted. It can also result from a high propensity for aggression, as with someone who readily enters into an altercation and allows it to escalate, even if there is the capacity to regulate its intensity. It is suggested (see the "Personality Disorders" chapter) that excessive aggression represents a personality disorder for two reasons. First, it tends to be an enduring and characteristic way of acting and reacting. Second, aggression is primarily a defensive response to circumstances that are perceived to be damaging if not opposed. The vast majority of aggression that occurs is defensive, and a lower level of aggression typically translates into aggression being expressed in circumstances where the benefits exceed the costs, such as for defensive needs. Aggression is a costly behavior, both in terms of energy expended and risk of damage. Elicited under the right circumstances, such as for defense, it can be highly evolutionary fitness enhancing. However, an extreme level of aggression often corresponds to circumstances where the costs can exceed benefits, typically detracting from evolutionary fitness, although if such behavior is rewarded it can intensify. As with other personality disorders a low level is generally adaptive, whereas an extreme and enduring expression is typically maladaptive.

Characteristic and enduring aggression in adults is currently viewed as being part of antisocial personality disorder. However, as we learned, the key component of antisocial personality disorder is deception and manipulation to enhance resource standing, based on the evolved dimensional templates of deceit and dissociation. Aggression can actually work against effective deception, and is more likely to result in injury or incarceration. As an example, many con artists are non-aggressive, working their deception in a very non-threatening fashion. Even if confronted many will simply deny the charge and withdraw. Where is the aggression?

It is quite likely the case that violent antisocial individuals have a high level of both deceit, seen here as the core to an antisocial nature, and aggression, resulting in violent antisocial behavior. In other words, two personality disorder continuums are interfacing to produce the manifestation of violent antisocial behavior. If there is only a high level of deceit the manifestation is that of a con artist or white-collar criminal. Their behavior is antisocial and victims definitely feel violated, at times more than with violent crime given the trust they placed in the person. If an individual rates high in aggression, but not deception, then the person is prone to excessive reactive and proactive aggression, such as the person who enters into fights with little provocation. The combination produces violent antisocial behavior where there is both deception and aggression, because there are few inhibitions to the aggressive acquisition of resources. In some instances, brain damage impairs regulation over aggressive responses, and also reduces caution in deceitful actions, the combination leading to more arrests and incarceration. Those individuals who are not deceitful but highly aggressive have aggressive personality disorder, whereas when deception and manipulation occurs, antisocial personality disorder is cited. These personality disorders are said to be interfacing when both occur. One option that might capture this occurrence is to name deceitful antisocial tendencies, deceitful personality disorder, and excessive aggression "aggressive personality disorder," and the regular interfacing of both dimensions "antisocial personality disorder."

The discussion of aggression has focused on externally directed aggression, but what about self-directed? There are those who cut and attempt to take their own life, and many more with so-called harsh superegos that relentlessly criticize themselves. It appears likely that self-directed aggression comprises a sub-dimension of aggression activated by certain conditions, resulting in increased self-criticisms, self-harm, and suicidal behavior, at least in those who have a propensity in this regard. Some people seem prone to it, while others are not, rarely considering suicide even when severely depressed. Furthermore, self-criticism, self-harm, and suicidal behavior might represent progressively intense dimensions within the sub-dimension of self-directed aggression, each with a range. More severe depression or borderline personality disorder can activate the more extreme levels of self-directed aggression in those with a higher propensity for this type of aggression.

Childhood Disorders

Several childhood disorders have already been discussed, as with oppositional defiant and conduct disorders, under the aggression continuum. Conditions including intellectual impairment, specific learning difficulties (such as for math and language), ADHD, and autistic spectrum disorders were discussed in the "Negative Symptoms" chapter. In addition, depression, anxiety, bipolar, schizophrenic spectrum, dissociation, eating, and reinforcement based disorders can all arise in childhood as part of the given continuum, with eliciting circumstances and expressions appropriate for the youth's age, often creating the illusion of discreteness. Personality disorders, or at least the defensive styles underlying them, start to appear in childhood-adolescence. Conditions clearly due to organic impairments, such as those involving motor function, tics, and elimination, are suggested here as being considered strictly neurological in nature, although reactions to them, as with depression and anxiety, are in the psychiatric and clinical psychology realm. An interesting potential condition emerging in DSM-5 is disruptive mood dysregulation disorder (DMDD).

DMDD is characterized by irritability, anger, temper outbursts, and as the name implies, problems regulating emotional states (Lochman et al, 2015; Rao, 2014). As a distinct disorder it does not appear valid, given that there is too much overlap with other conditions including depression, oppositional defiant disorder, conduct disorder, and ADHD (Alexson et al, 2012; Dougherty et al, 2014; Lochman et al, 2015; Roy et al, 2013). For example, Roy et al (2013) found that DMDD overlapped with oppositional defiant disorder in 88.2% of their sample, ADHD 74.5%, and depression 33.3%. Alexson et al (2012) using a longitudinal study design also found much overlap of DMDD with other conditions: Oppositional defiant disorder 58% and conduct disorder 61%, with these two conditions having the same rate of overlap reflecting the way they also overlap. Although DMDD does not appear to be a separate entity, emotional regulation constitutes a key dimension underlying various conditions, such as eating disorders and borderline personality disorder, as was discussed in the "Eating Disorders" and "Personality Disorders" chapters, respectively. Supporting the value of an emotional regulation continuum is a 14-year longitudinal study of 2,076 children and adolescents by Althoff et al (2010). Problems with self-regulation in childhood and adolescence resulted in elevated anxiety and mood disorders, disruptive behavior disorders, and drug abuse 14 years later (Althoff et al, 2010). Emotional regulation and the other forms of self-regulation discussed throughout the book, such as that over psychotic level cognitions, constitute continuums underlying mental illness and health.

References

Alexson, D., Findling, R.L., Fristad, M.A., Kowatch, R.A., Youngstrom, E.A., & Horwitz, S.M. et al (2012). Examining the proposed disruptive mood dysregulation disorder diagnosis in children in the longitudinal assessment of manic symptoms study. *Journal of Clinical Psychology, 73*(10), 1342-1350.

Althoff, R.R., Verhulst, F.C., Rettew, D.C., Hudziak, J.J., & Van Der Ende, J. (2010). Adult outcomes of childhood dysregulation: A 14-year follow-up study. *Journal of The American Academy Of Child & Adolescent Psychiatry, 49*(11), 1105-1116.

American Psychiatric Association (2013). *Diagnostic & Statistical Manual 5*. Washington, DC: American Psychiatric Publishing.

Begley, C. & Ellis, M. (2012). Drug development: Raise standards for preclinical cancer research. *Nature, 483*(7391), 531-533.

Bowins, B. (2004). Psychological defense mechanisms: A new perspective. *American Journal of Psychoanalysis, 64*, 1-26.

Bowins, B.E. (2015). Depression: Discrete or continuous? *Psychopathology, 48*(2), 69-78.

Dougherty, L.R., Smith, V.C., Bufferd, S.J., Carlson, G.A., Stringaris, A., Leibenluft, E., & Klein, D.N. (2014). DSM-5 disruptive mood dysregulation disorder: Correlates and predictors in young children. *Psychological Medicine, 21*, 1012.

Eme, R.F. (2007). Sex differences in child-onset, life-course-persistent conduct disorder: A review of biological influences. *Clinical Psychology Review, 27*(5), 607-627.

Fite, P.J., Colder, C.R., & Pelham, W.E. Jr. (2006). A factor analytic approach to distinguish pure and co-occurring dimensions of proactive and reactive aggression. *Journal of Clinical Child & Adolescent Psychology, 35*(4), 578-582.

Frick, P.J. & Dickens, C. (2006). Current perspectives on conduct disorder. *Current Psychiatry Reports, 8*(1), 59-72.

Greene, R.W. & Doyle, A.E. (1999). Toward a transactional conceptualization of oppositional defiant disorder: Implications for assessment and treatment. *Clinical Child & Family Psychology Review, 2*(3), 129-148.

Haller, J. & Kruk, M.R. (2006). Normal and abnormal aggression: Human disorders and novel laboratory models. *Neuroscience & Biobehavioral Reviews, 30*(3), 292-303.

Hofvander, B., Ossowski, D., Lundstrom, S., & Anckarsater, H. (2009). Continuity of aggressive antisocial behavior from childhood to adulthood: The question of phenotype definition. *International Journal of Law & Psychiatry, 32*(4), 224-234.

Keenan, K., Loeber, R., & Green, S. (1999). Conduct disorder in girls: A review of the literature. *Clinical Child & Family Psychology Review, 2*(1), 3-19.

Kempes, M., Matthys, W., De Vries, H., & Van Engeland, H. (2005). Reactive and proactive aggression in children—A review of theory, findings and the relevance for child and adolescent psychiatry. *European Journal of Child & Adolescent Psychiatry, 14*(1), 11-19.

Lochman, J.E., Evans, S.C., Burke, J.D., Roberts, M.C., Fite, P.J., Reed, G.M. et al (2015). An empirically based alternative to DSM-5's disruptive mood dysregulation disorder for ICD-11. *World Psychiatry, 14*(1), 30-33.

Loeber, R., Lahey, B.B., & Thomas, C. (1991). Diagnostic conundrum of oppositional defiant disorder and conduct disorder. *Journal of Abnormal Psychology, 100*(3), 379-390.

Prinz, F., Schlange, T., & Asadullah, K. (2011). Believe it or not: How much can we rely on published data on potential drug targets? *Nature Reviews: Drug Discovery, 10*(9), 712-717.

Rao, U. (2014). DSM-5: Disruptive mood dysregulation disorder. *Asian Journal of Psychiatry, 11*, 119-123.

Retz, W. & Rosler, M. (2009). The relationship of ADHD and violent aggression: What can we learn from epidemiological and genetic studies? *International Journal of Law & Psychiatry, 32*(4), 235-243.

Roy, A.K., Klein, R.G., Angelsolante, A., Bar-Haim, Y., Leibenluft, E., Hulvershorn, L. et al (2013). Clinical features of young children referred for impairing temper outbursts. *Journal of Child & Adolescent Psychopharmaocology, 23*(9), 588-596.

Rozin, P., Lowery, L., Imada, S., & Haidt, J. (1999). The CAD Triad hypothesis: A mapping between three moral emotions (contempt, anger, disgust) and three moral codes (community, autonomy, divinity). *Journal of Personality & Social Psychology, 76*(4), 574-586.

Shaver, P., Schwartz, J., Kirson, D., & O'Connor, C. (1987). Emotion knowledge: Further exploration of a prototype approach. *Journal of Personality & Social Psychology, 52*(6), 1086-1091.

Struber, D., Luck, M., & Roth, G. (2008). Sex, aggression and impulse control: An integrative account. *Neurocase, 14*(1), 93-121.

Turgay, A. (2004). Aggression and disruptive behavior disorders in children and adolescents. *Expert Reviews in Neurotherapy, 4*(4), 623-632.

Vanlaar, W., Simpson, H., Mayhew, D., & Robertson, R. (2008). Aggressive driving: A survey of attitudes, opinions and behaviors. *Journal of Safety Research, 39*(4), 375-381.

Viding, E., Fontaine, N.M., & McCrory, E.J. (2012). Antisocial behavior in children with and without callous-unemotional traits. *Journal of the Royal Society of Medicine, 105*(5), 195-200.

Weisbrot, D.M. & Ettinger, A.B. (2002). Aggression and violence in mood disorders. *Child & Adolescence Psychiatric Clinics of North America, 11*(3), 649-671.

Wood, R.L. & Thomas, R.H. (2013). Impulsive and episodic disorders of aggressive behaviour following traumatic brain injury. *Brain Injury, 27*(3), 253-261.

CHAPTER 12

Conclusion

In combination, continuums, regulation, and defense comprehensively define mental illness. Consistent with most natural occurrences, continuums characterize mental illness, with separate major dimensions, and also sub-dimensions within these, as covered in the various chapters (and also in the "Number of Diagnoses" section of the "Diagnostic Considerations" chapter). These continuums commonly interact, the interaction best referred to as interfacing continuums (or dimensions), insofar as comorbidity implies a worse outcome and co-occurrence more a random event: Dimensions interact for reasons other than random variation, and in ways that are not always negative, as with the hypomania-mania continuum defensively interfacing with the depression continuum. An interesting aspect of continuums, helping to reconcile apparent distinctions used to support discrete categories, is that quantitative variation yields qualitative variation as an emergent property. For example, melancholic depression is not discrete but represents a qualitatively different expression of the most intense level of the depression continuum. Unique circumstances can also foster the appearance of discrete entities, although they just activate a dimension, as with social circumstances eliciting anxiety.

Despite how integral regulation is to biological systems, its role in psychological processes is largely unrecognized. Healthy regulation characterizes mental health, while impaired regulation is instrumental in mental illness. Regarding depression and anxiety, compromised frontal cortical regulation of limbic system activity plays a prominent role. Adaptive and defensive hypomania progresses to dysfunctional mania when regulation over the hypomania-mania continuum is impaired. Psychosis transpires when cognitive regulatory control processes, normally blocking psychotic level cognitions from the conscious and awake state, are damaged. Personality disorders occur when milder and healthy defensive responses of select types transform into severe and enduring expressions, often due to impaired regulation. Compromised regulation generally contributes to the progression from healthy and adaptive levels on a continuum to unhealthy and maladaptive levels, a process seen with dissociation, food consumption behavior, and reinforcement-based disorders, in addition to the continuums already mentioned. A diverse collection of psychotherapeutic techniques, under the umbrella of cognitive regulatory control therapies, can help restore healthy regulation, as with cognitive behavioral therapy enhancing frontal cortex activity and dampening limbic system activity, in the case of anxiety and depression.

As an integral part of natural compensation and resilience, psychological defensive processes play a major role in mental illness and health. Hypomania acts as a defense against depression and even anxiety, with hyperthymic personality an ongoing expression conferring heightened resilience against depression. In addition, several mental illness continuums have defense as a core theme, such as personality disorders consisting of extreme and enduring expressions of normal defensive processes. Effective psychotherapy techniques readily follow from this conceptualization of personality disorders. The psychosis dimension includes cognitive distortions, with the milder range comprising a key defensive process—positive cognitive distortions—underlying many classical defenses. Dissociation in the milder range also constitutes a major defense mechanism template, utilized by everyone in the form of absorption. Positive cognitive distortions and milder dissociation (and the classical psychoanalytic defenses subsumed under these two templates) routinely defend against excessive negative emotions. Psychotherapeutic interventions focused on enhancing defensive processes, such as inducing hypomania and dissociation in the form of absorption, represent novel techniques capable of advancing treatment outcomes.

Continuums, regulation, and defense provide a unifying framework for psychopathology, linking diverse empirical results in a comprehensive fashion. Given the robustness of these constructs, the model places mental illness on a more scientific foundation, and much more so than the collection of discrete entities so characteristic of current diagnostic systems. Critics will point to the numerous empirical results seemingly supporting discrete approaches to psychopathology. However, when it is appreciated that most empirical research results are false, even when endpoints are hard, this "evidence based" approach quickly loses its luster; it becomes biased evidence based medicine. In the absence of sound theory, empirical results are prone to drift in false directions, away from true outcomes. By blending theory and empirical results, *Mental Illness Defined: Continuums, Regulation, and Defense* advances the quest for true outcomes, yielding a much needed paradigm shift.

Index

Made in the USA
Columbia, SC
17 September 2026

4518b2c2-e597-451a-ae54-8db29a2b3a30R01